DAIRY FARMING IN THE 21ST CENTURY

PRAISE FOR *DAIRY FARMING IN THE 21ST CENTURY*

'In this volume, Bruce Scholten brings together his long-standing research on dairying from around the world, making a unique and groundbreaking contribution to agri-food studies and agricultural geography. It is informed with an ambitious and critical approach to a wide range of literatures and empirical investigations. In particular, it blends ethical, political and environmental debates and perspectives, dealing with both production and consumption relations. It is a 'must read' for a wide range of scholars and practitioners interested in the conceptual and material cross-roads global dairying now finds itself.'

> **– Terry Marsden, Emeritus Professor of Environmental Policy and Planning, Sustainable Places Research Institute and School of Geography and Planning, Cardiff University, UK**

'Bruce Scholten's volume is an important contribution to the question of sustainable dairy farming. He thoroughly interrogates the ethical dimension of production, and demonstrates how ethics, the environment and political factors shape the face of the industry. The book uses evidence and fact in a rounded way and includes academic work as well as the observations of practitioners. As an aside, Scholten offers a valuable critique of how evidence is created and valued and the devaluation of expert knowledge and the subsequent costs. I particularly enjoyed his interrogation of the gendered nature of farming practice, a theme that is often overlooked when agriculture is seen as a sector rather than an occupation. This book is a delight to read; it is witty, engaging, and very clever.'

> **– Sally Shortall (PhD), Duke of Northumberland Professor of Rural Economy, Newcastle University, UK. Lead author, 2017 Scottish Government Report on *Women in Farming***

'As professor, researcher and mentor-cum-supervisor of university graduate students researching smallholder dairy development, including policies and climate change, over four decades, I have not come across a book that examines the political, ethical and environmental factors influencing dairy development in one volume like this. Writing on India's White Revolution, and the East Africa Dairy Development project (EADD), Bruce A. Scholten promotes sustainability and nutrition security, showing how village cooperatives, cold chains and technical assistance can empower women's income and family nutrition. We will see if more digestible feed, and additives such as seaweed, can enhance women's participation – while reducing ruminant methane which exacerbates global warming.'

> **– Stephen Gichovi Mbogoh (PhD), International Livestock Centre for Africa (ILCA), Professor Emeritus of Agricultural and Applied Economics, University of Nairobi, Kenya**

'This book provides extremely significant insights into environmental and social concerns related to the future of dairy farming in the Global North and South. Its engagement with key ethical debates and foregrounding of farming communities is outstanding, especially its abiding concern with animal welfare and insights into women's roles in dairy farming. Given concerns around livestock and methane emissions, Scholten's exceptionally valuable and timely perspectives will engage both a specialist audience and those more broadly interested in sustainable and just solutions to global warming and food insecurity.'

– **Pratyusha Basu (PhD), University of Texas at El Paso, author of**
Villages, Women, and the Success of Dairy Cooperatives
in India: Making Place for Rural Development

'In Chapter 5, Bruce Scholten highlights the importance of women farmers for international food security and sustainable development. Using the metaphor of the grass ceiling, he examines obstacles to women's success as farmers and the gendered economic disparities between men and women. Women's organizations and cooperatives, the growth of alternative food networks, organic production and organic certification policies provide the means for some women to break through the grass ceiling. Scholten explains how the grass ceiling differs among nations in accordance with geography, social structures and norms, government policy and consumer preferences.'

– **Lucy Jarosz (PhD), Professor Emerita, Department of**
Geography, University of Washington, Seattle, USA

'Dairy farming has become dominated by markets and investors, beyond control of family-scale farmers who get their hands dirty and break a sweat for a living. Bruce Scholten understands, both analytically from his academic background, and with his roots on the farm, that there is an intrinsic relationship between a herd of cows and a family, and between cows and cropland where their waste is recycled to enrich soil instead of becoming a concentrated pollutant. He articulates how eliminating these connections exploits people, animals and the environment, resulting in nutritionally-inferior food.

– **Mark A. Kastel, Executive Director, OrganicEye; co-founder of The**
Cornucopia Institute, US advocates for family-scale pasture dairying

DAIRY FARMING IN THE 21ST CENTURY

Global Ethics, Environment and Politics

Bruce A. Scholten

BLOOMSBURY ACADEMIC
LONDON • NEW YORK • OXFORD • NEW DELHI • SYDNEY

BLOOMSBURY ACADEMIC
Bloomsbury Publishing Plc
50 Bedford Square, London, WC1B 3DP, UK
1385 Broadway, New York, NY 10018, USA
29 Earlsfort Terrace, Dublin 2, Ireland

BLOOMSBURY, BLOOMSBURY ACADEMIC and the Diana logo are trademarks of
Bloomsbury Publishing Plc

First published in Great Britain 2023
This edition printed 2024

Series design by Adriana Brioso
Cover image © Matteo Grando/Unsplash

A catalogue record for this book is available from the British Library.

A catalog record for this book is available from the Library of Congress.

ISBN: HB: 978-1-8386-0452-3
       PB: 978-1-3503-7861-2
     ePDF: 978-1-8386-0453-0
    eBook: 978-1-8386-0454-7

Typeset by RefineCatch Ltd, Bungay, Suffolk NR35 1EF

To find out more about our authors and books, visit www.bloomsbury.com
and sign up for our newsletters.

*This book is dedicated to my linguist wife Martha Clemewell Young-Scholten.
We've walked dairy pastures worldwide and anticipate many more.*

CONTENTS

TABLES, SURVEY QUERIES AND FIGURES

Tables

Dairy survey queries

Figures

All photos are taken from the Bruce A. Scholten collection. All subjects have given permission for use.

PREFACE

Twenty years ago, my sister-in-law Johanna Young gave me an unusual picture from her spiritual retreat. She had photographed a cow, peacefully chewing seaweed and kelp on the rocky beach of Iona, a tiny island off Mull in western Scotland. Johanna suddenly died in August 2021. While her husband Lindley Rankine, my wife Martha Young-Scholten and family mourn her, the prescience of her photo, as I finished this book, is extraordinary.

Religions urge us to be good stewards of flora and fauna. However, as plastic pervades the oceans, and more animals endure lives of confinement for consumption by perhaps 10 billion humans in the twenty-first century, we are faced by more than a moral dilemma. That is because dairy and livestock sectors are prime sources of anthropogenic greenhouse gases (GHGs), and critics claim that switching from omnivore to vegetarian or vegan diets is necessary to save civilization from catastrophe. The UN's Intergovernmental Panel on Climate Change (IPCC) confirms that '[I]t is unequivocal that human influence has warmed the atmosphere, oceans and land . . .' (BBC 2021).

Our post-truth era, of narrow-casting on social media, allows more of us to affect politics as social influencers (*Economist* 2016). Experts are mocked, facts are politicized. Legislative stasis results when issues are kicked down the road like rusty tin cans. Deplorable examples include Covid-19 vaccines, and global warming.

The COP26 global climate summit – the twenty-sixth meeting of the parties to the 1994 United Nations Framework Convention on Climate Change (UNFCCC) – took place in Glasgow in November 2021. That same month, Reuters reported that the United States and China had agreed to phase out coal use, increase forest protection and lower the use of methane. Fossil fuel industries must stop methane leaks and flaring. This book is keenly interested in curbing methane cow emissions, most likely by mixing seaweed with digestible feed.

One catalyst for this book was knowing that mass-production of livestock was reaching unprecedented intensity, while researchers including Temple Grandin and Marian Stamp Dawkins revealed an overlap in human/nonhuman sentience and emotion. Yet, however one reconciles ethics with eating livestock, dairy devotees believe their stewardship of ruminants and soil can meet environmental challenges.

Why? Following the Pole Star north and west from Glasgow brings one to Iona. There, a bovine on the beach suggests mitigation for her enteric fermentation – and our existential climate threat.

FOREWORD

It is now over fifty years since I took up the study of dairying from the point of view of a geographer. Over the years this research has taken many forms, ranging from milk production in Victorian cities to an interest in the Indian dairy development project known as Operation Flood. Bruce Scholten joined me in this quest in 1992 and soon developed his own independent research themes that have included the consumption of organic foods in Seattle, India's 'white revolution' and US dairy organic politics. He is by far the best-placed scholar now to write about the political, ethical and environmental aspects of dairy farming in the twenty-first century.

Dr Scholten's book begins with the premise that dairy is part of the human make-over of the planet. Driven by population growth and the increased demand that comes with economic development, the consumption of milk and dairy products has soared. With less pasture for free-range grazing, many cows are kept on feedlots and fed on grains that are transported from a distance. This makes no sense for long-term sustainability.

The environmental issue is a related one, yielding some important insights into the impact of dairy farming. Apart from issues of pollution and landscape degradation, it is now generally accepted that livestock agriculture contributes about 15 per cent of greenhouse gas emissions. It is appropriate, then, that this book discusses the many attempts at mitigation that have been proposed and acted upon in recent decades. Most prominent has been the spread of abstinence from meat and dairy consumption. Vegetarianism and, more recently, veganism have become popular, with claimed benefits for human health as well as positive outcomes for climate change. Non-dairy products such as soya and almond milk now grace the aisles of most supermarkets and one senses the potential for a deep-seated shift in consumer habits.

A third strand in the book's argument is an ethical one. Dr Scholten suggests that animal welfare cannot be separated from economic considerations. The concentration of cows into vast enterprises reduces their longevity, an obvious cost to the industry that has to be addressed. High-yielding cows may also suffer compromised welfare, with pain being an everyday part of their short lives. One intriguing solution might be making seaweed part of their diet. This boosts disease immunity and, incidentally, also reduces methane – dairying's chief contribution to greenhouse gas emissions. The downside is a lower milk yield but this has welfare benefits because the animals are less stressed.

Finally, there is a discussion of the view that politics and commercial interests have skewed our diets and that we would be better off with the foods our great-grandparents would have recognized rather than obsessing about micronutrients.

This arises from the observation that many meat substitutes contain soy protein, coconut oil, corn starch and a lot of salt. We are not quite ready yet, it seems, to abandon milk and dairy products.

Dr Scholten's book is characterized by his usual wit and accessible writing style. It is both entertaining and informative and is another important building block in social science understandings of the dairy world.

Peter J. Atkins, Emeritus Professor of Geography, University of Durham, UK, author of *Liquid Materialities: A History of Milk, Science and the Law*

ACKNOWLEDGEMENTS

I am grateful to initial commissioning editor Tomasz Hoskins, his successor Atifa Jiwa, and assistant editor Nayiri Kendir for understanding in the gestation of this book. Thanks for encouragement from David Stonestreet who oversaw my 2010 book India's White Revolution for I.B. Tauris, now a Bloomsbury imprint. Thanks also to Tia Ali, Siân Lyshon, Sophie Campbell, Merv Honeywood, Zeba Talkhani, and Lisa Carden who assisted with the final editing of this present volume.

My sources share any acclaim for this book and no blame for any errors in it. Thanks to hundreds of survey responders, interviewees, farmers and vendors on crop and livestock chains for their input. I am grateful to academics, scientists and experts from all continents for information, especially on the intricacies of methane and climate. My nine-question *Dairy Farming in the 21st Century* survey (https://www.surveymonkey.co.uk/r/R3KR8W5) elicited relevant opinions from sixteen countries, launching this book project after 2017, when Professor Marcus Power of Durham University's Geography department advised earning a Certificate of Completion (2338308) from the National Institutes of Health (NIH-US) Office of Extramural Research training course 'Protecting Human Research Participants'. Thanks to Hannah Murray-Leslie and Peter Samson at Food Durham/ Durham Community Alliance UK for early survey distribution, and to Liz Charles who recruited me to the Alliance's advisory board in 2018. In the United States, Ed Maltby of the Northeast Organic Dairy Producers Alliance also spread the survey to the NODPA-Odairy list. Charles Benbrook revealed herbicide toxicity. Mark Kastel and OrganicEye assessed GMO dairy hormones and megadairy practices. Goldie Caughlan brought lore from PCC Community Markets in Seattle, and service on the USDA National Organic Standards Board. Steve Larson, my 'occasional editor' at *Hoard's Dairyman* magazine in Wisconsin, has been a North Star since 1987.

Appreciation also to the International Federation of Organic Agricultural Movements for information on dairy and climate in Bonn, and for hosting the 2017 IFOAM organic world congress in New Delhi. Correspondence and meetings in Bonn and Delhi with IFOAM's then President Marcus Arbenz and press officer Denise Godinho were helpful, as were chats with Brian Baker of IFOAM North America, and Sarah Henderson of Northeast Organic Farmers Association in USA. FiBL, the Research Institute of Organic Agriculture for Switzerland, Germany, Austria, France and Europe, has been a prime data source for decades; Helga Willer and Julia Lernoud there have been especially helpful.

Thanks to Atul, Yashodhara and Gandhali Bhide who strive for socio-economic empowerment via organizations including Rotary International. In Thane, near Mumbai, they hosted me and my wife Martha before and after visiting Amul and

Dudhsagar cooperative dairies in Gujarat. In Anand, Shri R.S. Sodhi, MD of Amul, whom I first met in 1998, ensured our every hour was filled by meeting professors and students at IRMA and Vidya Dairy, and by male and female farmers developing NDDB cow-and-climate-friendly solar water pumping, biogas and nutrient recycling. In Mehsana, home to India's largest cooperative dairy, Dudhsagar, thanks to Hon. Shri Vipul M. Chaudhari, Shri Dr. P. R. Patel, Executive Director MIDFT, Dean Dr. Dharmendra Shukla, Prof. B.P. Shah, and Ms. Akshita Sehgal of Mansinhbhai Institute of Dairy & Food Technology (MIDFT).

These people knew Shri Joseph Purathur, long-time assistant to the Father of India's White Revolution, Dr. Verghese Kurien, and my friend, before his untimely death in 2016. At MIDFT, I was honoured to give the Mansinhbhai Memorial Lecture on 15 April 2019. Thanks also to Ms. Nirmala Kurien, Roger Pereira, the Amul Girl, and the informal Dr. Kurien Fan Club, including dairy partisans Vivek Matthai and R.N. Bhaskar.

In Bangladesh, Mohd. Abul Kalam Azad of Milk Vita, and M. Shahidul Islam at the University of Dhaka, keep in touch. Sources in Africa include Stephen Gichovi Mbogoh at the University of Nairobi, Peter Ngaruiya of the Eastern and Southern African Dairy Association (ESADA), and Moses Nyabila (EADD). In Argentina, Jorge Perera assisted my *Sostenibilidad Global*. In Brazil, Felipe Machado de Silva is embarked on a fine career in rural networks. In Vermont, USA, Marla R. Emery, explicates forests and foraging. University of Washington Prof (Em) Lucy Jarosz, and Kate Ryan, Agriculture Program Coordinator, WSU Snohomish County Extension, help me explore grass ceilings in food networks. At the University of Texas-El Paso, Pratyusha Basu has co-written with me on Green and White Revolutions.

In North-East England, the World Heritage Site of Durham Cathedral has made tiny Durham (pop. 48,069) an official *city* under British law. For a quarter-century, my wife Martha and I have enjoyed the choice of a ten-minute walk to either the city centre or the 900-year-old Kepier Hospital Farm with 100 cows, bulls, calves and sheep on the River Wear. Another uplifting constant has been data from the UN Food and Agricultural Organization, so regards to FAO veterans Anthony Bennett, Brian T. Dugdill and Joe Phelan, and also Michael Griffin of Dairy Outlook Link.

Understanding ruminant methane was challenging, so gratitude to Atul Bhide for routing me to Deepashree Kand, a researcher in Europe, and also Milind Niphadkar, a cancer researcher now optimizing Indian cattle feed at Occamy Bioscience. Around Durham University Geography Department, Peter J. Atkins – officially retired but churning out books like the milk expert he is – has been a trustworthy sounding board. In Durham's Physics Department, Marek Szablewski had advice. Arborealist Ewan Anderson directed me to the Yorkshire Philosophical Society, whose Chair, Catherine Brophy, introduced me to Andrew Loftus, Neil Fuller's work on soil sustainability and the Oxford Climate Society.

Chapter 5, on the 'grass ceiling' that blocks women's access to farm ownership and management, benefited from Newcastle University's Sally Shortall, whose 2017 report to the Scottish Government dovetailed with my 2007 PhD observations on rural and urban women's attitudes and training. Smiles to Liz Oughton of Newcastle's Centre for Rural Economy. Best to Caroline Bell, co-director of Acorn Organic Dairy in County Durham.

I bid *Farewell!* to colleagues in the Rural Geography Research Group of the Royal Geographical Society with the Institute of British Geographers, like Henry Buller and Ellen Roe, authors of *Food and Animal Welfare*. In 2009, Chair Guy Robinson nominated me to edit *RGRG Newsletter* (https://rgrg.co.uk/newsletter), which lasted through the tenures of Keith Halfacree, Nigel Walford, and now Martin Phillips. It's been fun, with so many men and women writing about ruralities from Kenya to Malawi to Vietnam. After three decades in Germany and Britain, we are returning to Seattle and Puget Sound.

Goede dag! to female and male tractor-driving cousins around Lynden, Washington, USA for transcending grass ceilings (*Don't try tractor racing at home!*).

Guete Daag! to Hans Wolfisberg and wife, who graze 180 Organic Valley Jerseys on the Nooksack River, where I first lived. *Guten Tag!* to Rosi and Wes Jansen, whose Fine Feathered Friends bird shop in La Conner is part of their decades of pro-animal work.

In 2021, IPCC climate reports signalled a Code Red for humanity, with increased lightning, fire and floods in future. Ideally, this book will help academics, activists and other readers anticipate threats and opportunities, keeping this the best of all possible worlds.

CONVERSION TABLES[1]

Length

1 centimetre = 0. 3937 inches
1 inch = 2.54 centimetres
1 metre = 1.0936 yards = 3.2808 feet = 39.370 inches
1 kilometre = 0.6214 miles
1 mile = 1.6093 kilometres

Area

1 hectare = 10 000 square metres = 0.1 square kilometres = 2.471 acres = 11 960
   sq. yards
1 acre = 0.4047 hectares = 4 047 square metres = 4 840 square yards = 43 450
   square feet
1 square kilometre = 0.3861 square miles = 100 hectares = 247.1 acres
1 square mile = 2.5898 square kilometres = 254.98 hectares = 640 acres

Volume

1 litre = 1 000 millilitres = 61.026 cubic inches = 0.21998 Imperial gallons =
   0.26418 US gal.
1 Imperial gallon = 4.5460 litres = 1.20096 US gallons
1 U.S. gallon = 0.83267 Imperial gallons = 3.78528 litres
1 U.S. barrel = 42 US gallons = 34.972 Imperial gallons = 0.15899 cubic metres
1 cubic metre = 1 000 litres = 35.3148 cubic feet = 1.30795 cubic yards = 219.97
   Imperial gallons = 264.18 US gallons = 6.290 US barrels
1 m³ solid = 750 kg. fuelwood with 40% moisture

---

[1] Source: FAO (1987), 'Useful conversion factors – Appendix 4'.

Mass

1 kilogram = 2.2046 pounds = 1 000 grams
1 pound = 453.592 grams = 0.4536 kilograms
1 ton (UK) = 2 240 pounds = 1 016.05 kilograms = 1.01605 tonnes (metric tons)
= 1.12 US tons = 20 hundred weight (cwt)
1 tonne = 1 000 kilograms = 0.98421 tons (UK) = 1.10231 US tons = 2 204.62
pounds
1 U.S. ton = 2 000 pounds = 17.8572 hundred weight (cwt) = 907.184 kilograms
= 0.907184 tonnes = 0.89286 tons (UK)

Energy

1 kilowatt = 1.3405 horsepower
1 horsepower = 0.746 kilowatts
1 kilojoule = 0.2389 kilogram calories = 0.948 British thermal units (BTU) =
0.001 megajoules = 0.00027778 kilowatt hours
1 kilowatt hour = 3 412 British thermal units = 1.34 horsepower hours = 3 600
kilojoules = 3.6 megajoules

Economic & financial indicators: Currency Units per US$ (*Economist* 18 Aug 2021: 72)

USA/-	China/6.49	Japan/110	Britain/0.72	Canada/1.25
Euro Area/0.85	Norway/8.87	Russia/73.8	Switzerland/0.92	Australia/1.36
India/74.4	Argentina/97.1	Brazil/5.22	Mexico/19.9	Egypt/15.7
Israel/3.23	Saudi Arabia/3.75	So. Africa/14.7	Taiwan/27.8	Turkey/8.66

ABBREVIATIONS AND ACRONYMS

AMUL	Anand Milk Union Limited (co-operative), India
AOD	Aurora Organic Dairy
BCF	balanced cattle feed
CAFO	(Concentrated/Confined animal feeding operation)
CDC	Centers for Disease Control, USA
CiWF	CO_2e: Carbon dioxide equivalent
CH_4	methane, a flow pollutant
CO_2	carbon dioxide, a stock pollutant
CO_2e	carbon dioxide equivalents, e.g, CO_2e of methane is about 28.
CO_2-we	CO_2-warming-equivalent
COP	Conference of the Parties to UN
CSIRO	Commonwealth Scientific and Industrial Research Organisation
DEFRA	Department for Environment, Food and Rural Affairs, UK
DFA	Dairy Farmers of America
EADD	East Africa Dairy Development
EDC	endocrine-disrupting chemical
ESADA	Eastern and Southern Africa Dairy Association
EU	European Union
EPA: FAO	Food and Agricultural Organization of the UN
FAWC	Farm Animal Welfare Council, UK
FDA	Food and Drug Administration, USA
FiBL	Forschungsinstitut für biologischen Landbau, aka Research Institute of Organic Ag
G7	Group of the world's seven top economies, sans Russia after 2014 Crimea invasion
GHGs	greenhouse gases, e.g., carbon dioxide, methane, water vapour, nitrous oxide, ozone
GLY	glyphosate
GMO	genetically-modified organism (aka genetically-engineered)
GWP	global warming potential (https://www.epa.gov/ghgemissions/ understanding-global-warming-potentials)
GWP*	alternative usage of GWP
Hydroponics	Soil-less farming
IDF	International Dairy Federation
IFOAM	International Federation of Organic Agricultural Movements
LLCP	long-lived climate pollutant
IPCC	Intergovernmental Panel on Climate Change
LCA	Life cycle analysis
LO'L	Land O'Lakes, US cooperative active in overseas dairy development
N_2O	Nitrous oxide

NOP | AMS	National Organic Program | Agricultural Marketing Service, USA
NDDB	National Dairy Development Board, India
NIH	National Institutes of Health, USA
NODPA	Northeast Organic Dairy Producers Alliance, USA
NOSB	National Organic Agricultural Movements, USDA
OECD	Organisation for Economic Co-operation and Development
OMSCO	Organic Milk Suppliers Co-operative, UK
OV	Organic Valley dairy cooperative, USA
NDDB	National Dairy Development Board of India
PETA	People for the Ethical Treatment of Animals
SA	Soil Associate, UK organic advocate
SARA	subacute rumen acidosis in cows
SLCP	short-lived climate pollutant (opposed to Long-Lived CP)
UK	United Kingdom
UNFCCC	United Nations Framework Convention on Climate Change
US/USA	United States of America
USAID	U.S. Agency for International Development
USDA	US Department of Agriculture
US EPA	US Environmental Protection Agency
WHO	World Health Organization
WSU	Washington State University
WSDF	Washington State Dairy Federation

GLOSSARY

Affect human consciousness, desire, emotion, fear, pain reason, and intention arguably shared with animals, with-or-sans neocortex (*CDoC* 2012).

Agro-ecosystem eco-system on particular farmland.

Allogrooming animal social grooming, sometimes intensified in confinement.

Animals non-human mammals, though fish, fowl and insects are included increasingly.

Animal rights belief of vegetarians and vegans that humans should not exploit animals.

Animal welfare belief that humans may use, even eat animals if suffering is minimised.

Anthropocene epoch following the Holocene, when human effects on Earth appeared.

Biosphere global ecosystem of life from the ocean floor to the lower atmosphere.

Bovine spongiform encephalopathy (BSE) cow prion disease similar to human CJD.

Cognitive globalization evolving network of ideas shared in most countries.

Co-operative (also co-op, or coop) voluntary association to meet common economic, social and other goals. Examples: Organic Valley (US) and Amul (India).

Creutzfeldt-Jakob disease (CJD) human prion disease similar to Mad Cow disease (BSE).

Dairist person involved with dairying, especially in India.

Earthling (Collins) human inhabitants of Earth, as used in science fiction.

Farmgate price what farmers are paid for milk, crops, etc.

Food miles distance from farm to plate; said to average 1500 miles in USA.

Food sovereignty system, often localized, in which producers, distributers and consumers of food control food production[1] and distribution.[2]

Generations baby Boomers, born 1946–1964 (including Generation Jones, 1955–65); Generation X, 1965–80; Xennials, 1977–83; Millennials, 1981–96; Generation Z, 1997–12; and Gen Alpha: born 2010 or after (*Independent 22* Jul 2020).

Genetically-modified Organism (GMO) having genetic material modified – or engineered (GE) – in the laboratory. Early cases are GM/GE insulin and dairy hormone BGH/BST.

Glyphosate herbicide often used with genetically modified or -engineered (GM/GE) crops.

Grazing livestock-eating grasses and other plants on farm pasture or common land.

Holocene last twelve millennia since last major glaciation, before present Anthropocene.

Human rights basic rights (UN 1948 Universal Declaration of Human Rights).

Hydroponics growing plants in nutrient solution, not soil.

Ketosis stressed bovine condition similar to diabetes in humans.

Livestock farm animals, e.g., cows, pigs and sheep.

Locavore consumer prioritizing local food.

Mad Cow disease slang for prion disease bovine spongiform encephalopathy (BSE).

Metropole chief town in an area.

---

1. https://en.wikipedia.org/wiki/Food_production
2. https://en.wikipedia.org/wiki/Food_distribution

Monopsony market with a buyer dominant enough to set prices for rivals.

Neocortex part of human cerebral cortex dealing with perception, emotion, and cognition. Animals' lack of neocortex was taken as a sign of lack of consciousness, but that was later refuted by the *Cambridge Declaration on Consciousness* (*CDoC* 2012: 3).

Non-tariff trade barriers e.g., subsidies, anti-dumping duties, regulatory barriers, and voluntary export restraints.

North American Free Trade Agreement (NAFTA 1994) treaty reforming Mexican, Canadian, and USA tariffs. Followed by 2020 USA–Mexico–Canada Agreement (USMCA).

Organicist organics advocate.

Organic-industrial michael Pollan's (2001) term for corporate agribusiness competition with traditional family-scale organic farms (see Table 5.3a and 5.3b).

Pastoralist nomadic herder, or advocate of pasture grazing over confinement.

Pasture land with grass and herbage for farm animals to graze.

Pneumatic milk machine vacuum equipment to replace hand milking. Now used by robots.

Ruminants cows, deer, antelopes, sheep, and goats of suborder Ruminantia, which chew the cud and have a stomach of four compartments, one of which is the rumen. Professor Frank Mitloehner (UC Davis 2019) says seaweed in feed could dramatically cut the 200 lbs/100 kg of methane annually emitted by cows. Reductions of 60 per cent to 90 per cent may be possible with 1 per cent seaweed in digestible feed.

Seaweed seaweed, or macroalgae, refers to thousands of species of macroscopic, multicellular, marine algae. Types include brown, green, red and kelp.

Sentience awareness of pleasure, happiness, pain and distress. Since Descartes, scientists such as Marian S. Dawkins see human/nonhuman overlap in sentience and emotion.

Supply management production control, e.g., 1984–2015 European milk quota.

Sustainability (1987 UN Brundtland Commission) 'meeting the needs of the present without compromising the ability of future generations to meet their own needs.'

Chapter 1

DAIRYING FROM HOLOCENE HERDING TO ANTHROPOCENE CONFINEMENT

Introduction: Crisis? What dairy crisis?

The image of the pretty cow on this book's cover poses a question: 'Will these mountains retain enough ice and snow to water farmers' crops in river valleys in the twenty-second century?'

Dairy farming faces an existential crisis right now, however. It might not seem so, as over 6 billion of Earth's nearly 8 billion people consume milk and milk products. The dairy sector weathered early phases of the coronavirus pandemic well. China and Vietnam, which some Westerners assumed lactose intolerant, have increased production and consumption greatly since 1990. World consumption has climbed – if not in liquid milk, as in the United States, but certainly in fermented forms such as yogurt, and especially cheese pizza (Robinson 2018a and b). World production is about 81 per cent cow milk, 15 per cent buffalo milk, and 4 per cent for goat, sheep and camel milk combined (FAO-OECD 2021: 179–80). World per capita consumption of processed and fresh dairy products in kilos of milk solids is projected to rise from about 13 kg/cap to 15 kg/cap from 2018 to 2030.

This volume offers abundant information on dairying, some of which will be new even to seasoned observers. The glossary, bibliography and index are here to help. To avoid confusion, consider that dairy's methane emissions are a unique part of the overall climate crisis confronting us, as suggested by the book's subtitle: ethics, environment and politics.

Politics rears its head in national planning in emerging economies such as India, where forest and areas historically allotted to herders and marginal dairy farmers have been reclassified for industrial development (advocates of food sovereignty for indigenous people cast this as an archetypal excess of capitalist globalization). In developed countries, woke activist young people increasingly eschew cow milk for plant-based drinks, and demand political protections for animals whose lives they deem nasty, brutish and short in megadairy confinement.

Figure 1.1 Cow and calves on the 900-year-old Kepier Hospital Farm on River Wear, Durham, UK.

Ethics of eating other, possibly sentient, creatures has vexed humans for millennia. Thus, discussion of Jainism, veganism, vegetarianism and laboratory meat follows in succeeding chapters.

Environmental concerns demand emergency attention: Dairy's emission of about 15 per cent of greenhouse gases, especially of ruminant methane which is a faster-acting global warmer than carbon, could push average Earth's temperatures past 1.5°C above pre-Industrial Revolution levels, melting glaciers, inundating coastal areas and generating unprecedented patterns of floods and tornadoes. Dairy must confront such hard truths, if it is to be sustained into the twenty-second century. Fortunately, experts agree dramatic cuts in ruminant methane are possible by adding seaweed to cattle feed.

Chapter 5 combines the author's ideas (Scholten 2007a) on Women's Grass Ceiling with insights by others (Shortall et al. 2017), in the spirit of the 2030 Agenda for Sustainable Development (FAO-UN 2018), urging investments in the empowerment and training of women on all continents to engage in the growth, distribution and application of seaweed in ruminant agriculture to better themselves – and the planet.

This book does not have all the answers. But it suggests solutions to the climate crisis that could give humans more time to consider dietary ethics and farm politics.

Malthus, population and famine

What's a failed vegetarian to do? How should any of us – vegan, vegetarian or ravenous carnivore – consider food security, amid predictions that the Earth's population could reach 9.5 or even 10 billion by the year 2050? How can farmers feed us without converting remaining forests – which act as the world's green lungs – to grazing or crops? Technological solutions, in land management and animal control, have staved off the permanent famine implicit in the warnings of Englishman Thomas Robert Malthus (1766–1834) that human population tended to outrun food supply, but the welfare of farm animals often suffered as space for them shrank. According to United Nations (2017) estimates, the world population tripled from 2.5 billion people in 1950 to 7.6 billion in 2018. Around the globe, land previously committed to forest or livestock grazing is increasingly converted to high-value crops such as soybeans, palm oil and oilseeds that feed cattle far away (*Economist* 2010). Dairy's first problem is engaging with Malthus.

The initial chapter of this book lays out the world in which we find ourselves. Much of the discussion revolves around the United States as a key country in which dairying has undergone tremendous changes over the past half-century. We draw on academic sources as well as more popular sources given that the food we grow, raise and eat is one of the most important issues debated by consumers. As we will see, changes are underway.

Urban sprawl pushes periurban farming out in concentric circles, as population grows. In the US, the Brookings Institution (2017) reported that, although recovery from the financial crisis and Great Recession (2007–09), took an unusually long time compared to earlier downturns, previous flows of migrants from Snowbelt (Northeast and Midwest regions) to the Sun Belt (South and West regions) increased for three consecutive years. In the aggregate, less of the US remains strictly wilderness, and more is rural exurbs or suburbs. In my experience around

Seattle, three of the neighbourhoods I lived in during the 1960s and 1970s had equestrian fields offering riding lessons, before each morphed into houses or shops a few years later. In recent decades, the green dairy and beef pastures that graced areas around Puget Sound have turned into businesses, shopping centres and apartments, making Seattle the fastest-growing city in the country – albeit one now more renowned for transport gridlock than its verdant moniker, the Emerald City, suggests.

Dairy's second big problem worldwide is environmental. As humanity's eco-footprint deepens, it is difficult to balance concern for humans, animals including large mammals, bees and the microbes in our guts, with the environment. Some scientists argue that we have passed the tipping point for the sustainability of livestock agriculture. A meta-analysis published in *Science*, by Joseph Poore and T. Nemecek (2018: 987), of data from 38,700 farms and 1,600 processors producing forty assorted farm goods around the world, identified livestock agriculture as the priority in mitigating damage to atmosphere, land and oceans, claiming, 'Most strikingly, impacts of the lowest-impact animal products typically exceed those of vegetable substitutes, providing new evidence for the importance of dietary change.' In *The Guardian* (2018b), Damian Carrington (2018) interpreted their study to mean, 'Avoiding meat and dairy products is the single biggest way to reduce your environmental impact on the planet …' But, must livestock production be eliminated? This is the ultimate question, a question this book seeks to answer. Poore and Nemecek observe that the environmental cost of producing the same foods is variable. Therefore, significant gains could be made by addressing a few producers with the deepest environmental hoofprints. Dairy advocates such as Dr Jude L. Capper (2013) agree improvements and innovations should continue. Others suggest that, instead of banning the grazing of livestock on pasture, it would be more ethical and environmentally sensible to limit human population. That seems improbable, since China ended its one-child policy in 2016.

Ethics and climate

The questions we are exploring in this book, and to which we might or might not find answers, include the following: Are multi-thousand cow megadairies more climate-friendly, in terms of greenhouse gas and other emissions, than traditional small family-scale pasture-grazing farms? The United States Department of Agriculture (USDA) defines concentrated animal feeding operations (CAFOs) as those in which over 1,000 animal units are confined for over forty-five days a year. The US Environmental Protection Agency (EPA N.D.) monitors pollution and defines AFOs as agricultural enterprises where animals are kept and raised in confined situations. Typically, animal welfarists replace the word *concentrated* with *confined*, which CAFO advocates resist as pejorative. However, exponents of intensive systems (including Jude Capper) write of 'confinement and grass-based dairy farms' (O'Brien et al. 2014: 1835–51). The terms *concentrated* and *confined* are interchangeable here with CAFOs, but antithetical to traditional pasture-grazing systems.

According to Northeast Organic Dairy Producers Alliance (NODPA) communication officer Ed Maltby, the logistical limit for managed intensive rotational grazing (MIRG) is 1,000 cows. Recalling an organic farm in Massachusetts, he said: 'I know it can be done if you have a commitment to pasture-based systems' (Scholten 2014: 111).

Even if dairying has sufficient space on Earth, and is environmentally sustainable, activists question the ethics of animal welfare. In the United Kingdom, the Farm Animal Welfare Council (1997) listed 'Five freedoms' implicit to ethical farming: 1. freedom from hunger and thirst – by ready access to fresh water and a diet to maintain full health and vigour; 2. freedom from discomfort – by providing an appropriate environment including shelter and a comfortable resting area; 3. freedom from pain, injury or disease – by prevention or rapid diagnosis and treatment; 4. freedom to express normal behaviour – by providing sufficient space, proper facilities and company of the animal's own kind; 5. freedom from fear and distress. Intensive confinement dairying is most criticized on Point 1, via high-energy diets that boost milk production but ultimately weaken condition and limit longevity, and on Point 4, given the insufficient space in high-density confinement which limits freedom to express instinctive behaviours.

Overview: Intensive US dairying sets the world pattern for farm consolidation

This author grew up on a family dairy farm that began with twenty cows, all named, on forty acres carved from second-growth forest, a few miles south of the US–Canada border but not far from Vancouver. Over fifty years, our herd grew to ninety cows, plus a bull and twenty heifers (at its peak) on ninety acres. Today, such farms are no longer economic when producing conventional milk – nor even with an organic milk price premium. In the 1950s and 60s, we learned that our Dutch-American relatives in California were organizing farms with hundreds of dairy cows, but when a neighbour near Sumas, Washington, built a larger barn to milk a herd of 200, old farmers expected it to fail. That farm continues, but struggles to achieve profitability with 400 cows. In 1950, our Whatcom County had about 3,000 small-scale milk producers.

In 2022, Whatcom dairy farms number barely 104 averaging 400 cows – most of the animals have been absorbed by large megadairies. Most of Washington State's milk production has relocated over the Cascade Mountains to arid Eastern Washington, where huge megadairies rely on irrigation from the Columbia River for cows and cattle feed. This megadairy pattern, which originated around Los Angeles with Dutch immigrant ingenuity spawned in the tiny Netherlands, spread up the US West Coast and around the world. Bucolic images of cows munching meadow daisies faded around 1970, as cows were increasingly confined in feedlots year around, except for perhaps a dry period when cows healthy enough to be impregnated were allowed on fields before birthing their next calf.

The transition from small-scale dairying in mixed crop farming to intensive dairy monoculture is recorded in *Hoard's Dairyman* magazine. It was established in Wisconsin in 1885, and recently published Chinese- and Spanish-language editions for their growing markets. When this author was born in 1951, the US Department of Agriculture estimated there were 3.5 million farms with dairy cows. I have occasionally contributed to *Hoard's* since 1988, when the US had around 200,000 dairy farms. On 3 March 2022, *Hoard's Dairyman* circulated a benchmark article titled 'Dairy farm numbers slide below 30,000', a 90 per cent decrease in 40 years. A bellwether for this US dairy nadir had come twenty-five years earlier, however, when London-based magazine *Dairy News* (Scholten 1997b: 6) asked me to enumerate US dairy farmers, then declining toward 100,000. With cheeky British humour, the editors titled my article 'Bye-bye this American guy'. The article confirmed the decimation of small US family dairy farms, with consequent reductions in rural employment and community income.

The remaining, dominant, high-density 10,000+ cow megadairies produce ample cheap milk for consumers, but bring with them negative externalities including low animal longevity and welfare and the pollution of both the air and waterways (Scholten 2014). Succeeding chapters will detail these conditions. Here, readers may note that the world 2013 DeLaval Cow Longevity conference in Sweden acknowledged that the US set this intensive pattern, which has been adopted gradually by most industrialized, middle-income and developing countries. Some of the few exceptions are Canada which, unlike the European Union nations, retains its milk quota, and India whose co-operatives support women and marginal dairy farmers. China has some megadairies, with some facilities managed co-operatively, as is the case in Mongolia, a boon to small dairy farmers.

It seems logical that less developed countries with dairy sectors could maximize rural prosperity with voluntary co-operatives that improve family income, as shown by India's Amul model. Industrialized countries such as the US may provide enough jobs in services and (decreasingly) manufacturing to offset the loss of dairy jobs. But it spurs rural-to-urban migration – and puts the spotlight on the ethics of animal welfare in confined megadairies.

If seaweed in feed solves dairy methane, might it obviate plant-based trends?

Debates on such questions are underway around the world, and not just in rich countries where agribusiness sometimes ridicules climate activists as Greta Thunberg clones who are neglecting their schoolwork. India, an emerging economy but wrestling with food poverty in the COVID-19 pandemic, takes climate mitigation seriously as the Jet Stream fluctuates, endangering its largely rain-fed agriculture, and water tables in the Punjab. For example, the Mansinhbhai Institute of Dairy and Food Technology (MIDFT 2020) in Mehsana, linked to Dudhsagar co-operative dairy, hosted a webinar on 'Reducing Carbon Footprint in the Dairy Industry'. This is significant, as India bypassed the US as the world's top milk producer in about 1998 (Scholten 2010; Sundaresan 2014). It is becoming common knowledge that the methane burped out by cows, not carbon, is dairy's most worrying climate hoofprint. Weak jokes about flatulence are passé once it is obvious cow burps are the problem, and seaweed is part of the solution (more on this later). Consumers avoiding dairy drinks out of climate concerns might return to dairy if it breaks its methane curse.

In cities from Bangkok to Tel Aviv, plant-based foods are beginning to challenge the nutritional, environmental, climate and animal welfare practices of the US livestock model. Vegetarianism which includes dairy is not at all a new trend, as perhaps 40 per cent of India's 1.2 billion people are milk-consuming vegetarians (especially in the Northwest); less well known, however, is that some Indians are vegan, influenced by Buddhist, Hindu and Jain ethical traditions (India in Pixels 2014; Ipsos-MORI 2018). Adding to what is a complex situation are different perceptions of Brahman cattle, which are protected from human consumption in Hinduism, unlike water buffalo. The complexity increases when we discover that in the era of India's Prime Minister Modi, a Tamil Brahmin, Ms. Indira Nooyi, is claimed to head the world's biggest cow-meat supplier company, supplying PepsiCo's Frito-Lay Matador meat snacks in North America (*Muslim Mirror* 2016).

Great-grandmothers versus the modern obsession with micronutrients

Also in flux is the nature of food and nutrients explored, for example, by respected food pundit Michael Pollan in his 2008 book *In Defense of Food*. On US and UK chat shows, he has advised consumers to avoid anything their great-grandmothers would not recognize as food. Pollan (2008: 20–3) recounts the identification of macronutrients such as protein, fat and carbohydrates by Englishman William Prout (1785–1850), and circumspectly admires the addition by Justus von Liebig (1803–73) of the minerals nitrogen, phosphorous and potassium (N, P and K) to macronutrients in food – the same minerals he had identified as crucial to soil in agriculture. Although Pollan credits the identification by Polish biochemist Kazimierz Funk (1884–1967) of vitamins central to nutritional science, he (like nutritionist Marion Nestle) seems uncomfortable with scientific reductionism regarding food, blaming obsession with micronutrients for distorting the US diet. Epitomized by nutritionists' excoriation of dairy butter – in favour of margarine, containing unhealthy transfats – such campaigns left Americans more obese and prone to heart disease than people following Mediterranean diets replete with olive oil and including dairy products such as cheese. Likewise, E. Melanie DuPuis acknowledges how politics and commercial interests have skewed our diets (DuPuis 2015; *Epoch Times* 2016).

Michael Pollan tagged the hegemonizing of the grassroots US organic movement by agribusiness in his 2001 *New York Magazine* article on the aptly named *organic-industrial complex* (Scholten 2002). With his light touch, Pollan attacks obsession with micronutrients as an eating disorder. The good news, he writes, is that the last few decades expansion of farmers' markets and alternative food networks enable more families in many countries to eschew industrial diets in favour of fresh, local – *locavore* – and organic food. Objects of Pollan's suspicion include innovations in plant-based foods, such as meat substitutes from ingredients including soy protein, coconut oil and corn starch. Consider that von Liebig's identification of macronutrients N, P and K seemed to explain everything that mattered in human food and soil. It follows that one asks what elements may be missing from twenty-first-century foods concocted from soy, coconut and corn, which animal-based ingredients hitherto supplied. These are issues that purveyors of plant-based foods address – or sidestep – as their wares reach supermarkets faster than many Baby Boomers expected.

Vegconomist (2020b) reported that leading German discount supermarket entities ALDI Nord and ALDI SÜD have harmonized their vegan ranges under the brand 'Mein Veggie Tag' (My veggie day.) Products such as the ersatz meat Wonder Burger will soon be available in Aldi's 4,000 German supermarkets and 10,000 stores worldwide as well as in Trader Joe's stores in the US, where Aldi may soon be the third-largest grocery chain after Kroger and Walmart. Aldi's efforts have thus far won it two annual awards as most vegan-friendly discounter by the Albert Schweitzer Foundation. Millennials and Gen Xers alike may be impressed that Aldi won a 2020 award from People for the Ethical Treatment of Animals. PETA's moto is 'Animals are not ours to experiment on, eat, wear, use for entertainment, or abuse in any other way' (PETA 2017; Mance 2021: 17).

Also making an impact in the US is Pizza Hut's partnership with Beyond Meat, posing a vegan paradigm shift among pepperoni lovers (*Vegconomist* 2020). Beyond Meat calls its plant-based burgers, beef and sausages the future of foods, since they are made from plants such as beets and contain no antibiotics, cholesterol, hormones or genetically modified organisms (GMOs). Proteins are derived from peas, mung beans, faba beans and brown rice. Fats come from cocoa butter, coconut oil and rapeseed (canola) oil. Minerals include calcium, iron, potassium chloride and plenty of salt. Flavours and colours rely on beet juice extract, apple extract and natural flavours, eschewing synthetic additives. Carbohydrates establish texture with potato starch, and methylcellulose (plant-fibre derivative). Would such a culinary assemblage pass Michael Pollan's (2008) great-grandmother's test?

My test of a vegan Beyond Meat cheeseburger, at Cosy Club restaurant in Durham, UK, on 29 April 2021, was encouraging. The somewhat compressed patty tasted fine, if salty, though its thin vegan Gouda cheese slice was underwhelming. An added macaroni cheese fritter on the other half of the bun – both with lettuce, tomato, gherkin and onion – was delicious. Best of all was the distinct lack of remorse around animal-killing. But my own grandmothers might have asked, 'Where's the beef?'

At home a few days later, I compared an Aberdeen beef burger (from a trusted local woman cattle farmer) with a veggie sweet potato and black bean burger (from a Tesco supermarket). The beef burger was fried both sides to medium-rare, and tasted fine. The Tesco veggie burger emerged mushy, even after being baked in the oven for thirty minutes; barbecuing could have been more successful. *As academics are wont to say, more research is needed.*

If Beyond Meat, Tesco and rival offerings pass taste and mouth-feel tests for Millennials, Zennials, younger Gen-Xers, and Gen Zers, meat consumption will drop. That said, meat-heavy barbeques are non-woke tropes of Baby Boomer culture that may persist as long as we do. Also, the hesitancy of many Americans to receive COVID-19 vaccinations before long-term tests are complete suggests scientific safety and nutrition studies will be needed for wide acceptance of ersatz, analogue meat.

'Clean' meat from laboratories?

Non-plant-based 'clean meat' is on the horizon. Bill Gates, Richard Branson and late GE boss Jack Welch invested millions in laboratory-grown, tissue-engineered foods, citing UN-FAO estimates that meeting the meat demands of about 9.6 billion people by 2050 required 70 per cent more food, which in turn entailed deforestation and increases in greenhouse gas emissions by 77 per cent (CNBC 2018b). Whether or not family-scale farmers could compete with corporate power in analogue flesh chains requires political debate.

What are the unintended environmental consequences of a shift from pastured cows to plant-based 'milk?' Almond milk sounds viable until one quantifies the water costs of almond plantations in California's drought-ridden valleys, not to mention the damage to bee populations from pesticides in the nut-based monoculture producing the non-dairy stuff.

Of course, the attraction of so-called clean meat, compared to ersatz Beyond Meat, is that it is distinguished from fake or plant-based meat because it derives from real meat, grown from actual meat cells, presumably *sans* environmental deforestation, atmospheric loading and nutrient excretion linked to traditional dairy and meat production – not to mention the ethical baggage of sacrificing an animal's life. 'Clean' meat might have more traditional beef texture than the rival Beyond Meat vegan burger, and perhaps a better nutritional profile than such salty plant-based analogue meats.

Dilemmas for discussion

This book calls for a wider-ranging and deeper discussion of issues pertinent to feeding the world. Is a general shift from an omnivorous heavy in animal protein diet to a plant-based vegan diet, or a diet supplemented by laboratory-grown meat – without killing any more livestock – a better menu for our planet? It is important to consider other factors. For example, a 100 per cent shift to veganism is unlikely any time soon, given the fact that cows, sheep and goats eat plant matter inedible to humans, often on land unsuited to other uses, as researchers Christopher M. Wathes, Henry Buller, Heather Maggs and Madeleine L. Campbell observe in the journal *Animals* (2013, 2014).

The above concerns and their possible solutions are not the only ones confronting dairy farming in the twenty-first century but they are an important start. Forecasting sustainability in the human diet requires critical discussion of the complex interplay not just of considerations of human and animal health, ethics and the environment, but also cultural, social, economic, political, geographical and environmental factors. One point of departure is asking why some consumers in prosperous countries, and especially Millennials and Gen Xers, no longer view milk as what E. Melanie DuPuis (2002) called *Nature's Perfect Food*? Why do some see dairy animal milk as an unnatural commodity sourced via environmentally hostile methods that are intrinsically unethical, cruel – even sexist to animals – rather than the human-friendly resource portrayed by the traditional dairy industry? Why are many young people receptive to Kathryn Gillespie's (2014ab) feminist critique of dairying as a sector of *grievability* for female and male animals, whose violence is inherent to neoliberalism?

In extending the discussion, it's important to consider counter-arguments from agribusiness experts, who reject green developments described above in their belief that criticisms of intensive dairying are deployed by well-meaning but naïve urbanites lacking a historic, scientific and practical understanding of livestock farming and consumption. These experts include Jude L. Capper 2012ab, 2018ab; *JRS* 2016), whose papers and public voice have defended the environmental and animal welfare aspects of intensive confinement trends in post-1945 dairying. For example, Capper has consulted for the EU DairyCare project (*Dairy Site* 2013) on welfare and precision dairy farming.

What this book covers

This chapter, Chapter 1, presents an overview of milk production, processing and consumption from past to present, with examples from all continents (including Antarctica, where my fellow geographer Dr Charles Howie observed South American scientists keeping sheep for meat and, perhaps, milk). Interspersed in this volume are notes on the ethics of livestock farming, including views from Enlightenment rationalist René Descartes (1596–1650) to present-day biologist Marian Stamp Dawkins and philosopher Peter Singer.

To get a sense of what concerns people, three chapters in this book are devoted to responses from a range of 100 stakeholders to nine statements and questions or queries. Expert responders and those who made revelatory comments were retained, and ambiguous surveys culled to make an even 100.

Respondents ranged from academic food experts to farmers to activists – all consumers – speaking in their own words about their concerns regarding today's dairy industry. There is overlap among ethics, environment and politics in all chapters, but the sequence of survey questions guides discussion of answers and comments by pseudonymously named respondents from sixteen countries: Austria, Bangladesh, Brazil, China, Germany, Libya, Italy, New Zealand, Norway, Poland, Saudi Arabia, Serbia, Spain, Thailand, the UK and the US.

To vary pace, sidebars illustrate respondents' positionality, farming links and perceptions of how government, business and farmers' associations treat farmers, and how animals are treated. In Chapter 2, Politics, Family Farmers and Animals, the three queries to which these 100 responded were:

Q1. Farming is part of my family history.
Q2. Politicians, corporations and co-operatives treat our country's faily dairy farmers fairly.
Q3. My country's food system provides adequate animal welfare.

Chapter 3, Ethics and Animals, explores respondents' views on managing cattle, whether or not animals should be allowed to exercise instinctive behaviours such as grazing on pasture, whether they are healthy, whether they get what they want (Dawkins 2012ab) – and whether or not respondents are willing to pay more for humanely raised livestock products. The most poignant query (Q6) is on the ethics of eating creatures who seemingly share facets of human sentience such as affect, emotion, joy, pain, planning and humour (Singer 1990 (2nd edition of 1975 *Animal Liberation*), 2002; Dawkins 2012a; *Daily Mail* 2012; *Journal of Bioethical Inquiry* 2013). For decades, scientists ridiculed laypersons who ascribed human-like joy, pain and affection to animals as callow anthropomorphism. But, noted primatologist Frans de Waal warns the greater risk is not to anthropomorphize (de Waal 1999; Andrews 2020; Mance 2021: 11).

Q4. Cattle should be allowed natural behaviours, e.g., cows should graze fields >120 days a year.
Q5. I would pay a little more for pasture-grazed dairy products and meat.
Q6. It is not ethical to eat sentient animals like cows, goats, horses, pigs, and sheep.

Chapter 4, Environment and Livestock Agriculture, wraps up the discussion with respondents' views on the existential relationship between their diets, livestock emissions, environment and climate. Their responses reveal interesting contradictions with respect to their responses to the three queries discussed in Chapter 3.

Q7. Livestock ag unacceptably harms the environment & climate.
Q8. Vegan meals can be as tasty as those using ingredients from livestock.
Q9. Plant-based dairy and laboratory-grown meat substitutes could replace food animals soon.

Chapter 5, Women's Grass Ceiling: Nexus of Ethics, Environment and Politics, acknowledges that dairying is situated in communities and addresses this from the perspective of gendered work. The title of the chapter suggests this is a complex issue, and the chapter unites its ethical, environmental, and political aspects. It focuses on the US, but is based on World Bank employment data for all countries, and informed by 'Empowering rural women, powering agriculture', the UN-FAO policy document (2018b) in the 2030 Agenda for Sustainable Development. The FAO recognizes that women compose half of farm workers in developing countries, but suffer unequal access to resources, especially in Africa and Asia where most population growth is expected by 2050. To nourish and educate their own children, while helping the 821 million underfed people in the world (FAO 2018), women farmers need better training and infrastructure investment to increase yields. The political and ethical will to boost rural women's empowerment is calculated to 'leave no one behind' in the near term – and by meeting 17 UN (n.d.) Sustainable Development Goals it can help stabilize the climate in the long term. Chapter 5 combines my personal (Scholten 2007) and academic observations of the grass ceiling, with insights by Sally Shortall et al. (2017) in their report on *Women in Farming and the Agriculture Sector* for the Scottish Government, to understand how training can tip the balance to empowerment.

Chapter 6, Conclusions on Cows, Climate and Humans, reviews trends in Africa, Asia, Oceania, Europe, North & South America in the twenty-first century, combining insights from the US, EU and India, the leading global milk producers. (See: FAO Food Outlook 2014: 2013 World Dairy Production of 767 Million Tonnes: USA/91MT, EU-27/157MT, India/138MT, Africa). Global data help paint possible ethical, environmental and political futures for diets with or without dairy farming toward 2050 and the end of the twenty-first century. Lists of acronyms, abbreviations, a glossary, bibliography and index help navigate the text.

We now return to the discussion we began further above and delve into how the current situation developed. Again, there is particularly attention to the US as a key dairy country and trendsetter.

Dairy structures and the ethics of confinement

The trebling of Earth's human population in this author's lifetime, from 2.5 billion in 1950 to 7.7 billion in 2020, has reduced space for livestock pastoralism on common land or grazing on farms. As a result, the US and many other industrialized countries confine most dairy cows in barns or feedlots. Critics claim that such high-density stocking increases stress, pain and shorter lives for dairy animals than their grazing ancestors experienced.

Imagine if cows could vote. Although the US Department of Agriculture (USDA 2015) portrays a positive trend to increased food security with fewer cows producing more milk – an apparent example of what Jules Pretty (2009, 2011) dubbed sustainable intensification – it is doubtful that cattle on the ground would vote for intensive farming. For that matter, in his book *How to Love Animals* (2021: 3) Henry Mance notes: 'No one would vote for the looming mass extinctions of wild animals, certainly not the animals themselves.' Wild animal populations have fallen by 'two-thirds on average since 1970, according to the Living Planet Index', partly due to animal trading in Asia and elsewhere. British truckers hypothesize that diminished bug splatter on windscreens, compared to decades ago, is due to the overuse of arable pesticides. Wild habitat and biodiversity have shrunk due to expanding human population as well as the growing of soy and other inputs for cows in affluent countries that produce four times as much milk as a century ago, but have much shorter lives. It is no surprise that younger generations are turning away from the animal-based food strongly tied to intensive farming.

In this part of the chapter, we examine the twentieth-century shift from low-input extensive small-scale pasture-grazing farms to high-input, intensive, large-scale confined (aka concentrated) animal feeding operations, which Andrew Wesley and Heather Kroemer note are spreading from the US to the UK (*Guardian* 2018a). CAFOs have infiltrated the whole world, including China.

There is mounting evidence that the supposed efficiency of megadairies – concentrations of thousands of cows in feedlots – is overshadowed by negative externalities, i.e., cumulative dangers to human health by, for example, the overuse of livestock antibiotics (*Lancet* 2020). These threaten efficacy for human health, harm the environment via water pollution and compromise cows' welfare to the point that their lives are drastically shorter compared to their ancestors in the 1950s. At the same time, megadairies are blamed for weakening the socio-economic fabric of rural communities by bankrupting small fifty-to-100 cow family-scale farms that have less negative impact on animals and ecology.

Defenders of intensive dairying, such as Jude L. Capper, parry criticism by claiming modern feeding regimes are environmentally friendly and based on science (Capper et al. 2009; Capper 2017, 2018abc, 2020). Critics say intensive technologies maximize yield to the detriment of cow health, well-being and longevity (Dawkins 2012ab; Biagiotti 2013, 2014). Here it is useful to consider the fact that cows evolved to maintain milk for their calves, even when fodder is sparse. Now, cows in hyper-production dairies maintain milk yield even as their body condition drops, and when they are too weak to conceive another calf, they are culled. Manipulation of cows' natural diets and their instinctive behaviours, shifting from pasture-grazing to confinement in factory farming, can weaken well-being and shorten their lives. Indeed, dairy cow longevity in the US has halved since 1950 (DHI-Provo 2013; Scholten 2014). *What cow would vote for that?*

European research supports cows' pessimism. In the *Journal of Dairy Research*, Caja, Castro-Costa and Knight (2016: 138, 136–47) cite Capper et al. (2009), noting intensive dairying's reverse Malthusian production of more milk from fewer cows. The downside is heavy involuntary culling, based on 'reproductive failures and udder health issues, each comprising between a quarter and a third of total culling'. Longevity is tied to milk prices:

The reality is that productive lifespan averages 2–3 and rarely exceeds 3–4 lactations, the culling rate ranging from 21 to 36% in dairy cows, being greater in USA than in EU and being dramatically affected by milk price.

Human–bovine relations across millennia

In humanity's progress from hunting and gathering to agriculture, livestock became increasingly valuable, not only for food but also for traction power, and as a store of wealth in farming, transport, and economic transactions, respectively. The domestication of cows, sheep and goats occurred during the Neolithic Revolution, 9000–7000 BC (11,000–9000 BEFORE PRESENT) in Mesopotamia, and 3500–3000 BC (5500–5000 BP) in the Americas (Bellwood 2005; Meadow 1996). Knox and Marston (2007: 310–11) write that the domestication of draft animals occurred concurrently with the domestication of wheat and rice around 6500 BP.

This timescale may evoke pastoral images of cows lowing in meadows or rustic outdoor cattle pens. But the reality is redder in tooth and claw. Consider that modern-day bovines were domesticated about 8000 years ago from aurochs, *Bos primigenius*. Aurochs doubtless felt fear of tigers, and annoyance, at least, at humans pursuing them with spears. Humans' fear of aurochs was eventually mitigated by animal husbandry, which turned them from wild beasts into domesticated livestock.

As aurochs' progeny were bred for smaller size and docility, these modern cows' more aggressive cousins dwindled in number as agriculture encroached on their habitat. Aurochs were prey animals to predators such as sabre-toothed tigers, and became virtually extinct in the 1600s. Standing about two metres tall, aurochs were massive compared to even our biggest contemporary very high-yielding Holstein-Friesians. Modern cows and other herbivores can be seen not just as herd animals, but also still as prey animals loath to show weakness, lest they encourage attack by predators. Don Hogland and Bonnie Beaver, defenders of intensive dairying (*Hoard's Dairyman* Nov 2015: 735), warn that, 'The comfortable cow is a human illusion', based on unscientific anthropomorphism. Moreover, graduates of Netherlands-based *CowSignals Training* (2018) may detect dairy cows' suffering – and its opposite, comfort – otherwise hidden to some observers.

Understanding animal behaviour involving both fear and pain can help us parse concepts of the ethics and efficacy of livestock agriculture. Animals' fear of human handlers, and fears of confinement involving halters, milking machinery, stanchions or fences, can be obstacles to intensive operations. The abuse of animals in livestock agriculture has sometimes been excused by the religious logic that supposedly *dumb* animals do not suffer pain, on the spiritual assertion that they lack souls. Abuse has also been excused on the secular, anatomical logic that animals lack a cerebral cortex, neocortex or other neurological accoutrements. But Temple Grandin (1989), an eminent animal behavioural scientist from Colorado State University at Fort Collins, Colorado, has worked with others to dispel notions that the descendants of aurochs do not experience fear and pain, or should endure abusive conditions that, if they had to endure such conditions themselves, would mortify humans.

In her article in *Hoard's Dairyman* (2013: 684), Grandin praised scientists for contributions in understanding human–nonhuman interactions. One is Jack Albright, an emeritus professor of Purdue University who co-wrote *The Behaviour of Cattle* (Albright and Arave 1997; also, *Hoard's*, Nov. 1998: 787). Albright and Arave showed that tame dairy cows willing to approach people will give more milk. From her personal position on the autism spectrum, Grandin offers unique perspectives on animal perception. She writes that cows do not recognize human faces, but *do* remember places, smells, voices, distinctive clothing and certain objects. Therefore, to mitigate farm animals' fear of their keepers and to familiarize them with what they do recognize, it is crucial for humans to socialize with calves when they are young (a form of imprinting), and to make their newly calved heifer mothers comfortable in introduction to the milking barn. Harsh treatment, such as hitting cows with sticks or shocking them with electric prods, might be more prevalent on megadairies with untrained, non-family staff who do not feel invested in farm success. Such treatment reduces milk production and may embed a fear memory that permanently alienates a cow from handlers and surroundings such as milking parlours. What experienced dairy farmers knew – that kind treatment of animals pays off in milk yield – was validated by Albright and Arave's research.

Grandin (*Hoard's Dairyman* 2013: 684) relates that Australian Paul H. Hemsworth, at the University of Melbourne, estimated cow fearfulness by determining the degree of restlessness a cow exhibited when a stockperson neared her during milking. Hemsworth was lead author of a paper titled 'The effects of cognitive behavioural intervention on the attitude and behaviour of stockpersons and the behaviour and productivity of commercial dairy cows' (*Journal of Animal Science* 2002). The study involved two large experiments evaluating the effects of a training programme targeting attitudinal and behavioural variables in stock people. The results indicated that cognitive-behavioural interventions targeting the key attitudes and behaviour of stock people that regulate cows' fear of humans can improve milk yield. One intervention consisted of a cognitive-behavioural procedure designed to improve the attitude and behaviour of stock people to cows, and a control treatment, in which no intervention was attempted. Briefly, this intervention (Experiment 1) also revealed that cows at the intervention farms showed a significantly shorter ($P < 0.05$) flight distance to humans, indicating lower level of fear of humans. In Experiment 2, a significant ($P < 0.05$) increase was found in the milk yield of cows following the treatment. Similar treatment effects were observed on both milk protein and milk fat, two markers of milk quality.

Fear memories are important in human-non-human dynamics, and bovines' fear memories of people, places or objects may eventually be overridden but they may be unforgettable. At New York University, Joseph LeDoux has been credited by many observers, including Temple Grandin (*Hoard's Dairyman* 2013: 684), with locating fear centres in the amygdala (under the cortex in a more primitive part of the brain). It is not quite so simple, wrote LeDoux in a blog on *Psychology Today*

(2015). It is true that some humans and other mammals who suffer damage to the amygdala lose some fight-or-flight behaviour, but the amygdala contributes to a complicated detection system which long ago evolved in the brain.

With respect to pain, it is not always straightforward to detect when animals feel it. Those who might not detect animals' fear include farmers as well as city slickers. In Grandin's paper with Mark Deesing (2002), titled 'Distress in Animals: Is it Fear, Pain or Physical Stress?' for the American Board of Veterinary Practitioners, the authors parsed animals' separate but intertwined neurological and anatomical experiences of fear, pain and stress. They then went further, arguing that animals other than humans feel pain like humans do and seek to isolate it in their bodies via *pain guarding*. However, animals stop guarding to hide manifestations of their pain from potential foes, because that need overrides the need to prevent further damage to their injury. This illustrates why clinical observation of animals by hidden cameras are more revealing than observations by farmers, whose presence is known. Grandin and Deesing (2002: 2) state: 'All mammals pain guard after an injury. Dogs, cats, rats and horses limp and avoid putting weight on an injured limb. Poultry also engage in pain guarding after beak trimming and will peck less.' In an update to the paper, Grandin and Deesing (2002: 4) relate the case of a bull who appeared stoic when aware of observers, but suffered in private:

> We observed this behaviour recently in a bull that was being castrated with a large rubber band. When he was unaware of being watched, he laid on his side and was moaning. As soon as he saw us, he jumped up and behaved as if he was not in pain until we left.

The observation above shows that, as well as hiding physical distress, physical pain and fear from animal foes, prey animals also hide it from human handlers. (More discussion of predators and prey is found in Scholten 2014: 45, 77, 103, 122.) Sub-acute lameness is difficult to spot, but observation of cow visits to grooming devices showed 'lame and severely lame cows did not use brushes that were installed away from the feed bunk but continued to use brushes that were installed next to the feed bunk', according to R. Mandel et al. in *Journal of Dairy Science* (2018a). This suggests they need to display normal behaviour to avoid attracting the attention of predators. Cow handlers seeking to recognize animal ailments in other ways, for example by trying to identify visual cues like leg abrasions or visibly empty rumens that betray pain or dietary issues. This is a priority of the CowSignals organization, which enlightens farmers about bovines' cognitive characteristics (Dawkins 1998, 2007, 2012ab). CowSignals has trained farmers, veterinarians and livestock handlers in some forty-five countries in methods it claims keep cows healthier, living twice as long as most in intensive confinement dairying. Veterinarian and author Hue Karreman became the first CowSignals trainer in the US, linked to the Organic Valley dairy co-op and *Hoard's Dairyman* magazine (Karreman 2004, 2011, 2013; *Progressive Dairyman* 2013; Scholten 2014: xviii, 35, 122, 178–82, 217).

What this means is that in industrialized farming – with its various physical and psychological threats to cows – their distress is not as easily detectable as might be surmised and can therefore be disregarded by its advocates. Let's now turn to the era before plant-based milk came on the scene.

Milk-drinking in modernity

Drinking ice-cold milk was a joy of American culture in the mid-twentieth century. It was a pleasure after school sports., and became a staple with mass-produced foods such as cornflakes at breakfast or even at bedtime. But imbibing so much liquid milk is a recent phenomenon, a historical rarity. In most places, particularly in warmer climates around the world, milk was quickly turned into buttermilk, or processed for regional tastes into forms such as yogurt, butter and cheese.

In *Nature's Perfect Food* (2002), Melanie DuPuis relates how, after development of new processes in the Industrial Revolution (including widespread refrigeration), milk won status as a health food in Britain and the United States in the latter part of the nineteenth century. DuPuis writes that families aspired to at least one cow in the backyard for their needs. Manhattan Island had dairy farms in the late 1800s, and sheep grazed Central Park meadow until 1934. As industrialization proceeded, and farmland was converted to residential and business use, the backyard cow disappeared, and commercial firms offered doorstep delivery to families, from cowsheds commonly situated adjacent to urban breweries in New York City, London, Mumbai and elsewhere, according to historical analyses of milk, disease and pasteurization by Peter J. Atkins (1992, 2000, 2001a and b, 2010; *Hobby Farms* 2015). The low-degradability protein in brewer's waste was suitable for dairy cows and feeding it to them was an early step to sustainability. Sadly, however, increasing values of urban real estate ended in confinement of nineteenth-century urban cows who preferred grazing pastures. Cows stuck in muck and bereft of fresh air and sunlight, in unhealthy stocking densities, were an inducement to disease with parallels in twenty-first century factory farming. Tuberculosis was endemic in Britain, with urban cows' milk a vector for TB to other animals and humans (Atkins 1992, 2000, 2001a and b, 2010). This increased demand for clean, fresh milk, this time from country to city via milk train.

But disease remained a problem until Louis Pasteur showed, in 1864, that his eponymous Pasteurization process – i.e., boiling milk, wine, juice or beer – rid these liquids of most pathogenic microbes. It extended their shelf lives and prevented illness in consumers. However, Britain's blue-blood farming aristocracy resisted attempts to introduce pasteurization technology to the national cold chain. Similarly, in the US, as DuPuis notes in bitter irony, infant deaths in the late nineteenth century were statistically higher in prosperous New York social strata in which parents could afford to purchase milk, than among working-class households where parents could not. There were decades of delay in addressing microbes in milk. Atkins (2000), who pinpoints the TB eradication programme in England as occurring between 1900–50 (see also Atkins 1992, 2001a and b, 2010), has estimated that Britain consequently suffered hundreds of thousands of unnecessary human deaths due to tuberculosis before a large-scale eradication programme was finally agreed by national farmers' groups and the government in London; this involved health checks and compulsory euthanasia – putting down infected animals.

Writing on milk in India, the late P.R. Gupta, a publisher in New Delhi who specialized in dairy-related books, including the heavyweight annual *Dairy India Yearbook* (1997, 2000, and 2007 editions), also published a booklet titled *Traditional Milk Products from India* (2000), published online as a poster paper in an FAO e-mail conference on 'Small Scale Milk Collection and Processing in Developing Countries'. Gupta described a history of milk production and consumption in India where boiling at home offered simple sterilization. Households bought milk twice a day, as soon as possible after twice-daily milkings, and fermented surplus into curd for meals. Surplus milk unsold on farms was made into khoa, channa, paneer and ghee. Gupta (2000; personal communication, but now online) wrote how Indian milk-drinkers have taken steps to avoid disease:

> Milk and its products are consumed fresh and therefore the centres of milk production and consumption are close by. So, the need for expensive refrigerated storage and distribution is not necessary. This insistence on freshness in food has become something of an obsession in the Indian mind and is now an ingrained consumer mind-set that is not easily grasped by an outsider.

When, after the Second World War, pasteurization became global best practice against pathogens, and refrigeration became widespread, milk was ready for healthy, nutritious mass consumption. Since Gupta (2000), the picture has changed in India too, whose middle class of over 300 million people – including farmwives – routinely use small refrigerators. They chill traditional dairy products and, increasingly, high-value snacks such as flavoured yogurt from Amul, the leading farmers' co-operative brand based in Gujarat, north of Mumbai. Dairy farming is no longer based only in temperate climates where small-scale farms cater to the locals. Milk has joined other foods which typically travel 1,500 miles between farm and table. Food miles are further discussed below.

Marketing milk drinks: From Milky Way to Almond Joy

The story of marketing of milk during the twentieth century in the US, and the current trend to alternatives such as nut milks, illustrates how public opinion has been shifting first in response to knowledge about nutrition, then to animal welfare, and most recently to the environment. We playfully refer to this as Milky Way (= bovine milk) to Almond Joy (plant-based fake milk); both are also names of popular American milk chocolate bars.

An apotheosis of bovine milk, as a liquid icon of health, strong bones and strength, occurred in the mid-twentieth century US. Its popularity owed much to refrigeration. To improve children's nutrition, the UN-FAO held School Milk conferences on several continents in the 1990s. Organizer Michael Griffin stated the priority was chilling milk, because school children liked it cold but would spurn lukewarm milk (Scholten 2000: 174). In the advertising age of the 1950–60s, dairy co-operatives such as Darigold in the US Pacific Northwest bandied promotional straplines like 'Drink-A-Mugga-Milk-A-Day'. Another slogan that endured on Milky Way refrigerated semi-trucks on the US west coast was 'Make Mine Milk'. In the 1960s, adverts featured high-school athletes toasting sporting success with pints of ice-cold milk. Instead of quaffing champagne after the Indianapolis 500 motor race in the strait-laced Midwest, winners drank milk in the National Dairy Council's (2013) 'Milk Mustache' promotion.

That memorable advertising campaign has evolved. At the beginning of the twenty-first century, sports stars and celebrities with milk *moo-staches* were pictured in T-shirts asking 'Got Milk?' Soon after, the light-hearted slogan added another strapline – 'Got Cookies?' In 2013–14, The Milk Processor Education Programme (MilkPEP), based in Washington DC, funded by dairy processors, was yet another campaign to press for more fluid milk consumption with a campaign touting tickets to Super Bowl XLVIII. Sugary biscuits complemented after-school treats – no matter that they contributed to rising childhood obesity and tooth decay. This effort came at a time when kids had begun turning inward, eschewing playing ball games in sunny streets in favour of video games like Pokémon and Super Mario in darkened bedrooms. For example, the US National Institutes of Health (2013) reported that in the past thirty years, childhood obesity had more than doubled among children aged two to five, tripled among youth aged six to eleven, and more than tripled among adolescents aged twelve to nineteen. Sadly, that childhood obesity epidemic has now become global.

Despite a growing tendency by some to shun animal products as discussed at the start of this chapter, in India, where about 40 per cent of the population is vegetarian, dairy products –along with chickpeas and other legumes – continue to be vital sources of protein for strong muscles and of calcium for strong bones to resist osteoporosis. In fact, in omnivore cultures such consumption of dairy products has been, along with exercise and sports in healthy childhood environments, credited with boosting people's height, e.g., in the US as well as in the Netherlands and in the former Yugoslavia, which now holds records for the world's tallest people (*Atlantic* 2014). Anecdotal and empirical evidence for milk as a human-growth promoter (with immune-growth factor one, i.e., IGF-1) is plentiful. That explains why, after the 2008 Olympics, it was rumoured to be the reason the government of Vietnam pushed 'colossal growth' in domestic dairy development and imports from New Zealand and the US, to hasten the day that taller, stronger Vietnamese athletes would win their own Olympic gold medals (USDA 2011).

More on the vegan turn and analogue meats

The US 'Got Milk?' campaign of the early 2000s now elicits a worldwide Not Milk response. Consumption of dairy milk and milk products is unfashionable in some quarters. It's not *woke* in Millennial and Gen X terms. Plant-based foods such as almond and oat dairy substitutes, meat analogues or substitutes from soy and grain-based products are gaining traction in many countries. There's also interest in lab-grown meat, as discussed briefly further above. Why? Human health is certainly one reason. While meat delivers healthy protein, its cholesterol and saturated fats can trigger cardiovascular disease (CVD), atherosclerosis and obesity. There is a market for healthier choices. In February 2016, Allied Market Research estimated the global meat substitute market could earn revenue of $5.2 billion by 2020, with a compound annual growth rate (CAGR) of 8.4 per cent during the forecast period 2015–2020. Statista Research Department (Dec 9, 2021) projections were even more 'bullish', estimating the 2020 market value of plant based-meat at 6.67 billion US dollars, and expecting it to reach roughly 16.7 billion in 2026.

Investors are certainly interested in meat analogues and various forms of cultured, lab-grown, in vitro, synthetic and vat-grown meat and plant-based dairy milk substitutes. Current key players are becoming familiar names: examples include Amy's Kitchen Inc. (US), Beyond Meat (US), Cauldron Foods (UK), Garden Protein International, Inc. (Canada), Meatless B.V. (Netherlands), Quorn Foods (UK), Vbites Food, Ltd. (UK). Morningstar Farms (US), MGP Ingredients Inc. (US) and Sonic Biochem Extractions Limited (India). It is early days for the plant-based meat analogue industry, but it is stimulating innovations by past and future competitors in supply chains below them, and from consumers above them in food chains, according to Michael E. Porter (1979, 2008).

In social media, every action brings an equal reaction. It was only a matter of time before the activist group People for the Ethical Treatment of Animals (PETA) deployed an anti-milk slogan aimed at teenagers, satirizing the American dairy industry's 'Got Milk? Got Cookies?' campaign. In 'Got Zits?', their question to Midwest high-school students, PETA's advertising featured an attractive teen girl's face with a *milk moo-stache* – and several pronounced blemishes. As would be expected, PETA's campaign prompted countermeasures from the conventional livestock industry. The US National Dairy Council (2013) lambasted PETA for its 'sensationalist' attack. Such media exchanges reverberate with charges such as 'Milk is cruel' seen, for example, on innumerable websites. In *The End of Animal Farming* (2018: 118), Jacy Reese, co-founder of the Sentience Institute, calls moral outrage aroused by activist groups 'the nitromethane of a social movement, exploding in the engine to propel it across the finish line'. PETA calls itself the largest animal welfare group in the world. It is depicted by agribusiness entities as a fringe extremist animal rights organization that distorts facts about dairying. There is clear evidence of ferocity in advertising by non-meat-eaters in plant vs meat debates. This ethical position objects to an industry which PETA claims involves confinement, stress and the repression of sentient animals' natural behaviours, leading to shortened lives. There is compelling evidence that widespread practices around the world, in large-scale conventional and even intensified organic megadairies, not only compromise animal welfare and well-being but also negatively affect human health, threaten the environment, diminish biodiversity, weaken rural communities and – via emissions of greenhouse gases such as methane – destabilise the climate.

After 8,000 years of milk consumption, however, a switch to plant-based alternatives is unlikely to be universal. Much is wrong with modern dairying, but shifting to a plant-based diet with products from a few multinational companies could bring more socio-political problems than solutions.

Is dairy losing mainstream support?

There are signs that campaigns by PETA, and less aggressive groups such as Compassion in World Farming (CiWF 2020), are entering middle-class awareness and influencing dairy consumption. From 2016, the US Milk Processor Education Program (MilkPEP) promoted dairy consumption in its 'Milk Life' campaign, which featured milk *moo-stached* winter Olympic champion skier Maddie Brown and snowboarder Jamie Anderson of Team USA. Animal welfarists responded, pitting their own celebrities against pro-dairy athletes. Dairy has become a target of some athletes' condemnation. In February 2018, during the closing of the XXIII Olympic Winter Games in South Korea, a thirty-second anti-dairy commercial ran in television markets including Chicago, Dallas, Los Angeles, New York, San Francisco and Washington DC According to *Dairy Herd Management* (2018), 'Anti-Dairy Commercial Runs During Closing Ceremony of Olympics', the six former Olympians in the anti-dairy Switch4Good.org campaign included medallist Dotsie Bausch (USA, silver medallist in pursuit cycling, 2012) and Rebecca Soni, (USA, six-time medallist in swimming, 2008, 2012). Wyatt Bechtel observes that many of the anti-dairy athletes claimed that switching to a vegan diet made them stronger or run faster, and they were proud to be dairy-free. Bechtel noted (*DHM* 2018) the Switch4Good campaign was aimed at people worried about eating or drinking dairy for health reasons. Comments from the non-dairy athletes appeared to be about animal rights, though. In a campaign video, Dotsie Bausch said she was 'leaving violence out of her diet'.

MilkPEP replied that 90 per cent of US Olympians grew up drinking milk. But the advert for Switch4Good.org was a sign that altruism for animals is permeating sports ethics.

Dairy notwithstanding, questions on animal consumption remain. Meat and dairy analogues could render many animal welfare issues moot. According to Jessica Miley in *Interesting Engineering* (2017), Richard Branson thinks that by 2050, we will no longer need to kill any animals for meat. Miley said the UN-FAO reports that 13 billion hectares (32.1 billion acres) of oxygen-producing forest is cut each year for crops and pasture. The FAO estimates that livestock production consumes 26 per cent of ice-free land. Reports from the Worldwatch Institute and World Bank risk assessors have claimed an alarming 51 per cent of global greenhouse-gas emissions emanate from animal agriculture. These shocking statistics are contested, and will be scrutinized below.

Turning from Almond Joy back to Milky Way, it is difficult to see how traditional extensive farming, rather than intensive dairying, should, under enlightened management, be environmentally hostile. To begin with, dairy farming can build healthy topsoil teeming with worms and microorganisms. In a 1985 biography titled *W. D. Hoard: A Man for His Time*, Loren H. Osman described how Hoard, who had moved to the nineteenth-century Territory of Wisconsin from New York, educated Wisconsin farmers on how to renew their once bountiful soil, after grain yields waned. Hoard demonstrated that alternating between arable crops (for example, crops like oats that produce plant substitutes for milk) and grazing pasture revitalized fields, as cattle wastes added dry matter and improved tilth in the thin glacial topography. Nor does traditional dairy farming extol violence. Industry leaders have long encouraged farmers and handlers to treat animals with kindness, not least because their fortunes were intertwined. W.D. Hoard's exhortation on human–nonhuman relations is well known (Osman 1985: 1):

> The cow is the foster mother of the human race. From the time of the ancient Hindoo to this time have the thoughts of men turned to this kindly and beneficent creature as one of the chief sustaining forces of the human race.

Recall the discussion above of animal scientist Temple Grandin. She cites W.D. Hoard's rules in 'Reducing fear improves milk production' in the eponymous magazine, widely read by people in dozens of countries (*Hoard's Dairyman* 2013: 684):

> The Rule to be observed in this stable at all times, toward the cattle, young and old, is that of patience and kindness. A man's usefulness in a herd ceases at once when he loses his temper and bestows rough usage. Men must be patient. Cattle are not reasoning beings. Remember that this is the Home of Mothers. Treat each cow as a Mother should be treated. The giving of milk is a function of Motherhood; rough treatment lessens the flow. That injures me as well as the cow. Always keep these ideas in mind in dealing with my cattle.

Managing time and space

In the US in particular, since the mid-twentieth century, mainstream dairying – not only conventional megadairies but also organic megadairies – has strayed from the pasture-grazing model extolled by W.D. Hoard. It is partly a question of space. The non-grazing model is designed to feed cows the maximum of totally mixed rations (TMR) and extract the maximum of saleable milk. As a result, it is less – perhaps much less – animal and ecologically friendly than it should be. This is because the breeding, feeding and management practices of industrial-scale dairy farming tend to weaken cows' immune systems and truncate longevity. How long a cow lives is an important – perhaps *the* most important – marker of whether a cow has been given a good life. The fact that upwards of 40 per cent of cows on

US factory farms are culled due to their inability to conceive a second calf points to their leading the opposite sort of life (2013 DHI-Provo, now Amelicor).

In the US and elsewhere, on small-scale dairy farms of fifty to 1,000 cows, organic or not organic, these ruminants can have decades-long and relatively natural lives on pasture during the grazing season, punctuated by muddy winter weather when clean, dry barns shelter them with mangers full of sileage or hay, along with other commodities permitted under their milk processor's production model.

Some zero-grazed cows, in roomy feedlots and loafing sheds with 'specialized veterinary access and improved animal health monitoring' conducted digitally via robotic milking machines, can exceed more the four or five years averaged by cows in high-density factory farms (Scholten 2014; Buller and Roe 2018: 180–1). It turns out that pasture is the answer to many dietary and environmental threats that challenge cows' hoof, udder, dietary and reproductive health, and send too many of them to abattoirs long before their possible three-decade lifetimes. Intensive and less humane dairy farming has a range of environmental, economic and health outcomes which are examined further below.

Dairy and the Anthropocene

Human geographers describe agriculture as anthropogenic attempts to control time and space in the context of uncertain weather and animal activity. That's what we do. Despite our romantic, even adventurous, imaginings about hunter-gatherers, their Paleo diet involved grave risks of hunger and famine. Organizing farming communities was fundamentally a political process that culminated in producing economic surpluses that yielded enough food to not only store supplies against future food shortages, but also, when there were food surpluses, to motivate some members of the community to innovate, for example by designing tools to produce even greater surpluses, and accounting systems to manage such surpluses. This shift to agriculture had a knock-on effect among human populations; having once been 100 per cent dedicated to hunting and gathering everywhere, by the twenty-first century just 1 per cent and 2 per cent of citizens worked as farmers in countries such as the UK and US (World Bank 2019).

Managing space in a world of 7.6 billion people – a global population that may approach 10 billion around the year 2050 – is difficult. In the US and many other countries, urbanization increasingly limits pasture. Turning grass pasture dairy farms into confined animal feeding operations around cities such as Los Angeles, Nairobi or São Paulo is basically management of available space. Breeding the mighty aurochs into smaller, docile cattle reduced the space needed to manage them, making CAFOs possible, such Hobbesian confinement lowers bovine health and well-being.

The question today: Is it time to set our course for a world relying on plant-based milk substitutes? The first issue to be addressed is the provenance of such non-dairy foods. Where do the almonds, coconuts, oats, and soy originate that make these milk alternatives? How many hectares of rainforest are razed to grow coconuts or soy? Who owns these operations? Are they small-scale independent farmers in an ethos of food sovereignty? Or are they controlled by multinational corporations which depend on inputs including dangerous chemicals? Genetically-modified organisms (GMOs), not countenanced in organic farming, are also a consideration. For example, journalist Ann Garrison (2020) claims that GMO-linked agribusiness wins but small-scale farmers lose in AGRA, the Alliance for a Green Revolution in Africa, funded by the Gates Foundation. Pro-GMO and chemical aspects of some programs by the US Agency for International Development (USAID), and Land O'Lakes (LO'L) cooperative, elicit similar concerns on biodiversity.

Questions about what might replace dairy must be asked alongside the consideration of certain facts, particularly in countries where small-scale dairy farming still dominates. For example, 70 per cent of India's world-leading milk production is from smallholders, women and marginal farmers (Scholten 2010). The population of India means that space is an ever-present concern. So, this begs the question: If farmers in rich countries lack the space to graze cows, should milk powder and dairy products be imported from countries such as India where hill farmers might supply such dairy goods from cattle enjoying higher welfare than confined cows. This I have advocated in publications and presentations including the 2019 Mansinhbhai Patel memorial lecture to students, faculty and farmers at the Mansinhbhai Institute of Dairy and Food Technology (MIDFT 2022) at Dudhsagar co-operative dairy in Mehsana, India (Scholten 2007 *Dairy India Yearbook*, 2010 *India's White Revolution* book; 2018b *Rural History Today*, 2019a Vidya Dairy, 2019b *RGRG Newsletter*, Summer, 2019).

Turning back to innovations in dairy or meat analogues, how much of their ingredients involve genetically modified organisms (GMOs) which entail use of herbicides such as glyphosate, threatening human health as well as biodiversity loss? The World Health Organization's Agency for Research on Cancer (WHO-ARC) identified glyphosate as a probable carcinogen in 2015 (*British Medical Journal* 2019: 365; Benbrook 2007, 2012b, 2019). The Gates Foundation, which has invested in the purveyors of Roundup® glyphosate Bayer-Monsanto, is so concerned about court judgements on the toxicity of glyphosate that it invested $45 million toward the development of chemicals that could target pests with less collateral damage to the biosphere and humans. The new venture is called Enko (*Forbes* 2020).

Herbicides such as glyphosate have long been suspected as culprits in biodiversity loss. Straw, Carpentier and Brown (*Journal of Applied Ecology* 6 April 2021: 1–2, 1–10) found that Roundup® was a hazard to bees in farming and urban systems. Bees exhibited 94 per cent mortality with Roundup® Ready-To-Use® and 30 per cent mortality with Roundup® ProActive®, over twenty-four hours. The story turns out to be more complicated and confusing than at first assumed. Another pesticide, Weedol®, which does not contain glyphosate, did not cause significant mortality, demonstrating that glyphosate, the active ingredient in Roundup®, is not always the cause of bee mortality. The 96 per cent mortality caused by Roundup® No Glyphosate* supports this conclusion. The authors observed 'Roundup® products caused comprehensive matting of bee body hair, suggesting that surfactants, or other co-formulants in the Roundup® products, may cause death by incapacitating the gas exchange system'. They called for pesticide companies to release complete lists of ingredients in pesticide formulation, as lack of transparency hampers research for safe exposure levels for beneficial insects in agro-ecosystems.

Straw et al.'s findings do not mean that glyphosate is off the hook. As mentioned above, it is on WHO's list of likely carcinogens and there are court cases with respect to, for example, non-Hodgkin lymphoma victims. What this and other studies do highlight is the cocktail of anthropogenically made chemicals in the biosphere, and the need for regulators to mandate transparency to evaluate risks. In Chapters 2, 3 and 4 of this book, several respondents indicate their fear of leaving traditional meat and potatoes diets for unknown chemical formulations in plant- and laboratory-based dairy and meat substitutes involving multinational agriculture and pharmaceutical companies. Flawed agro-food policy involving such companies could have a range of tragic consequences. Boats left on the former shore of the Aral Sea, now miles outside its present perimeter, warn of that.

Time, space and food miles

Food miles became a hot topic decades ago, with public recognition that food in post-industrialized countries could average 1,500 miles from farms to dinner plates. This launched the locavore movement, alongside the organic movement (Murdoch and Miele 1999). In focus groups and surveys, Scholten (2007a, 2011) found consumers in groups of academics, firefighters, motorcyclists and others, generally had more trust in local food than organics from parts unknown. Local food and livelihoods were elements in preserving rural communities in policies, for example, of the European Economic Community's Common Agricultural Community (EEC-CAP, begun 1957), as well as a goal of India's Operation Flood (1970–96), which relied principally on small-scale owners of one or a few milch animals (Scholten 1997, 2010; World Bank 1998).

Pasture-based dairy farming thrives in temperate climates with around a metre of precipitation a year. This geographical perspective fits the locavore's ideal of local production and consumption. Organic farming has been seen as a solution to many problems identified in conventional agriculture. However, it turns out not to always be local nor does it always make the most environmentally appropriate use of space. There are ever more examples of large-scale organic megadairies where milk produced in arid states whose climate is not temperate, irrigation is required, cows are not routinely pastured – violating the USDA organic rules – and consumers are not local. Recently, milk was shipped 1,000 miles from arid Texas to processors in temperate Wisconsin, and then shipped out of that state. This situation would have befuddled W.D. Hoard, whose late nineteenth-century forty-acre, fifteen- to twenty-cow Wisconsin family farms exemplified Thomas Jefferson's ideals of agrarian democracy.

Animals in history

Let us now return to the issue of animal welfare, by first taking an historic perspective and then returning to the question of cow longevity, closely tied to how cows are treated.

Around the world, attitudes to living creatures, often based on religious beliefs, give primacy to humans, while granting varying degrees of care for animals including farm animals. In Asia, Buddhism, Hinduism and Jainism generally respect a spark of spirit in cattle that may, eventually, be reincarnated into a divine state. This has been amplified in the current tenure of Indian Prime Minister Modi, whose Hindutva ideology is a Hindu form of nationalism, and most or all beef eating is deplored. In the past decade, drivers of cattle transport vans have been attacked, and meat-eaters – including Christians, Muslims and Sikhs – marginalized. Secular critics say there are anomalies in Hindutva philosophy, claiming Brahmin priests historically ate beef, or that lighter-shaded Brahman cows are considered sacred because they give milk, but ignoring water buffalos – sister bovines – which are not always called cows because they are darker (*Times of India* 2015). Buffalo actually produce 70 per cent of the country's milk – much richer than cows' milk – and are also much more likely to be eaten. When it comes to diets in India, economics help explain why they vary among castes, social classes and faiths. A pure vegan diet may be more costly than diets including dairy and even meat products.

While strictures against killing bovines for meat vary somewhat among Buddhists, Hindus and Jains (Beauchamp and Frey 2014), the Abrahamic faiths pervading much of Africa, Asia, Europe, Oceania and the Western hemisphere have been more affected by a 'dominion' interpretation of scripture wherein the Deity creates humans in the Deity's image and give them, 'dominion over the fish of the sea, and over the fowl of the air, and over the cattle, and over all the earth ...' (KJV Genesis 1:28). This has been taken by some as carte blanche, not only to domesticate animals for traction, milk and meat, but – too often – to abuse them on farms, and for example, in bullfighting (which still continues in some countries). Yet, notes Janet M. Davis in *The Gospel of Kindness: Animal Welfare and the Making of Modern America* (2016), the carnivorous history of the US is leavened with ethical or religious communities rejecting meat. Strains of vegetarianism and veganism have always been present in America. Moreover, the dominion interpretation is softened in the Biblical (Genesis 8:1) rendition of the Flood, when the Deity promised human *and* non-human creatures alike, 'And God remembered Noah and every living thing, and all the cattle that were with him in the ark'.

In his long article on 'Animals, humans and the international legal order', Michael Bowman (2019: 133–4), an expert on treaty law at the University of Nottingham, agreed that even if Abrahamic religions had less regard for animals' spiritual status, their views overlap with Buddhism, Hinduism, and Jainism in realms from conservation to compassion, because, '... they may (for reasons of their own) be minded to support the conclusions even if they dispute the reasoning'. An historic instance of this is representation by all major world religions at the

World Wildlife Fund's twenty-fifth anniversary conference on Environmental Policy and Law in 1986. Bowman also notes Biblical texts urging kindness to animals in the Old Testament, and stewardship in the New Testament.

The notion of stewardship remains strong in parts of the US Pacific Northwest, where Christian faith communities dominate (Attfield 2006; Scholten 2014: vii, ix, 8, 110, 155, 159–69; *Bellingham Herald* 2017). Giovanni Roverso (*Whatcom Watch* 30 Dec 2020) describes how the Washington Conservation Corps monitors Bellingham's waterways productive for forestry, fishing and dairying. One example of a multigenerational small-scale family dairy enterprise managed sustainably is Appel Farms Cheese (*Bellingham Herald* 2017; Scholten 2014: 159). Owner Rich Appel says their 350 cows are in barns all the time, but a small percentage of the young stock grazes in summer months. Food miles are minimal: Appel supplies regional supermarkets with quark, Gouda, paneer, Gruyère and other dairy products.

Descartes' Error

Continuing our discussion on animal welfare, we turn from religion to philosophy and psychology. We see that academic discourse has undergone a paradigm shift from what neurologist Antonio Damásio (1994; *Times Literary Supplement* 1995) called Descartes' Error in relegating animals to fleshy but non-sentient machines. *The Cambridge Declaration on Consciousness* (2012) disputes Descartes' mind/body duality and, very importantly for our discussion of how cows should be treated, the rejection of this conceptual split opens the door to animal emotion, reason, pain and consciousness that are not altogether unlike that of humans. This academic re-evaluation of animals resonates with empathy for animal affect among consumers, expressed in the St Paul Declaration (IFOAM 2006; organic-market.info 2006; Scholten 2014: 288). The Declaration states that sentient animals be allowed to perform natural behaviours such as grazing naturally, outside, on grasses they evolved on. If one accepts overlap in human/non-human experience, and if one accepts that sentient humans have a duty of care to other sentient creatures, animal suffering in agriculture and other human activities becomes a major ethical concern (Dawkins 2012a; Wohleben 2017). Be kind. This resonates with an ancient contract between domestic animals and their keepers, exchanging their bodies or traction power for protection from predators. (This answer is still used by farmers when children ask why animals they know are slaughtered for food.)

In cognitive globalization, growing numbers of consumers are absorbing such ideas. In addition to turns to veganism, it is also possible that – if political and economic conditions permit – consumers could succeed in their demands for reform of factory farming and other meat-related practices. This is not to say proponents of animal welfare had identical reasoning. Sophie Riley (Scholz 2019: 148, 154; *Oxford Handbook of Animal Ethics* 2011: 61, 69), lecturer on animal law and policy in Australia, notes that from the time of St Augustine, wild animals were dichotomized into useful or harmful; i.e., ravens, badgers and foxes were vermin, but venison were useful. Riley (*OHoAE* 2011: 154) adds that advocates of anti-cruelty legislation included Jeremy Bentham (1748–1832), who based his views 'on animal sentience, while Kantian philosophies (doubting animal reason) justified anti-cruelty on the basis that those who were cruel to animals could also be cruel to humans'.

This book uses the term animal *welfare* instead of animal *rights* (see glossary). It is worth noting here that Bentham and Immanuel Kant (1724–1804) both wrote on domesticated and wildlife rights before Britain abolished human slavery in 1832 (Waldau 2011). As a rule of thumb, while advocates of animal welfare (perhaps CiWF members) are apt to argue for roomier poultry cages, advocates of animal rights (perhaps PETA members) are apt to argue *against any cages*. Hardcore defenders of livestock industries often accept initiatives to improve animal welfare, but mock efforts to extend human rights to creatures which do not understand litigation. Philosophers including the late Roger Scruton (1998) have discussed what duties humans have to farm animals, whether or not they have rights, per se. Definitions of consciousness, sentience and speciesism are critical. The ethical debate continues, but eventually may be trumped by political and environmental pressures.

How we view farm animals in the twenty-first century

For decades, the counsel of Temple Grandin has improved design of US abattoirs to minimize animals' distress and suffering before slaughter. Earlier in this chapter, the text referred to her writing in dairy trade magazines and her simultaneous veneration by corporate clients such as McDonalds, and – unusually – numerous animal welfarists. When an undercover video showing an Idaho megadairy abusing animals with cattle prods was shown on US news, it caused so much dismay that the industry's Center for Food Integrity created the Animal Care Review and Temple Grandin served as one of three on its expert panel. This move somewhat restored consumer trust (*Hoard's Dairyman* 2012). Grandin had been a go-to consultant in the crisis, but agribusiness trust was rattled by her candour. In an April 2016 *Washington Post* article, 'Why a top animal science expert is worried about the milk industry', Roberto A. Ferdman elicited Colorado State University Professor Grandin's views on the industry's short-lived supercows:

> What they've done is basically the equivalent of taking a car, putting it in neutral, and then dropping a brick on the accelerator until it blows up . . . These cows are constantly in the red zone.

As reported in media, Grandin elaborated, saying too many farmers were so obsessed with production that their cows suffer poor health. 'I call them bad dairies . . . .', said Grandin, whose forthrightness about genetically explosive bovines cooled relations between her and productivists who previously sought her approval (*Washington Post* 2016; *Hoard's Dairyman* 26 Apr 2016). *Farm Journal* (28 Apr 2016) reporter Anna-Lisa Laca asked, 'Why is Temple Grandin concerned about the dairy industry? Famed animal behaviour scientist, Temple Grandin, thinks dairy farmers have bred their cows to produce an amount of milk that is harmful to the cows' welfare.'

Animal welfarists considered Grandin's disparagement of some farms as expert evidence against an industry they perceived cruel. Numerous government and non-government organizations (NGOs) have since advocated for more compassionate animal welfare standards based on Grandin's statements.

One inspiration for animal advocacy has been the United Nation's 1948 Universal Declaration of Human Rights (UDHR), a moral force in improving the well-being of children, women, the differently abled and previously-otherized persons. It was not a great leap to apply some of the Declaration's elements to animals, especially to higher mammals and pets. In *The Oxford Handbook of Animal Ethics* (2014: 9), co-editor Tom Beauchamp pinpoints the influence of the UDHR in an analysis of 'Rights Theory and Animal Rights'. Of course, dogs or horses may be pets in one country's culture, but dinner in another.

From a philosophical perspective, it is worth noting that among observers recognising human rights are those who resist discussion of animal rights because non-humans are categorically not human. For example, although animals share some traits and behaviours with humans, the former's lack of a neocortex persuades some observers they are not conscious. Not all agree. *The Cambridge Declaration on Consciousness* was proclaimed on 7 July 2012 at the Francis Crick Memorial Conference on Consciousness in Human and non-Human Animals, at Churchill College, University of Cambridge (Low et al. 2012). Witnessed by Stephen Hawking and recorded by CBS TV show *60 Minutes*, *The Declaration* attacks that human-non/human demarcation (*CdoC* 2012: 3):

> The absence of a neocortex does not appear to preclude an organism from experiencing affective states. Convergent evidence indicates that non-human animals have the neuroanatomical, neurochemical, and neurophysiological substrates of conscious states along with the capacity to exhibit intentional behaviours. Consequently, the weight of evidence indicates that humans are not unique in possessing the neurological substrates that generate consciousness. Non-human animals, including all mammals and birds, and many other creatures, including octopuses, also possess these neurological substrates.

What does this mean for dairy farming? Consumers who empathize with bovines' instinctive behavioural needs, such as grazing and exploring fields (Scholten 2018a), and believe animals share human-like affective states of emotion, desire, fear, pain, even reason and some use of tools, will demand more sensitive welfare standards. Will they demand animal rights, too? The reason for use of the term animal *welfare* in this book is that it is less controversial than animal *rights* where some contend rights are derived by humans via politics. (Cows don't vote.) But better understanding of non-human faculties is making human condescension to 'dumb animals' – once widely thought incapable of pain or emotion – untenable in more of the Global North and Global South. Be kind first.

In response to careful studies of animals over the last half century, thinking has evolved from the fourth century, when St Augustine considered animals such as mice a category separate from farm animals. There is now wider appreciation of the ideas of Temple Grandin who with Catherine Johnson, in their book *Animals Make us Human* (2009), write that many pets and farm animals have emotional systems much like ours. Another influence is Peter Wohleben (2017), who argues in *The Inner Life of Animals* that there are important ethical implications to the fact a mouse is distressed when another mouse suffers.

Twenty-first century politics

The trajectory of increasing enlightenment and better welfare for farm animals has not always been uninterrupted. A *Universal Declaration for Animal Welfare* (UDAW) had been proposed in the year 2000 by an organization called World Animal Protection (previously known as the World Society for the Protection of Animals, which acts as its Secretariat). During the 1980s and 90s, WAP fought to prohibit bullfighting in Europe, and bear-baiting in Greece, Turkey and India. Such practices still continue and include bull-wrestling in Tamil Nadu (*Economist* 2017a). WAP is now supported by Compassion in World Farming (CiWF), the Royal Society for the Prevention of Cruelty to Animals (RSPCA-UK), the International Fund for Animal Welfare (IFAW), and the Humane Society of the United States. According to *The Oxford Handbook of Animal Ethics* (2014), WAP advocates higher animal protection standards.

In light of these developments, observers expected higher animal welfare standards in farming to be agreed at the United Nations level, but the Great Recession that began in 2007–08 in the UK and US put that on hold, and the COVID-19 pandemic had a similar effect. Public support has declined accordingly. A widely cited article in *British Social Attitudes: The 32nd Report* (2015) for the National Centre for Social Research (NatCen) titled 'Benefits and welfare: long-term trends or short-term reactions?', by Peter Taylor-Gooby and Eleanor Taylor (2015) found that public support for increasing taxes and spending more on health, education and social benefits for other people fell from 63 per cent in 2002 to 32 per cent by 2010. There was also evidence that taxpayers' concern for their poverty-stricken fellow citizens fell in the recession. This trend suggests altruistic concern for animals could recede as the COVID-19 pandemic, and grain shortages resulting from the 2022 Russian invasion of Ukraine, return millions of people back to food poverty and survival modes.

What is evident is that – in the context of populist politics represented by US President Donald Trump's 2016–21 tenure, and troubled Brexit politics of UK Prime Ministers Theresa May and Boris Johnson – animal welfare policies have been on a transatlantic rollercoaster. Organic groups (*Odairy* 2018 and 2019; *Meat + Poultry* 2018) revealed industry turmoil as the Organic Trade Association (OTA) joined the American Society for the Prevention of Cruelty to Animals (ASPCA) and the Animal Welfare Institute (AWI) as co-plaintiffs in lawsuits challenging the US Dept. of Agriculture's decision to withdraw painfully negotiated standards for organic livestock, just after President Trump's inauguration in 2017. They argued against USDA's decision to withdraw the Organic Livestock and Poultry Practices (OLPP) final rule. Laura Batcha, CEO of the OTA said USDA's attempt to kill this fully vetted regulation was a departure from twenty years of rulemaking in an aberrant move that had no historical or legal justification. The lawsuit challenged USDA's position that the agency need not consult with the National Organic Standards Board (NOSB), which was key in formulating fundamental regulations such as the 2010 USDA final pasture rule (Scholten 2014: 112–17). In *The Nation* (Mar 2018), Jasper Craven a warning by Michael Sligh, the inaugural chair of the NOSB, that big corporate players entering the $50 billion field must honour organic values. They did when values coincided with profit. Along with lyrical greenwashing.

In the UK, just twelve years after *The Cambridge Declaration on Consciousness*, animal welfare was also subject to a wrenching turnaround. After the public voted narrowly to leave the European Union on 23 June 2016, Britain's farm industry exerted its laissez-faire nature, which geographers Kevin Morgan, Terry Marsden and Jonathan Murdoch (2006) saw as being closer to intensive US agribusiness than to the German multifunctionality they promoted. In line with the European Model of Agriculture, Germany multifunctionality has balanced globally competitive farm production while preserving rural communities, tradition, biodiversity and open space for public recreation (Knickel, Renting and van der Ploeg 2004; Wilson 2007, 2011; Wilson et al. 2010).

Bullish agribusiness spokespersons claimed Brexit meant the UK could withdraw from EU animal welfare regulations, adopt profitable economies of scale and relax regulations on cattle and poultry density, thus increasing profits and contributions to the Treasury. The UK livestock industry might thus regain the beef export prominence it enjoyed before 1996. That is when many countries banned British beef, and the Ministry of Agriculture, Fisheries and Food (MAFF, later the Department for Environment, Food and Rural Affairs or Defra) admitted the link between Mad Cow disease and human Creutzfeldt-Jakob disease (BSE/nvCJD; see Scholten 2007). Brexiteers, including two-thirds of farmers, fancied they could renounce EU membership without losing its Four Freedoms of movement of labour, capital, services and goods (*Economist* 2006 and 2016). In the months following the vote, however, British farmers realized that Brexit would deny them a supply of Polish, Romanian and other foreign farm workers and truck drivers, given that most Britons avoid such jobs (*Farmers Weekly* 2017; *Farming Online* 2017; *Guardian* 2017b; Scholten 2017a).

In this Brexit scenario, intensified livestock and poultry industries could be a fiscal export engine, possibly to compensate for banks moving from London to Frankfurt and Paris. This was already happening in 2018 when *the Guardian* (2018a) reported a rise in the size of UK beef feedlots similar to US systems. Such prospects won quick support from some in the Conservative (aka Tory)

Party. In response, Britain's signature animal welfare organizations, such as the Royal Society for the Protection of Birds, vehemently countered suggestions that agribusiness could profitably treat Britain's cattle and poultry like crowded US CAFOs and battery chickens. This prompted cabinet member Liam Fox to deny the British public would countenance any US–UK trade deal that forced them to eat steroid-enhanced beef or chlorinated poultry, partly because this could tempt the lowering of animal welfare standards *(Guardian* 2017c). *The Guardian* had already revealed (2017d) that, despite previous assurances, a dozen US-style intensive beef units already dotted the UK. Jude L. Capper remarked that such economies of scale were almost inevitable, and that better use could be made of male calves by rearing them for beef on such feedlots, using feeds that people do not eat, including by-products from human food crop production.

After the Brexit vote, activist demonstrations held in the past against live export of veal calves to France and other destinations resumed, after BSE export restrictions ended. Veal exports had been – with fox hunting banned in 2004 – the target of a mass demonstration in London (Scholten 1995) before Mad Cow disease dominated headlines in 1996. By late 2017, it appeared that Britain's activist groups 38 Degrees and CiWF had restrained aggressive factory farmers, when Conservatives assured them that Brexit would be Green (Sky News 2017; see also UN-FAO 2014). But activists for animal sentience had only won one battle in a long war. Additional technical points on animal and human health were part of debates, and their relevance became painfully clear as the COVID-19 zoonosis spread from wet markets in Wuhan, China, to Italy and other countries in the worst pandemic since the influenza epidemic of 1918–19 killed more people than the First World War.

On 17 February 2021, shortly after the UK finally withdrew from the European Union, Labour MP Yasmin Qureshi (Qureshi 2021; *Telegraph* 2021b) deplored the Conservative Government's recurring turn against animal sentience:

> As you may know, under EU law, animals are recognised as sentient and therefore receive a certain degree of protection and consideration when it comes to Government policy making. However, post-Brexit, animals in the UK no longer have this safeguard.

Qureshi added that although animal sentience was part of Conservative pledges before the election, 'It is clear that animal sentience is not a priority for the Government, and it is becoming increasingly likely that it will not introduce animal sentience legislation at all'.

Conservative politicians, including Brexiteer Prime Minister Boris Johnson and Secretary of State for the Environment Michael Gove, faced difficulty pleasing farmers newly bereft of the EU farm subsidies they had long enjoyed, and (as noted) coping with the loss of farmworkers from EU countries, including those from Eastern Europe (Scholten 2017a). Brexit burdened an Exchequer keen on taxes from farm exports, and activists feared UK rules would revert to US standards to increase agricultural trade. The diets of Millennials and Gen X and Z voters diets are less heavy on meat than those of their Boomer parents and grandparents. But animal welfarists of any age might wonder how aware the late Francis Crick and Stephen Hawking, participants at the 2012 *Cambridge Declaration on Consciousness*, were of British indecision on sentience.

Welcome to the Anthropocene

It was in the late twentieth century that researchers familiar with geological quaternary studies gingerly hailed what was dubbed the new Age – or Epoch – of the Anthropocene, a time span in which humans are the dominant force shaping natural events. It is seen as the logical successor to what precedes it even though, as scientists reported to the International Geological Congress, the Holocene – the approximately 12,000 years of human agricultural development since the last Ice Age – was actually the first to be defined by human intervention (*Guardian* 2016). Humans had for millennia morphed Terran topography with deforestation, grazing and mining, but solar arrays and polytunnels are among the human activities accelerating change (Scholten 2018a).

In 2010, to mark the fortieth anniversary of Earth Day, established in the US by President Richard Nixon in 1970, *Environmental Science and Technology* published an article titled 'The New World of the Anthropocene'. Zalasiewicz et al. argued that human activity leading to mass extinctions, changes in atmospheric and marine chemistry and alterations to terrestrial features, could be geologically standardized in the sort of strata that mark epochs, and thus humans had written their own world, for better or worse. One of many examples is what concerns most modern inhabitants of the planet, namely the ubiquity of plastic in the environment that either has not been recycled or is not recyclable. The sources of the perhaps 79 per cent of plastic waste not recycled include not only consumers, homes and factories, but also farms (*Guardian* 2016). Plastic in rubbish heaps, on the roadside or in the sea also represents a material waste. As University of Delaware research has found, even single-use polyfolefins can be converted to diesel, jet and petrol-range hydrocarbon industrial gases by hydro-cracking.

In a *Hoard's Dairyman* (2016b: 579) article titled 'Farm plastic could be greener', I wrote that policy changes by the Wisconsin State Republican government had cut funding to state universities and farmers that supported recycling of agricultural plastics. Likewise, where I lived in County Durham of Northeast England, contracted fraudsters had lost, burned or buried much plastic waste instead of transporting it to specialized sites near Glasgow or the Netherlands. Poor governance exacerbates pollution: Too many UK food wrappers are marked *not currently recyclable*; this applies to a range of wrapping from chocolates to fruit to vegan meals. Governments could mandate that all farm plastic and food wrapping is recyclable. Non-biodegradable plastic harms sea life and will be apparent in sedimentary strata, eons hence. The Anthropocene is here. Whether or not humans survive attendant climate and oceanic changes is up to us – or Mother Gaia.

Accepting humans as shapers of a new geological epoch was a paradigm shift. Since the 1950s, wrote Damian Carrington in *The Guardian* (2016), human impact materialized in nuclear tests, plastic pollution and battery poultry has been so profound that the Holocene epoch must give way to the Anthropocene. Humans have become so numerous and powerful that they are physically recasting Earth's atmosphere (also via dairy methane), soil, waterways, biodiversity, temperature and climate. Germane to this book are pastoral scenes vanishing not only from post-industrialized countries but also emerging economies. Are we heading to a pasture-less world where everything will look like factories including processors of laboratory-grown meat, as in the dystopian 1982 film *Blade Runner*?

In this sort of world, lactating cows have virtually vanished into feedlot confinement. Today it is already the case in many regions of the world that the few cows left on pasture are part of organic dairy or beef co-operatives, or on hobby farms managed more for family tradition than profit – steers for beef, heifers or dry cows fortunate to be awaiting their next calf. All these bovines, of male, female or neutral gender had altered genetics which in turn altered their size, shape, longevity and other characteristics from their ancestors and, as the discussion above has pointed out, resulted in beings docile enough to seem to tolerate confined conditions.

Looking back to the twentieth century

How did we reach this point? On the advent of the Anthropocene in the mid-twentieth century US, farm activity changed from mixed farming with hogs, poultry and cattle on pasture and feed crops grown for them (the Midwest model), to monoculture, or to only a few crops such as alfalfa, soy and corn (aka maize) and to animals fed in central barns or feedlots but not grazing regularly on pasture. As well as cattle and poultry feed, corn was promoted as biofuel, after President George W. Bush's 2003 invasion of Iraq, amid attendant petroleum shortages. *The Economist* (2017b) noted similar changes in Britain: 'First, in the 1990s dairy farmers began to use corn as high-energy feed for cows ... As herds were moved into barns, and thus away from grass, more and more munched maize.'

It is now considered a truism that America's hamburger culture of the 1950–60s turned it into what Eric Schlosser (2001) dubbed a *Fast Food Nation*. Processed drive-in foods quickly replaced parts of people's diets that had been composed hitherto of home-cooked meals from simpler and healthier ingredients such as homegrown or locally grown fruit, vegetables and meat – traditional food recognizable by Michael Pollan's (2008) great-grandmother. What is less widely understood is that the standardization achieved by Ray Kroc in his McDonald's fast-food restaurants meshes so well with the ingredients and logistics of intensive confinement dairy facilities, i.e., CAFOs. Sociologist George Ritzer's (1993, 2004) 'McDonaldization' concept is applicable to many forms of late twentieth- and early twenty-first-century modernity, from fast food to franchised poultry farms, dairy farms and even social media. Not unlike the McDonald's chain, intensive dairy feeding systems developed in California suburbs were replicated in countries as disparate as Britain, Canada, China, Mexico and Turkey (*DeLaval Longevity Conference Proceedings 2013*: 3–4; Scholten 2014: 64–6, 129).

Dairy disruption in the mid-twentieth century is epitomized by the development of these intensive CAFOs, including by Dutch-Americans in Bellflower and other suburbs in the Los Angeles conurbation. Their grandparents' skill at maximizing production on small farms in the Netherlands was a competitive advantage in establishing dairy farms in periurban California cities, and then helped in innovating ever more intensive milk production. In recent debates, some academics, philosophers and activists claim that the characteristics of CAFOs – which include unnatural diets, genetic engineering, induced oestrus, artificial insemination and the separation of calves from mothers – constitute a forced reproductive dairy regime that is anything but natural. Broadcast of an anti-dairy advertisement during the Olympic games irritated the industry, noted Wyatt Bechtel (*Dairy Herd Management* 2018). In this context, maintaining herd health is challenging. There are various proposals to mitigate some of the problems which compromise herd health. For example, inside the dairy industry, Bill Gehm (2012) advocates the CoPulsation Milking System, blaming standard designs for chronic mastitis.

Politics is part and parcel of the dairy pastoral

As dairy farms in the US climbed economies of scale with herds of 100, 200, then 500, 1,000, 3,000 or 10,000+ milch cows, a food sovereignty political critique developed in which CAFOs represented the antithesis of Jeffersonian agrarian democracy. Bovine megadairies and poultry panopticons were light years from the modest national quilt of independent, multi-raced, self-provisioning forty-acre family farms in which relatives shared equity. Megadairies were oligarchic agribusinesses employing a domestic underclass of farmworkers – virtual serfs – composed increasingly of immigrant Latinx workers from south of the Rio Grande. Amy Trauger and Jennifer L. Fluri (2019: 73; 2008 *Food Inc.*) might find resonance between the evolution of US megadairies and poultry producers with Jan Douwe Van der Ploeg's (2009, 2010, 2020) arguments that states and neoliberal capitalism modernize subsistence economies toward consuming economies.

Some of the workers on Eastern Washington State megadairies emigrated from Mexico after their subsistence farms were overwhelmed by flows of cheap GMO corn from the US, following the North American Free Trade Agreement (NAFTA 1994). They were denied overtime pay for decades until the COVID-19 pandemic, when the Washington State Supreme Court improved their pay for work in hazardous conditions (*Seattle Eater* 2020). This made Washington the sixth US state to grant farmworkers overtime, and United Farm Workers' union official Elizabeth Strater said the ruling would impact jobs outside the dairy industry. The situation is ethically

> complex, because small- and medium-size family dairy producers seeking multi-generational sustainability, and working hard 24/7 amid falling real farmgate prices due to megadairy competition, were forced to increase their scale to the point they needed outside labour. Imagine their consternation when their family farm is, ironically, treated like factories in aviation or other industries. As a consequence, a group called Save Family Farming (2020) claimed their workers already averaged the highest pay rates in the US, and preferred the former salary system with variable hours.

A closer look at practices in CAFOs

In her PhD thesis at the University of Washington, Seattle, *Reproducing Dairy: Embodied Animals and the Institution of Animal Agriculture*, Kathryn A. Gillespie deplored not only the forced artificial insemination of female dairy cows, but also the little-known but painful electrical stimulation of male bulls for semen collection (2014b: 107–14). In her (2014a: 1321) article in *Gender, Place & Culture*, 'Sexualized violence and the gendered commodification of the animal body in Pacific Northwest US dairy production', Gillespie describes harrowingly the 'sexually violent commodification of both female and male animals in dairy production'.

European vegan activist Justine Butler has a PhD in molecular biology from Bristol University; she wrote for a non-academic readership in *Viva!* (2015) magazine, when she asked, 'Why milk is a feminist issue: What goes on behind the closed doors of the modern intensive dairy farm?' Butler blames cows' concurrent pregnancy and lactation for painful infections such as laminitis in hooves and mastitis in udders that cut cows' lives from a potential twenty or thirty years to about six. Her critique could be harsher: mainstream industry data (DHI-Provo 2013) show conventional US dairy cow longevity is nearer four in the US and five in the UK. Butler also refers to beliefs about animal sentience we have discussed above. In *Viva!* she cites John Webster, Emeritus Professor in Animal Husbandry at Bristol University, regarding non-human animals' perception of pain; because people assumed intelligence is linked to the ability to suffer, and animals have smaller brains, they suffer less than humans. Butler deems this a pathetic piece of logic.

Butler expands her argument to compare livestock farming to racism and slavery. She quotes American author and activist Alice Walker (1988), who summarized the message of Marjorie Spiegel's (1998) book *The Dreaded Comparison: Human and Animal Slavery* by stating that animals exist for their own reasons. They were not made for humans any more than black people were made for whites or women for men.

These are powerful ethical arguments. Contemporary society does not look easily on the conscious imposition of pain on sentient animals. Butler, also in *Viva!,* writes that milk comes from a grieving mother, parted just a day after delivering her calf, making this a feminist issue. Reading this alongside a photo of the chained rear legs of a newly calved cow might incline readers toward veganism. However, dairy farming experts would point out what was actually benign intent: in this case, hoof collars and chains are safety measures to prevent the cow's legs from splaying during a veterinary procedure.

That said, public sentiment has mounted against the trophy hunting of animals such as herbivore rhinoceroses and elephants, and carnivores such as tigers and wolves. It is relatively easy to justify these animals' sustainability by their assumed importance in biodiversity and ecology maintenance and general irrelevance in humans' diets.

But how do we compute the moral calculus of taking the lives of so many domesticated farm animals? St Augustine might have prayed, 'Please God, make me vegan – but not just yet!'

Paleo parallels: Ketosis in cows & diabetes in humans

Would *Homo sapiens* exist if our ancestors had not improved the protein quotient of their diets by hunting game on the African plain? Without the nutritious flesh of prey, we might not have evolved brains large enough to philosophize the ethics of domesticating and eating other creatures. Tatjana Visak, Robert Garner and Peter Singer (Singer is the paradigm-shifting author of *Animal Liberation* published 1975) address this in their 2015 book *The Ethics of Killing Animals*. In this present book, Chapters 2, 3 and 4 will discuss such issues further, prompted by the responses of 100 stakeholders – all of whom are consumers – to a set of key questions.

This prompts us to consider in more depth dairy's fourth problem: nutrition. Vegans question whether it is appropriate for humans weaned off mothers' milk to imbibe animal milk. Human and bovine mammals share similar woes. For cows, critics say one problem with non-traditional, non-pasture, high-energy feedlot diets featuring high-energy corn and soy, but insufficient fibre, is that they can lead to *over-condition* with symptoms such as fatty livers. Nutritionist Michael F. Hutjens of the University of Illinois warns farmers to 'keep some alfalfa in the ration' to balance corn and soy (*Hoard's Dairyman* 2018: 15). Studies by a team of scientists in Minnesota, New York and Finland (e.g., *Extension* 2016; Rajala-Schultz et al. 1999) identify susceptibility to ketosis in pregnant cows who have eaten a high-energy, low-fibre diet in the pre-calving dry period. Bovine ketosis is a hypoglycaemic state somewhat comparable to human diabetes, with a body condition score (BCS) of 3.5 to 4.0 or more, which is treated with glucose. Symptoms resemble milk fever, when a post-partum cow is down and cannot get up; treatment involves calcium – an on-farm treatment familiar to many reared on dairy farms.

Paul Biagiotti, author of *Practical Organic Dairy Farming* (2016), is a large-herd veterinarian, whose article 'Cow parallels to the human Paleo diet' (*Hoard's Dairyman* Dec 2017: 752–3) describes the nutrition of contemporary high-yield dairy cows in terms that resonate with diet-conscious humans. Biagiotti identifies

Dairy Farming in the 21st Century

dietary similarities between human hunter-gatherers and bovines in the Palaeolithic era, 50,00 to 10,000 years ago, before the dawn of agriculture. He explains the Paleo diet's 'premise is that by eating foods of a distant ancestral type and manner, we can approximate what evolution has decreed best suits our digestive tract and metabolism'.

Yet prehistoric diets were subject to feast or famine conditions, according to local circumstances. That is why, notes Biagiotti, human and bovine bodies evolved to store surplus nutrients in times of plenty as fat and protein, via hormones such as insulin and glucagon, for future use in times of hunger. Unfortunately for humans, alarming numbers of Americans and people in other rich countries – and more recently in middle-income and emerging economies such as India and China – develop Type 2 diabetes. This commonly results from obesity and an unbalanced diet consisting of processed carbohydrates and simple sugars, things that that were unavailable to human Paleo dieters and their prehistoric grazing bovine counterparts.

Human diets have come to warrant more scrutiny, amid sporadic signs that obesity and high intake of processed foods are cutting Americans' average lifespans in comparison to those in less rich countries (e.g., Costa Ricans now live longer). National Public Radio (NPR 2016) broadcast a story headlined 'Life Expectancy in US Drops for First Time in Decades'. The obesity epidemic is linked to deaths from heart disease, strokes, diabetes and possibly Alzheimer's. It could also be that doctors have reached the limit of what they can do to fight heart disease with current treatments. Here it's relevant that some human and bovine ills share their source in dietary problems.

Biagiotti concurs in *Hoard's Dairyman* (2017: 752–3). that post-partum fresh cows, which have recently calved, are prime subjects for 'fat cow syndrome' with insulin-resistant Type II ketosis as a major component in the syndrome Their fatty livers are incapable of delivering enough glucose to the blood, just when mammary glands require more. Losses to family farm income over US$100 per case mount quickly, but more serious are the long-term health implications for cows. Many high-yielding herds have significant proportions of cows suffering this bovine version of a human fast-food diet. Biagiotti (2014) blames 'cottonseed, corn – for both grain and silage – alfalfa, soybeans, and canola' which were not parts of their Paleo bovine ancestors' grazing.

As noted already, a surfeit of modern feedstuffs causes life-threatening ketosis in cows. Ketosis also increases the risk of milk fever. Accompanying acute ketosis is the silent phenomenon of – often undiagnosed – subacute rumen acidosis, or SARA. It is implicated in lameness, liver problems and, ominously, immune-system suppression which makes cattle prone to maladies such as displaced abomasum, mastitis, metritis and the inability to breed. Infertile cows are routinely given chances to conceive in just two further heat cycles. Failing that, they are culled. SARA exacerbates the cycle of weakness that has condemned almost half of America's cows to culling and slaughter before they have a second calf, or even reach their anatomical and production prime (Biagiotti 2014; Rajala-Schultz 1999; Mandel et al 2018; Paul Robinson 2010).

The penny drops on dairy welfare

Dairy consumption has become more globally significant even as objections to its practices grow. And while the conventional dairy industry has not been unaware of falling cow longevity, the bottom line for agribusiness will always literally be profit. Certainly, there are individual US farmers (particularly family farmers on relatively small-scale operations) who rally to positive goals of animal welfare, besides improving milk yield and knowing that they play a vital part in feeding the nation and filling gaps in the country's trade deficit with exports – despite making up barely 2 per cent of the population. To grasp how economics contributes to the situation we've been discussing, consider where dairy ranks among US exports. In 2017 for example, topping the list are soybeans, which account for $21.6 billion, but the dairy sector still contributed a weighty $5.4 billion as shown in Table 1.1 (USDA-FAS 2017). These statistics are given not to show current trade levels but to show the importance of dairy in trade, not solely domestic consumption.

Dairy, ninth on the list, had a hefty surplus after supplying the average American's per capita dairy consumption of liquid milk, butter, cheese, ice cream and yogurt – one of the world's highest consumption rates, of 646 lbs (294 kg) in 2016, up from 539 lbs (245 kg) in 1975. This was on a milk-equivalent, milk-fat basis.[1] If this dairy consumption of 646 lbs of milk equivalent per year sounds extreme, consider that it takes around 10 kg of cow milk to produce 1 kg of cheese (ratios vary by cows, goats or sheep). This is why aggregate dairy consumption can rise even if the drinking of liquid milk falls, or is in some countries virtually non-existent. *Give pizza chance?*

Indeed, Guy Robinson (2018ab) describes how dairy consumption has gradually spread and increased around the world, even in countries such as China and Indonesia where consumption of liquid milk or, in some cases other dairy products were not traditional dietary components. The *OECD-FAO Agricultural Outlook 2016–2025* (OECD-FAO 2016: 4) estimates that, 'By 2025, per capita

Table 1.1 Top US agricultural exports 2017, USDA-FAS

Commodity	Exports	Commodity	Exports
1. Soybeans	$21.6 billion	6. Wheat	$6.1 billion
2. Corn	$9.1 billion	7. Prepared Food	$5.9 billion
3. Tree nuts	$8.5 billion	8. Cotton	$5.8 billion
4. Beef	$7.3 billion	9. Dairy	$5.4 billion
5. Pork	$6.5 billion	10. Fresh fruit	$4.7 billion

Source: https://www.fas.usda.gov/data/top-us-agricultural-exports-2017, accessed 23 Mar 2018.

1. Source: USDA-FAS Dairy Data: Dairy products: Per capita consumption, United States, in lbs per person – 'Dairy products: Per capita consumption, United States [Annual] last updated 5/Sep/2017'.

consumption of fresh dairy products is set to increase to around 29 kg [64 lb] in least developed countries, compared to an average 56 kg [123 lb] in developing countries ...' Regional disparities within economies of similar income level are expected to remain.

It is no surprise that in this context practices anathema to good cow welfare are widespread. Geneticists and suppliers of feed, pharmaceuticals and other inputs have prioritized yield, pushing average annual rates of milk production per cow. In the US, production rose from about 12,000 lbs (5,455 kg) average per cow in 1980 to 20,000 lbs (9,091 kg) in 2007, and 23,000 lbs (10,455 kg) in 2017, representing a massive 12% increase over that nine-year period, according to the USDA National Agricultural Statistics Service (USDA[-NASS] 21 Feb 2018).

European Union yield per cow also rose, but less rapidly. In October 2017, Eurostat reported the average EU milk yield per dairy cow in the year 2016 had reached 6,941 kg (15,302 lbs), probably constrained by 1984–2015 milk quotas. Average milk yield was highest in Lombardia, Italy, at 9,870 kg (21,714 lb) per head, and lowest in Continental Croatia, at 4,534 kg (2061 lb) per cow.

Wherever cow productivity was pushed too hard, longevity fell, especially mong high-yielding Holstein-Friesians, the largest milch cow breed. However, in the early years of this millennium, too few data compilers and on-farm nutrition-feed staff recognized poor cow longevity; it was not common knowledge in the general population. Farmworkers on 10,000 cow dairies confided sadness to outsiders about culling young cows when they were still superficially young and sleek – but whose condition had been 'pushed' so hard that they were lame, had mastitis and could not conceive (Scholten 2014: 67, 125, 228). The dramatic reduction in cows' longevity – given that they have been able to live longer than 20 years – has now astonished people inside and outside the dairy industry.

Cattle handlers are uncomfortable if and when (perhaps at harvest time) feeding or milking routines break down, and a herd's cacophonous bellowing demands that their human keepers bring forage immediately. On the other side of the coin, herders enjoy the company of cattle that are well fed and cared for – a shared human/non-human feeling of well-being. Is this merely anecdotal evidence? Perhaps, but it is hard to disprove! A particular pleasure is pasture walking among cattle with apples, carrots or other treats in one's pockets. They are keys to popularity. It is psychologically significant that intensive dairy farms sometimes keep what effectively is a pet cow, a favourite cow who gets more daily attention and pampering than the cohort she has outlived. Her longevity of seven, ten or even more than twelve years can mask poor longevity in the farm's commercial herd. But as long as she keeps giving milk and births the occasional calf, she is allowed to live and represent the best aspirations of dairy life.

As the percentage of the US and UK population working as farmers fell from 3 per cent to 2 per cent between 1991 and 2017 (see Table 1.2), dairy farmers have been caught in a bind between the pressures of a round-the-clock job and the demands of processors and retailers seeking lower farmgate prices – whatever the real cost to animals, the environment or farm families. Numbers have not yet fallen to single digits in emerging economies such as India, but have plummeted nonetheless.

Table 1.2 World Bank (2017) Employment in agriculture (% of total employment) (ILO est.)

	1991	2017
India	64%	43%
UK	2%	1%
US	3%	2%

The decrease in these percentages in the US represents the consolidation of small family-scale herds into vast confinement operations. This restricts the possible incomes of remaining small farms, as does consolidation into just a few or one dominant processor, inviting charges of what economists term monopsony (USDA 2020). This is a serious trend in the organic sector, documented at Michigan State University by Philip Howard (2014; Scholten 2014: 74) in annual flow charts revealing acquisitions, mergers and spin-offs in 'Organic Industry Structures'. Sometimes, for example during the 2016–18 US milk glut, farmers had no choice of processers to which they could sell milk (*Odairy* 2018). A life-long dairy farmer from Kentucky, H.H. Barlow II, wrote to the editors of *Hoard's Dairyman* (May 10, 2018: 298; also Scholten 1997b: 6, 'Bye-bye this American guy'):

> In 1997, the US had 112,000 dairy farms with 9.4 million cows annually producing 155 billion pounds of fluid milk. In 2017, we had only 40,000 dairy farms with the same 9.4 million cows producing 215 billion pounds of fluid milk.

These statistics hide how grim the lives of dairy cows have become. And it has got worse. By 2020, barely 32,000 US dairy farms remained, and in 2022 there are fewer than 30,000. Consolidation, encouraged by President George W. Bush, pushed farm families along with cows. Farmer suicides mounted (*Guardian* 2017d). Above, farmer Barlow said he had been a free market advocate his entire life, but now advocated a 'national supply management program', hinting that the consumer trend to buy local would support what is, by any other name, a milk quota akin to Canada's system, or Europe's 1984–2015 milk quota. Supply management was not a new issue. In 1990 Congressional hearings, my father Bastian Scholten, President, Washington State Dairy Federation (1990), called for supply management, with nutrient component pricing, and herd buyouts as solutions to the milk surpluses that had begun to occur along with supermarket price swings, and weak dairy farmer income.

American voters are notoriously nervous about quotas because they are conflated with planned economies, socialism or even totalitarian communism. Hence the US dairy industry's choice of the phrase *supply management* for what in Canada or Europe were called milk quotas. Do quotas amount to a subsidy to industry, and form non-tariff barriers (NTBs) to would-be entrants to an industry? Yes (Scholten 1989a; 1989b; 1989c; 1990d; 2010a; 2010c). Economists routinely decry subsidies as political threats to efficiency, unless they are justified by market failure or special circumstances. However, while it would be unwise to subsidize factories making outdated buggy whips, protecting animal welfare and environment may be ethically justified in the face of less efficiency (Scholten 1990a; 2007c).

This is one the most difficult challenges facing dairy. Farmer Barlow's opinion is likely shared by observers who judge that the ethics of managing sentient creatures in the livestock industry, along with the existential need to manage anthropomorphic impact on the environment, amount to a special case for prioritizing animal welfare and environmental sustainability over economic efficiency. If a consequence of this policy is to lower the scale of new dairy farms from 20,000 in CAFOs to smaller grazing farms with herds from a few dozen to 1,000 cows that are physically able to walk between pastures and barn, so be it. Subsidies would guarantee a balanced outcome. An indirect good could be that rural communities prosper from the enhanced incomes of smaller, family-scale dairy farms, which in the aggregate employ more people per cow than do confined megadairies – and increase aggregate community prosperity. We consider these issues from different perspectives in Chapters 2, 3 and 4.

Why are farmers not compensated adequately? Supermarkets are one culprit. For example, in 2004, the UK's House of Commons concluded that supermarket multiple retailers, such as Asda, Marks & Spencer, Morrisons, Safeway, Sainsbury, Tesco and Waitrose, dominated price relationships with farmers. Eminent researchers Kevin Morgan, Terry Marsden and Jonathan Murdoch (2006: 149–50) agreed, largely because, 'the structure of the UK dairy sector, where producer-owned co-operatives are predominantly brokers rather than vertically-integrated processors, represents an organizational weakness that imposes a very heavy burden on producers'. Citing analysis from audit, tax and advisory service KPMG (2003), Morgan, Murdoch and Marsden (2006) wrote that this had led to the UK having the lowest farmgate prices in the EU. The attendant farmer woes (which in turn affect cow welfare) have taken the form of supermarket power, a bias towards commodity products, sectoral inefficiencies and a hostile regulatory environment. Again, if one accepts that pinched incomes induce farmers to compromise ethical care for animals and the environment when prioritizing their own welfare, there may be a case for restructuring the dairy sector, via a milk quota or other measures.

German discount grocery stores Aldi and Lidl have since eroded the market share of the major UK supermarkets, prompting restructuring of two, Asda and Sainsbury. The price position of dairy and beef farmers in the UK has also worsened, due to the growth of multi-thousand cow feedlots making inroads in the UK supply chain (*Guardian* 2018a).

From green pastures to the Green Revolution

Thus far the focus has been on cows rather than on the humans who work with them. Apart from noting an increase in farmer suicides in some countries, there has been little discussion of farmer welfare. Dairy farming is a calling, a quasi-religious vocation. It must be, or how else could farmers bear so many sixteen-hour days? In Chapter 5, we treat this issue from a gender perspective and ask whether there is a 'grass ceiling' for women in agriculture. Female and male farmers are typically born into farm families. Training begins by osmosis. If they inherited the farm, the compulsion – from themselves, family members and people in their communities – to retain the land in family control is strong. This issue also arises in the course of the 100 stakeholders' responses to a set of statements and questions presented in Chapters 2, 3 and 4.

But now, if you will, imagine a dairy farm in the 1940–50s. Morning milking began about 5 o'clock and, before evening milking twelve hours later, regular chores in winter included cleaning the barn, milking parlour and stalls when fields were too muddy for cows to graze every day. Daytime tasks included arranging breeding, building and fence repair, perhaps maintaining Dutch-style brick roads for cows to reach pasture without dragging their legs through mud, as well as drives to the auction, equipment dealers or bankers in town. Evening milking time varied according to the farm, equipment and number of cows. Dairy farmers had huge hands until pneumatic milkers superseded hand-milking after the Second World War. Then they still had pretty big hands, but for one reason or another, milking time seldom took under two hours. After night clean-up (critical in facilities where cow milk must have somatic cell counts/SCC 400,000 or lower), pre-partum, birthing and especially post-partum cows had to be checked for ketosis (and treated with glucose) or milk fever (and treated with calcium). If calves were born, farmers did not rest till the mother licked the calf to life, when it stood and suckled. Acute cases of ketosis or milk fever suffer also had to be checked on past midnight. The litany of dairy farm chores was infinite. Seasonal chores intensified activity. These included planting, weeding, harvest and replanting. For instance, ploughing, disking, harrowing and then replanting a degraded corn (aka maize) field with grasses and clover improved the depleted soil's chemical balance via the miraculous nitrogen-fixing nodules on legumes' roots. That was how pasture was reinvigorated for grazing cows. Artificial inputs were superfluous. After a few years, corn, oats or other crops could be replanted there with an expectation of renewed yields.

Production of nitrogen for armaments shifted to chemical agriculture after the Second World War, and the chemical intensification of conventional farming in the Green Revolution led by figures including Norman Borlaug and M.S. Swaminathan (Basu and Scholten 2012, 2013). Yields increased in response to artificial inputs. These were added to those in each cow's daily average of 20kg of cowpats. Veterinarian Hue Karreman (2013) explains that cows drink ten to thirty gallons of water a day and recycle much to the land. This washes into soil, boosting growth, before the next round of rotational grazing. Grazing on many farms proceeded with sporadic applications of chemical fertilizers, for years before Californian-style feedlot dairying swept the US.

Looking at the impact of world events further illuminates dairy's development from pasture to confinement in the US. In *Merchants of Grain* (1979), Dan Morgan tells the story of the Soviet Union's 1972 wheat coup. In collusion with the oligarchy of the world's five biggest grain distributors, the USSR had cornered the market. Morgan relates how, during the administration (1969–74) of President Richard Nixon, Secretary of Agriculture Earl Butz told US farmers to 'get big or get out' (see USDA 2001 for a Farm Typology for small, large and very large farms used in Scholten 2007ac, 2011b). Farming for the highest possible production became a patriotic duty. Butz was pushing Nixon's Food Power export policy quest to bolster the US dollar, after years of deficit spending to simultaneously fight the Vietnam War abroad, and the War on Poverty begun domestically, by previous President Lyndon Johnson. Many crops and livestock farmers acceded to Butz, sold to neighbours and moved to town. Others – younger, more ambitious or foolhardy – secured loans to multiply their herds. Many abandoned tie stall or stanchion barns for large loafing sheds and milking parlours to milk cows quickly for high milk yield. This reduced the need for land and skill in managed intensive rotational grazing (MIRG), and compromised bovine and soil health. Politically, 'Get big or get out!' became fighting words for environmentalists and greens.

More efficient infrastructure might relieve the strains of dairy life temporarily in some ways, but seldom brought farm families surcease for long. Dairy farmers heard incessant advice from experts to cull unprofitable cows after they hit their prime. Such advice unsettled farmers. Confused them. Over coffee after church, they discussed it. Suddenly a seven-year-old cow was considered old and headed for the knacker's yard. But there was that patriotic duty. American manufacturing and industry were facing competition from Japan, Korea and other countries in the 1980s, and farmers were expected to do their part by rationalising operations and innovating like non-farm businesses. Cows would lose their names and be numbered like widgets. In the US, this boosted a trend to larger herds in feedlot confinement that has continued ever since. In genetics the push was for larger cows with wider hips to ease calving and support fulsome udders. Annual average production gains of between 2 and 3 per cent were achieved, less often by natural breeding and increasingly by artificial insemination (AI) (Scholten 1989a; 1989b). Additionally, chemically induced oestrus rationalized AI for multiple breeding, lowering service costs – a fact known to few consumers in the general public, but a target of welfarists' wrath. High-yielding Holstein-Friesians eventually doubled, then tripled average yields from the 1950s onwards.

As mentioned above, US dairy farmers pled for 'supply management' in US Congressional hearings. They hoped for an American version of Canadian and European milk quotas (Scholten 1989b; Washington State Dairy Federation 1990; Eurostat 2017). This was denied by the neoliberal Reagan/Bush administrations to whom the word *quota* was political kryptonite in their philosophy which, superficially, denied public subsidies to few sectors except for the military and fossil-fuel production. To its credit, in 1986, the US federal government was able to bolster farmgate milk prices slightly with a herd buy-out and sale of surplus cows to China. Despite a brief rise in milk prices, respite did not endure. The push to 'get big or get out' continued, led by a wave of establishment of 400+ cow dairies (among which 1,000+ cow herds were about to become the minimum norm), often built on irrigated land in the spacious deserts of the West (Idaho and Eastern Washington), and Southwest (Texas to California). A few dry cows or heifers grazing on a post-harvest field near milking barns might hide confined hers from urban day trippers.

More than any other factor, it was agribusiness politics that in the twentieth century changed American dairying from mixed farms, from small-scale family farms, to intensive monocultural factory farms outsourcing inputs and feed. It was hard to find a four-leafed clover in the pasture. Corporate capital, not family inheritance and succession, dominated discussion. Can the genie be put back in the bottle? Perhaps.

Not all USDA policies have been inimical to small farms. This includes the organic farms whose numbers were increasing and which were established and certified as organic after Vermont Senator Patrick Leahy and colleagues passed the Organic Foods Production Act (OFPA 1990). In early 2018, during President Barack Obama's era, the USDA bowed to a petition from thousands of organic farmers who were protesting the imminent imposition of an organic 'check-off' scheme. The scheme was advocated by processors and traders such as the Organic Trade Association (Cornucopia Institute 2018a) and on the surface seemed like a step forward. Ostensibly, the check-off would promote sales of organic products. However, at a 2013 meeting of the National Organic Standards Board (NOSB), farmers complained it amounted to an unfair tax on their labours (*Odairy* 2018; Cornucopia 2018a). The check-off was abandoned. Another boon for farmers was a Safety Net for Dairy Farmers: the USDA had offered a risk-management program to protect producers from shifting milk and feed prices, and USDA Secretary Sonny Perdue extended the deadline until 8 June 2018 (USDA 2018e).

USDA help to the organic sector was not from a sense that this sector's products were *better* than conventional products in terms of nutrition for humans or welfare for animals. It is telling that the National Organic Program (NOP) was administered by the USDA's Agricultural Marketing Service rather than offices focused on ecology or nutrition. What the *market*-oriented USDA appreciated about the organic sector was the promise of economic growth; while it barely accounted for $9 billion in sales in 2002, by 2017 it approached $50 billion as the country's fastest growing consumer-driven farm niche. A bright spot in the otherwise grim COVID-19 pandemic was an announcement by the USDA from its NOP Organic Integrity Database that the number of certified organic operations worldwide grew to 45,578 in 2020 with 28,454 – over 62 per cent – in the United States alone. California led the US with 5,000 certified operations, while the Great Lakes Region, Iowa and Pacific Northwest rounded out the top ten (*Odairy* 2021; see also USDA 2016–17; also, USDA 2019). Who were these new consumers? Researchers at the Hartman Group near Seattle found organic milk adopters were often educated new parents considering organics for the first time as they weaned infants from breastmilk (Hartman Group 1997, 2004, 2006; Scholten 2014: 7, 68).

The organic turn

In the latter part of the twentieth century, some farmers resisted USDA Secretary Earl Butz's exhortation to intensify or leave agriculture. In a monopsony market, some were abandoned by their previous processor and they had to create new marketing links. A prime example of new links is from the US Midwest where, in February 1988, a few dozen organic farmers formed a co-operative called Coulee Region Organic Produce Pool (CROPP). Soon CROPP was shipping organic dairy, beef, poultry, vegetable, pork and egg products across the country under its Organic Valley (2018) or OV label. CROPP started a sister farm co-operative supplying organic hay and other forages to farms.

Organic grew. In 2008, a USDA survey found 3.5 per cent of US herds, 2.1 per cent of cows and 1.5 per cent of milk volume was organic (*Dairy Business* 2009). The Organic Valley co-op gradually expanded, partly by mergers of regional cognate organizations. By 2010, OV farms numbered around 1,200, as absorption of processers in Oregon and elsewhere pushed membership up, and by 2018 the number had risen to 2,000 farm members (*Coop News* 2017; Organic Valley 2018). More farmers began to feel they had options to going big, or getting out. They could join together with like-minded small farmers. In the twenty-first century, Organic Valley has also continued to foster organic fodder, forage and grain production. That effort was difficult, but continued into the 2010s with links to Organic Valley's thriving new grass-fed 'Grassmilk' line, which appealed to traditional grazers and consumers alike. This is akin to Germany, where milk from pastured cows keeps some farms thriving since the end of European Union milk quotas in 2015.

BY 2018, Organic Valley had become the US's biggest organic dairy co-operative, with most of its members small, family-scale operations by USDA definitions (Scholten 2007ac, 2014). All OV farms graze cows whenever possible, with herd health a priority, partly because consumers value the higher levels of healthful Omega-3 fatty acids in the grass-fed milk. Pictures of healthy families and cows on green pasture sell the grass-fed view effectively. Although the USDA National Organic Program (USDA-NOP) does not presently have a nutritional requirement for milk sold to consumers, the medical establishment's rehabilitation of milk fats as healthier than margarine suggests nutrition's role as a driving force (Benbrook et al. 2013, 2018). We return to discussion of these issues in Chapters 2, 3 and 4 when stakeholders, including consumers, share their views.

But all was not without debate. In what constitutes breaking news in the dairy sector, *Washington Post* investigative reporter Peter Whoriskey wrote a series of articles (starting 8 Jun 2017) sparked by a condemnation by the Cornucopia Institute's Mark Kastel of the USDA National Organic Program's (NOP) lax monitoring and enforcement of pasture-grazing rules. The target was Aurora Organic Dairy (AOD) in Texas. Were these organic cows spending the expected time grazing on pastures? Kastel said consumers were vulnerable to fraud and small family grazing farmers to unfair competition. Whoriskey observed this Texas megadairy for eight days, never finding more than 10 per cent of the 10,000-

cow herd on pasture. Through acts of 'commission and omission the USDA has been complicit' in alleged skirting of organic pasture rules, as Whoriskey quoted me in the *Washington Post* (28 Sep 2017).

In 2017 the Cornucopia Institute sued Aurora Organic Dairy, but did not win. (The loss surprised observers who recalled USDA threatened revocation of AOD's organic status in Colorado in 2007 for '14 wilful violations of organic rules' including pasture lapses.)

Peter Whoriskey's final articles in the *Washington Post* series (on 21 and 22 December 2017) described how scientists have developed ways to identify healthy Omega-3 and unhealthy Omega-6 fatty acids in milk (one reason that medical and consumer attitudes have swung to their recent pro-fat stance). *The Wall Street Journal* (3–4 Mar 2018) announced milk fat was rehabilitated, even fashionable, after decades in which the medical establishment touted plant-based margarine instead of dairy butter. In another boon to the organic dairy industry, Bhattacharjee et al. (2018) announced the development of spectroscopy technology that could monitor milk nutrients cheaply. This could improve enforcement of organic regulations, and increase consumer trust that the dairy products they eat are indeed from cows who grazed naturally on clover and grasses in meadows.

The Real Organic Project (ROP), based in Vermont, a farmer-led movement vaunting soil-grown and pasture-raised products, has joined the ranks of Organic Eye, Organic Consumers Association, and Cornucopia Institute (e.g., personal communication with organic pioneer Goldie Caughlan in Seattle). Participants in ROP include academics, consumers, politicians like Senator Patrick Leahy and activists such as Vandana Shiva. Besides distinguishing soil-grown and pasture-raised sustainable organics products under USDA organic certification from industrialized methods and megadairies, ROP counters agro-pharmaceutical hegemony embodied in new developments such as hydroponics or soilless farming, and plant- and laboratory-based substitutes for livestock-based foods.

Dairy trade amid embargoes

The US situation of the Organic Valley co-op was mirrored somewhat in other countries such as Britain, where the Organic Milk Suppliers Co-operative UK, established in 1994, was 100 per cent organic, farmer run and owned, with 270 members and an annual turnover of £100 million. OMSCO rose when powerful UK supermarkets and politicians crushed the MilkMarque co-operative in 1994 (Scholten 2014: 32, 219). Linked to the Soil Association, OMSCO managed 65 per cent of UK organic milk (Scholten 2018b), and is the largest dedicated organic dairy supplier in UK, the largest organic dedicated dairy co-op in Europe and the second-largest organic milk co-op in the world. Tantalisingly, in 2016, OMSCO and Organic Valley announced plans to ship surplus British dairy commodities and products to the US, where some would then be exported to prospering consumers in China. OMSCO-OV co-operation was already underway in 2017, with EU and UK hard cheese exported to the US, as noted in conference presentations in the UK and India (Scholten 2017b, 2018b). But there was trouble ahead. AGain, it was politics that drove trends.

Imbroglios involving Ukraine, between Russia and Western powers including the US and Europe, have had a significant impact on trade. In August 2014, in response to Western sanctions, Russian Prime Minister Dimitry Medvedev announced import bans on meat, fish and dairy items from the EU, US, Australia, Canada and Norway, according to Jennifer Rankin in *The Guardian* (2014a). In a separate article in the same newspaper that day, 'Russian food import ban leaves shoppers unaffected – or a bit peeved', Alec Luhn (*Guardian* 2014b) reported Moscow shoppers saying they supported Russian retaliation against the West. For them it was just 'Goodbye Parmesan, hello pelmeni. Goodbye brie, hello borscht'. But trivialities to elites can be existential threats to family-scale farmers. Economic sanctions added to food embargoes after Russia invaded Ukraine in 2022.

During the Cold War (1947–90), the US occasionally accused European countries with shared Christian democratic values, but social-democratic political philosophies to the left of Anglo-American politics, of weakness vis-à-vis the communist Soviet Union. Geographic proximity, i.e., geopolitics, was a factor. In the period around 2014, the German and British bark in trade sanctions against Russia was softer than the US bite – given the former countries' need, like Ukraine's, for Russian gas exports. Britain had, by the early 2010s, depleted its once-vaunted North Sea oil reserves. America, meanwhile, was weaning itself off its inefficient biofuel experiment, beloved by corporate Midwest grain producers. Fracking and shale oil technology had matured, and despite attendant water pollution, and evidence that fracking had triggered minor earthquakes in the US and the UK, these technologies contributed to rising petroleum stocks. Fracking was divisive, but Democrat candidate Joe Biden rode the fence to victory in the 2020 presidential election. On one hand Perdue wooed environmentalists by vowing to pay farmers to plant cover crops and put land in conservation, wrote Chuck Abbott in *Successful Farming* (16 April 2020). On the other hand, Biden claimed he was *not* against all fracking.

Britain's bark got louder (BBC 6 Mar 2018), when former Russian spy Sergei Skripal and daughter Yulia collapsed in a UK shopping centre. Then PM Theresa May blamed Russian agents wielding Novichok, a military nerve agent. May suddenly had to balance Brexit negotiations with an awkward request to Europeans to scold Russia for violation of Britain's sovereign borders against double-agent Skripal and his daughter. European unity was enhanced when France, Germany and other EU countries joined Britain's condemnation of Russia. What does espionage have to do with dairying? Such shenanigans and trade wars are no boon to farmers.

Although many US farmers voted for Donald Trump in the 2016 election rather than Hillary Clinton, their loyalty was tested after losing grain exports to Mexico which, irritated by Trump's plan for a new border wall, signed a bilateral trade deal with Argentina. On 5 June 2018, NBC News reported 'Mexico will impose 20 percent tariffs on US pork'. This recalled how President. Jimmy Carter, a peanut farmer himself, was abandoned by farmers in his 1980 loss to Ronald Reagan, after Carter banned US grain exports to the Soviet Union, following its 1979 invasion of Afghanistan. Like most economic actors, farmers prefer certainty. Trump deftly managed to retain significant farmer backing due to USDA subsidies for lost exports.

Farmers' worries were compounded on 22 March 2018, when President Trump unilaterally announced $60 billion of tariffs on imports from China. Earlier, Trump imposed tariffs on imported steel and aluminium, which impacted European suppliers, Japan and Canada. The peripatetic president then exempted Korea, Mexico and Canada, but did not entirely heal relations. Canadian PM Justin Trudeau excoriated Trump's tariff on steel imported from fellow NATO member Canada on national security grounds.

President Trump also led a shift away from the 1995 World Trade Organization agreements, and the principle of most-favoured-nation (MFN) status, which economists Bernard Hoekman and Michel Kostecki saw as fundamental to *The Political Economy of the World Trading System* (1995; CNBC 2018a). In tit-for-tat exchanges that marked his presidency, Trump made the credible charge that Chinese trade practices included stealing US firms' intellectual property. China riposted that it should not be penalized if its consumers did not fancy US products. Then Trump claimed, inaccurately, that China charged 25 per cent tariffs on US cars, while the US placed just 2 per cent on Chinese autos, echoing a complaint on US–German auto trade (CNBC 2018a).

In response to events on the Pacific Rim, UK farmgate milk prices went from poor to pitiful. In 2015, supermarket Morrisons asked customers to pay an extra 10 pence per litre of milk to help farm families (*Farming UK* 2015). More promising for UK small farm sustainability was new co-operation between OMSCO and Scandinavian-based Arla (2016) cooperative which produces conventional, free range and organic milk. A decade before, a Danish organic milk surplus prompted Arla to export to Germany, and this primed the pump for further exports across Europe, linking to the US and China.

Revisiting the Green Revolution

During the Cold War, when US farmers were urged to 'get big or get out', they were already able to depend on artificial inputs. Genetically modified organisms were a new kid on the block, promising to increase farm yields even more, with fewer (if any) inputs such as chemical fertilizers and pesticides. That was a false promise.

As outlined further above, the introduction of GMO crops turned out to involve the pharmaceutical company Monsanto, which developed Roundup®, the world's most-used herbicide. It is usually formulated with glyphosate, a long-suspected carcinogen, as recently ruled in US courts. Use of this and other herbicides and pesticides is problematic for organic farmers because they can drift to adjacent farms. They threaten the organic certification of neighbouring pasture and crops, posing health risks to animals and people that organic farming aims to avoid. There is attendant cost to organic dairy farmers, as prices of glyphosate-free organic feed and fodder are significantly higher.

Family-scale dairy and forage producers were exhausted by low farmgate prices in the pasture wars, and by the US government's relentless encouragement of agribusiness consolidation, not just in conventional dairying, but also by lax monitoring and enforcement of rules for organically certified megadairies (Scholten 2007c, 2010b, 2014). This further weakened farmers' bargaining power on the dairy value chain vis-à-vis processors, retailers and purveyors of seeds, pesticides and inputs. An egregious example is the $63 billion acquisition of US-based biotech firm Monsanto by German conglomerate Bayer, despite mass protests by the International Federation of Organic Agriculture Movements (IFOAM), and other greens in Bonn, Cologne and globally (*Euronews* 2018; *Hygeia* 2018; Benbrook and Benbrook 2018).

Since the 1990s, Charles Benbrook has led studies on glyphosate. Recently his daughter, graphics artist Rachel Benbrook illustrates his work, from Hygeia Analytics in Bellingham, USA (*Hygeia* 2018), showing how 37 million lbs (16 million kgs) of Monsanto's glyphosate were used in agriculture and landscaping in the decade after its introduction in 1974; this placed glyphosate seventeenth among US pesticides dominated by Atrazine, a herbicide used against weeds in cornfields, and banned by the EU in 2004 (Scholten 1990b; 1990c). Benbrook (C. Benbrook 1990; R. Benbrook 2018) noted that use of Monsanto Roundup® glyphosate nearly doubled between 1980 and 1990, yet Monsanto claimed residues in food and water were very low. But they were not as low as implied.

When Monsanto's patent expired about 1990, other companies began using glyphosate compounds on glyphosate-resistant GMO crops, and usage climbed to 25 million lbs around 1995. But the 1996 introduction of Roundup® Ready soybeans used with glyphosate brought a tsunami of glyphosate to the US, Canada and Argentina, where Binimelis et al. (2009) claimed a *transgenic treadmill* was spurring evolution of resistant superweeds requiring ever larger doses of glyphosate and chemical cocktails such as Dow's Dicamba. Glyphosate has been increasingly detected in water near conventional GMO cotton, soybean and corn fields in the US (Benbrook 2012b), and it is used in pre-harvest desiccation of alfalfa, barley, maize, wheat, potatoes, etc. Rachel Carson (1962) might have asked: Does glyphosate reach human bodies via crops and cow milk?

It's worth noting that the Genetic Literacy Project (2020) published a 2015 report by anti-GMO group Sustainable Pulse listing thirty-eight countries that had banned cultivation of GMO crops including Algeria and Madagascar in Africa; Turkey, Kyrgyzstan, Bhutan and Saudi Arabia in Asia; Belize, Peru, Ecuador and Venezuela in South and Central America; and twenty-eight countries in Europe. However, many of these countries, including the UK, allow import of food for humans and fodder for cattle which has been grown with glyphosate.

'MAMs vs Glyphosate'

US consumers were alarmed in 2014 when Moms Across America, with Sustainable Pulse and the Organic Consumers Association (Cummins 2020), found high levels of glyphosate in three out of the ten samples of breast milk tested: levels of 76 ug/l to 166 ug/l were allegedly 760 to 1,600 times higher than European Drinking Water Directive limits (*Natural Society* 2014). However, the Moms Across America study was disputed by Dr Michelle K. McGuire at Washington State University (*Science Daily* 23 July 2015, 'US breast milk is glyphosate free: Study is first independently verified look for the presence of Roundup ingredient in human milk', in *ScienceDaily*, Washington State University), and later with her team in *American Journal of Clinical Nutrition* (2016) 103(5): 1289, 1285–90):

> In conclusion, our data – obtained using sophisticated and validated methods of analyses – strongly suggest that glyphosate does not bioaccumulate and is not present in human milk even when the mother has detectable glyphosate in her urine.

Whether or not the WSU team's methodology was more rigorous than the Moms', the latter certainly wish no environmental- or food-borne glyphosate whatsoever in their bodies or their babies' bodies. One reason is that glyphosate is an endocrine-disrupting chemical (EDC) to which infants may be vulnerable (*Chemosphere* 11 Sep 2018).

I contacted Charles Benbrook in early 2021. His decades studying conventional and organic dairy systems are cited in this and previous publications (Benbrook 2007, 2012, 2019; Scholten 2014). In recent years, Benbrook has served as an expert witness for plaintiffs in litigation involving Roundup®-containing glyphosate and cases of non-Hodgkin lymphoma, trials ending in large judgements against newly merged Bayer-Monsanto. So, I asked for an update on the dispute between the Moms Across America group and the WSU team. Was there glyphosate in human breast milk?

Benbrook kindly replied: 'Back when I was a Research Professor at WSU, Monsanto hired Dr Michelle McGuire, a WSU professor of food science to test several samples of breast milk for glyphosate. She did and found none. Her husband worked in the dairy science department at the nearby Idaho State University. He was closely aligned with Monsanto and a proponent of rBGH, the genetically engineered bovine growth hormone given to cows to increase milk production. Both of them were part of Monsanto's network of third-party scientists. I had a meeting with them that was rocky. They are true believers. Milk is a tricky matrix to find glyphosate in. Was it there? Did they miss it? I do not know.'

Fairness suggested asking Michelle McGuire, since moved to University of Idaho, to comment on her WSU team's earlier conclusion that 'glyphosate does not bioaccumulate and is not present in human milk even when the mother has detectable glyphosate in her urine' (McGuire et al. 2016: 1289). Unfortunately, Dr McGuire had not replied to requests for comment, sent 30 March, 9 April, 26 May and 26 August 2021, and 24 March 2022.

Dairy farming in the twenty-first century

This chapter began by noting four key issues that apply to dairy farming today. The first is the recurring problem of Malthusian overpopulation of humans which leads to increasingly limited space to grow food for humans and raise animals on a finite Earth, and the attendant ethical and political problems of land and unequal resources among rich and poor countries. Second is the environmental impact of dairy farming on climate change, surprisingly equal to that of energy production and transport in our economies (FAO 2006). There are additional newly recognized factors not introduced in this chapter to be discussed in the final chapter. Third is the response to dairy's increasingly bad reputation in the form of a growing trend for plant-based foods as a solution to the ethical problems of dominating dairy cows and killing animals for food. Discussion included the admonition by Michael Pollan to shun what our great-grandparents would not recognize as food.

The twenty-first entury can be a turning point with respect to where our food originates. Trends towards industrialized farming and food processing, begun after the Second World War, can be countered. Frances Moore Lappé (1971) alerted readers to the environmental and moral impact of meat in *Diet for a Small Planet*. Debate, partly driven by activists' use of social media, has turned to dairy. Small-scale, co-operatively organized, sustainable dairy farming has the potential to redress many of the ethical, environmental and political wrongs of intensive dairy farming to animals, environment and farmers.

How often do cows graze to produce what often finds pride of place in our refrigerators? A visit to a Parmigiano Reggiano cheese facility in Reggio Emilia, Italy, makes a point. After a guided tour of the gleaming cheese-processing plant and warehouse, the guide took us to five dozen of the special red cows that make milk for connoisseur-level cheese. The cow barn was airy, clean and modern, but stocking density of the rare-breed Vacche Rosse red cows was high. Their ancestors grazed roomy fields, now covered by residences and a school. When feeding at the manger, or perching with forelegs on stalls, cows were licking the ears and flanks of their friends, in an atmosphere of tense boredom. As US veterinarian and CowSignals trainer Hue Karreman (2018) points out, when cows feel safe and happy, the herd spreads out on pasture, friends chewing cud with friends. Confined cows cannot spread out. It's like perpetual COVID-19 lockdown, bundled with family in a tiny apartment size (*Lancet* 2020). These were coping activities, less so natural behaviour.

The production of Parmesan cheese has come under scrutiny in Italy's Po Valley, where activists charged the head of a cheese association with lapses in animal welfare. He explained welfare had not been a priority because there was no direct link between cheese quality and the cows' living conditions. Compassion in World Farming (27 Nov 2017) issued a press release headlined 'The cruel truth behind Parmesan that is hard to stomach'. Emma Slawinski, Director of Campaigns at CiWF, said: 'What our investigators found was simply shocking and really exposes the misery of life in a factory farm'. She described underweight cows treated like milk machines with signs of lameness, 'Just so we can add a topping to our pasta. It's time to put these animals back on the land where they belong'.

Consumers around the world have become savvier. Chapters 2, 3 and 4 voice opinions of experts and stakeholders on a set of statements and queries on ethical, environmental, and political issues already mentioned above.

Chapter 5 addresses a topic only briefly referred to in this chapter: farm work. The focus is on dairy women and the 'grass ceiling' they confront. In the spirit of the United Nations 2030 Agenda for Sustainable Development (FAO 2018), the chapter is based on my research conclusions that, just as global institutions worked with India's National Dairy Development Board (NDDB) in Operation Flood 1970-1996 (Scholten 1997c, 2010c), to empower women, children and families in Amul-model dairy co-operatives, we can now paint on a global canvas. With investment and training, smallholder women in Africa and Asia, can help address environmental concerns with sustainable methane and solar technologies, and reducing ruminant methane emissions by mixing seaweed with cattle feed, showing ethical concern for animals while mitigating global warming.

As we have seen in this chapter, many issues interact in dairying in the twenty-first century. The most existential threat is climate change. Even if animal welfarists succeed in their demands for a phase-out of intensive zero-grazing confinement, the chances for long-term human survival lie in proportion to the extent we can limit dairy ruminant methane burps (along with the overall carbon hoofprint). In the final chapter of this book, we will examine what we know about cows' contribution to greenhouse gases to address the question of whether evidence strengthens the case for dairy alternatives.

Chapter 2

POLITICS, FAMILY FARMERS AND ANIMALS

This chapter, along with Chapters 3 and 4, presents the voices of 100 stakeholders from around the world who responded to a set of nine statements/questions (also referred to as 'dairy queries' below) with which they were asked to indicate agreement or disagreement on a five-point scale, between late 2019 and early 2020. Each chapter considers a set of three related statements shown at the start of the chapter. The respondents were encouraged to add comments about their responses to statements and many did so, in part because some of the statements were written to be provocative. Responses were not anonymous due to the need to ask respondents' permission to use their words in this book. However, pseudonyms have been used, unless noted.

Figure 2.1 Bovine sculptures at Mahabalipuram, UNESCO World Heritage Site, near Chennai, India.

Figure 2.2 Prof. C.S. Sundaresan introduced us to milk villagers in Orissa, India.

What role will consumers play in the status and nature of dairying as we move further into the twenty-first century? Given that what happens in dairy farming is influenced greatly by those who drink and eat what cows produce, these chapters give voice to consumers. Respondents, from low- to high-income groups, were recruited on social media sites such as the Rural Geography Research Group of the Royal Geographical Society (RGS-IBG: rgrg.co.uk/), on this author's Academia. edu and LinkedIn sites, at meetings and in social media for the Food Durham advisory board in the Durham Community Alliance in the UK, and in US email fora such as Odairy in the Northeast Organic Dairy Producers Alliance (NODPA). Respondents were also found via his linguist partner's networks, by means of snowball sampling in which early respondents referred the survey to acquaintances or colleagues.

(Author's note: Surveys were emailed to some participants in US/UK doctoral fieldwork and focus groups of academics, firefighters, motorcyclists and others (Scholten 2006c, 2007a, 2011, 2013a). It may be interesting that, while most participants manifested more trust in local food than organics, and that academics were the keenest organic consumers, it was motorcycle racers, despite the stereotypes surrounding bikers, who often adopted organic or local food from farmers' markets and had well-reasoned views on food. Firefighters who regularly cook in the station houses were also keen on gardening and local food.)

Snowballing drew 100 respondents from Baby Boomers to Gen Z, though none from Gen Alpha, born from 2010. (Baby Boomers were born between 1946 to 1964, Generation Jones from 1955 to 1965, Generation X from 1965 to 1980,

Xennials from 1977 to 1983, Millennials from 1981 to 1996 and Generation Z from 1997 to 2012.) Informants hailed from Austria, Bangladesh, Brazil, China, Germany, Libya, Italy, New Zealand, Norway, Poland, Saudi Arabia, Serbia, Spain, Thailand, the UK and the US.

This Chapter 2, along with 3 and 4, comprise respondents' replies to survey questions, alongside sidebars and text adding relevant information. A variety of opinions from consumers was attracted, including people whose identity is also that of farmer, activist and government environment officer. Indeed, respondents' professions varied greatly: some had expertise in aspects of the ethics, environment and politics related to livestock, while others were experts in technical and educational aspects of dairying. Most were middle class, but a few had passionate views on animals and food despite their low income. Ages ranged from teens to nonagenarians. Some might have been unable to distinguish a cow's front from its back, but as we will see from their responses, they felt livestock are implicated in planetary sustainability.

Responses to these statements can be quantified as percentages of these 100 stakeholders' responses to each choice, and these results have led discussion of each question. These percentages and the stakeholders' comments should not be equated to what we might discover by conducting a randomized survey of many more than 100 participants. Rather, these statistics and particularly the comments are snapshots that serve to give a face to the topics discussed in the previous introductory chapter. To provide a context for each statement, there is more discussion of background information that underpins that statement. These voices echo the conclusion in the preceding chapter, that the outlook for dairy farming in the twenty-first century is unclear and likely to remain unsettled for the foreseeable future.

Queries 1, 2 & 3

Q1. Farming is part of my family history.
Q2. How politicians, corporations and co-ops treat family dairy farmers.
Q3. My country's food system provides adequate animal welfare.

To what extent was farming part of the respondent's family history? This first statement sought to determine the respondent's positionality when they responded to other questions. But, before we delve into the responses, background on recent paradigm shifts is useful. We begin with the existential threat to life on this planet as we know it, namely climate change, and what we now know about dairy's contribution and then return to one of the themes running throughout this book, animal welfare.

Traditional pastoralists were stunned in 2006, when the UN Food and Agricultural Organization (FAO 2006) in Rome released *Livestock's Long Shadow (LLS)*. The cover of the 390-page report portrayed a long-horned bovine casting an elongated shadow at sunset. Whether it presaged the end of millennia of livestock farming was for readers to interpret. But lead researcher Henning Steinfeld and team of Pierre Gerber, Tom Wassenaar, Vincent Castel, Mauricio Rosales and Cees de Haan estimated that livestock account for 9 per cent of carbon dioxide (CO_2), 35–40 per cent of methane (CH_4), and, and 65 per cent of nitrous oxide (N_2O), in total global anthropogenic greenhouse gases (GHGs) (FAO et al. 2006). Dairists assuming they were innocent bystanders in the anthropogenic production of climate-destabilizing greenhouse gases were shocked. Many continued to blame atmospheric carbon loading primarily on the burning of wood and coal during the Industrial Revolution and the subsequent use of petroleum for power generation, factories, automotive transport, and more recently, military and civil aviation – not cows. But such creatures were prodigious emitters of methane.

Pastoralists preferred competing studies. Pitesky et al. (2009: 33) denied claims by Steinfeld et al. (2006; 2010) that livestock emissions outweighed transport. Capper and Cady (2020) further vexed pastoralists, claiming the reason livestock in Europe and the affluent US had relatively small GHG emissions compared to the developing world, was partly because they were eating special feed in confinement. Albrecht Glatzle (2014), an agricultural biologist from University of Hohenheim, Stuttgart, who had worked in Botswana, Morocco and Paraguay, defended the livestock industry, attacking baseline assumptions in FAO publications.

Nevertheless, there was a growing consensus in the scientific community that Steinfeld et al.'s early estimate of livestock greenhouse gas contributions of 18 per cent (including the smaller subset of dairy) was realistic. Cow burps were not the only villains attacking Mother Gaia's climate. The vertical integration of oligopolistic beef finishers in North America depended on global streams of soybeans and other cattle feed that ultimately released millions of metric tonnes of carbon from deforestation from the rapidly increasing monoculture plantations carved from Amazonian or Asian rainforests.

Pastoralists protested their virtue. After all, had not cattle grazing for meat, dairy and traction power, pulling carts and farm implements, been part of the human tapestry for millennia, since retreat of glaciers in the Pleistocene epoch, before spreading across non-icy areas of Earth in the Holocene? Was it not more likely that historically recent innovations, such as jumbo jets, boosted pollution? Another incisive defence by grazing dairy families was to blame what Professor Tim Lang of University College London called 'food miles' for deepening the energy and carbon hoofprints of global agriculture: a Chicago study showed food that travelled 1,245 miles in 1981 travelled 1,518 food miles in 1999, a 22 per cent increase in that time 'with the national food system using 4 to 7 times more fuel' than in localized systems (Lang and Heasman 2004: 235–9). The stereotype of a diesel freight truck belching smoke from twin stacks, or jet aeroplanes flying flowers and veg from Nairobi to Amsterdam, deepened suspicion that aviation was culpable for atmospheric emissions. To what extent? Fear of food miles boosted locavore food and dairy systems in California and Washington States. But reasoned analysis by observers such as Jude L. Capper (*Hoard's Dairyman* 2012) clarified the fact that bulk shipments in ocean freighters and freeway trucks could, for some foods, be greener than local systems. *Horses for courses.*

A nuanced locavore argument is made by Guy Watson (2021), founder of Riverford Organic which delivers 80,000 weekly boxes to British customers at the time of writing. Since 2018, Riverford is 74 per cent employee-owned. *Wicked Leeks*, Watson's online blog, claims local can be international, explaining Riverford's reluctant decision to buy a farm in West France (supplying spring crops of lettuce, cabbage, chard, turnips and broad beans), because it requires fewer polluting road miles to its Devon base than the alternative 250-mile route to the Lincolnshire Fens in the UK.

Slowly, more agriculturalists have admitted more blame for the Anthropocene. Pastoralists continue to laud grazing as the best animal-friendly way to build fertility and biodiversity in soil while sequestering carbon. In 2011, organicists from the Rodale Institute in Pennsylvania, USA, argued in detail that farms have thrived and could continue to thrive without synthetic chemical inputs that endanger waterways, in long seven-step organic crop rotations, while fields acted as major carbon sinks. At the beginning of the twenty-first century, few everyday consumers, or even farmers and foresters, realize how much deforestation has contributed to greenhouse gas build-up in the atmosphere. In the Age of the Anthropocene, the built urban and rural environment and overall material output of human activity, including concrete, steel and plastic, was estimated to exceed the overall natural biomass on Earth (*Nature* 2020 Elhacham et al.). Considering the home shopping delivery frenzy, requiring the building of more distribution centres during COVID-19 pandemic lockdowns, this was credible.

The Malthusian thesis was revived vis-à-vis human nutrition: Earth has insufficient space to hack pastures out of forests to graze enough cows to supply the 10 billion people who may inhabit it by the end of the twenty-first century, consuming milk and meat on the scale that Americans consumed them in the 1950 and 60s. Bill Gates and Richard Branson echoed this message, attracting investors to their plant-based food projects. But Gates (2021), who sagely predicted the current COVID-19 pandemic, was dead earnest in ameliorating the conflict between human development and environmental apocalypse. *The Economist* review of his 2021 book *How to Avoid a Climate Disaster* on 21 February 2021 quotes him saying that decarbonizing electricity is the 'single most important thing we must do'. How can dairy be part of climate solutions?

Animal welfare

Mariana von Keyserlingk and Dan Weary, at the University of British Columbia Dairy Education and Research Centre (UBC 2017), have experimented with weighted gates to show that cows often prefer grazing outside on grass fields under a starry night sky – rather than eating rations of fresh feed. Indoor housing provides fodder, water, hygiene and security, noted von Keyserlingk, but does not allow cows to express instinctive behaviours like exploring new pasture (*Scientific Reports* 2017).

Grandin on i) abuse & neglect; ii) boredom & restrictive environments

Livestock's link to environmental change is now vexing consumers in more demographics, who accept its links to new climatic patterns in droughts, fires, storms, melting poles and glaciers. Storybook images of Heidi tending cows in Swiss mountain meadows have given way to the realities of dairy cattle in distressed confinement, videoed by undercover welfarists from groups such as Compassion in World Farming (CiWF) and People for the Ethical Treatment of Animals (PETA), who argue cruelty is too often implicit in animal farming. Lifelong observation of dairying persuades me otherwise.

In a blog post, Temple Grandin (2011) divided animal welfare concerns into two categories: i) abuse and neglect; and ii) boredom and restrictive environments. These can inform analyses of the following scenes.

One peaceful scene involved a dozen black water buffalo tethered at their manger, under a thatched roof in Mujkur village in Gujarat, India, in 2019. The Indian cows seemed peaceful, not bored, and were entertained by frequent contact with passing villagers.

Another scene was the speciality Parmesan cheese farm and factory in Reggio Emilia, Italy, referred to in Chapter 1. It featured red cattle (Vacche Rosse) that were producing milk for butter, ricotta and other dairy products. These Italian cows were beautiful and clean, but seemed nervous. The fields that once surrounded the facility had been covered by suburbia. Without grass under hoof to exercise instinctive grazing impulses, the densely housed, bored cattle had few behavioural outlets besides social grooming, i.e., *allogrooming* – licking each other's necks and hard-to-reach areas.

The breeding and feeding technologies that extract maximum milk can weaken their immune and reproductive systems to such an extent that barely half of intensively managed cows are able to produce a second calf before slaughter (Biagiotti 2013; Scholten 2014). Britain's Prince Charles lamented the state of intensive dairying in which cows typically die after four years in US herds, and five in British equivalents. The leading milking-equipment maker DeLaval (2013; Scholten 2014: 122, 129, 194, 208) recognized this as a worldwide problem, convening a 2013 conference on longevity in Sweden. There, UBC researchers Jeff Rushen and Anne Marie de Passille presented a paper on 'The Importance of Improving Cow Longevity', pointing out that illness or reproductive problems leading to involuntary culling occurred due to poor housing and management practices, which amounted to poor cow welfare.

In contrast, low-technology marginal and family-scale dairying in India may be easier on animals, even in zero-grazing systems, where individualized care promotes bovine welfare and well-being via frequent attention. Joseph A. Purathur, long-time assistant to Dr Verghese Kurien, before becoming deputy general manager for Dudhsagar Dairy co-operative communication at in Mehsana, Gujarat, told me after investigation: 'One of our experts in the animal health department says the longevity of cows in co-operative dairying averages 17 years' (Scholten 2014: 209). That is four times US conventional rates.

Poor animal welfare increasingly pricks human consciences. This is the legacy of philosopher Peter Singer (1975/1990, 2002) and animal behaviour researcher Marian Stamp Dawkins (1998, 2007, 2012a and b). As discussed in the previous chapter, it is clear that (*Pace, Descartes!*) dairy cattle share some human-like aspects of consciousness – including emotion, empathy and will – that have been long denied in the Western canon. Animals – even fish – that were assumed to be unconscious automatons are joining apes in exhibiting self-recognition. Evidence for Piscean self-recognition in mirrors was found in experiments with a cleaner wrasse (*Labroides dimidiatus*) by evolutionary biologist Alex Jordan at the Max Planck Institute in Germany (*Quanta* 2018; *PLOS Biology* 2019).

Linking mental states such as hunger to animal behaviour in theory-of-mind experiments can yield valuable empirical data. Marian Stamp Dawkins (2012ab) urges researchers to pursue tangible, measurable facts, by asking if animals are healthy, and then determining if they have what they want. Stamp Dawkins may concur that the UBC weighted-gate experiments revealed dairy cows often *wanted* to graze pasture in fresh air even more than fresh fodder in a stuffy shed (Keyserlingk and Dan Weary 2017).

Challenging our culinary status quo, recent research and development, production and marketing of plant-based food and analogue meats has advanced the prospect that humanity could eventually sustain itself on what are argued to be more environmentally friendly vegetarian or vegan diets. As was pointed out in Chapter 1, plant-based diets designed to meet human needs – or tastes for meat and dairy products – could, potentially, make ethical questions of dairy animal welfare moot.

Criticism of animal welfare has increased in demographic shifts, concurrent with criticism of intensive livestock farming, and openness to vegetarian or vegan diets. Further complicating the politics of such questions was the UK's 2020 'Brexit' from the European Union which increased its need for a trade deal opening the door to US or Australia imports made with dairy hormone rBGH/rBST, meat boosted by steroid pellets, and GMO seeds for cattle fodder grown with herbicides such as glyphosate.

Responses to this first statement, 'Farming is part of my family history', confirm what we know from statistics about the decline in farming participation worldwide. This is important in shaping consumers' beliefs because falls in farm employment reduce the percentage of relatives with direct knowledge of current farm conditions and policy debates. Before we turn to what respondents had to say, let's look more closely at what lies beneath the shift mentioned in Chapter 1.

Q1 Farming is part of my family history.

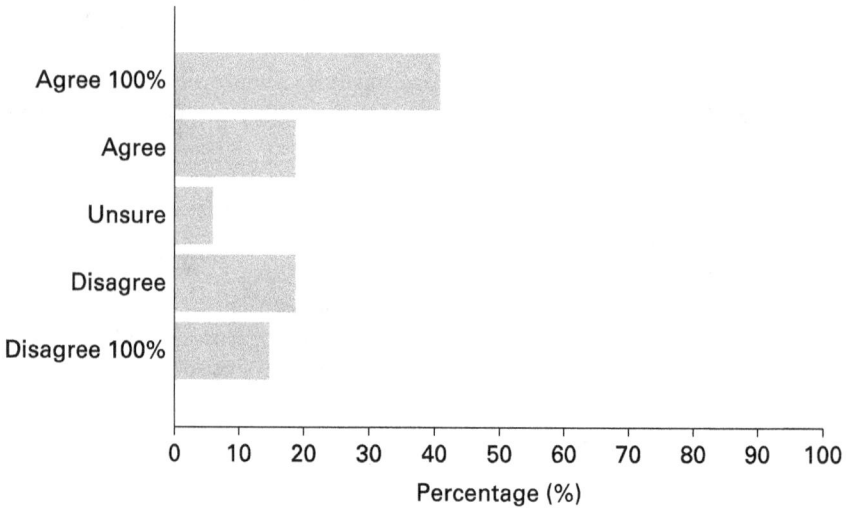

Employment in agriculture as a percentage of total employment has fallen for most countries in recent decades; according to the World Bank (2019). The US has become a major agricultural exporter, but its rationalized ag sector employs barely 2 per cent of the population, down from 3 per cent three decades ago, statistics that were presented in Chapter 1. The US Department of Agriculture Economic Research Service put this in perspective in its report on 'The 20th Century Transformation of U.S. Agriculture and Farm Policy', noting that 41 per cent of Americans were employed in agriculture in the year 1900; 21.5 per cent in 1930, when ag GDP was 7.7 per cent of total GDP; 16 per cent in 1945 after the Second World War, when ag GDP was 6.8 per cent of total GDP; 4 per cent in 1970, when ag GDP was 2.3 per cent of total GDP; and 1.9 per cent in 2000–02, when ag GDP was only 0.7 per cent of total GDP (USDA 2005).

At the University of Sheffield in the UK, D.B. Grigg wrote, 'Until the 19th century agriculture employed at least three-quarters of the world's workforce' (1975: 194, 194–202). Grigg's data showed rapid labour shedding in this sector during the twentieth century via new technology. Looking at trends between 1900–70, we see:

- All developed countries had agriculture as 59.4 per cent of the total labour force in 1900 and 23 per cent in 1970;
- Developed countries (excluding USSR & E. Europe) had ag as 48.1 per cent of total labour force in 1900 & 13 per cent in 1970;
- Developing countries had agriculture as 77.9 per cent of the total labour force in 1900 and 65.2 per cent in 1970.

Taken globally, agriculture accounted for 72.1 per cent of the total labour force in 1900 and 31 per cent in 1970.

Farm employment in the UK (which in 2021 imported about 30 per cent of its food), has fallen from 2 per cent to just 1 per cent in the three decades of my residence in North-East England. A century ago, in 1920, it was 54.7 per cent (Grigg 1975).

Stanley Lebergott (1966: 123) wrote about the UK and US – templates for industrializing nations – in his chapter on 'Labour Force and Employment, 1800–1960', in a book for the US National Bureau of Economic Research (NBER), noting: 'Both nations had reached a peak of agricultural employment in 1910 – the United States clearly, the United Kingdom somewhat less clearly – and both then began an uninterrupted descent from that peak by a 10% decline.'

Clearly, industrialization and urbanization have gutted farm employment in the Group of 7 (G7) most industrialized countries in the twentieth and twenty-first centuries, and these forces continue that process in developing economies. But changes have been so swift in historic terms that among our 100 respondents, 18 per cent agreed, and 41 per cent still 'agreed 100 per cent' that farming was part of their family's past. Only 18 per cent disagreed 100 per cent that farming was not part of their family background. Below, anonymized respondents speak in their own voices.

Food Wars shrink farm employment

When farmers, dependent on the environment in the primary sector of the economy, found themselves to be a shrinking portion of the population employed in a shrinking part of national output, many sought profitability by shedding workers and emulating the secondary sector of industry, manufacturing and processing. Farmers looked to scientific and technological champions, e.g., aviation, chemicals, digitization and pharmaceuticals – activities that dominate global economies.

In their book *Food Wars: The Global Battle for Hearts, Minds and Markets* (2004), UK academics Tim Lang and Michael Heasman paint this as a battle between the conflicting paradigms of ecologists versus life science actors. Ecologists favour traditional extensive methods including mixed arable and livestock farming, crop rotations building organic soil health in local food and fibre networks. On the other side in the Food Wars are life sciences advocates such as Jude L. Capper (2013: 233), who promote saving Planet Earth by 'Productivity metrics that enhance sustainability [including] milk and meat yield, growth rates, feed efficiency, calving rate, parasite control and use of growth-enhancing technologies'. Additional methods may entail switching from organic methods to synthetic fertilizer, pesticides and other inputs; soilless farming with hydroponics; vertical farming in urban skyscrapers; and intensified livestock production by abandoning pasture-grazing for globally sourced, high-energy soybeans, etc., in feedlot confinement. Milk yield would be maximized with chemically induced oestrus, artificial insemination, embryo transfer (Morris and Holloway

2014), GMO hormone rBGH/rBST for milk yield and robotic milking systems (RMS) delivering tasty concentrated grain pellets tailored to each cow's stage of lactation, plotted on her digitized dataset, when she decides it is her milking time.

Some worry that Earth's dearth of available land for extra farm production – along with rising population numbers – will force conversion to vegan diets, plant-based or analogue meat-like foods, or laboratory-grown cell-based meat alternatives. Putting aside the ethical, environmental, cultural, nutritional and climate concerns regarding foods not based on livestock farming, it is the *political* aspects of such a switch that most frighten some. There is fear of complete domination of farming and food chains by multinational corporations, resulting in the full industrialization of farm and food economies, robbing the livelihoods of people engaged in extensive livestock pasture farming.

Impossible Foods, which supplies Burger King with Impossible Burgers, slashed grocery prices of plant-based meat to compete with real beef (*New Yorker* 2019; *Plant Based News* 2021). It is developing a vegan-based 'milk'. While this is attractive to many Generation Xers, Xennials, Millennials, Gen Zers, and Gen Alphas, it clouds the horizons of under-capitalized livestock farmers. Can family farmers – or even their co-operatives – compete with a meat-analogue company whose stock opened with a market capitalization of $7.6 billion in 2020?

Farmers are not just fighting for their incomes; they are also trying to justify their best practices, as scientific consensus strengthens that dairy emissions contribute too much to Greenhouse Effect. We are far from meeting goals (to limit global warming to 1.5°C to 2°C by the end of the twenty-first century), set in the Paris Agreement (UN-FAO *2018*).

Q1. 'Farming is part of my family history.'

Voices of the stakeholders

What do the comments that respondents added to the simple statement in Q1 tell us? Those who agreed 100 per cent elaborated on the role of farming in their families. (**Names are pseudonyms unless noted.**)

Tom Charles, 44, is a carbon-management officer in a Northern England county which numbered 350 coal mines after the First World War. He wrote that farming was a few generations back in his family, but he had no connections now.

Sue Tracker, 62, is a college teacher living near Hartford, Connecticut. She says: 'My grandmother was born on a dairy farm that remained in the family and actively producing until the 1970s. I visited the farm but never worked on it.'

Kate Ryan, in her 60s, is the agricultural programme co-ordinator, WSU Snohomish County Extension, in Washington State. Her family were, 'Farmers as far back as I know about'.

Kal Charge, 70, owns a motorsports business near Seattle. There was farming in his family, but 'in generations past – not currently'. It did not escape his notice that farmers who once depended on horses or tractors increasingly bought small, moderately priced four-wheelers from motorcycle shops.

Vern Godin, an aerospace technical consultant in his 60s, has always been keen on nutrition and water quality. 'My dad's family were farmers in New England, and then moved out to the Pacific Northwest where my dad worked in dairy processing plants.'

Elaine Oordt is a 60-year-old gardener and horticulture lecturer who defies the 'sausage and chips' (French fries) culture of North-East England by buying ingredients for vegan meals from local hill farmers. 'I've always lived in farming areas of Durham and buy farm produce.'

Juan Siena is a Spanish teacher in his 40s; one of his previous jobs was owning a café in County Durham, UK. 'My parents and grandparents were coffee bean farmers in Colombia.'

Nan Toner, in her 70s, is a retired teacher in Chester-le-Street, England. 'One of my great-uncles was a farmer. I spent a lot of time visiting farms with a relation who was a vet in Normandy, France.'

Stevie Hart, 60s, an IT system engineer and author, motorcyclist and wrestler from near Seattle noted: 'Some of my family have been small-scale farmers. As far as I can tell, they all were, before they came here in the 1800s, and for some time after.'

Berta Racarden, 50s, is a civil servant at the United Nations in New York. Her family is in Spain: 'Both sides of my family were small dairy farmers.'

Celia Cremen, 30s, was born in the US, and now is a teaching assistant and graphic designer at a university in Northern England. 'All on my Mom's side in Greeley and Kersey, Colorado. We went to the farm every year for the family reunion. We pet the pigs, ate the fried chicken, rode the 4x4s, the "whole hog", if you'll excuse the pun.'

Ken Mentzer, 40s, is an ex-military author and motorcyclist. 'My great-grandfather and great-great-uncle farmed vegetables in the Yukon, then (with their sons) wheat in Oregon.'

Karen Suttler, 60s, retired office worker, skier, hiker and environmentalist from Salt Lake City, and participated in the anti-Kaiparowits Coal Power plant in Southern

Utah in the 1970s. Of her family, she recalled: 'Mainly sugar beet farming in Utah and Idaho dating back to the 1800s.'

Some of the above respondents indicated farming was part of their family history in the settling of North America, and others commented on the effects of the Second World War on Britain, France and Europe. They reappear below, along with others who have not yet been quoted.

Q2 Politicians, corporations, and cooperatives treat our country's family dairy farmers fairly.

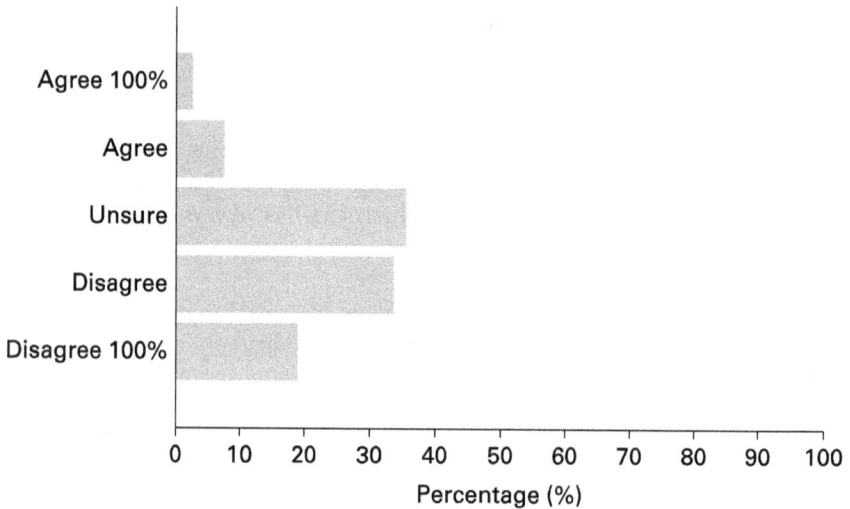

*Q2. 'Politicians, corporations, and co-operatives treat our
country's dairy farmers fairly.'*

Query 2 begs debate. In fact, responses show a pattern different from the – factual – first statement which revealed that less than half of the respondents did not have farming in their family history. Moreover, the total of US dairy farms fell during their lifetimes, from about 350,000 in 1980 to 70,000 in 2005, and 30,000 in 2020.

The *Journal of Dairy Science* (2006) reported an epochal plunge of 74 per cent in just a quarter of a century. Yet in the same period, the number of US cows fell by only 17 per cent, while average milk production per cow increased 60 per cent from 5,394 to 8,599 kg per lactation. Such productivity increases sound positive to an economist, but as was discussed in Chapter 1, the trend accompanies a troubling rise in involuntary culling and in turn worsening longevity, a welfare situation that has turned Millennials, Gen Z, and Gen Alpha consumers away from dairy.

But responders indicated uncertainty. Let us therefore revisit and extend the discussion of animal welfare along with politics, begun in Chapter 1, before we examine comments individuals added after responding to the second statement.

When creatures we now know are capable of emotion such as dairy cows endure more aches and pains than their great-grandmother bovines, it demands ethical consideration. It also raises the question of whether the sacrifice of the livelihoods of men and women nurturing small dairy farms is worth consolidating into 10,000-cow megadairies. As the number of farms declines at a rate of 4 per cent per year, in July 2020 the USDA expected just 31,500 licensed dairy herds to still be in operation at the end of 2021. With the population of cows relatively stable, but numbers of dairy farmers declining precipitously, the political clout of farmer voters dwindles to almost nothing.

Historically, of course, many family enterprises – from buggy-whip makers to corner food shops – closed after the advent of automobiles and supermarkets. The difference is that livestock agriculture affects the well-being of living creatures capable of pain, pleasure and emotion. Livestock agriculture also plays a central role in local ecologies and global climate. Thus, when the animal welfare, environmental or ethical aspects of intensive megadairies seem untenable, it is ammunition for small farmers demanding that politicians enforce more sustainable regulations. Other stakeholders also have a voice.

Over 50 per cent of respondents completely or partly disagreed that politicians, corporations and co-operatives treat family dairy farmers fairly. There is intended ambiguity in the query, which helps account for 36 per cent being unsure about it. After all, politicians, corporations and co-operatives are different types of entities which change over time. The question drew acute comments, a selection of which is presented below.

As Chapter 1 showed in reference to events in the USA since the Second World War, politics has more often than not been a negative influence on the economic sustainability of small pasture-grazing dairy farms. Organic farmers were hoping things would improve but during President Trump's administration they were nonplussed in January 2017, when one of the new president's first acts was to quash a comprehensive list of organic standards that had been negotiated by farmers, processors and other entities for a decade. Trump and the then USDA Secretary Mike Pompeo said organic and conventional cattle should follow the *same* welfare standards. However, that did not mean conventional should follow organic. It was especially discouraging to people in the organic movement who, from passage of the Organic Foods Production Act (OFPA 1990), as well as USDA development of national standards for organic products, and establishment of the National Organic Program after the year 2000, wished to carve a regulated market for milk from pasture-grazed cows that were treated like treasured animals, not machines.

The European Union (née EEC, now EU) had smaller, more extensive dairy structures than the US conventional dairy sector, which from the mid-1960s became a wild west of intensification in ever larger concentrated or confined animal-feeding operations. Europe had a milk quota system from 1984 to 2015 in order to cap farm intensification and slow urbanization. In 2022, Canada still had a milk-quota system which in many respects fosters well-being of farmers and animals. Emerging economies such as India, Mexico, Thailand and countries in the East Africa Dairy Development project (Scholten 2013b) are climbing the dairy technology ladder, but their intensification and the prevalence of CAFO feedlots does not rival the Unites States', though China may be catching up.

Keeping alive the dream of pasture-grazing is why progressive farmers and ethical consumers rallied around organic dairy certification labels. Only the most cynical envisioned that the total of US conventional dairy farms would fall to barely 30,000 in 2021 – and that agribusiness would bring the same megadairy apocalypse in the USDA National Organic Program, because the NOP failed to enforce the 2010 final Pasture Rule, or remove loopholes on replacement of cows burned out on 'organic' megadairy CAFOs (Cornucopia Institute 2015). Many believe that proper funding of the NOP would have beefed up monitoring and enforcement enough to halt that process in its tracks. Below, respondents give their views.

Voices of the stakeholders

Above, we mentioned Tom Charles, a carbon-management officer in a Northern England county characterized by hill farms. Despite having no connections to farming in his family, he disagreed vehemently with the suggestion that farmers were treated fairly by politicians, corporations and co-operatives. This and other responses below and in the following two chapters indicate that while consumers may have no current first-hand knowledge of farming, they have strong, well-reasoned views that reflect a general awareness of what has been discussed in this book. There was a range of strongly expressed views revealing considerable discomfort if not outright trust of the current situation.

New Zealand is similar in many ways to other post-industrialized countries, yet its landscape is extolled for grazing cows on verdant pasture, as well as the pristine ecology that that served as a backdrop for Hobbits in the *Lord of the Rings* film franchise. An academic with a family farming background, responded to the statement, 'Politicians, corporations, and co-operatives treat our country's family dairy farmers fairly' from his positionality as professor of environment:

> It has varied over time by the categories listed. Most of the time they have been regarded as crucial to the country's development and operating without a fault. This reflects the grip of farmer politics which is slowly being rejected.

That rejection is connected to the conversion of traditional sheep ranches into large-scale dairy operations with a total of 6.11 million cows in 2021 from 5.92 million in 2010 (*Statista* 2021ab). It may be that the newer and larger NZ farms built to feed China's appetite for cheese and other milk products make it harder to disperse point pollution. Sadly, *The Economist* (2017c) reported cow manure carrying campylobacter, E. coli and whatnot, has sullied river water quality (66 per cent of rivers are allegedly unsafe to swim in), and their bovine methane (CH_4) burps have increased greenhouse gases (GHGs) by 23 per cent since 1990.

Unsurprisingly, experts argue that cow numbers must fall to cut GHGs by 30 per cent below 2005 levels by the target year of 2050.

The responses from respondents in both the UK and the US, whether they are from those directly involved in farming or from consumers, emphasize the problems the dairy sector is confronting in their countries. ***Pseudonyms are used, unless noted.***

Nan Toner, 72 and a retired teacher, from Chester-le-Street, UK, lamented: 'Farmers do not get the recognition they deserve.'

Richard Beakins, a retired social scientist in his 70s from North-East England, blamed corporations: 'The corporate strangulation of the milk price is killing dairy farming in some regions; the government's bovine TB policy needs upgrading. It is failing at the moment.'

Nanci Barnes, 50, an academic specialist on rural broadband from Scotland, was unsure of farmers' treatment: 'I don't think in the current market of large corporations and cheap consumerism that farmers get a fair price for the product, and in return we the public aren't willing to pay more. Take profit off of this and that doesn't add up to much of a living.'

Harold Daniels, in his 40s and an IT and social services consultant in Newcastle, UK, grew up near a dairy farm but was unsure about the statement, saying: 'My impression is dairy farming has changed unrecognizably in methods and market forces. Necessary standards and sometimes unfair commercial pressures seem to have created a sanitized, mechanized industry. Is the question of fairness to do with recompense, or the wider cultural changes with which they are inextricably bound? My assumption is small dairy farmers may be more greatly affected culturally, but may have more of a local market to achieve better returns.'

Hans Wolfisberg, 50s, of Swiss origin, is directly involved in farming as the owner of an Organic Valley dairy farm in the US Pacific Northwest, where he practises rotational pasture- grazing. He was aware of the harsh economic situation of small farmers described in an article we shared from the *Journal of Dairy Science* (2006), saying: 'Too many family farms are exiting the industry.'

Elizabeth Henderson (real name), activist author in her 60s wrote: 'My family has not had any farmers for way more than two generations! Though I do not know how many [. . .] I am not a vegetarian. I will eat fish and meat that has been raised by organic farmers I know and trust.' She is Co-Chair of the Policy Committee for the Agricultural Justice Project Board of the Northeast Organic Farming Association of New York. She was not the only respondent blaming government-fostered price structures that have slashed the real price of milk in 1975 terms, while bankrupting small farmers. She agreed: 'Through corporate power and consolidation, the price structure is deliberately created to underpay dairy farmers.'

Tina Dice, age 31, is another dairy farmer, in this case a third-generation family farmer living near Poughkeepsie, New York. Her first-hand knowledge of farming led her to disagree 100 per cent with the industry's overall treatment by politicians, corporations and co-operatives. But she does not fault co-ops as much as other entities.

Although not a farmer, Liz Cordell, in her 50s, is active in New York State organic dairy networks. She agreed with the statement, adding an anecdote: 'When I was contemplating farming as a career choice, my father asked if I realized how hard my grandparents worked to get OFF the farm. Now governments have set up a commodity system which is a race to the bottom.'

Karl Harvest, in his 60s, lives in Wisconsin and is a US-certified organic dairy pioneer. He disagreed that politicians, corporations and co-operatives treated family farmers fairly and blamed all players, saying: 'Co-operatives have gotten so large they don't need the business of small farmers, corporations pit farmers against each other all over the world in globalization, prices fall to below costs of production and corporations have plenty of cheap commodities. Politicians support an unfair system because, in most cases, industry funds their campaigns.'

Len Monroe, a retired journalist in his 70s, still farms part time. He also lives in Wisconsin, a state whose car licence plates proclaim it 'America's Dairyland'. However, the state is losing hundreds of small farms as western megadairies dominate production. (Recall from Chapter 1, how Aurora Organic Dairy in Texas shipped milk – from cows likely not grazing in verdant meadows – to Wisconsin, ignoring that state's comparative advantage in the ability to pasture cows.) This is ironic because Wisconsin's arable top soil was revitalized with dairy-cow waste in the nineteenth century. After decades that saw California-style confinement operations erode price structures of Wisconsin's small farms, Monroe is seen as a man of integrity who cares about cows and farm families. He also disagreed 100 per cent that politics, corporations and co-ops were fair to farmers. Twenty years ago, he told me: 'When co-operatives get too big, they treat small farmers the same as do corporations.'

In his 60s, Randy Grein (real name), an IT system engineer and author, former motorcycle racer and wrestling coach based near Seattle, commented: 'Like anything else, we give corporate farms preferential treatment. Family farms, not so much. They get screwed at both ends of the economic equation.'

Berta Racarden, who is in her 50s, was born in Spain, before earning a doctorate in the UK and subsequently taking a job with the United Nations in New York. She disagreed that farmers were well treated, recalling conditions in her native region: 'The EU has pretty much wiped out small dairy farmers in Southern Europe, where non-mass farming was the norm rather than the exception. You can't compete at the prices they set to sell the milk unless you supersize and become another massive dairy corporation.'

Harold Zinn, 60s, another organic dairyman in New York state, did not agree that politicians, corporations and co-ops treated family dairy farmers fairly. His sentiment was shared by other respondents recruited in online dairy forums, including Len Brady (in his 50s) and Nancy Thomas (in her 30s), both of whom found profitable dairy farming a challenging proposition. Several organic farmers across the United States, including members of the Northeast Organic Dairy Producers Alliance, spoke out on the *Odairy* email list, deploring poor monitoring and enforcement of standards by the USDA National Organic Program. This, they argued, has led to encroachment by corporate megadairies in what small family grazing farmers hoped would be their domain. This is the deplorable situation investigated by journalist Peter Whoriskey (*Washington Post* 2017b).

Happy Larson, in her 60s, a care-giver/adoption counsellor on the Olympic Peninsula of Washington State, said: 'No farmers in my maternal (all railroaders in rural Nebraska), or paternal (all copper miners in Butte, Montana) lines, but as an adult, I have attempted to create a hobby farm, with vegetables, berries, fruits, chickens, sheep and llamas – the animals for fibre.' This farm includes a super hen, 'Gertie'. Happy was unsure whether other farmers were treated well by politicians, corporations or co-operatives, 'Nationally, I believe family dairy farmers are experiencing challenging times due to a lack of thoughtful financial policies. Many are looking for alternative ways to enhance their earnings, i.e., energy production, Locally, however, Clallum County has approved a new tax to preserve farmland which includes [some] historic dairy farms.'

Kate Ryan (real name), 60s, a part-time farmer and Washington State University Extension co-ordinator in Snohomish County, recalled: 'My family were farmers as far back as I know about . . . until my father declared, "If I never milk another cow again in my life, that will be fine."' Do politicians, corporations, and co-operatives treat our country's family dairy farmers fairly? No. But she put some of the onus on farmers, describing the political silence of America's scant, remaining family dairy farmers. 'Unfortunately, part of the problem is overall farmer reticence to whine, complain or become activists. That, and the overall declining numbers of farmers, renders their collective voice barely a whisper. So, it's easy to ramrod just about any crap legislation through, when the folks who know how bad it is have to stay home and milk the cows – not head to the halls of government to rattle cages in a loud and noticeable way.'

Melanie Porta, in her 70s, a retired science teacher reared on a Washington State dairy farm that, like most in America, ended up being sold, unsurprisingly agreed 100 per cent that unfairness characterizes farmers' treatment by politicians, corporations and co-operatives.

Rita Carter, in her 60s, a retired accountant in Oklahoma, disagreed 100 per cent with the idea that politicians, corporations and co-operatives treat US family dairy farmers fairly. She blamed 'Subsidies to pour out milk rather than sell; government price controls; creating industrial dairy farms that result in buying out or destroying family dairy farms'.

By the same token, many advocates for the USDA National Organic Program tried to design the NOP to strengthen the resilience of smaller farms. Would things improve under President Joe Biden? Biden named Tom Vilsack, who was Secretary of Agriculture in Barack Obama's era, to take up that mantle once more. Sadly, organicists fear Vilsack is a monoculture champion who ignores the benefits of organic methods to soil, biodiversity and human and animal health.

Tim Finley, 65 (real name), aerospace engineer, motorcyclist and former racer based near Seattle, had family farm lore substantiating how politicians, corporations, and co-operatives treat dairy farmers. Like several others above, he lauded co-operatives, making a central point not to be forgotten: 'The co-ops do well, but the rest don't.'

Is this pessimism justified? As noted above, in July 2020, the USDA expected farms to continue exiting at the rate of 4 per cent per year, with only 31,500 licensed dairy herds left at the end of 2021. The number fell below 30,000 early in 2022. (More in this vein will appear in the next chapter, with respect to how this has affected animal welfare, in the responses to Query 4: Cattle should be allowed natural behaviours: For example, cows should graze fields at least 120 days a year (see also *New York Times* 2007; Scholten 2014: 112–15.) But not all responses indicated pessimism, as the feedback below indicates.

Kristin B. Cremmer, in her late 80s, a retired farmer living between Seattle and Mount Rainier, said politicians, corporations and co-operatives treat small dairy farmers fairly. Likewise, she agreed US animal welfare levels were adequate, while adding that cattle should graze pasture at least 120 days annually. They did in her youth, but few do today.

Now we turn to responses from other countries.

Brijit Deana Caldera, a 41-year-old lawyer in Brazil, disagreed 100 per cent that those farmers get fair treatment from government, business or co-operatives: 'In Brazil, the only option for small producers is to sell milk through co-operatives. They pay [only] pennies for the litre.'

Not all respondents in other countries agreed so vehemently that dairy farmers suffer poor treatment by politicians, corporations and co-operatives. A positive view is often connected to systems with farmer-centric agricultural ministries and large voluntary co-operatives.

Badur Banglar, a 55-year-old staffer in the Milk Vita co-operative in Bangladesh, believes co-ops treat the country's dairy farmers fairly. Interestingly, he includes politicians and corporations in those who demonstrate fairness. There are sound reasons for his positive view of public-private-market performance, because the dairy sector still plays a vital role in the country's nutrition and economy.

Taking a macro view, I co-authored a chapter with FAO veteran Brian T. Dugdill titled 'Avoiding Dairy Aid Traps: The cases of Uganda, India and Bangladesh' for a book edited by Alpaslan Ozerdem and Rebecca Roberts, *Challenging Post-Conflict Environments* (2012). Dugdill was reared on a Yorkshire farm before graduating from Reading University and working for Asda, one of the large supermarket chains in Britain. After the 1971 Bangladesh war of independence from Pakistan, he was recruited by the FAO to help reorganize Bangladeshi dairy chains. Scholten and Dugdill (2012) used FAO documents – and Brian's Bangladeshi experience – to relate how untimely dairy commodity aid disrupted market stabilization. Dugdill described the 1980s FAO efforts he led in Uganda, and I (Scholten 2010c) detailed how Uganda and India brought their dairy sectors into functional equilibrium.

Eashav Taalin, a 40-year-old college administrator and dairy researcher in India, agreed that 'Politicians, corporations, and co-operatives treat our country's family dairy farmers fairly.' His opinion is valid because – similar to Bangladesh – India values co-operatives such as Amul and Dudhsagar, which return around 75 per cent of the retail price to farmers, boosting family health and education indicators.

Jong Wei, in his 20s, an undergraduate student from Beijing studying in Spain, reported no family history of farming, but expressed the view that Chinese farmers received fair treatment from politicians, corporations and co-operatives. From a non-farm background, he might have nonetheless been aware that after the 1949 communist revolution, farmers were subsidized by the central government, until reforms in the Deng Xiaoping era when commune land was released to individual farmers. In the last decade, China has accelerated dairy imports from countries in Oceania and elsewhere, including the US, while adopting domestic intensive dairying. Some of these large animal concentrations have helped low-income farmers by sharing capital costs of barns and equipment in quasi-co-operative structures. This is an intelligent political solution to changing economic situations, which reportedly has also been applied in Mongolia. However, research is awaited on environmental, ethical and animal welfare aspects of such operations.

Bertran Kiung, another Chinese respondent, a PhD student in his 30s living in Newcastle, UK, was unsure about the statement, saying: 'We didn't have any fields and we never did farming from my grandparents' generation [...] Now, I don't know if farmers are treated fairly. We come from different countries, so the answer could be different. Even the same country, I think it also depends on the regions, corporations and co-operatives.' His comments show an understanding that anthropomorphic effects on animals and environment vary from one location to another.

Below, the comments of respondents in some Asian and European countries pattern similarly to those in the US and Britain. As most respondents had completed secondary education, and others were studying for or already completed tertiary degrees, this may be due to cognitive globalization, i.e., rising worldwide awareness of issues relating to ethics, the environment and politics.

Nisit Omsin, a 45-year-old teacher in central Thailand, did not agree that farmers get a fair shake. He is animal friendly, but questions why consumers should pay more when the moral responsibility for animal welfare lies on government powers that set standards in society.

In Europe, Natan Worisky, a teacher in his 40s who moved from Poland to Spain and converted to Islam, disagreed that farmers received fair treatment. He was critical of the European Union's Common Agricultural Policy (CAP) for demolishing too many small mixed farms in favour of monoculture.

Karl Rikard, a 21-year-old student in Spain, but originally from Serbia, also disagreed with the idea that farmers were treated fairly. In comments, his Generation Z attitudes included concern for animal welfare and an openness to vegan food, while doubting plant-based or laboratory grown meat would soon replace traditional fare.

Bernice, 19 years old and another student in Spain, said that farmers are not treated fairly. 'If you do a little research, you realize the little money farmers receive for the enormous effort they make.' She thought cattle should enjoy grazing outside and added that she favoured veganism and plant-based or analogue meats, foreshadowing the discussion to come in the following chapters.

We wrap up Chapter 2 with responses to the third statement with which respondents were asked to agree or disagree.

Q3 My country's food system provides adequate animal welfare.

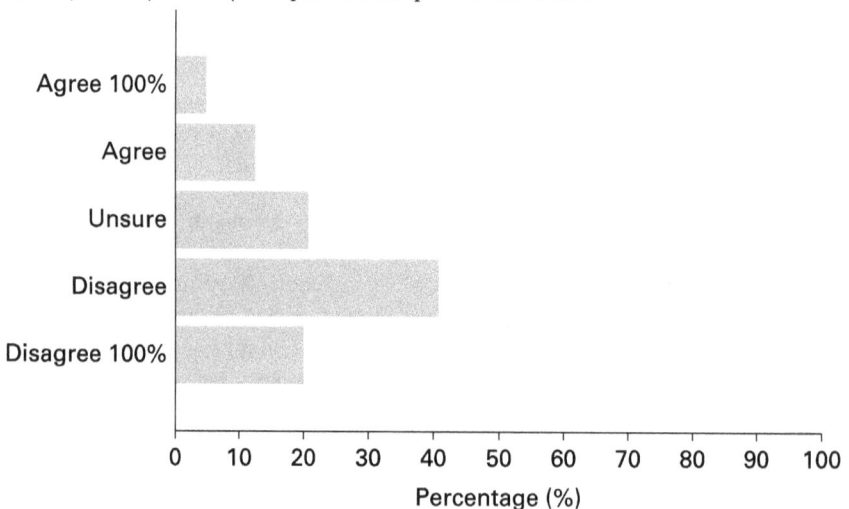

Q3. 'My country's food system provides adequate animal welfare.'

Unlike responses to the second statement, these skew to disagreement with the statement. Only 5 per cent of respondents agreed 100 per cent that their country's food system provides adequate animal welfare, while 61 per cent responded that it did not.

Unease is driven partly by media reports, from animal welfare activists' alarms on the deleterious effects of intensive confinement practices on livestock well-being and longevity, as well as effects upon the environment in point pollution, and global impact on atmosphere with carbon, methane and nitrous loading. As has already been noted several times, induced oestrus, artificial insemination and GMO dairy hormone rBGH/rBST together have helped boost average milk yield where farming is intensive, for example in the US, by 60 per cent in 25 years. *The Journal of Dairy Science* noted that over 1981–2006, the US cow population decreased by only 17 per cent, as the tally of dairy farms fell by 74 per cent (*JDS* 2006). This pattern permeated the global conventional dairy sector.

Was this upheaval justified on environmental and ethical grounds? Perhaps politics were moot because few voters knew farmers. But consumers increasingly learn that densely occupied megadairies push cows to early culling and barely four years' longevity (Biagiotti 2013; Scholten 2014). Many Americans heard Colorado State professor Temple Grandin on National Public Radio, or read in the *Washington Post* about her condemnation of dairy farms that prioritize short-term productivity over animal well-being and longevity (*Washington Post* 2016; *Hoard's Dairyman* May 25, 2016). Grandin had advised McDonald's and other corporations on animal welfare, but finally deplored 'bad dairies' adding: 'They make up most of the farms in the United States, and their cows are so wrecked by the time they stop milking they can barely be used for beef.'

A spokesperson for the National Milk Producers Federation said: 'No farmers want animals that are unhealthy, because that's bad for cows and even worse for their owners.' But many consumers find Professor Grandin's judgement on an industry that recently grew a huge Holsten named Gigi who produced 75,000 lbs of milk in one year – three times the contemporary yield, in a sector which already burns out cows faster than many intensive dairies can replace them.

Let's again start with responses from the countries identified as demonstrating questionable practices with respect to animal welfare.

Voices of the stakeholders

Ken E. Tillman, retired and in his 60s, has more time for gardening now that he is retired from aviation, industry and university work in the US. His memories of 1950–90s US family dairying evoked this distressing memory: 'Before we had the loafing shed with free stalls, our cows would bed down on wood shavings in the 1950 stanchion barn overnight, especially during blizzards. Come into the barn in the morning and it's warm and muggy, hoarfrost on the windows, and the air smells like Holstein breath. Cozy, but not easy for a cow to get up with their front hooves stationary because of the stanchion. As a result, we'd sometimes get the sorry sight of a "stepped-on teat". Parts of it could be missing; lots of blood and also milk, when it is time for milking. That is a big reason we built the loafing shed. We had lots fewer stepped-on teats with the new loafing shed.' Such injuries required stitching by a veterinarian, as well as daily treatment, entailing losses in time, milk and money. Concern for cow welfare helped drive dairy architecture from stanchion barns, to free stalls or cubicles, even before widespread adoption of labour-saving milking parlours, and to loose housing on sawdust, straw or sand according to Roger Martinot (*Britannica* 1998; Dairy Group 2010). Knowledge of bovine anatomy is essential to safe free stall design. In 2013, at the National Organic Standards Board (NOSB) meeting in Portland, Oregon, a well-meaning but flawed rule was proposed to increase minimum width of free stalls. The idea was to enhance cow freedom of movement, but the rule change was abandoned when discussion clarified that instead of more lateral space, more headspace in longer stalls was *critical* for cow mobility.

Hans Wolfisberg, 50s (real name), a dairyman of Swiss origin with a herd of cows whose milk ships to Organic Valley co-operative, said he was happy with his own farm's situation. But he was critical of the level of animal welfare on US intensive megadairies, saying: 'We can always do more.'

Views expressed by Daniel Schappen, attorney-at-law in Lenzburg, Switzerland, echo those above. He agreed 100 per cent that his country does, indeed, treat family dairy farmers and cattle fairly. This includes the humane laws which mandate that cattle must be stunned before slaughter (*Futurism* 2018). Images of Brown Swiss cows grazing Alpine meadows merit government subsidies for such tourist attractions. *Heidi pastoral?* Like the cover of this book.

In bucolic New Zealand, academic Steve Marton, 60s, had no illusions about animal welfare, 'Not a priority. Animals may be romanticized but at the farm-face are often treated as without feeling.'

Near Seattle, USA, retired 86-year-old Kristin B. Cremmer said she believed cows had generally good welfare. In her nine decades, the area in which she farmed had enjoyed decades of dairy grazing. She does not note this, but it should be pointed out that population pressures have now overrun many pastures with residential housing.

Rick Carlinni, 50, author and veterinarian on conventional and organic farms on all scales, in eastern and western US states, disagreed vociferously with the idea that cow welfare was optimal: 'The government is biased towards "factory farms" and agribusiness.'

Happy Larson, a hobby farmer liveibg in the Pacific Northwest, deplores intensive farming methods: 'I don't think there is a reliable, overarching system which promotes, monitors, or regulates animal welfare. Slaughter houses and over-crowded feed lots and poultry "factories" are disgusting, shameful, and saddening. On the other hand, the movement to provide animal "producers" as well as "martyrs" with more humane living conditions seems robust.'

Kate Ryan, 60s, the WSU university agricultural-programme co-ordinator, unequivocally disagreed that the US provided adequate animal welfare: 'Animal welfare still comes down to individuals. All the legislation in the world cannot overcome an attitude that cows, poultry, hogs are nothing more than a commodity. I had an incredible conversation with a large-scale dairy farmer years ago. When I asked about their use of [GMO dairy hormone] rBST, he proudly proclaimed it was because he loved his cows so much that he gave them rBST. Same farmer is still grumbling their co-op insisted they stop. Too many people with too many uninformed opinions ... or worse opinions informed by falsehoods.'

For Elizabeth Henderson, activist author and organic farmer: 'CAFOs predominate, animal prisons.'

Mandy Alt, 60s, homemaker in Houston, Texas, has no background in farming, and her family is in the oil business. Nevertheless, surrounded by the Lone Star State's beef culture, she commented: 'It's horrendous the way cattle in the USA are treated.'

Josie Suttler, also in her 60s and a retired office worker, skier, hiker and environmentalist in Salt Lake City, disagreed that farm animal welfare was sufficient because: 'Factory farms are becoming the norm, and animals are suffering more and more to keep up with demands for quicker production.'

Rita Carter, a 60-something Midwest retired office worker, disagreed 100 per cent that all cows were treated well, saying: 'Just take a look at any factory meat farm, with its goal of maximum output with minimum cost. The results are overcrowding, antibiotics overuse, genetic engineering to grow ever larger and faster than normal, and inhumane treatment.'

Another US respondent in his 60s, Tanner Cross, is a medical worker with roots in Seattle, Washington, and Irvine, California. In Irvine, his enthusiasm for Alta-Dena raw non-pasteurized milk, yogurt and cottage cheese was curtailed when it was acquired by Dean Foods in 1999. He still works with patients in the Philippines, and his daughter in Europe works with NGOs in Francophone Africa. He commented: 'I have seen videos of the treatment of farm animals, cows and chickens. It is a huge turn-off to me.'

Mega dairies do not yet predominate in the UK, making it unsurprising that views expressed there were more nuanced.

Elaine Oordt, a 60s-something gardener and horticulture lecturer in North-East England, was optimistic about, '[Especially] traditional and organic farmers – but not the industrialized factory so-called farms'.

Tom Charles, the 44-year-old carbon management officer in a Northern English county, has no family farming background but observed that: 'Animal welfare is quite good, but could be better.'

Harold Daniels mused: 'It depends. Do you view animal captivity for "renewable products", such as milk, an appropriate [fair] way of treating animals? Can some species only have lives with this purpose in mind (i.e., where do wild cows and wild pigs go to live?). And if you agree with farm animal products (including fish?) as appropriate, then beyond the legal framework, what aspects of welfare should be prioritized? This should be embedded in the culture of farming.'

Neil Barnes, 50s, does not agree that animal welfare was adequate because, 'Intensive farming is used extensively and I believe much intensive practice provides inadequately for animal welfare'.

Richard Beakon, 73-year-old retired geographer in North-East England, observed: 'Dairy cows suffer more stress than is reasonable.'

Karl Zillener, 40s, disagreed that the UK food system had adequate animal welfare but tempered this with optimism when he added: 'I am heartened by partnerships I have seen between farmers, food industry corporations and researchers in animal welfare at Newcastle University. However, I think there is a lot more that can be done.' This is noteworthy. For decades, many Britons fancied they had better welfare standards than the US and some continental countries. It is apparent that public–private initiatives are now attempting to rectify perceived lapses.

Celia Crème, who grew up in the US and is now in her 30s, detests hypocrisy. In the UK she works as a teaching assistant and graphic designer. She disagreed 100 per cent that animal welfare was adequate: 'Every country wants its citizens to believe it's "taking care of it", that while other countries might treat animals badly, "we are the good guys . . . So, citizens don't have to feel guilty about the consumption of meat and dairy. Unless we go back to farming locally on small-scale, with animals and the eco-system prioritized above profit, levels of animal welfare will not be adequate.' In fact, she has become a vegan.

Karl Rikard, the student in his 20s from Serbia but studying in Spain, was unsure about dairy animal welfare. Though pro meat-eating, he was receptive to meat analogues.

Bernice, another student in Spain, disagreed 100 per cent that the country's food system provides adequate animal welfare: 'It is a better system than other countries, but the animals are still very overexploited and mistreated.'

Regarding Brazil, lawyer Brijit Deana Caldera wrote: 'The situation of dairy cattle is not as bad as beef cattle. But the worst situation is chickens.'

Voices from China are less critical. Bertran Kiung, a PhD student from China studying in Newcastle, UK, disagreed with the idea that animals are treated well saying: 'I think my country [China] doesn't. Actually, the rules and regulations from the government may require farmers or slaughterhouses to give animal welfare ... but some farmers or companies may not follow strictly.'

Chapter 3

ETHICS AND ANIMALS

In this chapter, we continue to listen to the voices of stakeholders, the same sample of 100 individuals from the previous chapter. This chapter presents responses to the three next specific statements shown in the box below. These lead on from the third statement in the previous chapter, 'my country's food system provides adequate animal welfare' and were designed to elicit more in-depth and multi-faceted comments. Before turning to responses, let us consider certain developments in dairy farming in the 2000s.

Figure 3.1 The venerable Kepier Hospital Farm once tended pilgrims to Durham Cathedral, North-East England. It still grazes hundreds of cows, calves, bulls and sheep.

Figure 3.2 Italy's Benedictine monks produced superb Parmigiano Reggiano cheese from Vacche rosse 'Red cows' 800 years ago. Now, when urbanization covers pastures and confines them in barns, bored cows lick each other to pass time.

Dairy Queries 4, 5 & 6

Q4. Cattle should be allowed natural behaviours, e.g., cows should graze fields >120 days a year.

Q5. I would pay a little more for pasture-grazed dairy products and meat.

Q6. It is not ethical to eat sentient animals like cows, goats, horses, pigs and sheep.

Two steps forward, one step back

In an early victory around 2007, by the Cornucopia Institute and its bovine and small farmer advocate allies, California and Idaho organic megadairies were threatened with organic decertification before they desisted or reduced stocking density. This resulted in the 2010 organic dairy Pasture Rule (*New York Times* 2007, 2010; *Odairy* 2007; Scholten 2007c, 2010a proceedings, 2014 Scholten: ix, 7, 65, 90, 117, 150, 226, 230; Whoriskey 28 Sep2017 *WaPo*). But those in the USA who expected the 2010 Pasture Rule to settle the contretemps were disappointed by lax monitoring and enforcement by the USDA National Organic Program, which was, unfortunately, too underfunded to have the necessary teeth. We return to this issue in Chapter 6, Conclusions.

Origin-of-organic-livestock rule

The administration of President Barack Obama seemed ready to usher in a new green era in 2009 when First Lady Michelle Obama planted an organic garden on the White House lawn. But Obama was so engaged remedying the 2007–08 Great Recession and subprime mortgage crises that green issues received less attention than anticipated.

The US organic dairy situation deteriorated further under President Trump, when long-negotiated welfare regulations were cast aside. The need for a new 'origin-of-organic-livestock' (OOL) rule was further ignored – prolonging a loophole that Cornucopia Institute (2015) co-founder (in 2004 with Will Fantle) Mark Kastel said allowed industrial-scale megadairies, mostly newbuilds in the desert West, which gamed 'the system and competitively disadvantaged the family farmers who milk cows and follow the spirit and letter of the law [. . .] These dairies burn out their cattle and send them to the hamburger plant, sometimes just a year or two after they start milking them, and then replace them with conventional cows'.

The absence of a meaningful OOL rule meant industrialized 'organic' farms still get away with not replacing aging cows sustainably, as farms traditionally did. So, they buy pregnant heifers (young cows who have not yet calved for the first time) from heifer farms which had raised them on conventional fodder, and used antibiotics in their first year of life, before switching to truly organic fodder only in their second year. This loophole dramatically lowered costs for organic megadairies (Cornucopia Institute 2018b). The ruse was one by which 'organic' megadairies were crushing authentic mom and pop organic grazing farms in America's 'Dairylands' such as Washington, Wisconsin, New York and New England. One of the first to warn the public of this corruption of organic integrity was Mark Kastel, co-founder of OrganicEye, a project of Beyond Pesticides (a public interest group overseeing the Environmental Protection Agency, advocating elimination of toxins in food), before it became independent in 2022. Kastel et al have continued to disseminate Action Alerts urging 'USDA: Stop "Organic" Factories from Milking Conventional Dairy Cows' (Organic Eye 2019).

Cows on quasi-organic megadairies – essentially feedlot CAFOs – burn out young if the operators push them to lactate 25,000 lbs per year. Except for technical requirements notionally outlawing antibiotics and other substances prohibited on the National Organic Standards Board (NOSB) list, intensively managed organic cows can burn out as early as their sisters in conventional CAFOs, who are fed a diet of imported soybeans and grain. They might graze outside on pasture just enough to fool folks on a Sunday drive that the operation honoured the NOP rule of 120 days annually on pasture.

Fraud in 'organic' imports

Fraudulent certification of imported soybeans, legumes and other cattle feed from South Asia, Central Europe and elsewhere has been a major problem in US organic dairying. In late December 2018, Peter Whoriskey reported in the *Washington Post* that the farm bill signed by President Trump included 'efforts to curtail imports of fraudulent "organic" food into the US'. However, the *Kansas City Star* (2020) also provided documentation that domestic US fraud was rampant, including $142 million of fake organic grain and GMO soyabeans. Nobody died, as far as we know – but legitimate US organic grain growers lost income. Six babies *did* die during the scandal of toxic melamine in adulterated milk powder imported from China. Seattle nutritionist Goldie Caughlan, then a spokesperson for Puget Sound Consumer Coop (PCC) Natural Markets, had shared rumours of this scandal with me years earlier. BBC News (2010) reported that in 2008, toxic melamine had been detected in milk products in one out of five dairy companies in China, where it killed those babies and made 300,000 babies ill. It is unknown if exported milk powder caused deaths overseas. Melamine, used in plastics, fertilizers and concrete, can be used illegally to adulterate milk, making it appear to have a higher protein content, but it is dangerous to children's and adults' kidneys (BBC 2010).

One night in 2004, my farmer father and I chatted after church about economic pressures on family-scale farmers who practise traditional pasture-grazing in the National Organic Program. Dad laughed ruefully, recalling the 1950 and 60s, 'When we were almost organic!' True. We grazed cows and spread their winter manure from the barn onto pasture. Occasionally we applied sacks of co-op fertilizer to a field converted to corn, oats or alfalfa – or vice versa. Nitrogen-fixing clover was part of field rotations to keep soil quality high. Raised in a family of Dutch-American dairy farmers, Dad, President of the Washington State Dairy Federation (1990), asked congressional hearings for 'supply management', an Americanism for a European- or Canadian-style milk quota. Their reasoning was that such supply management could stave off bankruptcy for more families, and give their cows a little breathing space. But some fourteen years later, I told him, then recently retired, how agribusiness megadairies – one funded by a Harvard University endowment fund (also landgrabbing in Brazil: see *Grain* 2020) – were devastating family-scale farms in the organic dairy sector, just as 100-year-old family grazing dairies were turned out of business in his era. After an intake of breath, Dad said: 'I always thought pasture belonged to us and our cows, not agribusiness.'

The Cornucopia Institute and the Organic Consumers Association (Cummins 2020), I told my Dad, joined with Puget Consumer Coop around Seattle to organize a boycott of dairy products by Aurora Organic Dairy and Horizon Organic brands (Scholten 2008, 2014: 107). Supporters criticized high stocking density, and lack of sufficient pasture-grazing on their 'organic' operations. Horizon Organic (NOFA 2006), which wished to protect its animal-friendly brand, reacted to the Seattle embargo by improving stocking density, and regained lost spots in dairy cases. *But CAFO rustlers were about.*

Whither the USDA 2010 organic Pasture Rule?

I reflected on conversations with my Dad, while monitoring reports from family farm watchdog, the Cornucopia Institute (2006, 2014). It wasn't what organic was supposed to involve. The Institute had filed complaints against Aurora Organic Dairy (AOD), a company established in 2003 by Marcus Peperzak, and based in Boulder, Colorado. As a result, in August 2007, AOD was sanctioned by the USDA,[1] forced to reduce their stocking density on a 4,200-cow Platteville, Colorado farm, and to end deceptive labelling after the USDA investigated violations of federal law. In August 2007, AOD entered a consent agreement with the USDA, and agreed not to sell as 'organic' milk which came from cattle that were not raised organically according to federal law. An agreement was reached by the USDA and Aurora which resulted in the dairy agreeing to reduce the size of its herds and provide cattle with pasture-grazing in the growing season (Scholten 2010a, 2014: 112–17).

On announcement of the USDA-NOP final Pasture Rule in 2010, pastoralists thought they'd won a war, but it was just a battle. AOD did not give up. Their market position was different from Horizon's. To continue supplying milk for Costco's, Safeway's and Walmart's own labels, it built more 'organic' megadairies in Colorado and Texas. With few animals visible outside large barns, there was scant evidence that they were following the letter and spirit of the 2010 Pasture Rule. So, in 2017, *Washington Post* journalist Peter Whoriskey (2017b, c and d) staked out an AOD factory farm in Texas. Over several days of good grazing weather, he observed very few of its 10,000 cows grazing.

To anyone who interpreted the rule to assume that cows always graze outside in good weather, published photos showed violations of the USDA final 2010 pasture-grazing rule. Was the matter settled? No. Pastoralists suffered an unexpected, crushing defeat by the Trump administration, when, in September 2017, the USDA ruled the operation was in compliance with organic rules. Whoriskey wrote that two officials had flown to view the dairy that June – but it was far from a surprise dawn raid – a fact scorned by pioneers of an earlier, grass-roots-based organic movement, before US national organic sales topped $47 billion per year (*Washington Post* 2017d; *Denver Post* 2017)

As farmer and soil scientist Francis Thicke exited the USDA's National Organic Standards Board, he warned organics was at a crossroads: it could

---

1. https://en.wikipedia.org/wiki/United_States_Department_of_Agriculture

either kowtow to commercial interests, or work with consumers to maintain integrity (*Odairy* 3 Nov 2017). Thicke scorned lax NOP enforcement in the Texas case: 'How smart was it to tell Aurora, "Hey, we're coming. Get your ducks in a row"?' In April 2021 Thicke articulately renewed requests that the USDA honour the initial sustainable visions of the organic movement (NFFC 18 May 2020).

Richard Mathews, former assistant deputy of the USDA office that oversees the NOP, had investigated Aurora for the USDA a decade previously. In 2007, when AOD was cited for 14 'willful' violations. he said (*Odairy* 3 Nov 2017): 'The investigators should have gone in unannounced – they should have shown up at the door with a subpoena and said, "Give us your records."' Charlotte Vallaeys, a senior policy analyst at *Consumer Reports* (previously at Cornucopia Institute), agreed: 'We consider unannounced inspections to be a critical component of a labelling program's verification system … Unannounced inspections would be especially important if a complaint has been received, and could be investigated by showing up unannounced.'

In the *Washington Post* (2017d) and the *Denver Post*, Peter Whoriskey summarized: 'But the USDA investigators who visited Aurora did not conduct a surprise inspection, although they were legally empowered to do so and the allegations warranted one […] USDA officials were in contact with Aurora officials and arranged the review days in advance. Moreover, while the USDA said records proved that the dairy had been operating organically, officials have refused to release those records.' As a result, the 2010 Pasture Rule – the Holy Grail of organic litigants – was moribund in the Trump era.

Origin of Livestock (OOL 2022) rule prevails

Hope was rekindled that President Joe Biden, inaugurated in January 2021, would more strictly enforce organic dairy rules. However, pastoralists and greens were dismayed by Biden's reappointment of Tom Vilsack who, in his previous pro-agribusiness tenure as USDA Secretary under President Obama, allowed Roundup® glyphosate to be used on farmland, even to be sprayed to desiccate hay crops shortly before harvest, giving the chemicals little time to disperse.

But the Democratic administration made a crucial commitment to organic integrity, by closing notorious loopholes in Origin of Organic Livestock (OOL) rules that tempted intensive organic megadairies to cull cows young, because they could easily replace them by converting heifers from conventional farms, raised on antibiotics and pesticide-sprayed GMO feed. USDA published a Final Rule on Origin of Livestock on 29 March 2022. USDA's National Organic Program will oversee the new rule, which, when implemented in 2023, will allow a dairy livestock operation transitioning to organic, or starting a new organic farm, to transition non-organic animals only *once*. It prohibits organic dairies from sourcing any transitioned animals. Once a dairy is certified organic, animals must be managed as organic from the last third of gestation (*Odairy* 29 March 2022).

Q4. 'Cattle should be allowed natural behaviours, e.g., cows should graze fields >120 days a year.'

Stakeholders show awareness of the events described above, even if not in detail. Overwhelming agreement met the query of whether cattle should be allowed natural behaviours, such as grazing on fields at least 120 days a year. As mentioned earlier, in the US, 120 days per year was the minimum grazing period, with minimum 30 per cent dry matter content, established in the 2010 USDA organic Pasture Rule involving farmer groups such as NODPA and farmer advocacy group, the Cornucopia Institute, based in Wisconsin, against megadairies such as Horizon-Dean Foods and Aurora Organic Dairy.

Q4 Cattle should be allowed natural behaviours: For example, cows should graze fields at least 120 days a year.

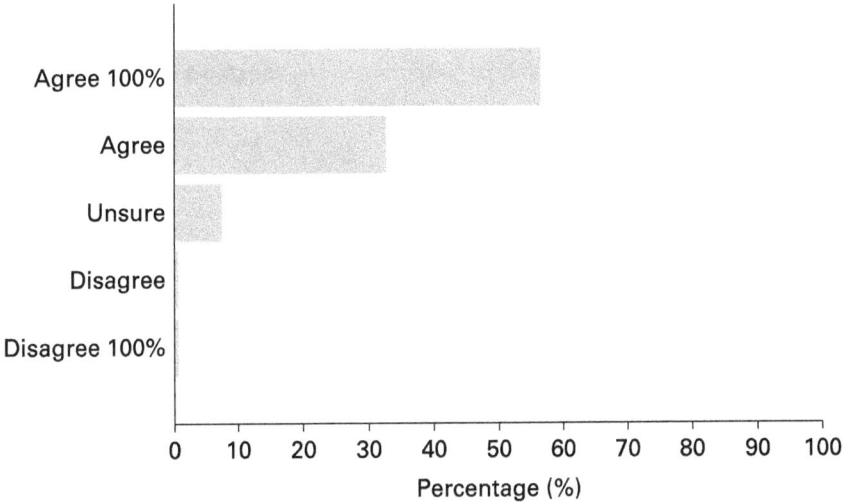

Voices of the stakeholders

We again start with respondents from the US, which allows us a window into whether people there are aware of trends in dairy farming relevant to statement 4 over the last several decades. The first two responses are from those with direct knowledge of dairy farming and their responses reflect this; however, so do responses from those in the consumer-only category. (See previous chapter for their ages.) Again, pseudonyms have been used unless otherwise noted.

Jim Goodman (real name) in Wisconsin, the first US dairy farmer to be certified organic, thought it obvious that cattle be allowed natural behaviours: 'Of course they should, especially if they are supposed to be managed under organic certification. Natural behaviour might put production on a more sane scale, and farmers might be able to remain small and make a profit.'

Kate Ryan (real name), the agricultural programme co-ordinator for WSU Snohomish County Extension, agreed 100 per cent that cattle should express natural behaviours but thought the 120-day rule was too minimal: 'Only 120 days? That leaves cows in the dark loafing shed, or worse (tiny feedlot paddock) 245 days/year! Still a miserable existence, but better than 0 days outside. Thinking about things like this makes me wish I could be a vegan, but I love dairy and meat waaaaaay too much!'

Interestingly, Tim Finley (real name), ex- motorcycle racer, aerospace technical consultant and from a farming family echoed Kate Ryan's response. He was sensitive to nutrition, and scathing about what George Ritzer (1993) dubbed *The McDonaldization of Society*: 'Thank you, McDonald's!' He was adamant that cattle welfare depended on extensive grazing periods: '120 days is not enough IMHO.'

Happy Larson, the caregiver/adoption counsellor near Sequim, USA, agreed cattle should express natural behaviours. She mentioned 'Cows with Guns', a 1996 ditty by Dana Lyons, favoured by animal welfarists in Washington State: 'As the song says, "We will fight for bovine freedom and hold our large heads high; we will run free with the buffalo or die .... (https://youtu.be/a5s5qGg01nE).'

Ned Harold, communication specialist for an oil multinational in Washington state, had farming in the family in previous generations, but was a 'townie' whose Dad ran a barber shop. He advocated grazing as the norm: 'Depends on the farm, possibly 365 days' if conditions permit.' He was upbeat about treatment of farmers and dairy cows, but did he accurately perceive changes from a small farmer's perspective? In his lifetime, county farms had moved from extensive pasture to intensive feedlot methods. Passing motorists may assume that fields of fodder – alfalfa, silage, hay – are some sort of arable crop for humans such as oats or mustard, while cattle graze pasture elsewhere – perhaps behind a big barn that dominates the landscape.

Townies might not always notice the slow change from small grazing farms to intensive confinement, perhaps because the new landscapes appear more orderly, with cattle confined behind feedlot walls. Although cows are not stretching their heads under fences to catch 'greener grass' along roadsides, CAFO operators typically allow a few non-lactating dry cows to graze outside buildings, for a month before they birth calves. Motorists wondering where the rest of the herd is may assume they're grazing *behind* the barns. Contemporary agricultural scientists argue the ethics, environmental externalities and politics of confinement versus pasture-grazing, but the debate came into focus decades ago when Kate Ryan, recalled her dairist dad's words: 'Nowadays they shut cows in a barn, where they bring them fodder, then haul their manure back to the fields, when the cows were perfectly capable of handling those chores, themselves.'

Stevie Hart, engineer with applied systems engineering which is applicable from IT to dairying, agreed 100 per cent that cows should graze at least 120 days annually: 'Cows used to do this, but efficiencies argue otherwise. We need to find a way to manage them better while allowing for pasture, which produces healthier animals, less need for antibiotics and satisfies the ethical issues.'

Berta Racarden, civil servant in New York City originally from Spain, agreed 100 per cent that cows be allowed natural behaviours: 'Why not give small farmers subsidies so they can reach this goal? All the small farmers that were wiped out in Southern Europe allowed their cows to graze pretty much on a daily basis.'

Nancy Centuri, market gardener selling in Seattle Neighbourhood Farmers' Markets, lives in the Snoqualmie Valley (Jarosz 2008). With a farm background, she is wary of government, business and even co-operatives. She believes animals need to express instinctive behaviours, saying: 'When grazing is available cattle should graze always.'

Karen Suttler, retired office worker, outdoorswoman from Salt Lake City, also agreed 100 per cent that cattle should express natural behaviours: 'Yes, in an ideal world, but cattle farms are all about profit and an animal's "natural behaviours" obviously don't fit into the profit equation, so I'm guessing not many cows are grazing 120 days a year.'

Kal Charge, motorsports business owner on Puget Sound, provides an example of what Karen Sutter noted. He withheld opinions on fairness to farmers or about animal welfare because he lacked direct knowledge – as did some respondents in occupations like aerospace fabrication. Should cattle express natural behaviours? He expressed commercial acuity to the bottom line: 'Seems like a natural thing to do, [but] not sure how it would impact the economics of the industry.'

Turning to UK responses, we also start with someone directly involved in dairy farming, Caroline Bell (real name), a second-generation co-manager with Graham Tweddle of Acorn Dairy (12 Dec 2019), a family organic dairy farm, and bottler, featuring doorstep delivery service in North-East England. The operation is a century-old family farm that converted to organic two decades ago. Significantly, Caroline and co-director Graham mix seaweed containing iodine with cattle feed to boost cows' immune systems, and reducte methane emissions from the cows' burps. They claim research shows spring and summer grazing on grass, clover and herb leys produces organic milk richer in antioxidants, and healthy Omega-3 fatty acids. In her responses to the first three statements, Caroline agreed that politicians, corporations and co-operatives interact fairly with their business. But she is concerned about animal welfare in intensive UK livestock farming, where producing cheap meat for supermarkets is the main driver. Bell's family dairy achievement relies on carefully managed extensive rotational grazing, on pastures receiving annual rainfall of 641 mm or 25.2 inches annually, in average annual temperature of 8.8°C /47.9°F. She agrees 100 per cent that cattle should graze fields at least 120 days a year: 'I would argue more 180+ days or as long as weather and grass conditions allow (whichever is the longer and is in line with Soil Association organic standards). However, there is more to cow welfare than turning her outside for half a year.' One thing that helps is eye-to-eye contact between farmers and cows in fields or loafing sheds. Extra points for bringing apples or carrots!

The non-farmers in the UK were united in their views that cows should graze.

Tom Charles, county carbon management officer in rural Northern England, agreed 100 per cent that cattle should graze at least 120 days a year and so did Richard Beakins, retired social scientist, market gardener and dairy historian. He agreed that cattle should express natural behaviours: 'I hope zero-grazing mega-farms do not become common in the UK.'

Nanci Barnes, academic and company director from Scotland, also agreed 100 per cent that cattle be allowed to express natural behaviours: 'Why would you put an animal in a shed, other than to shelter from the weather? Pretty sure quality of the product is much better than quantity. This also counts for quality of life for livestock.'

Elaine Oordt, gardener and horticulture lecturer, in North-East England, praised 'especially traditional and organic farmers but not the industrialized factory so-called farms.' She agreed cattle should be allowed natural behaviours, which was: 'Exactly what happens at the Acorn Organic Dairy and Sacriston farms I buy from.'

Loren Marton, a youth and community worker who travelled rural North-East England for his job, and had grandparents who farmed, said: 'I think politicians can use throwaway comments on agriculture. Big companies can also treat small farmers unfairly.' Was UK animal welfare adequate? 'I think this is true on the whole.' As for Query 4, about grazing fields at least 120 days a year, he agreed: 'This would seem to make sense for any animal.'

An Antipodean professor saw geographical variability on the practicality of cows grazing fields 120 days a year: 'It's relatively easy in New Zealand, but probably hard in other places. Winter grazing outside in poor conditions is being challenged at the moment in NZ.'

Bertran Kiung, a PhD student in Newcastle, UK, orignally from urban China who in his responses to the first set of queries in Chapter 2 felt farmers in China were treated fairly, expressed a view with respect to Query 4 that contradicted this, saying: 'It is true … under many circumstances … their natural behaviours are deprived by humans, by the farmers and the companies. In order to get as much milk as humans can, they deprive the rights of new-born calves and lambs to drink their mother's' milk. I feel very sad!'

Q5. 'I would pay a little more for pasture-grazed dairy products and meat.'

This statement goes to the heart of consumer behaviour: will customers pay a little more for cows who've grazed in verdant pastures? Yes. Nearly 90 per cent of respondents (57 per cent of respondents agreed 100 per cent and 32 per cent agreed) were sympathetic with paying a little more for pasture-grazed dairy products and meat. This is hardly surprising – if connotations of healthy freshness did not assist marketing, manufacturers would not utilize images of happy cows on green pastures.

Q5 I would pay a little more for pasture-grazed dairy products and meat.

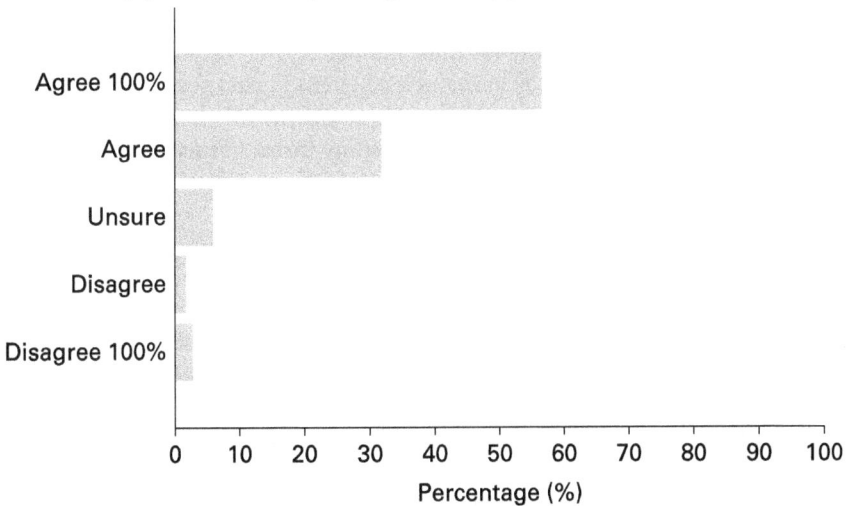

Voices of stakeholders

Starting with someone with direct knowledge of dairy farming, Kate Ryan (real name), agrees 100 per cent that it's worth paying a little more for pasture-grazed dairy products and meat: 'Heck, the poor farms stuck with the iron-clad dairy co-op system are not making money, and that is just plain stupid. I have no problem paying the $13 a gallon that the raw milk dairy wants. It's definitely worth it.'

Many US respondents said they already paid more.

Tim Finley (real name), aerospace technical consultant, was critical of animal welfare in industrialized agriculture, which he believes sacrifices nutrition and contains toxins such as glyphosate. He believed the so-called organic milk from some megadairy suppliers of supermarket own brand organic milk was nutritionally inferior to responsibly-produced conventional milk. So, he agreed 100% with paying more for pasture-grazed dairy products and meat: 'I do that already as it is.'

Ben Elliot, a retired aviation maintenance manager based in Gig Harbor, Washington, 'grew up on a subsistence type farm in Maine', and has more confidence in traditional extensive farms than in intensive agriculture's treatment of farmers or animals. He agrees 100 per cent to paying a little more for pasture-grazed dairy products and meat: 'I do. I pay US $5.99 for two quarts of grass-fed milk.'

Marie Nuancz, a teacher in her 60s and journalist based near Chicago, had farming on her mother's side of the family, three generations back. In her responses to the first set of questions, she was unsure about treatment of contemporary farmers, and disagrees with the overall state of animal welfare conditions. Regarding 120 days per year grazing she said: 'Sounds good, but I am no expert.' She agrees 100 per cent with paying a little more for pasture-grazed dairy products and meat: 'For years I have chosen to pay more for milk and butter from responsible producers who do not use bovine growth hormone [BGH/rBST], and seem to have fewer antibiotics in the feed. I did a blind taste test, comparing the healthier milk with cheaper, factory farmed milk and noticed that my throat burned or tingled after drinking the latter, probably from the chemicals in it.'

Berta Racarden, civil servant in New York, originally from Spain, agrees 100 per cent with paying more for ethically reared dairy and meat: 'I already do. I would rather eat less meat of better quality than the hormone-full meat found in most US supermarkets these days.' She deplores the ubiquity of steroid-boosted meat in the US, as well as the use of the dairy hormone rBGH/rBST, whose use has, to her approval, fallen away except in the most intensive operations. Such synthetic GMO dairy hormones, and beef steroid pellet growth-boosters, are banned in the EU. Since Brexit in 2020, however, many Britons fear future UK–US trade deals could bring such products to their supermarkets.

Josie Suttler, retired from office work, and with more time for outdoor pursuits and ethical consumption, agreed 100 per cent with paying more for quality food: 'And I do! It's hard to trust store-bought items like "cage free" or "free range" so I would like to see a more definitive standard to assure consumers that they are indeed purchasing from an ethical source. When I purchase beef, I go to nearby local farms.' Consumers like her were frustrated when animal welfare regulations negotiated a decade in the USDA National Organic Program were shelved by the Trump administration in 2017.

Rita Carter, retired accountant in Oklahoma, says 'I absolutely already do!' pay a little more for pasture-grazed dairy products and meat.

But Kal Charge, with his business hat on as owner of a motorsports business on Puget Sound, quipped a commercial response on paying more for pasture-grazed dairy products and meat: 'How much is a little more?'

Bertran Kiung, the student from China who was studying in Newcastle when he responded to the dairy survey, echoed Kal's response saying that, while he said he would pay a little more for pasture-grazed dairy products and meat, 'What do you mean "pay a little more" here? More time, more care to animals, more money? If money, I think most people prefer paying less to paying more.'

In the UK, we first turn to a response from Caroline Bell, the co-director of Acorn Organic Dairy: 'Finding organic meat is relatively easy in our local farm shops & mainstream retailers. I always choose this over any other premium brands, but we do not eat meat every day.' Bell and co-director Graham Tweddle, her brother, say customers appreciate tastier organic milk and improved cow health boosted by clover for added antioxidants. Seaweed mixed with cow fodder is rich in iodine, boosting immune response, cow welfare and environmental sustainability (CSIRO 2016; *The Lead* 2020 and 2021; *Progressive Dairyman* 2019; NODPA 2019). These cows produce only about 6,500 litres of milk a year, so their stress is less – *and well-being and longevity greater* – than in intensive dairies targeting 10,000 litres a year.

Nan Toner, retired teacher from Chester-le-Street, UK, agreed 100 per cent with the idea of paying more for pastured milk and meat: 'We have Arla Farmers Milk. This should be applied to other consumer goods.' She understands that co-operatives like Arla help small family-scale dairy families remain economically viable in a world dominated by industrialized production, processing and marketing distribution – not to mention trade wars.

Celia Cremen, university teaching assistant and graphic designer in Newcastle, UK, underlines welfare points in her 100 per cent agreement with paying a little more for dairy products and meat if cows are pasture-grazed, 'And also not forcibly impregnated, caged, prodded, hooked up to milking machines until their udders are covered in weeping sores, etc.'

Karen Saren, retired onto her farm, is on a low budget. Would she pay more for pasture-grazed dairy products and meat? 'I probably would if I could afford it.'

Some responses from non-farmers in the UK exhibited more scepticism than those from US consumers. They do not trust farmers to adhere to high standards and are not always happy with supermarket offerings.

Richard Beakins, the retired social scientist and market gardener in North-East England, is an expert on the British dairy industry since the eighteenth century. He would pay more for pastured dairy and meat – 'But only if produced with higher environmental and welfare standards'.

Nanci Barnes, the academic specialist on rural broadband working in Norway, agreed 100 per cent with paying a little more for pasture-grazed dairy products and meat, noting: 'Difficult to find in Tesco supermarket because their pricing mechanism reflects the consumer and distribution market rather than production – I would much prefer co-operatives that offer fair trade and animal welfare. We can also just eat less meat if it is more expensive – we are omnivores so meat should not be high on our diet.'

Elaine Oordt, gardener and horticulture lecturer in North-East England, agrees 100 per cent to pay a little more for pasture-grazed dairy products and meat and shows her priorities: 'I am not well off, but I would do without new clothes to maintain my standards for food.'

Harry Cremen, an ecommerce manager in Newcastle, UK, disagreed 100 per cent with any chance of paying more for pasture-based milk or meat, but explained: 'I'm a vegan so I wouldn't pay for any animal products.'

Bernice, student in Granada, Spain, was disappointed by the average levels of animal welfare in the country. She agreed that cattle should graze 120 days annually, adding: 'They should even do it much longer.' Would she pay any more for pasture-grazed dairy products and meat? 'I don't eat meat or drink milk, but I think I would.'

Omsin, a teacher in central Thailand, disagreed that farmers got a fair shake in response to the first set of queries, and is animal friendly. But he wonders why consumers should be expected to pay more, when the moral responsibility lies on the agricultural powers that be, especially in politics and business, saying: 'I am totally with pasture-grazed dairy products and meat, not just paying a little more for it.'

Eashav Taalin, professor of dairy education and research in Gujarat, India, says farmers are treated fairly in India. This is likely because the Amul-model dairy farmers' co-operatives propagated in the world's biggest ever dairy development programme, Operation Flood (1970–96), return about 75 per cent of retail prices to small, marginal and even landless male and female farmers (Scholten 1996, 2010). The erudite academic agreed 100 per cent that cows should graze fields at least 120 days a year, and similarly agreed with paying a little more for pasture-grazed dairy products and meat. However, he was unsure about animal welfare; perhaps this links to zero-grazing strategies adopted two decades ago amid India's population growth.

Dairy co-operatives co-operating globally

Arla Foods, mentioned above, is a global dairy company and co-operative that began in Denmark and Sweden in 1881. In 2014, Arla had farmer owners in seven European countries: Sweden (3,356), Denmark (3,156), UK (2,956), Germany (2,763), Belgium (955), Luxembourg (236) and the Netherlands (52). A few years later, Arla noted it was owned by 12,700 dairy farmers across thirty-two countries including Denmark, Germany and the UK, with about 2,700 British dairy farmers (Arla revenue was €10.3 billion in 2017).

In February 2014, the United States, European Union (EU) and other countries imposed sanctions against Russia and Crimea after the Russian invasion of Ukraine. The trade embargo cut European dairy exports to Russia in 2014, and the situation of small dairy farmers became more precarious when EU milk quotas that began in 1984 ended in 2015, spurring laissez-faire competition akin to that which caused about 90 per cent of US dairy farmers to quit or merge with neighbours since 1980 (Scholten 1989ac, 1990d; BBC 2015; *Hoard's Dairyman* 2016a).

Dairy farmer numbers fell in the UK, which was then still in the EU, along with the farmgate price paid by big supermarkets. The Farmers Milk label was created by Arla to give shoppers the opportunity to pay a little extra on each container to help Arla farmers. In product differentiation, Arla also markets organic milk, as well as free-range milk from cows grazed on pasture. To help parents, Arla Big Milk added Iron, Vitamin D and Vitamin A, to give children extra vitamins and minerals with their breakfast cereal (Arla 2016). The UK Soil Association certified Arla schemes according to its organic standards on animal welfare, increasing consumer confidence in nutritional and ethical considerations such as animal welfare and well-being.

The Arla co-operative and the UK Soil Association also worked together on a scheme to export organic milk from Europe and the UK to the US Organic Valley dairy co-op. This included organic cheeses from the UK to the US, then shipped to China for consumers there. In 2017 sessions at the Royal Geographical Society (with IBG) in London, and the IFOAM world organic congress in Delhi in 2017, I described how – despite slings and arrows of trade embargoes – co-ops working internationally can help sustain family-scale farmers (Scholten 2017 IFOAM).

Q6. 'It is not ethical to eat sentient animals like cows,
goats, horses, pigs, and sheep.'

If stakeholders judge current intensive farming practices negatively and are willing to pay more for dairy products from humanely raised cows, might they go further and shun animal products all together? We have already seen in one response to Query 5 that some are.

Q6 It is not ethical to eat sentient animals like cows, goats, horses, pigs, and sheep.

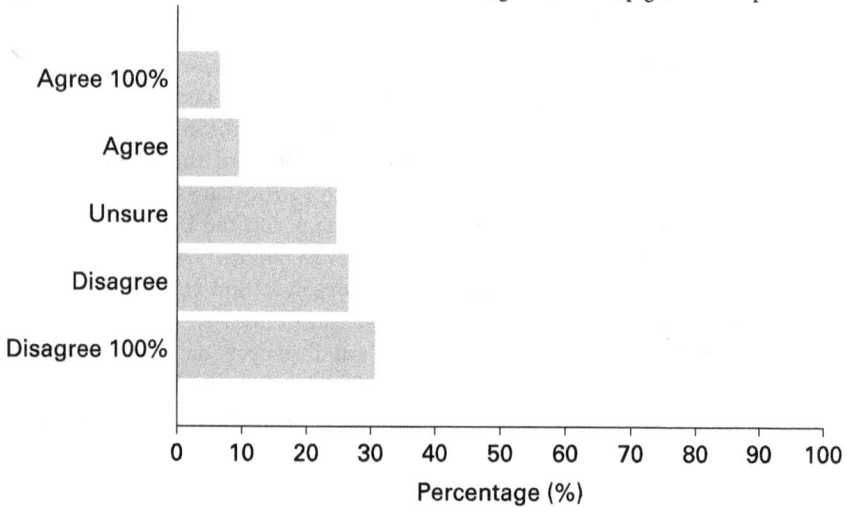

Only 7 per cent of respondents agreed 100 per cent that it is not ethical to eat traditional farm animals; just 10 per cent 'agreed' it is unethical to eat them. One quarter (or 25%) were unsure, as 27 per cent disagreed. At the other end of the scale, the largest group, 31 per cent, disagreed 100 per cent that it was wrong to eat meat. That is, a combined 57 per cent do not question the ethics of eating meat. If Query 6 was difficult for respondents to answer, neither were all comments straightforward. Rueful remarks reveal respondents' torn emotions (what academics call *affect*), split between their passionate hunger for meat, and troubling reflections on the ethics of carnivorism, or fears about negative impacts of livestock supply chains on local ecologies, biodiversity or, ultimately, global climate.

Whatever the ethics of eating other creatures, it is not unnatural, in historical, or pre-historical terms. There is evidence of carnivorous practices we would consider highly unethical not just among humans but also among other living creatures. For example, Tom Fletcher, Honorary Research Fellow in Palaeobiology at the University of Leicester, and his team claim that the megalodon shark, which lived 15 to 3.6 million years ago and stretched fourteen metres), gave live birth to babies two metres long – that is, larger than an average adult human (*Conversation* 2022). How did the babies grow so big? Fletcher's team say it was cannibalism; they ate their siblings in the womb. Natural? Yes. *Baby shark ethics are red in tooth and maw.*

The peskiest word in this intentionally ambiguous statement is the word *sentient*. This takes us back to issues discussed in Chapter 1. Are cows, goats, horses, pigs and sheep *sentient* – in ways comparable to human sentience? French natural philosopher René Descartes denied it. In the twentieth century, behaviourist psychologist B.F. Skinner (1904–90) did little to dissuade people who regarded animals as unconscious machines driven by instinct, but incapable of human-like cognition, planning, language, emotion or pain. *Think about that, when your cat curls up beside you on the sofa.*

Again, we begin with Americans who work directly in farming.

Voices of the stakeholders

Elizabeth Henderson, the activist author and farmer, disagreed: 'We are all part of the cycle of life and death. Why is it worse to slaughter a goat than broccoli for food?'

Kate Ryan, agricultural programme co-ordinator, dissected the question with expertise evoking the philosophy of lacto-vegetarian Jainism in India, which eschews eating even plants such as potatoes, onions and other roots. She disagreed 100 per cent that it is not ethical to eat sentient animals: 'We could certainly debate sentience in critters . . . and then we would need to debate the same for trees and plants.' She added: 'I'm pretty sure the carrot has a loud, silent scream as it is ripped from the comfort of the only home it's ever known, and it's every bit as anguished as the hours-old calf being ripped from its mother's side. Guess I don't understand how it's horrid to eat a chicken, but have no problem with predators taking down critters to feed themselves and their families. Isn't it the same thing?'

Luke Quoral, 70s, a retired rock radio disc jockey and transport union leader in Denver, Colorado, was a thoughtful meat-eater, whose family and friends actively discussed such issues from Buddhist, Marxist and Presbyterian perspectives. He disagreed that it is unethical to eat meat, but: 'we must make the taking of a life a sobering, painless process. We need to give thanks to the animal that will sustain us.'

Jim Goodman, the Wisconsin dairy farmer who was the first certified by the USDA National Organic Program, defended livestock being raised for its meat: 'We need to realize that animals play a vital role in holistic farming systems. While we should cut way back on meat consumption if we choose to eat meat, there is a place for animals. We also need to realize that in indigenous farming cultures, animals are vital for work, to utilize crop waste and as a source of protein for the farm family that is cheap and can provide nutrients to recycle into the system.'

Happy Larson, near Sequim, USA, expressed views indicating that she was unsure about vegetarianism, veganism and the ethics of eating sentient animals: 'Intellectually, yes! But when I smell a barbecuing hunk of meat or visit an Omaha Steakhouse, I find my ethical bravado weakens and I happily scarf down the poor animal. Medium rare, please.'

Ken Mentzer, disagreed 100 per cent that it is unethical to eat animals such as cows, goats, horses, pigs and sheep: 'Humans did not invent carnivorous behaviour out of an ethical lack, or a cruel mentality. Humans did not invent meat-added diets, at all. Meat offers health benefits. You have to kill to have meat. You also have to kill living things in order to eat vegetables. Calling cows, goats, horses, pigs and (especially) sheep "sentient" pushes the lexical limits of the term.'

Randy Grein saw ethical dilemmas in carnivorousness: 'There are arguments several ways here. At the very least we should treat animals humanely, something we fail in spectacularly now.'

Kal Charge, motorsports business owner, who takes his best clients to Ruth's Chris Steakhouse in Seattle, disagreed 100 per cent that it is unethical to eat farm animals: 'Really!'

But there are some who *do* agree that the practice is unethical.

Rita Carter, retired accountant, explained her decision not to eat farm animals: 'It is difficult for me to view intelligent animals only as "meat". This was a large part of my decision to become a vegetarian at the age of 22.'

Harry Cosin, in the UK, evidenced his 100 per cent disagreement that it is not ethical to consume animals: 'I'm a vegan.'

Other UK responses were similar to the US respondents in the conflicted sentiments.

Richard Beakins, perfectly articulated the carnivore's ethical conundrum when considering veganism: 'My head says yes but then … there are bacon sandwiches …'

Tom Charles had said he was willing to pay more for pastured meat, but unsure about the ethics: 'I am eating less animal products these days. I think we've grown quite complacent in our attitudes to meat and sanitized the process for the consumer.'

Harold Daniels, familiar with dairy farms, was unsure about eating cattle, saying: 'Too many contextual things here, and whether personal or communal ethics are in question. Sentience as a focus can be problematic. Seeing life forms as disconnected, compartmentalized entities rather than connected, influencing each other multiple ways, is an important and arbitrary distinction, moored in cultures of need and ownership. Environmental concerns are huge. There is no final answer to this, because there can be no universal ethical position without contradictions and compromises for all involved.'

Nanci Barnes, academic and company director from Scotland, now in Norway, was unsure if it is ethical to eat sentient animals like cows, goats, horses, pigs and sheep: 'Don't all living beings think or have awareness, including the animals we eat? I think if we had closer connection with our food and respected what we eat, rather than just consumed them we may act differently. This seems a world gone by. Sadly, our society is very disconnected from the world that supports its lifestyle. It now would need to be packaged as Ethical Eating to catch society's eye.'

Elaine Oordt, horticulturiat in North-East England, disagreed that it is unethical to eat meat, noting her '... reduced meat diet with fairly treated animals'. She augmented her opinion with the observation that: 'Much of upland Durham is unsuitable for growing anything but turf, and the grazing improves habitat for wildlife.'

Loren Morton, community worker in rural North-East England, disagreed that it is wrong to eat farm animals: 'Happy to eat animal-based food in moderation.'

Nan Toner, retired teacher, in Chester-le-Street, UK, added caveats to eating cows, goats, horses, pigs and sheep, but responded similarly to American Randy Grein: 'It is a personal choice, but I expect animals to be slaughtered in a humane way.'

Views from other countries are, in response to this statement, more like those in the US and UK: conflicted.

Bertran Kiung, PhD student in Newcastle, UK, from China, disagreed 100 per cent that it is ethical to eat sentient animals: 'There should be ethics. They became food for humans since old times, but in this modern time [sic], we should establish ethical rules for these animals. For example, how to reduce their pain and how to treat them when they are raised in the farms. I saw some farmers treated animals very badly in the videos. It is terrible.'

Jong Wei, an undergraduate from Peking, studying in Spain, reflected China's hunger for meat and dairy. He disagreed 100 per cent that it is unethical to eat sentient animals.

Juan Siena, Spanish teacher from South America, unexpectedly agreed that it is unethical to eat farm animals, as he previously owned a café serving meat in Durham, UK.

Badur Banglar, staffer at a dairy co-operative in Dhaka, Bangladesh, agreed it is not ethical to eat sentient animals like cows, goats, horses, pigs and sheep. This is surprising, as 90 per cent of Bangladeshis follow Islam, and many who can afford it are meat-eaters. Perhaps he misunderstood the question – or the word 'sentient' gave rise to ethical qualms.

Perhaps Celia Cremen, UK teaching assistant, best sums up responses to this statement: 'If it's necessary for human survival, like it was for many years, then yes. But starving humans have also eaten other humans, so ... There are so many better choices these days – better for the planet, and for our bodies. We just aren't built to eat this volume of animal products at every meal, every day. And our ecosystems aren't made to support it either.'

Chapter 4

ENVIRONMENT AND LIVESTOCK AGRICULTURE

We now continue with the more specific statements. The seventh query was written to elicit comments in addition to what respondents shared in their responses to queries in the previous chapter. The eighth and ninth queries aimed to gauge the extent to which respondents might be prepared to adopt vegan, vegetarian or meat-alternatives.

Dairy Queries 7, 8 and 9

Q7. Livestock ag unacceptably harms the environment & climate.
Q8. Vegan meals can be as tasty as those using ingredients from livestock.
Q9. Plant-based dairy and laboratory-grown meat substitutes could replace food animals soon.

Q7. ' Livestock agriculture harms the environment and climate unacceptably.'

Q7 Livestock agriculture unacceptably harms the environment and climate.

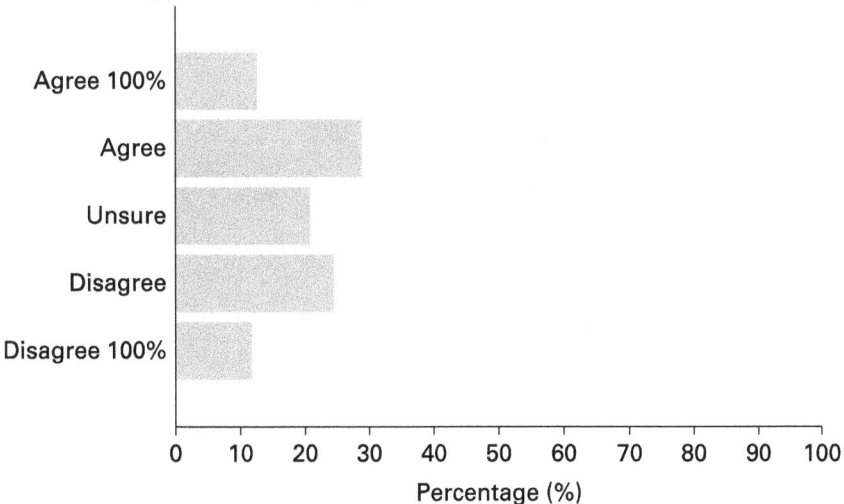

Figures 4.1 and 4.2 Pasture dairy farming in Cumbria, UK, sequesters carbon in soil, enriches milk with healthy Omega-3 fatty acids, and enhances animal welfare.

Comments featured in the previous chapter indicated concern about the environment. It is therefore not surprising that considerable worry was expressed in responses to the statement that livestock agriculture harms the environment and climate unacceptably, with 13 per cent agreeing 100 per cent with the proposition and 29 per cent in agreement. What is somewhat unexpected, given the voices we've already heard in Chapters 2 and 3, is that 25 per cent disagreed and 12% disagreed 100 per cent. The level of uncertainty, at 21 per cent, is high. Their comments will reveal the basis of their responses to the statements.

Now it is over a decade and a half since the FAO (2006) report 'Livestock's long shadow' surprised many people with its claim that dairy and meat production emitted prodigious amounts of greenhouse gases (GHG) into the atmosphere. Before 2006, wood fires, coal, petroleum and jet fuel were prime suspects. Recognition has been spreading that production of cattle feed, on land cut from previous forests, sacrifices Earth's green lungs. This heats and acidifies oceans, diminishing phytoplankton which absorb carbon and emit oxygen into the atmosphere. But the problem was not just carbon loading. Knapp et al. made it clear in *Journal of Dairy Science* (2014: 3231) that cattle emissions of methane (CH_4) and nitrous oxide (N_2O) are potent allies of carbon dioxide (CO_2). The pronounced – if shorter half-lived – effect of methane on climate volatility makes it dairy's Achilles' hoof. So, Life Cycle Analyses (LCA) convert methane into carbon dioxide equivalents (CO_2e). *In a bad rhyme – with cows it's less carbon hoof print than methane breath mint.* We return to dairy's contribution to GHGs topic in the final chapter of this book.

Voices of the stakeholders

We start with the UK this time, with Tom Charles, the county carbon-management officer in Northern England. He linked production methods to the length of livestock's long shadow: 'It's mainly due to demand and drivers for cheap products. I'd like to think it could be well managed at lower intensity.' He has reason for optimism, as J.R. Knapp et al. (*Journal of Dairy Science* 2014: 3231) tout prospects to cut enteric methane and other greenhouse gases:

> Research over the past century in genetics, animal health, microbiology, nutrition, and physiology has shown intensively managed farms have GHG emissions as low as 1 kg of CO_2 equivalents (CO_2e)/kg of energy-corrected milk (ECM), compared with >7 kg of CO_2e/kg of ECM in extensive systems.

This broadly supports Steinfeld et al. (FAO 2006), recommending intensive feedlots over pasture-grazing – but disappoints pastoralists. At this point, grazers tend to fall back on their argument that pasture can act as a carbon sink, sequestering GHGs.

Some respondents, for example retired teacher Nan Toner, grappled with the contention that livestock agriculture unacceptably harms the environment and climate but were not exactly sure how: 'I think it does harm the environment, but it could be done more sensibly with less waste. I disapprove of the excess consumption that is encouraged in some developed countries.'

Loren Marton, youth & community worker whose grandparents had a farm, simply agreed, saying: 'At the moment some effect to climate is attributed to agriculture.'

What becomes evident from these responses is a shared conviction that if farming is done right (not intensively), the environmental footprint is reduced.

Tim Sands, artisan cheesemaker in his 40s, based in North-East England, disagreed that livestock ag was universally harmful to environment: 'In isolation, no. In conjunction with other man-made pollutants, yes.'

This view was shared by Richard Beakins, retired geographer, who said he has for decades been unsure of dairy effects upon climate: 'There is methane, but then there are many sources for that.' Quite right: for example, Sir David Attenborough's film series *Blue Planet II* showed big methane volcanoes erupting from the seabed of the Gulf of Mexico (BBC 2017).

Karl Zillener, in his 50s and a lecturer in linguistics in Northern England, agreed that livestock agriculture unacceptably harms the environment and climate, but had a nuanced take: 'I think the effect varies quite a bit by animal and farming technique.' He has heard grazing cows might produce more methane than cows in feedlots; this is the position of Steinfeld et al. (2006), which disappoints traditional graziers. Grazers hope the combination of seaweed with digestible grasses and feeds can dramatically lower methane emissions.

Elaine Oordt, the gardener and horticulturalist keen on hill farming in County Durham, disagrees that livestock agriculture causes unacceptable harm: 'Humans do more damage but we are not suggesting removing them, are we?'

Caroline Bell, with direct experience of dairy farming in her role as co-director of organic Acorn Dairy, disagreed 100 per cent that livestock agriculture unacceptably harms the environment and climate. She pointed to positive developments, saying: 'I see an improvement in the soils on our farm and research from Sustainable Food Trust, among others, shows extensive, mixed, organic farming improves soil and is a benefit to the environment in terms of carbon and soil fertility for the future.'

Nanci Barnes, the Scottish company director and geographer working in Norway, agreed livestock agriculture unacceptably harms the environment and climate, with this caveat: 'Large scale livestock agriculture does – again it is the production/consumption paradigm. Recent research illustrates seaweed pellets or substitutes reduce CO_2 emissions from animals – good news. But intensification of agriculture and over consumption are the real culprits – a bit of societal change required but just on burger consumption alone this is a massive thing to tackle.' She is right to finger the production/ consumption paradigm, which links economic growth to degradation of natural resources. Geographers David R. Harvey (1997, 2003), and Geoff A. Wilson (2007) have written that multifunctional farm and forestry policies can balance economies, social amenities, and environmental sustainability.

Neil Barnes, company co-director and consultant, said he'd remain a carnivore but agreed that 'Intensive agriculture unacceptably harms the environment and climate'.

Hans Wolfisberg, a US-based organic dairy farmer, defended his traditional rotational pasture-grazing system, declaring, 'Confined animal feeding operations harm the environment!' He targeted CAFOs for high-density point pollution, and extra GHG emissions due to global sourcing of fodder and other inputs. He noted that consumer pressure is now forcing many corporations and co-operatives to stop sourcing milk made with the GMO dairy hormone rBGH/rBST. But Wolfisberg added that few shoppers know conventional megadairies subject cows to chemically induced oestrus – a complaint of CiWF and PETA animal welfare activists – mentioned in previous chapters. That may be seen as an ethical issue. It is also a practice which intensification proponents (e.g., Capper et al. 2009; Capper 2017, 2020) defend as efficient for maximizing milk production. However, consumer fears are increasing that such practices stress bovines, weaken their immune systems and make them more vulnerable to zoonoses which affect humans and animals alike.

Nancy Thomas, organic farmer and part-time barista, looked more favourably on her organic co-operative than politicians and corporations. On our previous queries about cow welfare, she agreed 100 per cent that cows should graze at least 120 days a year and that it is ethical to eat farm animals. She disagreed 100 per cent that livestock agriculture harms the environment and climate unacceptably, emphasizing that, 'When done properly, with grass-fed ruminants, it actually heals the land by sequestering carbon into the soil.'

Three American respondents are less equivocal. Elizabeth Henderson, the arable farmer and founding member of the Northeast Organic Farming Association in the US, expressed the view that, 'As practised today in the US, most livestock agriculture pollutes and abuses.'

That view was shared by 31-year-old Tina Dice, a farmer from Pine Palms, New York: 'The way that it is currently done, yes that is fairly true.'

Also agreeing with the contention that CAFO dairies pollute was Jim Goodman, the pioneer Midwest organic family farmer: 'Yes, we raise too many livestock, eat too many animal products and do not integrate animals as part of the farming operations.'

Kate Ryan, agricultural programme co-ordinator in Washington State, agreed that large-scale intensive livestock agriculture harms the environment and climate unacceptably: 'As the vast majority of current livestock production takes place under less-than-ideal conditions, yeah, it's [harming] the environment in a lot of places. That said, it certainly doesn't need to be that way [...] there are plenty of small-scale farms showing how it can be done correctly.'

Ken E. Tillmann, retired aviation technician, was raised on a Dutch-American dairy farm, where work seemed endless. He still has nightmares in which his parents died and – just as mortifying – he is left with responsibility for the farm and cows, 24/7. He reckons that by some measures, livestock do unacceptable harm to climate and environment. He knows politicians, corporations and co-operatives can be unfair to farmers, disagrees 100 per cent that the United States has adequate animal welfare, and agrees 100 per cent that cows should graze pasture at least 120 days per year – or every day that weather permits.

There were also Americans who partly or completely disagreed that livestock agriculture unacceptably harms or is a major culprit in environmental and climate issues. They seem to be speaking from their personal experience of small farms that are less likely to do so.

Len Monroe, retired dairy journalist and part-time farmer in Wisconsin, denied that livestock agriculture unacceptably harms environment and climate. So did several others.

Rick Carlinni, author and veterinarian with US organic and conventional farm, co-operative, and multinational corporate experience, disagreed that livestock harm the environment and climate unacceptably: 'Current data does not support this premise.'

Nancy Centuri, organic market gardener in Snoqualmie Valley selling in Seattle Neighbourhood Farmers' Markets. She disagreed 100 per cent that livestock agriculture harms the environment and climate unacceptably.

Melanie Porta, retired science teacher who grew up on a Washington State dairy farm disagreed 100 percent that livestock ag is antithetical to environment and climate. Ben Elliot, retired aviation maintenance manager who grew up on a small farm in Maine but now lives on Puget Sound, disagreed 100 percent that livestock agriculture unacceptably harms the environment and climate, specifying: 'At least for family farms where animal population does not overload the land.'

Karen Saren, retired farmer near the Mount St Helens National Volcanic Monument, was unsure about – and startled by – the idea that livestock farming emits dangerous amounts of greenhouse gases: 'I have never heard of this before.'

Herbert Thomas, a grazing organic dairy farmer in Maine said, 'CAFOs and outdated or undereducated farming techniques, harm the environment.'

When Happy Larson, entertained the prospect that livestock farming entails unacceptable harm, she commented, 'I understand that the water consumption, the methane, the E. coli, the use of animal land and all the rest do not serve our planet well.' Moving on to the issues in the next two queries, she added that [plant-based], 'Impossible Burgers are amazingly delicious and greatly reduce the issues noted. Unfortunately, they're not that great for health due to the amount of salt and added fats. A better choice, long term, however, when some of the health concerns are successfully addressed while keeping the amazing flavour.'

Rita Carter, retired accountant in Oklahoma, agreed 100 per cent that livestock agriculture harms environment and climate: 'It's a known fact, for example, that industrial livestock farming is the leading contributor of pollutants to lakes, reservoirs, and groundwater systems, leading to pollution of our drinking water and the death of aquatic life.'

For retired office worker, skier and hiker Karen Suttler, livestock agriculture definitely harms the environment and climate: 'Yes, it does generate global greenhouse gas emissions, and is one of the leading causes of deforestation, biodiversity loss, and water pollution.'

Some respondents were more succinct in their comments, like Tim Finley: 'I can bear witness to that.'

Stan Danilow considered *Query 7: Livestock agriculture unacceptably harms the environment and climate.* This businessman – who owned a woodstove business committed to reducing GHGs –had no family farming history, but liked seeing cattle graze pasture, and was prepared to pay more for humanely produced dairy products.

Some American respondents were more ambivalent in their responses and comments. Mandy Alt, a homemaker in Houston, Texas, said she was unsure whether livestock agriculture threatened environment and climate: 'I waffle on this issue as it is so ingrained.'

Tanner Cross, medical worker with roots in Seattle, enjoyed Alta-Dena raw non-pasteurized milk, yogurt and cottage cheese in California before its acquisition by Dean Foods. He was disappointed when local farms moved from Los Angeles, due to high land prices, residential pressure and concerns about dairy waste and water quality. Does livestock agriculture unacceptably harm the environment and climate? He replied: 'I can only say this. East of where I live in California, they have moved almost all the cows to a different state. I believe Utah. But not sure of that.' Actually, many dairy farmers *did* leave Arcadia, Bellflower and Dairy City for the San Joaquin Valley, where 10,000 cow megadairies became the new norm, and cow ammonia and crop dust raised air quality concerns among California environmental authorities (Scholten 2006d, 2014: 97, 140).

Ken Mentzer, ex-military, motorcyclist, disagreed 100 per cent that livestock agriculture unacceptably harms the environment and climate: 'Farming, like any other professional discipline, can be pursued with higher or lower standards. Highly professional, ethical farming is not a contradiction in terms. Farms, and farmers, are more important than farming critics.... That is, if you like to EAT.'

Kal Charge, whose responses thus far come from his positionality as a business owner and concomitant faith in science-driven market capitalism, understands there are environmental and climate issues for livestock (as there are in the motorsports industry, now switching from petrol to electric energy): 'Yes, there is a negative impact on the environment, but I generally agree that much of it is being addressed – albeit a bit slowly.'

Randy Grein agreed livestock ag harms environment and climate, but suggested solutions could be engineered: 'Corporate practices, certainly. We can neutralize that impact, which likely will mean lower production, but I think we can handle that.'

Responses from the rest of the world are similar to those above.

Badur Banglar, staffer in the Milk Vita co-operative in Bangladesh, was unsure that livestock unacceptably harm the environment and climate. That may be because the country's dairy practices are broadly sustainable. Cattle waste is recycled on fields, and refrigeration systems are more climate friendly than earlier ones subject to freon (CFC) leaks,such as those addressed by the 1987 Montreal Protocol to protect the ozone layer.

Bernice, 19-year-old Gen Z student, in Granada, Spain, had agreed 100 per cent that it is not ethical to eat sentient animals like cows, goats, horses, pigs and sheep. She also agreed 100 per cent that livestock agriculture unacceptably harms the environment and climate. Among Millennial and Gen Z respondents, there may be a pattern of saying first, it is not ethical to eat sentient animals, and second, that livestock farms harm environment and climate.

Benjamin Ricardo, age 29 and a primary-school teacher in Spain, wanted animals to graze pasture traditionally, and was unsure about the ethics of eating them. He agreed livestock agriculture unacceptably harms the environment and climate but: 'Just when it's done without control or a scientific/ecological base.'

In New York, Berta Racarden, unpacked Query 7: 'Livestock agriculture harms the environment and climate when taken to a scale that is inappropriate. Small subsistence farming took place in the past without harm to the environment in the proportions we see today. It is massive livestock agriculture that is harmful, not livestock agriculture per se.'

Bertran Kiung, Newcastle PhD student from China, seemed to think deeply before expressing opinions; these evolved and became more nuanced in the process of addressing each query. He disagreed that livestock agriculture unacceptably harms the environment and climate saying: 'It depends . . . Because cattle graze grass and produce waste, it can harm the earth or soil. But farmers can sow the grass in time and reasonably use the waste. It doesn't necessarily harm the environment.'

Similarly, Ileni Fharad, Newcastle University PhD student and teaching assistant from Libya, had no family farming history and assumed farmers and animals were treated well. She wanted animals to graze pasture, but was unwilling to pay more for pastured produce. She disagreed 100 per cent that it is unethical to eat animal meat, and disagreed 100 per cent that livestock farming unacceptably harms environment and climate.

Omsin (no surname), teacher in Thailand, disagreed that environment and climate suffer unacceptably from livestock. When this author visted rural Isan province in North-East Thailand in 2004, agricultural methods and technology were comparable to those used in the US between 1950 and 1970. There were some farms with over 300 dairy cows, but the cows were moderate producers milked with belted DeLaval type vacuum machines in airy sheds, not on the shiny fifty-cow carousel milking parlours now seen in Mexico, New Zealand, Australia and the US.

Commenting on technological change in global dairying, an Antipodean professor of environment agreed dairying had some negative environmental impact, saying "The numbers don't stack up on complete substitution', referring to non-dairy substitutes for animal products.

1. https://www.collinsdictionary.com/submission/4923/Piscetarian

Q8. *'Vegan meals can be as tasty as those using ingredients from livestock.'*

Q8 Vegan meals can be as tasty as those using ingredients from livestock.

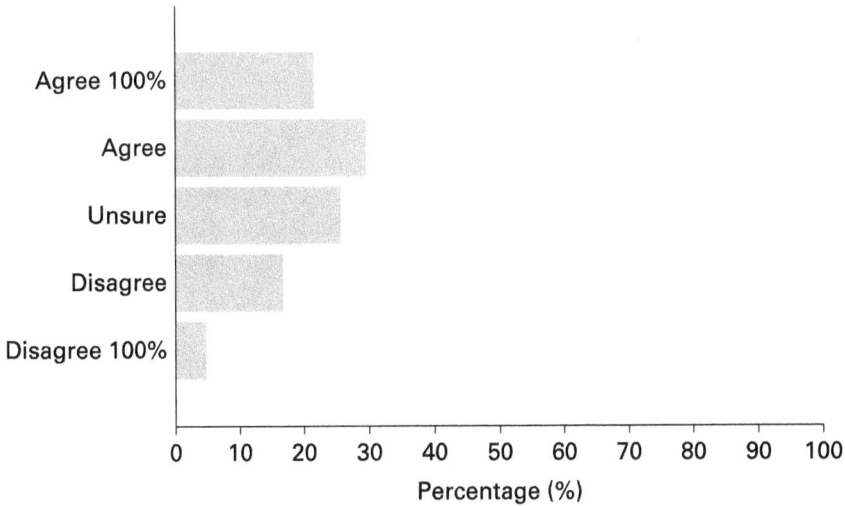

Percentage (%)

Plant-based foods are trending. A robust 22 per cent of respondents agreed 100 per cent, that vegan meals can be as tasty as those made with meat, and 30% agreed. Their comments suggest that some confused the word *vegan*, which denotes food made entirely without animal dairy or meat products, with vegetarianism, which allows dairy products, or even with Piscetarian vegetarianism,[1] which allows fish, but not poultry, game or red meat. Only 5 per cent disagreed 100 per cent that vegan meals were uninspiring compared to the 'meat-and-two-veg' diet so common in both the UK and the US. Yet this enthusiasm for vegan options prompts the question: will vegan food seem as tasty if eaten *every* meal, week after week? Experienced eaters say the answer has much to do with herbs and spices. As indicated in Chapter 1, the alternative food industry is growing exponentially and much of this has to do with reception of such foods, e.g., ready meals, by those accustomed to the flavours of animal-based products.

Voices of the stakeholders

Assuming such meals would be made from scratch rather than purchased as ready meals, Tom Charles, county carbon management officer, in Northern England, agreed vegan meals can be tasty: 'They are getting better, but most people lack the knowledge to prepare them, and they are often seen as lacking something. This is changing, though.'

Harold Daniels disagreed, explaining that vegan meals were dull 'without seasoning, which usually isn't easy to produce, or needs to be shipped in, depending on where you live. Taste surely has to be a mid-rank consideration, unless we are in a consumer society where taste is sometimes the only selling point for a product with no nutritional value. Many localized, traditional and market-driven cultural factors here, which are helpful or not.'

Richard Beakins, retired social scientist and dairy expert agreed vegan meals can be as tasty and suggested that aspirants, 'Read Yotam Ottolenghi'. Although Ottolenghi[2] is not personally a vegetarian, he celebrates veggie dishes without trying to make them taste like meat.

Nanci Barnes had personal insights on various diets, but was unsure about the relative tastiness of vegan/carnivore diets: 'Personally having been a vegetarian for fourteen years, then [returning] back to an omnivore diet, and now a "happy food" consumer, vegan has never floated my boat. Vegetarian food at our London geography conference in 2019, before COVID-19, was evidence of that!!! Sustainably resourced, distributed and marketed food is the way to go – so the Tesco big guys would need a different supermarket business model.'

Neil Barnes, company director and consultant in Scotland, agreed vegan meals can be as tasty as those with ingredients from livestock. His comments did not disclose whether or not he would enjoy eating vegan at *every* meal for the rest of his life.

Elaine Oordt, gardener and horticulturist in North-East England, agreed 100 per cent that vegan meals are as tasty as those derived from livestock: 'Yes, I regularly eat vegan meals and cook them for guests at our B & B. But I also eat meat – my late husband described us as ethical omnivores.'

Loren Marton, youth & community worker in North-East England, agreed 100 per cent that vegan meals could excite taste buds like carnivorous fare, but cautioned: 'I think a lot of work would need to be done first.' It may be a long and winding road to universal veganism.

Celia Cremen, in Newcastle, UK, is a vegan who enthusiastically agreed 100 per cent that vegan meals can be tasty as meat-based options: 'Even more so. You can bite into your burger with gusto, without getting those weird bits and wondering what they are. And if you choose whole foods, you can eat loads without worry about weight gain, cholesterol, etc.'

In the US, agricultural programme co-ordinator Kate Ryan knew much about food, farming and animals, but less about veganism: 'Can't say I've enjoyed any 100% vegan meals, but then I tend to avoid them like the plague. Miss the heme.'

Some with direct experience in dairy farming welcome such foods. Tina Dice, dairy farmer from Pine Palms, New York, was open to vegan food, but oncerned about nutrition: 'Vegan meals might possibly taste good. But they are definitely less nutritious. And still bad for the environment, re. mono-cropped soy and corn and wheat, tillage and chemical use.'

Ken Mentzer agreed that vegan meals can be as tasty as those incorporating livestock products, but added observations on ethics and nutrition: 'Vegan meals can in some cases [taste good], but most often are not.'

Happy Larson has, travelled widely in Africa and Asia, where meat is not always on the menu. She agreed 100 per cent that vegetarian and vegan food can match the tastiness of meat. How is that possible? 'It's all about the spices, the herbs and, unfortunately, the salt.'

Such sentiments raise the question of how nutritious plant-based diets are. Decades ago, friends who were then in their late twenties adopted a vegetarian diet. This carpenter and his family ate a Mexican-style diet of beans, rice, vegetables and some dairy. In snowy winter months, they developed chronic colds and flu. Even though theirs was a lacto-vegetarian diet, not strictly vegan, a doctor urged them to return meat to their diet for B vitamins and dietary iron, i.e., heme/haem. Their immune systems improved and they continued to eat some meat in their vegetable- and legume-rich diet.

Ken E. Tillmann, raised on a dairy farm, retired from aviation maintenance and office work, benefits from years of work as a chef in an Olympic National Park resort. He remains a fine cook, gourmet even, but has always relied on meat as a central component in meals. He described himself as, 'Unsure [about vegan dishes]', but his eggplant parmesan has such marvelous texture, diners assume it is made with veal.

Randy Grein shared what is easily observed among those in the younger generations, that many are shifting to alternative-food diets. He partly agreed vegan meals can be as tasty as America's carnivorous mainstream and noted, 'My son went vegan this year and my wife has had to give up most meat and dairy . . . I've not cared that much, and while the new "meatless meats" do not taste like meat to me they are quite good – just different.'

We consider Berta Racarden in the context of where she works: New York City where alternative food companies are now listed at the New York Stock Exchange. NYC has been called a vegan mecca, where strict vegan dishes are available at approximately 150 Chinese, Japanese, Korean and other dining establishments (in fact, Chinese cuisine has a long history of meat-substitute dishes). She agreed 100 per cent that vegan meals can be as tasty as those using ingredients from livestock: 'It is a matter of taste, but there is no reason vegan meals should be less tasty.'

Those we've heard from before are open-minded about vegan foods.

Kal Charge, motorsports entrepreneur near Seattle, likes steak and was unsure about the taste of vegan food, but his marketing finger was the wind for the next big thing: 'I've not tasted enough vegan meals to know. Perhaps the Burger King meatless hamburger will be a good test.'

Ned Harold, communication specialist for an oil company near Bellingham, Washington, had opportunities to sample cuisines across the US, when he worked for a company with its own plane. His verdict on the tastiness of vegan meals was measured: 'Some are, some are not.'

Karen Suttler agreed 100 per cent, lauding vegan food as 'Very tasty, and no animal cruelty involved'.

Rita Carter has so much experience with meatless diets that she seems to welcome diets *sans* livestock products: 'I was a vegetarian for most of my adult life. I found vegetarian cooking to be much more diverse than my previous diet of meat, quite delicious, and healthy.'

In the rest of the world, we find similar responses. Brijit Deana Caldera, a lawyer in Brazil, is critical of livestock practices in her responses to other queries and agreed vegan food can be as tasty as meat dishes.

A New Zealand earth sciences academic was alert to the political-economic implications to Oceania if plant-based foods, analogue meats or laboratory-grown meats replaced his country's massive dairy and meat exports. He agreed vegan meals can be as tasty as meat-based ones, while cautioning on health and nutritional grounds 'But taste is only one criterion of a vegan diet, the pro's and con's need to be listed in each context'.

Q9. Will there be a complete shift to meat substitutes?

Q9 Plant-based dairy and laboratory-grown meat substitutes could replace food animals soon.

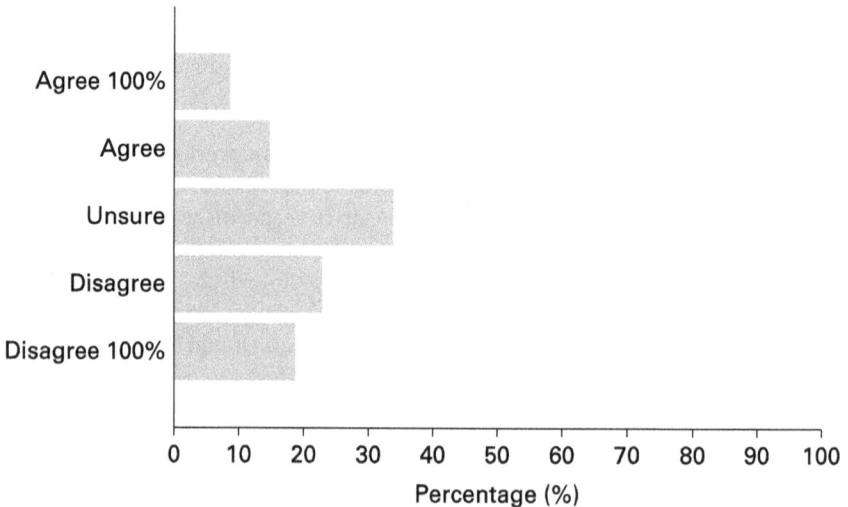

Our 100 stakeholders welcome animal product substitutes, as long as they are tasty, and many agreed they are. But 'unsure' is the overriding reply to this final query – accounting for 34 per cent of respondents – to the prospect that plant-based dairy and laboratory-grown meat substitutes could replace food animals soon. Only 28 per cent either agreed or disagreed 100 per cent. Rather than presenting their comments first, we return to what underlies the turn away from consumption of animals, and in the process highlight a range of issues discussed in Chapter 1. Much what is debated is and will be in the mainstream media and will influence the views and in turn the behaviour of stakeholders worldwide. It is crucial that all the facts are considered and questions addressed when the issues are not clear. Stakeholders' comments appear at chapter end. Many of these show awareness of the points discussed first.

A shift to substitutes has been pushed by animal welfarists who altruistically question the ethics of livestock management systems in which sentient creatures suffer boredom, stress, actual pain, truncated lives, varying in different production systems, generally bifurcated into pasture (grazing) or feedlots (confined CAFOs). Politics are also driven by human self-interest, engaged by evidence that the burgeoning human population's appetite for dairy and meat flirts with cataclysmic climate change (FAO 2006; Goodland and Anhang 2009; Gates 2021). Zero Population Growth advocates shrug their shoulders in despair, at humankind's awkward attempts to solve Malthusian crises on finite planet Earth, foreseen in Paul Ehrlich and Anne Ehrlich's 1968 bestseller *The Population Bomb*.

Such fears were downplayed by Republican candidate Donald Trump, who, as he touted the benefits of 'clean coal' to voters in the 2016 and 2020 presidential campaigns, claimed that radical Democrats not only wanted to take away Americans' guns, but also their hamburgers (2020b). President Biden reversed former President Trump's climate politics by returning to the Paris Climate Agreement, adopted by 196 Parties at the Conference of the Parties, COP 21 Paris, on 12 December 2015, and entered into force on 4 November 2016 (We will visit COP26 below.) Its aim is to limit global warming to well below 2°C, preferably to 1.5°C, compared to pre-industrial levels. Biden dodged right-wing charges that he would seize guns, outlaw cheeseburgers or even stop fracking for petroleum. He pledged a paradigm shift from petroleum to a sustainable electric-and-hydrogen economy, promised to reduce greenhouse gas (GHG) emissions – not least by converting federally owned vehicles including presidential limousines, National Park trucks and US Army tanks from petroleum to hybrid or pure electric power. This could provide enough well-paying infrastructure jobs to strengthen middle-class prosperity, well-being and mental health.

How does climate change link to livestock? An apparent increase in climate-related disasters suggests quests for Trump's vaunted clean coal are retrograde. Massive range fires in Australia, and drought-ridden California, have recently decimated flora and fauna, leaving land vulnerable to erosion, as they emit atmosphere- and ocean-warming carbon (Howitt et al. 2018). Climate pessimists believe transcontinental dust from such fires reaches the Himalayas, decreasing albedo effect, hastening snowmelt in a feedback loop. Ultimately this means less glacial melt into India's rivers for agricultural irrigation, interspersed with glacial fragmentation disasters, such as one that caused devastating damage to a hydroelectric dam and killed 170 people in the Dhauliganga river valley of India (*Telegraph* 2021a). These disasters force us to confront the ethical, environmental and political implications of food systems. Whole Life Cycle Assessments are probably the best means to model dairy and meat systems. But they are complicated and, in the examples below, one study often challenges the assumptions, accuracy and political or bureaucratic affiliations of other studies.

How realistic is a world shift to plant-based foods? After all, meat-eating has been a driver in human evolution and brain development, hunting, military activities, and holistic farming for millennia. Who would argue that humans need smaller brains? Most cultures utilize the consumption of meat to mark seasons, religious ceremonies, rites of passage and so on. Vegetarian cultures which do not eat meat, often source protein and other nutrients from milk products and eggs. Vegan societies (such as Jains) eat plant-based foods, including whole grains and legumes, and meat and egg substitutes made from sorghum, peas and beans. Such diets are generally responsible for only minimal greenhouse gas emissions.

Dairy and greenhouse gases

In the *Journal of Animal Science* (1999) Harper et al. showed methane emissions from grazing cattle were about four-times higher than those from feedlot cattle. Similarly, Doreau et al. (*Journal of Animal Science* 2011: 19) concluded: 'In summary, our results show that a very high concentrate diet for finishing young bulls (86%) strongly decreases methane emission ... compared to diets based on hay: concentrates (49:51) and corn silage: concentrates (63:37).' Imported soybean concentrates helped reduce methane, and a small uptick in nitrous oxide and carbon dioxide emissions was offset by methane reductions.

2006 was a nadir for people who altruistically wished to see cattle exercising natural behaviours, grazing grass pasture and not confined in barns or feedlots. As aforementioned, a paradigm shift began with publication of Henning Steinfeld and team's (UN-FAO 2006) report for the Food and Agricultural Organization titled *Livestock's Long Shadow*, which highlighted an alarming 18 per cent (cut, after criticism, to 14.5 per cent in the FAO report by Gerber et al. 2013) share by dairy and meat systems to climate-warming greenhouse gases carbon dioxide, methane and nitrous oxide.

This was a very unpleasant surprise, as it vied with the contribution by transport whose auto and aviation emissions previously topped the suspects list for carbon loading. It required time for scientists and laypersons to understand that carbon dioxide was not the only dangerous greenhouse gas among methane, nitrous oxide, ozone and water vapor. Steinfeld's report (FAO 2006) was an eye-opening multiple of previous benign estimates of ruminant animals' GHG emissions, perhaps 3 per cent to 5 per cent of the anthropologically linked total. Traditional pastoralists claimed innocence with regard to GHG emissions by projecting blame on intensive CAFO feedlot operations, which notoriously sourced inputs an average 1,500 miles from suppliers, and in turn trucked milk trans-continentally, improving shelf life with microfiltration that critics claimed harmed nutrition.

Three years later, in 2009, the FAO (2006) estimate of livestock accountable for 18 per cent of GHG emissions and its comparison of land-use change by transport and livestock sectors, was attacked by Maurice Pitesky, Kimberly Stackhouse and Frank Mitloehner (*Advances in Agronomy* 103, 2009: 1–40; Scholten 2014: 189) who set direct livestock emissions (enteric fermentation, manure, and respiration) at less than 3 per cent of total human-related emissions.

More farmers and activists were alerted to the dangers of greenhouse effect from carbon loading. Awareness grew slowly that methane was a dangerously strong greenhouse gas persisting one or two decades, while carbon dioxide was less dangerous but persisted for a century or more. Livestock produced methane, levels of which varied with the amount of cellulose in the forage or the mix of grain digested in ruminants' multiple stomachs.

Livestock and dairy emissions

For years, the term 'carbon footprint' was shorthand for anthropogenic GHG emissions. Gradually, climate scientists and activists understood methane was dairy's Achilles' heel. Its permutations were mysterious, and not a little irritating. It helps to bear in mind that Frank Mitloehner, the acclaimed scientist at University of California Davis who co-authored Pitesky et al. (2009), eventually accepted the FAO (2010) estimate that the livestock sector emits about 14.5 per cent of global GHGs. In a 2019 video, Mitloehner said cows and other ruminants account for just 4 per cent of greenhouse gases produced in the US, and beef cattle for just 2 per cent of direct emissions. Mitloehner was interviewed in a documentary by Amy Quinton titled 'Making cattle more sustainable' (UC Davis 2019). Chapter 6 will summarize conclusions on GHGs.

If carbon dioxide and methane weren't complicated enough, ruminants also release nitrous oxide in urine and manure. Climate journalist Sabrina Shankman (*Inside Climate News* 2019) notes N_2O is 300 times more potent than carbon dioxide, and also depletes the ozone layer. But since N_2O, like methane (CH_4 is about thirty-five times more potent than CO_2), has a shorter half-life than CO_2, treating it is nuanced. Nitrous oxide is related to nitrogen (N), a problematic that divides extensive and intensive approaches to farming. Nitrogen is necessary to crops and pasture, but since German scientist Justus von Liebig synthesized nitrogen fertilizer in the nineteenth century, it has been overused in most regions of the world, from India to Britain's Lake District, which regulates its use on littoral farmland (Scholten 1997a: 181).

Intensive feedlot CAFOs are hotspots of point pollution with huge manure lagoons which, if not agitated (i.e., regularly stirred to add oxygen) generate climate-unfriendly N_2O from manure pits. Dairy farm chores for teens on family farms include monitoring and mechanically stirring, or agitating, lagoons. Extensive pastoralists mock this technological scenario, saying it's simpler to release imprisoned cows onto pasture, to deliver the nitrogen naturally. Why don't intensive farmers let cows graze pasture and drop cowpats? Land scarcity is the excuse in some quarters. Historically, dairying is conducted on urban peripheries, so that fragile milk does not deteriorate before processing into durable buttermilk or cheese, and these heavy foods are close to consumers (Atkins 2010). For example, many California dairy farms were suburban orange groves converted to pasture. As urbanization encroached, farmers sold outer pastures to new home owners, moved cows from grass pasture to feedlot confinement near the milking parlour, intensified fodder production on remaining area, and outsourced extra hay and inputs from afar. Urbanization of those orange groves was complete when dairy farms (some managed by my relatives) had to move from, say, urbanized Bellflower to the San Joaquin Valley now suffering drought (Howitt et al. 2018). *The beat goes on.*

Dairy farming's contribution to greenhouse gases and the existential threat to the climate

Understanding or at least being aware of these details is crucial in weighing whether the future of dairy farming should be a return to small operations or whether dairy's contribution to GHGs is unacceptably high and, together with other negative factors we've discussed, should instead point to a shift away from consumption of animal-based products.

In a 2010 follow-up to *Livestock's Long Shadow* (FAO 2006), an FAO team led by Pierre Gerber and advised by Henning Steinfeld, issued *Greenhouse Gas Emissions from the Dairy Sector: A Life Cycle Assessment* (FAO 2010: 50) which reiterated that enteric methane emissions per kilogram of milk are relatively low in intensive systems compared to extensive systems, but noted, 'the fraction of methane coming from manure storage is relatively high (15% to 20%, compared to less than 5% in the extensive systems of the arid and humid zones)' – that is why manure lagoons must be agitated regularly. Dairy families beset by low farmgate prices, and needing to enlarge herds for profitability, realized that to keep green credentials, best practice now included anaerobic digesting technology for manure pits. (The switch was already underway in 2001, at the National Dairy Leaders Conference in Sun Valley, Idaho on 9/11, when I breakfasted with family friends. They were installing an anaerobic digester on their 300-cow farm near Portland, Oregon, with financing from Enron and Pacific Gas & Electric. USDA incentives accelerated installation of anaerobic digesters by families who moved their herds from pasture to CAFO feedlot management. Critics claimed digesters did not eliminate discharges into groundwater, but acknowledged that if manure is spread quickly, little methane is emitted (McKenzie 2019).

Small-scale biogas units in dairy villages in India share similarities with higher-tech anaerobic digesters in the US (Scholten 2019b). A properly managed anaerobic digester, utilizing a Combined Heat and Power (CHP) unit, reduces odour from slurry and reduces pathogens in the slurry which otherwise could cause crop disease, by breaking down microorganisms in the absence of oxygen. Dairy-fish-crops-biogas systems have been promoted in dairy industry development programmes by FAO-UN in various countries, including Bangladesh, Ethiopia, Mongolia, Thailand and Uganda (Scholten 2015: 461; Dugdill et al. 2013). The end product of the process is methane-rich biogas, used for smokeless household cooking and lighting in villages, and similar purposes in intensive feedlot CAFOs world-wide. Technology continues to improve treatment of nitrogen and phosphorous in cattle waste on big US dairies (*Farm Journal's Milk* 2020).

Pastoralists were disappointed by the conclusion of Steinfeld et al. (FAO 2006: 236) that, if projected future global demand for livestock products is to be met, 'it is hard to see an alternative to intensification', and as an answer to pollution, 'intensification will lead to gradual reductions of resource use and waste emissions across the board'. In other words, CAFO feedlot confinement was to be the solution to cattle on grassland that emitted relatively more methane (but less nitrous oxide in the absence of anaerobic manure digesters). They granted that intensive systems generated appreciable CO_2 emissions in global supply chains and transport miles, but assumed these were cancelled by higher methane emissions because the grass such ruminants munch has higher cellulose content, resulting in greater enteric fermentation (belches, etc.), than the easily digestible concentrates and fodder fed to fancy CAFO feedlot cows! That said, seeding grasslands with easily digestible legumes cuts emissions. When I was five years old, my father pulled up red and white clovers to show me the root nodules making this possible.

Nevertheless, Steinfeld admitted that if all livestock switched from extensive to intensive systems, marginal gains in GHG reduction might diminish – while local areas would endure increased emissions from manure, fossil fuel and other inputs. *Livestock Science* found that farmers seeking cost-effective GHG mitigation often turned to less replacement of dairy cattle and replacement of concentrates by single by-products grown near their farms; switches like this could increase cow longevity, decrease transport emissions, and achieve total mitigation of 310 to 360 g CO_2-equivalents per kg milk, a significant reduction of 25 per cent–30 per cent compared to 1990, with low costs (Vellinga et al. 2009: 185; 186–95).

According to Steinfeld et al. (2006) the lower level of emissions per unit of product in intensive systems compared to extensive dairy systems explains how US herds produce more milk with fewer cows over time. This is driven by two factors: easier digestibility of the animals' largely out-sourced feed, and higher genetic milk productivity level. Unfortunately, enhanced genetics and easily-digestible fodder do *not* necessarily improve longevity.

Because cattle grazing high-cellulose pasture emit more methane than intensively raised animals, and livestock on grassland use more land than confined ones, there is less forest available to absorb GHGs. The UK Agricultural Development and Advisory Service (ADAS 2017) estimated that cattle raising accounts for 26 per cent of Earth's ice-free land for grazing and 33 per cent of global arable land for livestock feed crops. Africa and Asia are driving world demand for livestock products; it was projected to double by 2030, so serious thought was given to retaining and expanding forest for climate stability. *Pastoralists muse that if world population had stabilized at 1950 levels, at 2.5 billion compared to 7.8 billion in 2020, cattle would have more room to graze.*

Goodland and Anhang's critique

More *merde* hit pasture fans in 2009, when *World Watch Magazine* (Nov/Dec 2009; also Goodland and Anhang 2011) featured 'Livestock and Climate Change' by Robert Goodland and Jeff Anhang (2009). Englishman Goodland (1939–2013) attended McGill University in Canada for degrees in biology, tropical ecology, and a subsequent PhD on ecosystems in Brazil. He began consulting for the World Bank in 1975, and became their first full-time ecologist in 1978, engaged in socio-environmental mitigation of dams and other projects. WB colleagues included Nobel Prize winner Joseph Stiglitz. Goodland continued working on global environmental mitigation and renewable energy after retirement in 2001, and will be remembered for his and Anhang's 2009 *World Watch Magazine* critique of Steinfeld et al.'s *Livestock's Long Shadow* (FAO 2006). They criticized Steinfeld et al. (FAO 2006) for failure to develop a true whole life cycle analysis in estimating GHG emissions in livestock systems. The criticism would boomerang. Goodland and Anhang topped FAO estimates (14.5 per cent–18 per cent), ascribing a shocking 51 per cent of annual worldwide GHG emissions to cows, pigs, poultry, etc. Recalculating *Livestock's Long Shadow* (FAO 2006), they focused not just on carbon or fossil fuel or methane reductions, or on forest protection and regeneration – but on all at the same time. Goodland & Anhang (2009) claimed Steinfeld had:

- Overlooked animal respiration, which doubles livestock's annual GHGs: 'Carbon is released from ecosystems as carbon dioxide and methane by the process of respiration that takes place in both plants and animals' (FAO 2006: 85). Goodland and Anhang imply Steinfeld et al. (2006) were stuck in an outdated paradigm assuming carbon dioxide and livestock respiration are balanced by photosynthesis. But (Goodland 2013ab) maintained this is invalidated by unprecedented livestock and feed production, deforestation and burning during the twentieth and twenty-first centuries.
- Overlooked land already in use for livestock in their report. The FAO only included change in land use and deforestation which is small by comparison.
- Underestimated the disruptive GHG effects of cattle methane (CH_4) in different time frames. FAO considered CH_4 to be twenty-one to twenty-five times stronger than CO_2 over a 100-year time frame. Goodland and Anhang

recommend the International Panel on Climate Change (IPCC) twenty-year time frame, which boosts methane's global warming potential (GWP) to 72.

Goodland and Anhang (2009) also claimed Steinfeld et al. (FAO 2006) misallocated, or excluded, livestock deforestation in countries such as Argentina, and excluded farmed fish for cattle feed and human consumption.

Reader response was so strong that a linked article of criticisms and responses was published the following spring in *World Watch Magazine* (Mar/Apr 2010). Over the next half decade, fissures widened between FAO- and World Bank-linked research teams. After Goodland's retirement from the World Bank, he remained active on issues in Malaysia, Indonesia and climate circles generally. He wrote a letter to *Global Change Biology* (published 2014: 2042–4) faulting the Steinfeld (FAO 2006) conclusion of a mere 18 per cent livestock contribution to anthropogenic GHGs, due to their 'failure to develop a true-life cycle estimate'. Goodland repeated their estimate for the World Bank (Goodland and Anhang 2009) that livestock accounted for 51 per cent of human-linked GHGs. Then Goodland twisted the knife, saying Steinfeld et al. (2006) were 'disadvantaged by including no specialist in environmental assessment (the profession of Jeff Anhang and me)' (*GCB* 2014: 2042–4). Goodland also faulted the FAO (2006) for forgetting most experts agreed climate mitigation required capping atmospheric carbon by the year 2020, and cutting all GHG emissions 80–95 per cent by the year 2050 – a failure inexplicably letting them 'project a doubling in livestock production by 2050, paired with only minor prescriptions for reducing GHG emissions'. *Was this joined-up-thinking?* Goodland was right to fault it.

Observing World Bank projects since 1975 may have given Robert Goodland a sense that, when FAO cut its (Steinfeld et al. 2006) estimate of livestock's total anthropogenic emissions from 18 per cent greenhouse gases to 14.5 per cent (FAO 2010), it acted more from regard for the livestock industry than climate science. He seemed to imply the FAO had vested interest in cattle propagation, while his World Bank view prioritized risk assessment that ensured wider global economic sustainability. Goodland and Anhang (2009) hinted the International Meat Secretariat and the International Dairy Federation allied with the FAO to downplay livestock's role in climate disequilibrium. Others feared Goodland was manipulated by a petroleum industry tired of blame for climate change. It may have felt that blame shared is halved.

When invited by FAO Rome, Berlin and Beijing to explain their *World Watch Magazine* claim that livestock accounted for 51 per cent of greenhouse gases, Goodland (2009) noted that after the FAO began in 1945, global human population tripled and livestock sextupled by 2009 (Chomping Climate Change 2014):

[L]ivestock have changed from being one of many sectors dependent on natural capital to being today's top determinant of the future of natural capital. [. . .] livestock are the leading driver of deforestation, while consuming up to half the catch of marine organisms and as much as half of all crops brought to market.

Declining fish stocks, including humble krill, hint at the hollowness of the arguments made by those sustainable intensification advocates who claim shutting cows in sheds and feeding them soybeans and fishmeal concentrates is a long-term remedy for livestock GHG emissions. Humanity's heavy CO_2 footprint has already smashed that pipedream. Goodland urged the FAO to moderate livestock production and consumption. A 25 per cent cut in livestock products would discomfit fellow policy makers and millions (or billions!) of meat-eaters and livestock producers, he acknowledged, but their children might thank them in the long run.

Robert Goodland was a gadfly, challenging World Bank colleagues, government departments and commercial interests to curb global warming. He cofounded Chomping Climate Change (2014), an online source which, after his death, continued to urge reforestation of the Earth's green lungs, and switching to meat and dairy substitutes. Green allies included former Beatles songwriter and vegetarian Paul McCartney.

Another was Ethan Brown, who says he ate a lot of meat on his flexitarian way to starting Beyond Meat in 2009. Brown explains that five plant basics – amino acids, lipids, water, trace minerals and trace carbohydrates – can be converted from plants to fake meat. These five basics could defeat the apocalyptic Four Horsemen signified by climate change, animal welfare, natural resource scarcity, and human health (*Business Insider* 2015). Meanwhile, efforts to limit average earth temperature rises to 2°C by the year 2100 lagged.

Pasture vs intensive beef & dairy

Where CAFOs are held to contribute less to GHGs, this adds ammunition to calls for continuation of the practice. One robust defender of intensification in US-style livestock systems has been Jude L. Capper. She obtained her BSc and PhD on ruminant nutrition and behaviour from Harper Adams University in the UK, before a faculty stint at Washington State University in the US, and work as an independent consultant, before returning to Harper Adams. In her presentations in agricultural events, trade magazines such as *Hoard's Dairyman* (2012), and academic journals, she has advocated the use of biotechnology and genetic modification to achieve production efficiencies in crops, beef and dairy production. In 'The Environmental Impact of Dairy Production: 1944 compared with 2007' (*Journal of Animal Science* 2009), Capper, R.A. Cady (of Elanco which bought rBST from Monsanto) and D.E. Bauman note the impressive milk production gains from fewer cows in the US described in previous chapters. In Capper, Cady and Bauman's defence of biotechnology, such as glyphosate-resistant Bacillus thuringiensis (Bt) maize for cattle feed, and genetic modification in the recombinant bovine somatotrophin (rBST/rBGH) dairy hormone, they maintain that these reduce resource use, water use, land committed to production and human labour, while reducing GHG emissions (Capper et al. 2008).

During this period, Charles 'Chuck' Benbrook, then at Washington State University and the Organic Center in Washington DC, addressed the Cow of the

Future Project by agribusiness to alter diets and animal nutrition, rumen function, genetics and herd structure, in order to cut methane emissions 25 per cent by 2020 (Knapp et al. 2011). Benbrook's support came from the Packard Foundation, Aurora Organic Dairy, Horizon Organic, Organic Valley, Stonyfield Farm and WhiteWave Foods. (These entities were capable of infighting themselves, not to mention sometimes tricky relations with family-scale dairy farmers.) Concerned that conventional agribusiness would ignore cow health and longevity, Benbrook devised the *Shades of Green Dairy Farm Calculator*, which details four scenarios: significantly, Jerseys making under 50 lbs of milk a day on year-round grass pasture in Scenario 1 averaged 6.3 lactations over 8.5 years and won the race to sustainability, beating the confined GMO-enhanced conventional Holsteins making over 70 lbs of milk a day that averaged only 2.3 lactations in 4.3 years (Benbrook Oct 2010, 2012a, 2014; Scholten 2014: 210-12). Scenario 4 cows had very high emissions because archaea microorganisms released methane in megadairy manure lagoons – another reason anaerobic digesters are mandated on megadairy CAFOs. Life-cycle analysis by Benbrook (2010, 2012a) found organic pasture-based dairying had a lighter environmental hoofprint than intensive confinement dairying – which contradicts the verdicts in favour of feedlot intensification by Steinfeld et al. (2006), Goodland and Anhang (2009) and other studies. If cows could vote, animal welfarists imagine them voting for 6.3 lactations grazing pasture over 8.5 years, rather than 2.3 lactations in a boring feedlot over 4.3 years.

In 'A case study of the carbon footprint of milk from high-performing confinement and grass-based dairy farms' by Donal O'Brien et al., conclusions were – unsurprisingly – more favourable to CAFOs than in Charles Benbrook's studies (*Journal of Dairy Science* 2014: 1835–51). In her 2013 article asking 'Should we reject animal source foods to save the planet?' in the *South African Journal of Animal Science*, Capper acknowledges the steep demand rise for dairy and meat accompanying the human population rise to 9.5 billion by the mid-twenty-first century, and laments the difficulty of getting consumer acceptance of 'modern best practices and technologies'. She concludes that consumers can only be served by 'collaboration between producers, veterinarians, other allied industry and academia in order to ensure that animals are bred, fed and cared for using management practices and technologies that will enable them to perform to their genetic potential' (Capper et al. 2009: 243).

As we saw in previous chapters, Jude L. Capper's support of intensive megadairies was industry mainstream in the US. But 'organic' megadairies in the desert have also been contributing to the bankrupting of family-scale organic certified grazing farms across the country. Visitors to the UK were surprised to see cattle grazing outside London-to-Edinburgh trains. Britons have been less tolerant of the US 'get big or get out' mentality. Consumers and small farmers resisted the opening of an 8,100-cow megadairy at Nocton, Lincolnshire, in 2010 (*Guardian* 2010; *Daily Mail* 2016; Ipsos-MORI 2018) when a MORI poll, commissioned by Compassion in World Farming (CIWF), Vegetarians International Voice for Animals (VIVA) and World Society For The Protection Of Animals (WSPA), found 61 per cent of people in Britain would not buy milk if they knew it was produced in large-scale indoor sheds. But since 2016, Brexit has threatened that status.

A decade later, Capper spoke to the Royal Norfolk Agricultural Association, saying that for every negative story in the media, farmers needed not to 'debunk' negative environmental or animal welfare media stories, but to 'pre-bunk' stacks of positive stories, generating 'a tidal wave of factual information' to counteract 'bad news bias' (*Eastern Daily Press* 2020). Consider that the average herd size in the UK was at the time 148, with scant megadairies, compared to 273 cows in the much larger US (USDA 2019). After Oxford University students, worried about greenhouse effect, voted to ban beef and lamb in their college dining halls, Capper rightly pointed out that only 65 per cent of the UK is suitable for grazing. She said, 'We hear a lot about how beef is the enemy and beef is bad, but we really do need to look at our fossil-fuel consumption far more closely.' Perhaps it was more logical to ban long-haul London-to-New York flights, each of which produced the carbon equivalent of raising 50.8 kg of beef per passenger – over double the annual UK consumption of 18.2kg per person. Capper also claimed the carbon footprint of beef production is about four times higher in Latin America than in Western Europe, and that milk yield varies from 2,000kg per year in India to 11,000 kg per year in the US. She said if every cow in the world had the same 8,140 kg yield as the average UK cow, the world could maintain its total dairy supply using 181 million fewer dairy cows, i.e., 69 per cent fewer cows. Perhaps choosing her words carefully, Capper added: 'Having said that, I'm not pushing for US-type dairying [...] It isn't just about pushing and pushing for higher yields. It is about improving everything on our farms.' UK cows are probably not pushing for US-type dairying either.

Veganism?

Did Henning Steinfeld (FAO 2006) think a switch from carnivorous to vegan diets could mitigate climate and save the human race? Perhaps, but others saw the FAO and Steinfeld instead as defenders of livestock ag – whose negative effects on climate they had pussyfooted around with low GHG estimates of 14.5 per cent–18 per cent. When interviewed on the future of the EU livestock sector by Sarantis Michalopoulos (*Euractiv* 2019), Steinfeld said, 'Veganism is certainly not for everyone'. This was especially true for women, young children, people in food deserts or in lower-income quintiles. He went on: 'A vegan diet is often deficient in iron, zinc, calcium and vitamin D [...] supplementation to a vegan diet may be costly and may require access to a diverse set of pulses and vegetables that may not be readily available everywhere.' Steinfeld knew veganism is problematic because the global livestock sector can be seen through four lenses: food and nutrition security; livelihoods and economic growth; animal health and welfare; and climate and natural resources use. Technical innovation in any one area may cause unintended disruptions in others.

To wit, Goodland and Anhang (2009) who estimated livestock GHGs at 51 per cent of the global total (nearly three times Steinfeld et al.'s (FAO 2006) estimate of

18 per cent, suggested replacing some contemporary livestock products with alternatives such as whole grains, and meat and egg substitutes. Was veganism knocking on the door? Such dietary shifts might allow reforestation for increased large-scale carbon sequestration (Bellarby et al. 2013). Unfortunately, Goodland's deadline was 2017. *That ship has sailed.*

A dose of practicality was added to this contretemps by the UK Agricultural Development and Advisory Service (ADAS 23 Oct 2017). A paper titled 'Grazed and confused?' from the Food Climate Research Network reminded us the world is variegated. Regions such as Britain's Pennine mountains unsuitable for arable crops may be indefinitely suitable for hill farming of beef and dairy grazing. However, green hopes that grass pasture offered unlimited potential for carbon sequestration were truncated by FCRN advice that, while proper management increases soil carbon stocks rapidly, such increases can fall to zero in as little as 30 years when the soil is saturated.

IFOAM, co-ops and quantifying the world's *non-certified* organic land?

Progressive dairy farmers, pastoralists and animal welfarists were allies of the Arla and Eko Holland organic co-operatives in Europe; in the UK, OMSCO worked with the Soil Association in the UK. There was also collaboration in the US with the Organic Valley dairy co-op, as part of an organic cheese supply chain to China (OMSCO 2019; Scholten 2019a).

Such organizations, among 750 member organisations in 117 countries, are linked to the International Federation of Organic Agricultural Movements (IFOAM) based in Bonn, Germany, which with the Research Institute of Organic Agriculture (FiBL) in Switzerland, publishes *The World of Organic* Agriculture, edited by Helga Willer with others including Minou Yussefi, Neil Sorensen, and Julia Lernoud. After years accessing IFOAM-FiBL publications, and in preparation for writing this book, I travelled to IFOAM Bonn, in April 2017, where I enjoyed lunch with then President Marcus Arbenz. Chats with Arbenz, press officer Denise Godinho and others encouraged a realization that, as bound as their organic principles are to science, they are practical about working with conventional agriculturalists and innovators. This means that, if IFOAM can show conventional actors more sustainable ways to grow food and fibre, they do so with good will. *It takes a village.*

At the IFOAM organic world congress in Delhi, November 2017, we heard IFOAM President Arbenz speak on positive growth in organic acreage and farmers internationally (Scholten 2018b: 8). FiBL's Julia Lernoud, from Argentina, also spoke, piquing my interest with their attempt to quantify the world's *non-certified* organic land. This is congruent with ideas first proposed by a Catholic priest decades ago for semi-nomadic Rabari herd people to export 'Dairy organics from the Green Hills of India' to that country's metropoles and later to global cities abroad (Scholten 2007ef, 2014). In an email to me (2 April 2019), FiBL's Helga Willard acknowledged that quantifying so much of the world's hinterlands would be a 'huge project!', because of difficulty in obtaining accurate, comparable data from all countries. Perhaps UN-FAO can help regularize data collection internationally. Meanwhile, it helps that data from Sikkim – an Indian state with the goal of becoming 100 per cent organic – is based on Tracenet, the Indian government's database for certified organic farmers. Mapping the earth is easier said than done, but progress can be made section by section. Also taking part in symposiums in the 2017 IFOAM organic world congress in Delhi (Scholten 2018b: 8) was Brian Baker, who is acutely aware of the economies and diseconomies of scale in different supply chains. From his base in Eugene, Oregon, IFOAM North America President Baker builds strategic partnerships with 750 member organisations in 117 other countries.

Emails and meetings in Anand during April 2019, with Shri R.S. Sodhi, long-time managing director of the Gujarat Cooperative Milk Marketing Federation (GCMMF in Amul.com), were informative. Amul is India's leading dairy farmers' co-operative, and Sodhi said it was already spearheading more co-op societies among Rabari hill people, and making progress, but long supply lines in hot climates were formidable obstacles. Milk is so fragile that it deteriorates quickly. Rabari hill areas are largely pristine environmentally, theoretically making them eligible for organic certification as pastures for high-value organic dairying. But hill areas suffer continuous encroachment by urbanization. So, there is a growing need to achieve among hill people the same income, health and education benefits for women, children and men won in Amul's Operation Flood, sponsored by the World Food Programme of FAO-UN between 1970 and 1996, in *India's White Revolution* (Scholten 1997c, 2010). *It can be done.*

Reconsidering organic dairy farms

Due to his decades of research, publication and advocacy on wide-ranging farm issues, the name of a certain US-UK researcher surfaces regularly. As research professor, Charles 'Chuck' Benbrook at the Center for Sustaining Agriculture and Natural Resources (CSANR) at Washington State University, and scientific advisor for the Oregon-based non-profit organization 'Organic Center' from 2004 to June 2012, Benbrook (2010, 2012a and b, 2014) published studies such as comparisons between extensive organic pasture farms and what had become the new convention of intensive CAFO feedlot operations. At some scales Benbrook found favourable outcomes for the organic position, especially when superior cattle longevity bolstered farm income. Aspects of Benbrook's work are discussed in more detail in *US Organic Dairy Politics* (Scholten 2014).

Benbrook helped evidence the benefit to human nutrition of organic pasture-based milk, with colleagues including Gillian Butler, Latif Maged, Carlo Leifert and Donald David, based at Newcastle University's Nafferton research farm in North-East England, near Hadrian's Wall. Their studies found extra healthful Omega-3 nutritional fatty acids in grass-fed organic milk, and lower unhealthy Omega-6 fatty acids, replicated in an eighteen-month study in the US (Benbrook et al. 2013, 2018). When these news stories went viral, it was a boon for the sustainability of both conventional and certified organic farmers who achieve a maximum number of lactations with pastured cows.[3]

Benbrook (1990; 2020) documented the near-doubling of Monsanto Roundup® glyphosate herbicide use between 1980 and 1990. Glyphosate was remarkably ubiquitous. With a class I was teaching (*Sostenibilidad Global*) in 2000 at the National University of Tucumán in Argentina, we visited a small organic dairy farm. The hospitable manager gave us tea, while casually showing us how he killed weeds around his house – though not the fields – with Roundup®. He assured us it was not used on cows' pasture or their corn and hay crops!

As noted in an earlier chapter, in 2018, German multinational Bayer bought Monsanto for $63 billion at just the wrong time, when thousands of cancer victims were suing Monsanto over Roundup® glyphosate. Bayer announced it would drop Monsanto's 117-year-old name and be known only as Bayer. Benbrook gave expert testimony regarding the toxicity of glyphosate as part of litigation around non-Hodgkin lymphoma (NHL), resulting in $12 billion punitive damages on Bayer-Monsanto (Benbrook 2018; *Bloomberg* 2020). Geeks in pro-chemical life science online chatrooms sometimes called Benbrook a shill for the organic industry. One such geek claimed Roundup® glyphosate was safe enough to drink, but backed down before trying it on TV (*Huffington Post* 2015).

On 24 January 2020, Reuters reported that three huge court judgements had been awarded to plaintiffs. Bayer-Monsanto tried to negotiate a $10 billion award to all victims without admitting responsibility, but a larger judgement was awarded, and did not preclude further litigation.

Besides carcinogenic effects to humans, and diminishment of farm and soil biodiversity, another negative aspect of Roundup glyphosate was its diminished effectiveness over time. In Argentina, Rosa Binimelis, Walter A. Pengue and Iliana Monterroso (2009: 623–33) published an influential paper titled '"Transgenic treadmill": Responses to the emergence and spread of glyphosate-resistant

---

3. With daughter Rachel Benbrook, a graphic artist in coastal ecosystem management and science education, Chuck Benbrook set up Hygeia Analytics in Bellingham, Washington. Hygeia archives papers, congressional testimony, etc. One output is an interactive video on glyphosate titled 'The lowdown on Roundup, Part 1' (2017; https://vimeo.com/225190429). Pastoralists also value Hygeia Analytics' links to articles by Lukas Rist et al. (2017) in the *British Journal of Nutrition* such as 'Organic milk and meat enhances the nutritional quality of human breast milk', with Conjugated Linoleic Acids (CLAs).

johnsongrass in Argentina'. Binimelis et al. described the 'GMO treadmill' in which higher doses of glyphosate were required to combat weeds, before farmers resorted to chemical cocktails with herbicides from rival manufacturers, such as 2,4-D, a component in the defoliant Agent Orange used during the Vietnam War.

On 4 May 2014, the Natural Society reported that the Organic Consumers Association, Moms Across America and Sustainable Pulse found 'high' levels of glyphosate in three out of ten samples of breast milk. (Turn back to Chapter 1 for more details on this controversy.) Meanwhile, organicists insist organic milk and meat enhance the nutrition of human breast milk (Rist et al. 2007; *Hygeia Analytics* 2016).

Sustainable intensification

Unfortunately, the macro state of global trends and people's growing appetite for dairy and meat cannot continue ad infinitum. Cognizant that world population may reach 9.5 billion people around the year 2050, and that global demand for meat could double by then, Sir Jules Pretty coined the term 'sustainable intensification' (2009, 2011; *Huffington Post* 2013). This denotes increasing agricultural production without cutting more of the forests which function as the Earth's green lungs. With African and Asian demand for livestock products projected to double by 2030, more deforestation threatens climate stability. However, climate-change-denying President Trump returned protected US areas to logging and oil drilling, while Brazilian President Bolsonaro released more Amazon rainforest to development, livestock feed crops and cattle production. So, it is no wonder that Pretty and other leading scholars agreed with Steinfeld who wrote: 'The principle means of limiting livestock's impact on the environment must be ... intensification' (Steinfeld et al. 2006: 236; also Bellarby et al. 2013). These are chilling words for extensive pastoralists, but as Gordon Conway noted in *Huffington Post* (2013), sustainable Intensification is often incorrectly associated only with high-input, industrial agriculture (though India's Amul and Dudhsagar dairy co-ops show that need not be the case).

Yields might be increased by economies-of-scale in larger production units, but smaller grazing farms could also benefit from innovations in biotechnology, data analysis, and inputs such as seaweed (CSIRO 2016; *The Lead* 2020 and 2021). It is easier said than done. Around the world, we have seen significant downsides to Green Revolution crops which compromised soil fertility, depleted food nutrients and depleted groundwater in India's Punjab and other areas. The post-Second World War dairy intensification that spread from California to other countries boosted milk production but sacrificed bovine longevity in its concentrated or confined animal feeding operations, as we have discussed in previous chapters (Basu and Scholten 2012, 2013; DHI-Provo 2013). In proper scenarios of sustainable intensification, groundwater levels would be stabilized, and bovine well-being would not be compromised by ketosis, laminitis, mastitis, infertility and the other maladies that characterize CAFO feedlots, where nearly half dairy cows go to slaughter, too burned out to conceive a second calf (Rajala-Schultz et al. 1999; Biagiotti 2014).

When extensive mixed livestock and crops farming gave way to intensive monoculture in the US, Europe and elsewhere in the second half of the twentieth century, it impacted negatively on soil fertility, water quality and biodiversity by reducing habitats for seasonal birds, shellfish, animals and insects – not least due to misuse of artificial fertilizers such as nitrates and phosphates. Monsanto introduced GMO canola, a type of rapeseed, to North America in 1994 with assurances that glyphosate, the herbicide the seeds were genetically modified to resist, would replace chemicals atrazine and DDT which were more toxic to humans. But promises that minimal doses of glyphosate would always control weeds proved wrong. *Weeds read Darwin, too.*

Green America (2013) disseminated a *Washington Times* report that the EPA had been lobbied to raise permitted glyphosate levels in oilseed crops, sesame, flax and soybeans, from 20 parts per million (ppm) to 40 ppm. Glyphosate contamination limits for sweet potatoes and carrots were boosted from 0.2 ppm to 3 ppm for sweet potatoes and 5 ppm for carrots – fifteen and twenty-five times previous levels respectively. Not everyone was surprised.

In recent years, US court judgements for cancers attributed to Bayer-Monsanto's Roundup® glyphosate put the ongoing legality of the herbicide in doubt. In 2019, Mexico banned imports, citing the World Health Organization's warning that glyphosate is a 'probable carcinogen'. Doubt increased on New Year's Eve 2020, when Mexican President Andrés Manuel López Obrador (AMLO, as the head of the National Regeneration Movement is nicknamed), honoured campaign promises to not only stop the use of glyphosate, but also to halt the cultivation of GMO corn or maize (*Common Dreams* 2021).

For decades, glyphosate drifting endangered Mexico's genetic heritage as the world's premier maize hearth. Mexico's prohibition represents invocation of the precautionary principle, which the Reagan and Bush administrations had rejected in favour of the risk–benefit principle advocated by the agro-pharmaceutical industry (Scholten 1990b; 1990c). AMLO's blow to glyphosate and GM maize could portend the eventual end of glyphosate, in the suite of inputs required with GMO crops. But, Bayer-Monsanto develops biotechnologies to circumvent objections to its notorious herbicide. How free of unintended consequences will the next iteration of biotechnology be? Before Bayer-Monsanto answered that question, it sought to defend glyphosate.

Monsanto owner Bayer AG and industry lobbyist CropLife America quickly pressured Mexico to abandon its glyphosate ban, just as it fought Thailand's attempt to ban the herbicide on health grounds in 2019. The Organic Consumers Association (OCA) disseminated a report in *The Guardian* (2021) that glyphosate partisans in the Office of the US Trade Representative (USTR) were hoping to jinx AMLO's ban, by claiming it was non-compliant with President Trump's US–Mexico–Canada Agreement (USMCA) trade deal, which came into effect on 1 July 2020. CropLife warned that if Mexico extended the precautionary principle to pesticide residue levels in food, it could jeopardize $20 billion in US annual farm exports to Mexico.

(US exports of GMO corn displaced thousands of Mexican peasant farmers, exacerbating domestic rural-to-urban migration and illegal migration to the US.)

The big question is whether or not glyphosate residue survives in milk, meat or eggs; results in an article in the *Archives of Animal Nutrition* were indeterminate because it (like GMO dairy hormone rBGH/rBST) supposedly disappears in a cow's digestive system (Flachowsky et al. 2005). But with glyphosate used on perhaps 90 per cent of exported US crops, its trade partners were nervous.

Unintended consequences in the twenty-first century's white, green, blue, brown and yellow food revolutions suggest a global switch to plant-based vegan food, meat analogues and nutritionally suspect laboratory-grown meat by the year 2050, entails environmental and health risks, especially for the poor (FAO-UN 2003, 2005). Quorn, the venerable meat substitute using mycoprotein derived from a natural fungus, does not satisfy all palates.

But food chemists are skilful: above, one of my dairy survey respondents was delighted by the 'amazingly delicious' taste of new plant-based Impossible Burgers, but nonetheless worried about its high salt content and nutritional profile. Recently proposed soy protein *chicken-like* analogue meats, or Richard Branson and Bill Gate's *clean meat* grown from bovine cells in laboratories, evoke sci-fi speculation – and revulsion in others. Nevertheless, consumer interest, commercial innovation and investment suggest plant- and lab-based foods *will* play increasing roles in decades ahead. Below, respondents assess survey Query 9, repeated here with responses to the statements for the reader's convenience.

Q9 Plant-based dairy and laboratory-grown meat substitutes could replace food animals soon.

Q9 Plant-based dairy and laboratory-grown meat substitutes could replace food animals soon.

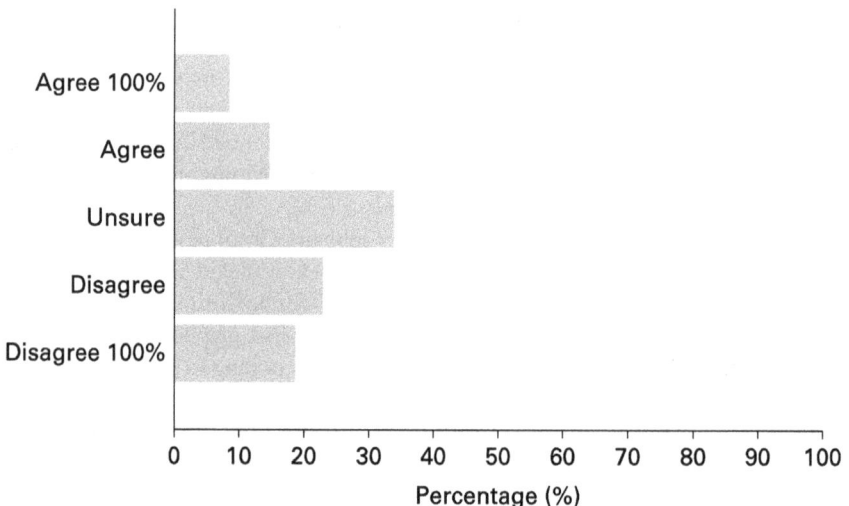

Stakeholders' voices

Age was not a specific variable when these stakeholder voices were collected. We have, however, occasionally referred to certain generations' preferences and behaviours and these are evident in comments in response to query 9. *Whither dairy farming?*

Celia Cremen, an American Millennial working in Newcastle, UK, agreed 100 per cent that plant-based dairy and laboratory-grown meat substitutes must replace animal-based food: 'If they don't, the planet is sunk! Putting aside the whole animal welfare question, and question of whether or not humans are even meant to digest animal products. . . . World-wide reduction of traditionally reared meat and dairy, has the power to dramatically slow climate change. Save the humans!' Her partner Harry, agreed 100 per cent, too. Both are vegans.

Two younger respondents, PhD students in the UK, were unsure. Originally from China, Bertrand Kiung agreed vegan meals were tasty and said that he hoped plant- and laboratory-based foods could soon replace animal products, 'But it really depends on whether people would like to accept it, and whether they would like to give up the real meat, or change their mind'.

Ileni Farad from Libya also agreed vegan meals can be tasty, but put conditions on future food regimes: 'Plant-based dairy, yes. But laboratory-grown meat is an absolute no-no.'

Mary Tufts, in her 40s with a new doctorate in migration geography from a Northern English university, once ran a business selling organic beef and lamb and promoting small farmers and animal welfare. She agreed plant- and laboratory-based foods could replace livestock.

Some of the older (40s and older) respondents just did not have an answer. Tom Charles said: 'I don't know, sorry.'

Tim Sands, artisanal cheesemaker in County Durham, UK, agreed vegan meals can be tasty. But he was unsure if vegan and analogue meats would soon prevail over established foods.

Harold Daniels took a global stance in his comments, noting that: 'If you look at China, this seems to be going the opposite direction. It'll only happen if it's enforced, or much cheaper than current sources. We should research new food sources, but limiting this to poor simulations of existing food preferences seems "market driven".'

Other older UK residents, includng those who grew up elsewhere were sceptical.

Richard Beakins, retired food geographer living in North-East England, disagrees that plant-based dairy and laboratory-grown meat substitutes could replace food animals soon: 'I doubt this will happen in the next twenty-five years.'

Elaine Oordt, in North-East England, tempered her agreement that plant-based dairy and laboratory-grown meat substitutes could replace food animals with an intriguing question: 'What are the environmental costs?'

Caroline Bell, co-manager of family-run Acorn Organic Dairy in North-East England, was unsure about the tastiness of vegan food. She was loath to criticize vegan products, but expressed annoyance that some vegans panned all animal-based foods.

Karl Zillener, originally from the US and a linguist in Newcastle, said vegan meals can be as tasty as those from livestock, but doubted they would replace traditional fare.

Likewise, Vern Veldman, with family farming history in his native Netherlands, agreed 100 per cent on the earlier query that cows should be on pasture at least 120 days per year. While the ethics of eating animals gave him pause for thought, he was unsure of the chances that plant-based foods or laboratory-based meat analogues could soon replace traditional omnivorous diets.

Sena Omar, university lecturer in northern England, from Syria, agreed vegan food could be tasty, but also doubted whether it would soon replace traditional omnivorous diets.

Loren Morton, youth & community worker North-East England, is sceptical about an imminent shift to plant-based dairy and laboratory-grown meat, writing: 'I think a lot of work would have to be done first.'

Nanci Barnes has alternated between vegetarian and omnivore diets. Could plant-based dairy and lab-grown meat substitutes replace food animals soon? 'Always willing to try, I did eat Quorn a lot until they changed the recipe – now I prefer vegetarian [food] or ethically sourced meat.' Her partner Neil's comment was equivocal: 'Plant-based [or] laboratory-grown meat substitutes could replace food animals, BUT I don't believe this is necessary.'

Two other professionals, Georgina Thahl and Bernd Insley (pseudonyms), neither with farming backgrounds but who support the idea of 120-day grazing minimums, show concern for animal welfare and the effect of livestock on environment. They find vegan meals tasty but doubt they will soon dominate human diets.

Ernest Anderson is a civil servant in Tyne & Wear, England. He made no comments, but his answers reveal an animal-friendly person coming to grips with ethical and environmental issues. He had no farming family history, but disagreed that farmers or their animals got fair treatment. Cows should graze pasture at least 120 days a year, he indicated, and he questioned the ethics of eating them. He agreed livestock harm the environment and climate unacceptably, agreed vegan meals can be tasty, but was unsure plant-based dairy and laboratory-grown meat substitutes could replace food animals soon. Perhaps we are all a little unsure.

Juan Siena, a Spanish teacher from Colombia, who has been studying and working in Northern England, comes from a family of coffee bean farmers in South America. Previously he owned a café in the UK that served meat, yet this thoughtful man expresses some pro-vegan opinions. He agreed it is not ethical to eat animals, that livestock agriculture harms the environment and climate unacceptably, and that vegan meals can be as tasty as those using ingredients from livestock. Will plant- and laboratory-grown meat substitutes replace food animals soon? He was unsure, but added: 'I hope so.'

Benny Meong, lecturer from Hong Kong, teaching in North England, uploads foodie photos on Facebook in his (minimal) spare time. He was unsure of farmers' place in political spaces, but understood animal welfare was adequate in Britain, and he would pay a little more for meat if the cattle were allowed to graze on pasture. He was unsure about the ethics of eating sentient animals, or their effect upon environment and climate. Vegan meals can be tasty, he believed, and suspects plant-based dairy and laboratory-grown meat substitutes could replace food animals soon.

Nan Toner, retired teacher in the UK, agreed, adding a proviso others may agree with: 'I do think vegan meals are tasty, but I prefer to have a more varied diet.' She was unsure about future food regimes without animals and commented: 'It does not appeal to me.'

There is less evidence from respondents in the US, regardless of their ages, that they expect an animal-free diet to prevail anytime soon.

Nancy Thomas is a dairy farmer in her 30s and so committed to the farm lifestyle that she supplemented income by work as a barista. She agreed vegan meals can be as tasty as those using livestock, but doubted they would soon dominate.

Pasture-based livestock agriculturalist Nancy Grove, who lives in Ames, Iowa, was sceptical of the food value of plant-based dairy, or what Bill Gates, Richard Branson and late GE head Jack Welch called 'clean meat'. She agreed: 'Vegan meals can be tasty, but don't provide the same nutritional profile.' Could they replace meat and dairy? She agreed: 'Yes, plant- and lab-based food could replace food animals. But should they? They should replace conventional meat and dairy, but not [pastured] livestock, who are managed in a way that benefits our environment.'

Three farmers/farming activists were also unwilling to predict a meatless future.

Organic dairy farmer Hans Wolfisberg was open-minded about vegan food and analogue meat, but doubted plant-based dairy and laboratory-grown meat substitutes would soon replace food animals.

Mark Kastel, cofounder of industry watchdogs the Cornucopia Institute and Organic Eye, had documented adulterated feed in the Mad Cow (BSE/nvCJD) disease, and cow ailments due to GMO rBGH/rBST hormone tests, so plant- or laboratory-grown dairy and meat analogues prompted his suspicions. Will plant-based dairy and laboratory-grown meat substitutes replace food animals soon? Kastel answered: 'Based on the profit motive, they very well might. Based on true nutrition and safety they could be quite risky.'

Co-founder of Northeast Organic Farmers Association in Massachusetts, and a community supported agriculture (CSA) farmer in New York State, Elizabeth Henderson vehemently disagreed that plant- or laboratory-grown dairy and meat analogue products would soon supplant livestock: 'Vegans do not have a clear grasp on life, death, farming, food realities. Highly processed foods are not preferable to natural foods.'

Nathan Charles, farm owner in Anneville, Pennsylvania, gave answers that were a litany of pastoralist views. His family history was in farming, which he felt was unfairly treated by institutions; he disagreed that US animal welfare was adequate, and advocated cattle graze pasture at least 120 days per year. He also disagreed that it was unethical to eat livestock, disliked the taste of vegan food, and disagreed 100 per cent that plants and lab meat would replace livestock in the food chain.

Kate Ryan, agricultural programme co-ordinator in Washington State, considered the political ramifications of a global food regime of plant-based dairy and laboratory-grown meat: 'Unsure. Depends on whether you're asking me what I think will happen, or what I want to happen. I think fake meat will become way bigger than it should be, which feeds nicely into the corporate takeover of ALL food. Don't think it should happen, and quite frankly I think "lying meat" should be outlawed.'

Other family and organic farmers in their 50s and older expressed similar views. While some were open-minded about plant-based foods, their responses reflected their thoughts about the future of their own and friends' farms.

Missy Cordon, organic dairy farmer near Hammond, New York, was equable about US animal welfare: 'There are violators that need to be caught, but all in all, I believe animal welfare is good.' She was passionate about pasturing their milk cows, '...to improve health and welfare'. Regarding dairy's effects on environment and climate, she said: 'Agriculture can be a point source of pollution, user of toxic chemicals, etc. But not all farms choose to farm that way.' About vegan tastiness, she was unsure: 'Don't know. Never tried any of them.' She disagreed that plant-based and lab-based food would soon replace traditional fare: 'With GMO soybeans and who-knows-what as the ingredients? I am sure that some consumers will choose them, and that's fine. But I wonder about the long-term health implications and the effects of putting more land under continuous cultivation. Cows can graze during the season, eating grass that is a perennial crop.'

Jim Goodman, retired from family-scale organic pasture-grazing in Wisconsin, agreed 'without a doubt' that vegan meals could be tasty. But he disagreed that plant- or lab-based meat will soon replace traditional food: 'Probably not soon, but more and more plant-based and lab-grown products will be developed. Not sure I am excited about it. Guess I'd rather eat the plants than turn them into "milk".'

Len Monroe, retired editor, who still farms part-time in the same state as Jim Goodman, enjoys a good steak with blue-cheese dressing. He defends dairy's continuing role in nutrition, and disagreed that livestock agriculture unacceptably damages the environment or climate. He also disagreed 100 per cent that vegan meals are as tasty as traditional fare – or that they'll soon replace it.

Kristin B. Cremmer, octogenarian retired farmer in Enumclaw, Washington, disagreed that livestock unacceptably harmed climate and environment. She was unsure of the tastiness of vegan meals – or whether plant- and laboratory-based meat could soon replace the farm products she grew up on.

Harold Zinn's answers exuded traditional small farmer nous. An organic dairy farmer, in New York State, he might trust his dairy co-operative, but scrutinized politicians and corporations carefully. He thought US animal welfare was okay, at least in his co-op. Of course, cows should graze outside. He paid a little more for organic food that he did not raise himself. Eating sentient animals was ethical. He did not agree that his methods polluted the environment or fostered climate change, and he disagreed 100 per cent that vegan meals were as tasty as his, or that they'd run farmers like him out of the supermarket.

Rick Carlinni, 50s, veterinarian and author with experience on all types of US dairy farms, with insights on multinational processing and marketing, believes sustainable dairying will continue. He is unsure of the tastiness of vegan food, and disagrees that plant-based dairy or laboratory-grown meat substitutes will replace food animals soon.

Ken E. Tillman spent his youth on a US grazing dairy farm, and is sensitive to negative environmental aspects of intensive dairying. Friendships with Buddhists in Thailand have increased his reflection on the ethics of eating sentient animals. However, he is unsure if three vegan meals a day would be culinary satisfaction guaranteed – and doubts plant- and lab-based meals will soon overtake the dairy farm diet he thrived on.

Another American Buddhist, Maureen Isle, an advertising reviewer on Wall St, New York, expressed similar views. She appreciated the farming rurality of her native Hawaii, where her Punahou School was attended by President Barack Obama. She knew little of the national or global livestock sector, but Nichiren Shoshu Buddhism infuses her empathy with animals, who she thinks should be able to express natural behaviours. Yet, she was unsure about the ethics of eating sentient animals, whether or not livestock farming harmed environment and climate, the tastiness of vegan meals – or vegan hegemony in future human diets.

Karin Tyne, dairy and creamery owner in Othello, Washington, thought vegan food could be tasty. But she disagreed 100 per cent that plant- and lab-based foods will soon replace livestock. A societal switch to veganism would put her creamery out of business.

Letty Barton, organic dairy farmer with Northeast Organic Dairy Producers Alliance in the US, had pro-organic pasture and farmer sentiments – with a loving nose for beef in the oven. Was dairy harmful to environment and climate? She was: 'Unsure. It all depends on the system of production'. She disagreed that vegan meals were as tasty as meat-based, adding: 'If plant- and lab-grown food replaces dairy and livestock, it would be to the detriment of consumers' nutrition'. Her partner Len disagreed 100 per cent that dairy harmed environment and climate.

There were those who were older whose comments were similar to the younger practicing and potential vegans of whom Luke Quoral, in his mid-70s, was one. A retired rhythm & blues radio disk jockey, later transport union leader in Denver, Colorado, he was highly critical of dairy's effects on our biosphere. He agreed vegan meals can be tasty as livestock-based ones, and agreed 100 per cent that plant-based and lab-based foods could soon overtake traditional foods.

A host of other respondents from the US varied in their responses about animal welfare and the ethics of eating meat but doubted plant-based dairy and laboratory-grown meat substitutes will replace food animals soon. These include Melanie Porta, who was raised on a dairy farm but switched to another line of work, Noraleen Binyon, a retired Boeing aerospace worker in Seattle with family farming history, and Nathan Norris, a software engineer with no history of farming

Happy Larson recalled trekking through Bangladesh with her husband after college graduation in the 1970s, after which she attacked a Big Mac cheeseburger with gusto. Now she agrees 100 per cent that plant-based dairy and laboratory-grown meat substitutes could replace food animals soon: 'Just look at Burger King stock/quarterly earnings. Just talk to the McDonald's manager who is getting weary of telling people "Soon, soon … They are engaged in test marketing in Toronto." Toronto? Geez, just give us an Impossible Big Mac. I have "chicken" nuggets in the freezer. Haven't tried yet.'

Faron Ingineur, PhD, retired toxicologist, commented from his professional stance as a toxicologist. He agreed livestock agriculture harms the environment and climate unacceptably. He was unsure whether vegan meals can be as tasty as those using ingredients from livestock, and disagreed 100 per cent that plant-based dairy and laboratory-grown meat substitutes could replace food animals soon.

Sue Tracker, college teacher and writer from near Hartford, Connecticut, had memories of her grandparents' farm, but was unsure of contemporary farm policies. She called herself a 'Cutatarian' because she liked meat but refused to eat animals too cute to eat, like the ponies she and her husband rode on holidays in Iceland. Or bunnies. She was unsure about both livestock effects on environment and climate and the tastiness of vegan meals, but actually agreed plant-based dairy and laboratory-grown meat substitutes could replace food animals soon.

Kal Charge, motorsports business owner on Puget Sound, kept his marketing hat on when asked if plant-based dairy and lab-grown meat could replace food animals soon: 'It will take a couple of generations to eliminate meat – look at electric automobiles.'

Tanner Cross, medical worker from Seattle, had lived in California where he was a fan of raw milk, before working in the Philippines. He agrees 100 per cent that vegan meals can be tasty, but doubted plant- and lab-grown meat substitutes would soon dominate.

Denzell N. Loral had no farm background, and was unsure how politicians, corporations and co-operatives treated farmers. He hoped cows graze pasture at least 120 days a year, and was willing to pay more for livestock products managed humanely. He agreed 100 per cent that livestock harmed environment and climate, and that vegan meals were as tasty as traditional meals based on meat – he also agreed that plant-based dairy and laboratory-grown meat substitutes could replace food animals soon. He is a club motorcycle racer and his risk-taking may reflect the attitudes of green Oregonians portrayed in a *Portlandia* (2011) satire, 'Ordering the Chicken'. In it, 'woke' diners walk out when the server cannot guarantee the chicken had a happy life. Beef connoisseurs may similarly spurn factory-farmed meat in favour of grass-fed, organic red meat (Food Revolution Network 19 Dec 2012). Green household trends in Portland and Seattle are also compared by Helen Jarvis (2006). Food ethics are complicated.

Karen Saren, retired farmer near Mt St Helens, seemed to lament the past golden age of local family dairy and crops farming, now increasingly isolated by shifts to globalized food chains. Her initial exposure to ideas in *Livestock's Long Shadow*

(FAO 2006), i.e., the link between livestock emissions of greenhouse gases and climate change, was via this dairy survey. She was unfamiliar with some ethical, environmental or political dairy issues, but was sceptical that plant-based dairy and lab-grown meat substitutes would supersede the food her family produced. She is not alone.

The remainder of responses from Americans over forty are much the same. Almost none of them predict a complete shift away from meat and dairy anytime soon. Some express doubt about plant-based food's nutritional value and provenance.

Rita Carter, retired office worker in Oklahoma, has been a vegetarian consuming milk and egg products since she was twenty-two years old. Regarding plant-based dairy and laboratory-grown meat substitutes, she commented: 'I think that is a direction in which we are headed. However, I don't believe it is a health alternative. I don't like the idea of any lab-grown "food". I believe humans are designed to eat non-GMO foods grown naturally.'

Randy Grein, IT system engineer and author living near Seattle, agreed plant-based dairy and laboratory-grown substitutes like the Impossible Burger must be taken seriously. Recall from his response to Query 8 that his son had gone vegan. But he warned how safety problems could develop: 'Lab-grown substitutes will always be more expensive, but they don't have to be hugely so. The big problem is, continued pressures to reduce cost will introduce hazards we don't see right now – either new kinds of pollution or contamination by toxins. We need a strong regulatory system to prevent that.'

Kenny Harold, president of an aerospace company on Puget Sound, had a family farm background, was unsure about farmers' current treatment by politicians, corporations or co-operatives, but agreed 100 per cent with cows grazing pasture at least 120 days a year, and would pay more for humanely produced food. He disagreed that livestock agriculture harms the environment and climate unacceptably. Vegan meals could be tasty, he admitted, but disagreed 100 per cent that food animals would soon be replaced by vegan options.

Like other respondents suspicious of high salt content and low nutrition density in meat substitutes, Mandy Alt, a homemaker in Houston, Texas, had reservations about a future food regime of plant-based dairy and laboratory-grown meat substitutes: 'Futuristic is right. I've seen nothing yet that approaches acceptable in meat substitutes. The USA options I've seen have unhealthy nutritional profiles.'

From Spain with a dairying background on both sides of her family, Berta Racarden, disagreed that plant-based dairy and lab-grown meat substitutes could replace food animals: 'I doubt any lab-grown food would be as healthy as a natural product. You only need to fake something when you cannot do without that item. Why do you need to turn these veggies into something they are not? Perhaps the solution is to change the diet and make it more vegetarian, not to process these things to turn them to something else.'

Rod Scheu, lighting specialist near Seattle, had a family farm background, but was unsure of how fairly farmers are treated. He agreed 100 per cent that US animal welfare is adequate, and that cows should graze fields at least 120 days a year. He thought it ethical to eat meat, and disagreed 100 per cent that livestock agriculture unacceptably harms the environment and climate. Vegan meals can be as tasty as those using ingredients from livestock, he agreed, but disagreed 100 per cent that plant-based dairy and laboratory-grown meat substitutes could replace food animals soon.

Tim Finley, aerospace technical consultant and former club motorcycle racer, is critical of many elements of human food chains. He is open to vegan food, but disagrees 100 per cent that plant-based dairy and lab-grown meat substitutes could replace food animals soon: 'Processed content, no thanks.'

Ernie Graham, former national championship motorcycle roadracer, bicyclist and technician, splits his year between Seattle and Costa Rica. He is unsure how US farmers fare these days, but disagreed that the country's animal welfare is adequate, partly because not all US cattle graze 120 days a year on pasture – compared to Costa Rica, where most do. He agreed that livestock harm the environment and climate, that agreed vegan meals can be tasty and that plant- and lab-grown meat substitutes could advance.

Ken Mentzer, Gen X ex-military man, motorcyclist and author, had dystopian forebodings about leaving our omnivorous diet: 'The replacement of natural foods with laboratory food will be as inferior as every other highly processed food has been to date. Let's not curse our children with eating packaged field rations throughout their life.'

Nancy Century is an organic market gardener selling in Seattle farmers' markets. She disagreed 100 per cent that vegan meals can be as tasty as those using ingredients from livestock, and also disagreed 100 per cent that plant-based dairy and laboratory-grown meat substitutes could soon replace animals.

Karen Suttler retired office worker, skier and hiker from Salt Lake City, observed too much carnivorous behaviour to believe plant-based dairy and lab-grown meat adoption was imminent: 'I can't see animal products disappearing anytime soon. With people eating steaks every night, and bacon cheeseburgers on every corner, it's not a change that will be easily accepted by a still very large number of meat-eaters. And then there's the Keto diet, bacon, bacon and more bacon.' The Keto diet she mentions was popularized by a Hollywood producer to obviate the use of anti-convulsant drugs for a child's epilepsy. It has also been applied to a number of other illnesses (Gano, Patel and Rho 2014).

Dawn Roue, retired in Seattle, had a family farming history, and disagreed that farmers or livestock were treated fairly. She loves animals and uploads photos of the intelligent crows she delights in feeding in a nearby alley. But she was unsure about other farm policy issues.

Ned Harold, communication specialist for an oil company near Bellingham, Washington, had farming in previous generations. He disagreed 100 per cent that plant-based dairy and laboratory-grown meat substitutes could replace food animals soon.

Stakeholders based outside the US and the UK expressed a diversity of views.

Harald Classen, retired teacher in Vienna, Austria, said farming was part of his family's history, but he disagreed that farmers or farm animals were treated fairly. Cattle should be allowed to perform instinctive behaviours such as grazing pasture, and he would pay a little more for farm products raised humanely. As to tricky Queries 6 to 9, he was unsure about the ethics of eating sentient animals, whether livestock agriculture harmed environment and climate unacceptably, whether vegan meals can be as tasty as those using ingredients from livestock, and whether plant-based dairy and laboratory-grown meat substitutes could replace food animals soon.

Eashav Taalin, college administrator and dairy researcher in Gujarat, India, agreed 100 per cent that it is unethical to eat sentient animals, and that vegan meals can be as tasty as those using ingredients from livestock, but was unsure that plant-based dairy and laboratory-grown meat substitutes could replace food animals soon. Might he be a vegetarian considering veganism?

Harriet Vassen, financial employee in Sassenheim, Holland, left no comments, but her answers were thought-provoking. Her family history did not lie in farming, and she was unsure how fairly politicians, corporations or co-operatives treated Dutch farmers. She disagreed that The Netherlands practised adequate animal welfare, agreed cows should graze fields at least 120 days a year, paid more for food from humanely treated animals, and thought it was ethical to eat them. She was unsure about the livestock sector's harm to environment and climate and the tastiness of vegan meals, and doubted plant-based dairy and laboratory-grown meat substitutes could replace food animals soon.

Karl Rikard, 21 and a student from Belgrade, Serbia, disagreed that farmers or livestock are treated fairly. He was a meat-eater, but unsure of effects on environment and climate. He agreed vegan meals can be tasty, but disagreed 100 per cent that they will soon replace meat.

Twenty-year-old Jong Wei, a Chinese student living in Spain, had no family farming history, but said farmers were treated fairly in China. He was unsure about cows' need to graze 120 days a year, and disagreed 100 per cent that it was unethical to eat animals. He did agree vegan meals were tasty but doubted they were the future.

Natan Worisky, a Polish linguist now teaching in Spain, agreed 100 per cent that vegan meals are tasty – perhaps out of sync with the sausage- and chorizo-loving places he has lived. But he agrees plant- and laboratory-based food could soon replace meals based on livestock.

Richardo Nontales, an English professor in Brazil, came from a non-farming family, but suspected both farmers and animals deserved fairer treatment. He was unsure on technical points such as 120 days' minimum grazing, but found meat-eating ethical, and preferred meat-based meals to vegan ones. That said, he reckons plant- or laboratory food could soon replace livestock-based fare.

Brijit Deana Caldera, another Brazilian lawyer, is less carnivorous than her above-quoted husband, Richardo. She agreed it is unethical to eat sentient animals, agrees vegan meals are tasty, and that plant- or lab-based meat could soon replace livestock. These are difficult issues. Might she be a pescatarian vegetarian experimenting with vegan food?

Daniel Schappen, lawyer in Lenzburg, in the canton of Aargau, Switzerland, agreed vegan meals can be tasty, but doubted plant-based dairy and laboratory-grown meat would soon replace the pretty Brown Swiss cows grazing pastures around his medieval city. Locally, a Dutch-born woman who sought Swiss naturalization was rejected by neighbours who resented her public animal welfare objections to traditions of putting bells around cows' necks (*Independent* 2017). If the woman believed belling cows was animal abuse, she might reconsider after reading a report by St Andrews zoologist Andrew Whiten (2021), evidencing culture among animals such as chimps in a wildlife preserve in Zambia, who followed a fashion for wearing grass earrings after one named Julie started the trend.

Bensulamin Belman, staffer at the Milk Vita co-operative in Bangladesh, was unsure whether vegan meals can be tasty as those using ingredients from livestock. He also disagreed that plant-based dairy and laboratory-grown meat substitutes could replace food animals soon.

Omsin, teacher in Samut Prakan, a province in central Thailand, found the survey online. He remains unsure about the ethics of eating sentient animals and about the tastiness of vegan meals. He is also unsure that they will soon replace contemporary omnivore diets.

The voices of the youngest respondents to the survey wrap up responses to the nine dairy queries. Do they represent a future in which food production occurs exclusively in the large-scale operations or laboratories of multinational corporations rather than on small farms in the community?

Bernice, a nineteen-year-old student in northern Spain is vegan, agrees 100 per cent that her food is tasty, and agrees 100 percent that plant-based dairy and laboratory-grown meat substitutes could replace food animals soon.

Nora, from Granada, Spain, and also nineteen, has farming in her family history. She is unsure how politicians, corporations and co-operatives treat farmers, but disagrees 100 per cent with present levels of welfare, and believes cows should be allowed to graze at least 120 days per year. She agrees 100 per cent that livestock farming harms the environment and climate unacceptably, that vegan meals are tasty, and like her Spanish compatriot, agrees that plant-based dairy and laboratory-grown meat substitutes could replace food animals before too long.

Benjamin Ricardo, 29, a Spanish primary-school teacher, is an omnivore, but was critical of welfare levels in his country and wanted animals to graze pasture more. He was unsure about eating sentient animals, but believed they could be raised sustainably without impinging on environment or climate. Finally, he agreed vegan meals could be tasty, and were capable of replacing present omnivore diets.

Some conclusions on cows and climate

First of all, in our Age of the Anthropocene, it is necessary to establish the best scientific consensus on links between livestock and the shadow of impending climate doom. As the best future forecasts are often rehashes of the past, it is likely that for decades to come, pockets of grazing will persist, in the green hills of India (Scholten 2007acf, 2019ab), Britain's Pennines, the foothills of the Andes or former Amazonian rain forest, while consumption of plant-based dairy and lab-grown meat substitutes will increase in the metropoles which Saskia Sassen (1991) dubbed global cities: these hyper-urban spaces, such as London, Paris, New York and Shanghai, have more in common with each other than the hinterlands they attempt to command and control.

A worldwide switch to a vegan diet could solve some ethical, environmental and political problems, but would entail social disruptions, particularly for the livelihoods of workers on animal food chains. There is a limit to our human environmental footprint, even if everyone goes vegan. It is up to us to assess risk scenarios. Are omnivore, carnivore, vegetarian, vegan – or freegan – consumers, willing to eat ambient meat but not order it killed? These are lifestyle labels. Even tougher are ethical questions on how dairy and meat products are to be produced. Do you like animals? Are they your friends? Do we eat our sentient friends?

Good luck! This recalls one of Durham University Geography Department's annual climate lectures, delivered around 2008. The speaker was a risk assessor from the City of London, with a different take on global warming than World Bank risk assessors Goodland and Anhang (2009), who claimed ruminant livestock were culprits in the climate crisis. The speaker, who doubled as a pundit on radio and TV talk shows, challenged students and faculty to consider the political possibility that the Cassandras of climate catastrophe were actually left-wing socialists, intent on subjecting personal liberties to state control. (The hypothesis was already in the air, if you will, and resurfaced between 2019 and 2022, over the wearing of masks during the COVID-19 pandemic.) Next, he described how industrial risk assessments for environmental crises, epidemics, storms and so on were calculated by insurance companies in metropoles like London, New York and Tokyo. Then he suggested that, while the street noise of Green groups touting sustainable solar and wind power, versus retrograde groups defending 'clean coal' dominated media, the strategic decisions on food and climate would ultimately be made by insurance actuaries in global cities.

We are participants in an existential double- or triple-hermeneutic. That's a pedantic way of saying climate science is politicized by economic and ethical interests, corporations and co-operatives, wrestling for votes. But voters are fickle, reacting to the last newsfeed while politicians rush to the front of shifting mobs. Climate events like the black swan winter storm that wrecked Texas power and water grids in February 2021 can shatter predictions in a trice. 'Once-in-a-century' climate events seem to have become annual routine.

It's not all bad news for pastoralists cleaving to images of cows grazing meadows. But astute readers may be unsurprised that venerable intellectual Noam Chomsky sees the climate crisis as exacerbated by neoliberal forces wielding fake news in class warfare.

Chapter 5

WOMEN'S GRASS CEILING: NEXUS OF ETHICS, ENVIRONMENT AND POLITICS

Introduction

The FAO recognizes that women compose half of farm workers in developing countries, but suffer unequal access to resources. To nourish and educate their own children, while supplying the world's roughlyy 821 million underfed people (FAO 2017), women farmers need better training and infrastructure investment to

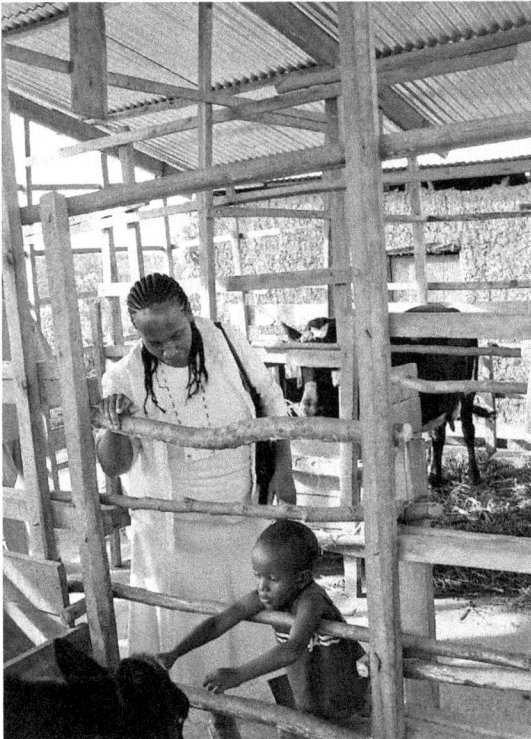

Figure 5.1 Dairy Africa 2010 conference goers visit a Rwandan woman's smallholding.

increase yields and family incomes. The political and ethical will to boost rural women's empowerment is calculated to 'leave no one behind' in the near term – and by meeting 17 UN Sustainable Development Goals, it can help stabilize climate in the long term. Unfortunately, the 2019–21 coronavirus pandemic lockdowns, which necessitated the home teaching of children during school closures in many countries, halted women's rise through urban glass ceilings and rural grass ceilings. It is past time that education, training and investment in rural women's human capital matches their prominence as the female face of farming (FAO-STAT 2012; *Guardian* 2012).

Here are my personal and academic observations of the 'grass ceiling' in doctoral fieldwork (Scholten 2007a). Further inspiration comes from insights by Shortall et al. (2017) in their report on *Women in Farming and the Agriculture Sector* for the Scottish government, to illustrate how training can tip the balance to empowerment. The focus is on the US and UK, but based on World Bank employment data for all countries, and inspired by the FAO policy document (FAO 2018) 'Empowering rural women, powering agriculture', in the 2030 Agenda for Sustainable Development.

First of the FAO campaign's key messages is that gender equality is essential for attaining food security, nutrition and achieving its 17 Sustainable Development Goals (UN n.d.). A precursor to equality in dairy farming is literacy. 'Dairy extension is needed to assist dairy farmers, particularly women, who are mainly involved in dairy operations (e.g., milking, barn cleaning, and manure management) that affect the production of good quality milk', conclude Didanna et al. in their 2018 study of smallholder dairying in Ethiopia and selected countries.

Female and male farmers are typically born into families who work on the land, but urbanites – including early career, limited-resource, socially disadvantaged, minority and female aspirants – have become leaders and innovators in organic dairy and crops movements in the US and other countries (Scholten 2007a, 2014; USDA 2019). A key requirement for farm managers or owners is the desire to farm. Support, from family members and communities, to retain the land in family control helps. Dairy farming is a calling, a quasi-religious vocation. It must be. Otherwise, how could farmers bear so many eighteen-hour days?

Whither aurochs?

Imagine three blindfolded people asked to describe a giant aurochs. From each position they report the contours and feel of hips, udders, muzzle – maybe even the rasp of a bovine tongue amid methane-rich breath. (Blindfold or not, no witness stupidly allows hands past the muzzle into a mouth full of bone-crushing teeth!) But the descriptions could sound nonsensical to other observers around the creature.

The situation is much the same when fair-minded people, from different positions, focus solely on the ethics, or environment, or politics of dairy farming in the twenty-first century. Ideally, they could doff blindfolds and discuss the whole cow, which is more than the sum of her parts. An ethicist may stress animal welfare. An environmentalist may measure greenhouse gas-breath effects on climate. A political economist may ponder how two-metre-high hips and shoulders to be harnessed for pulling ploughs, udders for milk yield, and the amount of forage aurochs need for maximum productivity. Ultimately, do we need aurochs? The clock is ticking on the decision, as global institutions (FAO 2006) implicate cattle in climate change that threatens the nutrition and safety of as many as 10 billion Earthlings.

How best can humans avoid climate catastrophe, while managing the nutritional, health, educational and income needs of us all? The answer rests with the elephant – or aurochs – in the room: women.

This truth was recognized by Asian policy makers in the twentieth century. In China, Communist Party Chairman Mao Zedong brought legal equality to grateful women, and enlisted them in agricultural collectivisation. However, Helen Gao, a social policy analyst whose grandmother was a journalist in the 1950s, notes (2017) studies showed women performed demanding tasks but seldom reached management, and earned less than men; more valued jobs with large animals or machinery were usually reserved for men – while women managed most home and childcare

In India, women in small, marginal and landless households generally manage cash from milk sales in Amul-model dairy co-operatives. Amul is headquartered in Anand, Gujarat, where Dr Verghese Kurien led Operation Flood 1970-96, the world's largest dairy development programme linked to the World Food Programme of the UN-FAO (Scholten 1997c, 2010c; World Bank 1998; ILRI 2000; Basu 2009; Bhardwaj 2011; Bhaskar 2011; Business Standard *IJAR* 2018). Today Amul has 3.6 million members. Pratyusha Basu (2009) found women-run dairy co-ops were particularly successful in improving family incomes, health and literacy for children.

A few hours by car from Anand is Mehsana, the base for Amul's sister brand Dudhsagar Dairy, and India's largest co-operative processing plant, for 520,000 mostly smallholder members. Next door is the Mansinhbhai Institute of Dairy & Food Technology, which espouses commitment to women's empowerment and taking care of rural milk producers, most of whom are women (MIDFT 2019). The Dudhsagar co-op, like Amul, returns around 80 per cent of retail prices to farmers. MIDFT aims for 50 per cent enrolment of daughters in its technology courses, because women's leadership is a driving force in village economies. In an 15–16 April 2019 research visit to Mehsana, MIDFT Dean Dharmendra Shukla, and MIDFT Executive Director Dr P.R. Patel explained to this author that female students attend Women's Leadership & Awareness Programmes, giving them impetus for active participation in villages.

In an update of FAO policy, in their article 'Dairy Industry Development Programmes: Their Role in Food and Nutrition Security and Poverty Reduction', Dugdill et al. (2013: 334, 313–54) note the 'incredible success of Operation Flood', and cognate efforts such as Milk Vita in Bangladesh, and the East Africa Dairy Development (EADD) project (Scholten 1999, 2011, 2013b). These entail positive indicators for women, children and their wider communities as income, health, education and literacy improve. Women's initiatives in emerging economies share goals with Washington State Dairy Women (*Hoard's Dairymen* 2019) in the US; they sponsor scholarships for female 'Dairy Ambassadors', who educate students, consumers and the legislature on the nutritional and environmental benefits of sustainable dairying, while preparing for leadership.

Women, solar and methane

Today, India's White Revolution continues with the National Dairy Development Board's (Scholten 2010c; *RGRG Newsletter* Summer 2019) Dairy Plan-Phase 1, in which women are managers of both renewable energy and nutrients in villages. In April 2019 research for this book, we visited Mujkuva Village, about 20km from NDDB headquarters in Anand, Gujarat, north of Mumbai, where ten houses, linked to the bovine biogas system, enjoy smokeless cooking fires and electric light for children's study and family evenings. The 1,000-village pilot is blooming to 5,000 across India. An NDDB technician emphasized that, just as in Operation Flood, women manage cash derived from the sales of new biogas slurry and compost products to crop farmers. Old-tech methane extractors used heavy concrete modules. New PVC 'pillows' are easier to bury, use and repair. Women also control *Kobas Dam* (aka dung money) with (a) liquid-and (b) solid-micronutrients, and (c) phosphate-rich organic manure (PROM) for replenishing organic and non-organic soils that have been strained by up to three annual maize or fodder crops. Solar pumping uses tech licensed from a private firm, via solar panels for the irrigation of crops and pastures for cattle fodder.

In the past, many farmers *liberated* electricity from the grid. Now subsidized solar panels and pumps help decide which crops to plant and not over-irrigate. Example? Tomato yields were poor and took too much water in one area, so a farmer switched to wheat and sold surplus electricity back to the grid for future credits (Tushaar Shah et al. 2018).

A decade ago, a leader of India's Green Revolution, Dr M.S. Swaminathan, lamented that there would never be a second green revolution, because it had turned into a greed revolution driven by proprietary science and monopolistic control, while ignoring small farmers (*Open India* 2011). Another reason was the dearth of knowledge of biology and chemistry taught in agronomy classes. Too many farmers over-applied nitrate chemical fertilizers, not knowing how to balance nitrogen, phosphorus and potassium. Fortunately, the NDDB Dairy Plan's *Kobas Dam* programme trains girls and women in advanced knowledge and technology, helping them transcend the grass ceiling that hitherto blocked them from management and ownership.

Training is key for women if they are to manage and profit from emerging technologies. Efforts are underway around the world inspired by 'Empowering rural women, powering agriculture', the FAO 2030 Agenda for Sustainable Development (UN-FAO 2018). The goal is to advance the well-being of women, families and their animals, feed growing populations, and mitigate climate change.

Training and family experience determine women's expectations in agriculture. This chapter is based on my extended family's experience in twentieth-century North America, when every female *and* male cousin learned to operate tractors and farm machinery, and milk cows at around the age of ten – excellent preparation for farm management. Later, my academic fieldwork (Scholten 2007) identified a grass ceiling, which, with insights by Sally Shortall (2017 et al.; Shortall 2019) in their report on *Women in Farming and the Agriculture Sector* for the Scottish government, suggests how education and training tips the balance to women's empowerment.

How the grass ceiling is made and unmade

Mao Zedong said that 'Women hold up half the sky'. The United Nations estimates they also do half the farm work. While women farmers exceed 25 per cent of world population, participation in farming is little indication of ownership or the power to make decisions on crops or livestock, and women's productivity suffers from limited access to assets, inputs and services. A subtle-but-dense 'glass ceiling' (USDL 1995: 13–15) impedes women's career progress in agriculture as in other sectors (Scholten 2004; Wilson 2007). One example, in the US with its history of pushing for gender equality, is Carly Fiorina; she led Hewlett-Packard from 1999 to 2005, but her presidential campaign failed in 2016. Unlike Argentina, Bangladesh, Ceylon, China, Germany, India, Israel, Liberia, New Zealand and the UK, the US has never had a female chief executive. History, from President Nixon's 'Food Power' policy of export-led agricultural (aka ag) intensification in the 1970s, to President Trump's 'America First' policies of the 2020s, unearths evidence of how changes in social norms (*Economist* 2020; Kahneman & Tversky 1979; Mill 1836) and politics can make such a grass ceiling more or less permeable.

Longitudinal data reveal changes in US women's decision-making power in agrarian transitions due to market-led development, government policies such as the Organic Foods Production Act (OFPA 1990) and National Organic Program (2004; see Scholten 2014). In our age of urbanization, World Bank (2019) statistics show anomalies, bucking the trend of workers exiting agriculture for industry or service sectors. These data show that, between 1991 and 2019, US male agricultural participation remained comparatively stronger than women's.

Ancillary questions are what government policies, and which social trends, have affected women's empowerment in agriculture? Male ag participation has likely remained strong, partly due to USDA Food Power policies in the Nixon administration, 1969–74, to boost exports. Such 'get big or get out' US governmental policies abandoned mixed extensive farms for intensive monoculture, embracing highly capitalized machinery that stereotypically attracts men more than women.

Meanwhile, a counterforce has been pulling woman back to farming methods linked to nature (Murdoch and Miele 1999; Whatmore 2002). Predating Nixon,

Rachel Carson's 1962) book *Silent Spring* warned of biodiversity loss via agro-chemicals like atrazine, DDT and 2,4-D. The US organic movement grew in response to food scares including diseases such as Mad Cow (BSE/nvCJD 1980-2000s; see Smith 2003; Scholten 1990abc, 2007abd), foot and mouth (FMD), and the advent of genetically modified organisms in seeds and GMO dairy hormones (Scholten 1990c). Women have been prominent in organic and alternative food networks (AFNs) and farmers' markets, which quintupled from 1,755 in 1994 to 8,284 in 2014 (USDA-AMS 2014; Scholten 2014: 117).

This chapter combines past and recent research to envisage how more women can transcend the grass ceiling to empowerment. It includes data (USDA-ERS 2013) on increasing numbers of farm operators on a timeline of benchmarks such as grain embargoes, industry consolidation, co-operatives and farmers' markets, showing US women's share of farms and ranches in eleven sales classes. It also refers to interview data from a report to the Scottish government (Shortall et al. 2017) suggesting the backgrounds that help women navigate the grass ceiling vis-à-vis changing public policy – even pandemics.

General vs gender-based decline in agricultural participation

As noted above, women farmers account for over one-quarter of the world's population (NIRD 2018), while worldwide and in the US, as shown in Table 5.1. World Bank data from September 2019 show steady falls in agricultural (ag) employment for men and women in virtually all developed and emerging economies between 1991 and 2019.

Assessing the Grass Ceiling – Methodology

Participation in farming is a stepping-stone towards ownership and the power to make decisions on crops or livestock. But the grass ceiling that hinders their career

Table 5.1 US & World employment in ag (% total employment) (World Bank – Sep. 2019).

https://data.worldbank.org/indicator/SL.AGR.EMPL.ZS?contextual=ag-employment-by-gender&locations=US
US Total ag employment fell from 2.777% in 1991 to 1.41% 2019.
US Female ag employment fell from 1.261% in 1991 to 0.743% in 2019.
US Male ag employment fell from 4% in 1991 to 1.978% in 2019.

https://data.worldbank.org/indicator/SL.AGR.EMPL.ZS?contextual=ag-employment-by-gender&locations=1W
World Total ag employment fell from 43.8% in 1991 to 28.141% 2019.
World Female ag employment fell from 43.475% in 1991 to 27.509% in 2019.
World Male ag employment fell from 44.008% in 1991 to 28.544% in 2019 (modelled ILO est.).

trajectories is illuminated by 1982–2007 statistics (USDA-ERS 2013) on Women Farm Operators, in the context of Nixon's Food Power policies of the 1970s, the Organic Foods Production Act of 1990 and the National Organic Program launched in 2004. The last fifty years have seen upheavals involving grain embargoes, dairy industry consolidation and co-operative mergers. Fortunately, correlations do appear on the five-decade timeline regarding US women's roles on farms and ranches in eleven sales classes. While women have been increasingly visible in corporate communications in US dairy sectors, it is not easy to assess what extent they wield power on the ground – or simply furnish feminine masks to patriarchy. After all, pay and power are more coveted than roles as supernumeraries.

Longitudinal data, referred to below, help explain changes in women's decision-making power, due to market-led development and government policies. We will examine the US Organic Foods Production Act (OFPA 1990) and National Organic Program (2004; Scholten 2014) against the World Bank's findings of steady falls in ag employment of men and women in virtually all developed and emerging economies between 1991 and 2019 (Table 5.1 above). What government policies and social trends affected women's ag empowerment? I hypothesize that US male ag participation remained strong, partly due to gender norms, in response to US Department of Agriculture (USDA) Food Power policies to boost exports in the Nixon administration, in the context of budget and trade deficits during the Vietnam War. As noted in earlier chapters, President Nixon's USDA Secretary Earl Butz famously touted such 'get big or get out' USDA policies, which entailed abandoning mixed extensive farms for intensive monoculture operations, embracing highly capitalized technology and heavy machinery that may attract males more than females.

After clarifying the origin of the terms and concepts 'glass ceiling' and 'grass ceiling' below, we move on to describe how male ag participation is linked to Nixon's USDA export policies and subsequent neoliberal policies. Discussion then shifts to a green counterforce – largely social – that has been pulling woman back to farming methods linked to nature. Then we return to the grass ceiling to consider its current (non-)permeability, drawing on mixed qualitative and quantitative methods which were employed in researching and writing my doctoral thesis (Scholten 2007a) culminating in this chapter. Initial 2000–03 literature reviews informed field research in alternative food networks (farms, farmers' markets, farm shops, box schemes, etc.) around Puget Sound and Seattle in the USA, and my base at Durham University near Newcastle in the UK.

The methodology for my PhD (2007a), my book *US Organic Dairy Politics* (2014), and this present book, used snowball sampling in which different sets of respondents could recommend the SurveyMonkey to others. The separate projects drew on travels, research and interviews in Africa, India and elsewhere.

In broaching the interplay between government macroeconomic policies and how they impact the microeconomic activities and aspirations of women in rural societies, we find an example of a double or multiple hermeneutic among changing ideas of feminism, masculinity and the shifting psychology of social norms which compete with the idea of a rational homo economicus i.e., a person who makes all life choices on the basis of financial advantage rather than, say, traditional gender roles or professions.

The grass ceiling

The glass ceiling

US management consultant Marilyn Loden (2017; BBC 13 Dec 2017) recalled coining the phrase 'glass ceiling' for an invisible barrier on women's career paths in 1978. She noticed that female panellists in a discussion about aspirations 'focused on the deficiencies in women's socialization, the self-deprecating ways in which women behaved, and the poor self-image that many women allegedly carried'. Loden concluded that an 'invisible glass ceiling' blocked career rise beyond the lower rungs of middle management – but that this barrier was 'cultural not personal'. Loden's phrase went global. Lydia Aziato (2017), Dean of the University of Ghana School of Nursing, noted that Loden's 'glass ceiling' first appeared in an *Adweek* article in 1984, and in a 1986 *Wall Street Journal* headline, before the Merriam-Webster Collegiate Dictionary adopted the popular phrase in 1993.

While the focus here is women, there are implications for other marginalized or vulnerable groups. The United States Federal Glass Ceiling Commission defined the glass ceiling as 'the unseen, yet unbreachable barrier that keeps minorities and women from rising to the upper rungs of the corporate ladder, regardless of their qualifications or achievements' (USDL 1995: 13–15; USDA 2012).

Glass to grass ceiling

After the expression 'glass ceiling' leaped from Marilyn Loden's management theory into feminist theory, and then into quotidian world discourse, its resonant corollary 'grass ceiling' – specific to farming – developed independently. This author imagined he created it himself in doctoral fieldwork between 2002 and 2003, in which he observed farmers' markets and alternative food networks (AFNs) around Newcastle and Durham in North-East England, and Seattle, Washington state. Despite the 2001 foot and mouth disease zoonosis, North-East England was a hive of farm-to-farmers-market activity. Seattle and Puget Sound in Washington state featured an organic certification system led by Miles McEvoy, who later led the National Organic Program (NOP; Keating 2009; USDA 2019) until 2017. The women-led Seattle Neighborhood Farmers Market Association (SNFMA; Jarosz 2008; Scholten 2007a, 2014) was part of forty to sixty Washington state farmers' markets and AFNs in which women worked in management, media, certification and political lobbying, as well as farmers, mentors and apprentices in rural–urban food chains and direct marketing. My thesis sources included longtime progressive activist Goldie Caughlan who balanced her job as nutritionist and spokesperson for Puget Consumer Cooperatives (PCC) and supermarkets with national work, such as negotiating organic livestock rules, set 2002 with the USDA in 'the other Washington', the US capital in the District of Columbia.

Fieldwork quickly suggested to me a hypothesis that I dubbed the 'grass ceiling'. To my eventual regret, I was not first to devise the term, which nevertheless garnered numerous references in the resulting thesis, Consumer risk reflections on organic and local food in Seattle, with reference to Newcastle upon Tyne (2007: 65–6, 103, 119 (Tab/Fig), 120 (Tab/Fig), 117, 274, 291). Similar references marked the differently titled, commercially published book, *Food and Risk in the US and UK: Seattle and Newcastle Academics, Firefighters, Motorcyclists and Others Reflect on Organic and Local Food* (Scholten 2011b). Geoff A. Wilson's (2007) book *Multifunctional Agriculture* cited my presentation 'A Grass Ceiling is haunting America's rural economy: Comparing a US alternative agro-food network to those in the UK and Germany' (Scholten 2004). But, a literature search found the phrase used three years earlier in Margaret Alston's (2000) book, *Breaking Through the Grass Ceiling: Women, Power and Leadership in Agricultural Organisations*.

The historical context of gendered US agriculture: Government policies

In our increasingly urbanized age, World Bank (2019) data show anomalies that buck the trend of workers exiting agriculture for industrial or service sectors, hinting that, between 1991 and 2019, US male ag participation remained comparatively stronger than women's, due to the USDA's notorious 'get big or get out' policies boosting intensive monoculture in national supply chains. Although bigger tractors and combines in the Nixon years shed local labour, added foodmiles in transport and worsened point pollution and biodiversity loss, they were claimed to be economically efficient in stabilizing US consumer food costs, while supplying food exports to sustain the national economy.

Examining President Nixon's 'Food Power' policy of export-led ag intensification in the 1970s, and President Trump's 'America First' policies of the 2020s, suggests how politics, and changes in social norms (*Economist* 8 Feb 2020; Kahneman and Tversky 1979; Mill 1836) can raise or lower such a grass ceiling. Today, male participation in ag remains slightly higher than women's, but ratios vary by country (*IJAR* 2018; ILRI 2000).

Historic benchmarks from 1970 to 2020 include the following. In 1971, almost thirty years on from the end of the Second World War, President Nixon abandoned the 1944 Bretton Woods monetary system that had pegged the US dollar exchange rate with other currencies at $35 an ounce of gold. This was the harbinger of neoliberal economics promulgated by President Ronald Reagan, and UK Prime Minister Margaret Thatcher. UK geographers Kevin Morgan, Terry Marsden and Jonathan Murdoch critiqued the provenance of Anglo-American capitalism in their (2006) book *Worlds of Food: Place, Power, Provenance in the Food Chain*. The US farm policy of parity, by which President Franklin D. Roosevelt sustained small farmer incomes vis-à-vis urbanites in the Great Depression (1929–39), was defended by 1952 Democratic presidential candidate Adlai Stevens, and advised by economist John Kenneth Galbraith. But parity was set aside by Republican

President Dwight Eisenhower, and gradually abandoned in the Nixon and Reagan administrations.

On the microeconomic level, these incentivized farmers to raise scale by adding milking cows, and confining them to feedlots, supplied with high-energy but soil-depleting maize planted fence row-to-fence row with monocultural Green Revolution technologies, and inputs such as soybeans sourced from afar. This was to reach the macroeconomic goals of bolstering US farm exports, and balancing trade deficits boosted by spending in the domestic War on Poverty, and the Vietnam War abroad.

Morgan, Marsden and Murdoch (2006) saw that, compared to neoliberal Anglo-American agricultural policy, the European Economic Community's (EEC) Common Agricultural Policy (CAP) retained a multifunctional approach (Wilson 2007). Policy aims included the social welfare goal of limiting rural-to-urban migration by sustaining populations in remote farming communities, and preserving the natural amenities of forests (even wilderness) for city and rural dwellers, by subsidizing production of dairy and arable food and fibre when necessary. The CAP did not restore EEC food security until the end of the 1960s. Yet, US-UK neoliberal policy makers criticized CAP subsidies as wasteful to Europeans and unfair to producers in other countries, including their own.

Post-war European industrial and service sectors gradually rallied, nearing pre-First World War levels. Economists call this ramping-up of production toward the limits of the world's production possibilities frontier (PPF). Greater trade increased technology transfer and efficiencies that caused a fall in farm labour. Decades of World Bank (1970–2019) data show farm employment rates falling, especially in developed economies, though the vast US Midwest helped maintain its status as a food exporter.

The historical context of gendered US agriculture: Food scares and science wars

Yet as US agriculture intensified, there were curious developments on gender frontiers. A relatively higher proportion of males remained in US ag than in some developed economies, as heavier machines were designed not just for harvest, but as metal carousels big enough to rotate fifty cows during milking. Multi-crop farming was left behind in a switch to monocultures in which pests were suppressed by chemicals such as atrazine and DDT, instead of multi-cropping and crop rotation. Cultural voices such Frances Moore Lappé decried waste and global food insecurity as negative externalities of the meat-based US diet, dependent on imports of foreign soybeans in *Diet for a Small Planet* (1971). The late twentieth-century legacy of superficially cheap food has led to rampant food waste, from fields to households in many countries (*Economist Intelligence Unit* 2017).

Ever since Homer's mythical Achilles revealed his gender by selecting a sword amid a display of women's accessories, men have been stereotyped as fond of weapons, tools and heavy machinery. Consider the Trojan Horse. By the same token, women are stereotyped as oriented to home, hearth, nature and organics. Whereas US male ag participation remained strong, a grassroots force pulled women toward paradigms variously described as extensive, natural or organic. Predating Nixon, Rachel Carson's (1962) book *Silent Spring* warned of toxicity in food chains and biodiversity loss due to chemicals introduced to farming after the Second World War. The US organic movement grew in response to such scares, as well as chronic zoonoses such as tuberculosis and foot and mouth disease (FMD). The mid-1980s brought more primal fear in the form of new variant bovine spongiform encephalopathy (nvBSE), or Mad Cow disease presenting in humans as new variant Creutzfeldt-Jakob disease (nvCJD) (Scholten 2007ab). With the 1994 commercial sale of recombinant bovine growth hormone/recombinant bovine somatotropin (rBGH/rBST) in the dairy sector, consumer fears of intensive dairy farming grew. Mark Kastel, author of the *Down on the Farm, the Real BGH Story: Animal Health Problems, Financial Trouble* (1995), identified serious problems in the eponymous title of his report for the Rural Vermont Rural Education Action Project.

US diabetics welcomed GMO insulin for their treatment, but consumers in the US, UK, EU and other countries resisted synthetic dairy hormones out of concern for animal harm and the potential tainting of human food. Jeffrey M. Smith (2003, 2009) who founded the Institute for Responsible Technology, also deplored Monsanto's GMO dairy rBGH/rBST (and Roundup®-dependent crops). These dairy hormones were banned in Canada, the UK, EU and parts of Asia and Africa, but not the US. Agri-pharmaceutical corporations blamed public uncertainty over biotech inputs on fear of science, but Americans put higher priority on healthy eating and farming (Pew Research Center 2016; *PeerJ* 2018), to the extent that a celebrity chef called farmers the real rock stars (Phillipov and Goodman 2017).

US introduction in the 1990s, of genetically modified seeds tolerant of glyphosate, elicited consumer distrust. Increasingly, even consumers who assumed GMO foods were safe to eat feared the loss of biodiversity entailed by GMO monoculture. Industry promises that GMO technology would reduce the aggregate quantities of herbicides and pesticides deposited on crops faded, as greater amounts were needed to counter evolving weeds among GMO corn, cotton and soy (Benbrook 2007). Multinational pharmaceutical companies flexed their muscles, for example, lobbying an academic journal to retract a paper critical of the herbicide by Gilles-Eric Séralini et al. (2012, 2014; *Economist* 2013).

The 1981–93 Reagan–Bush administrations marked abandonment in the US of the precautionary principle inherent in the 1958-era Delaney Clause, in favour of the risk–benefit approach advocated by biotechnology proponents (Scholten 1990b; Scholten 1990c; Scholten 2007b; Smith 2003). This reflects US policies of maintaining global economic dominance via new technologies such as GMOs, as had been the case with autos, aviation, and TV in previous product cycles.

Consumer attitudes were changing. Although the Hartman Group (1997, 2004, 2006) near Seattle found little difference in young men's and women's organic food buying habits, surveys determined that when new parents (especially highly educated ones) weaned babies from human breast milk, many turned to organic bovine milk, which was perceived as untainted by BSE and other risks. In 2016, a survey of 1,480 US adults by Pew Research Center (2016) titled 'The New Food

Fights' found 75 per cent of Americans believed organic foods were healthier than conventional foods, and women and men had similar views on organic and GM foods, adding: 'However, women tend to care more deeply about the issue of GM foods than do men, a concern that is quite consequential for people's views and behaviours about food.' This was borne out in my research in both the UK and US (Scholten 2007a) finding women more likely than men to eat organic food themselves and to serve it to guests in home meals (**Tables 5.2a and 5.2b, below**).

Food scares from the 1960s through the 1990s pushed some US consumers away from conventional intensive food systems Scholten (2006a). Many women were pulled toward alternative food networks (AFNs), often as actors prominent in urban markets linked to local and organic farms (Scholten 2014: 72). In 2018, Olivia Taylor-Puckett (2018), manager of the venerable Lawrence Farmers' Market in Kansas, USA, wrote in *Women Farmers Weekly* that most of its eighty-seven vendors were women, with twenty-three of those businesses female-run or co-owned. She described a contradiction between the old image of a man on a tractor on a vast field and the new, diversified farms run by women with plant and animal products marketed by them. Taylor-Puckett explained: 'Women in particular are taking advantage of the cornerstones of market culture: connection with customers and other farmers, low entry cost, ability to diversify products offered, community building, and capturing a larger share of the customer dollar.' Trust in organics and suspicion of GMO farming methods and inputs motivates increased women's participation. (This is also the case in Europe, where 28 per cent of farm managers are women (Eurostat 2019; FAO-STAT 2012.)

Some questions on women's empowerment that were inexplicable decades ago might be answered here. The process involved a literature review connecting early questions to later conclusions, my doctoral (2007a) corpus of US-UK food network data, interviews with informants hinting at the factor of heavy machinery in agricultural success, and twenty-first century data from global, national and academic institutions. Recent research (Shortall et al. 2017) reveals attitudes to heavy machinery among women of urban and rural origins, which (coupled with their knowledge of the actors and supply chains that maintain such technology, as well as access to capital) help explain how some women transcend the grass ceiling to farm ownership or management.

Is the grass ceiling becoming more permeable?

Women's increasing empowerment in agriculture

As mentioned, the United Nations Food and Agricultural Organization (FAO 2018) targets women's empowerment in its goals for 2030. The World Bank's (2 March 2018) feature story 'Breaking the "Grass Ceiling": Empowering Women Farmers' reflects consensus that improving women's incomes and decision-making authority has positive leveraged effects on children's and family health, education, professional attainment, as well as mitigating population growth by delaying marriage and childbirth (NIRD Nov 2018). This is not surprising, as my academic study on *International Dairy Product Aid & Trade 1960s–1990s focusing on the EU and India in Operation Flood* (1997), identified benefits for women and families, before the World Bank published similar conclusions (Candler and Kumar 1998). My book *India's Operation Flood* (2010) showed that raising women's central roles in dairy development raised family incomes, health, education, literacy and well-being. Pratyusha Basu's (2009) book on *Villages, Women, and the Success of Dairy Cooperatives in India: Making Place for Rural Development* underlines such family-friendly outcomes, especially in women-only co-operative societies.

It is important to distinguish not just how many women participate in farming, but how numerous they are among high-level farm owners and operators, and on what pay grade. What percentage of women break through this grass ceiling to manage the largest agri-corporations, co-operatives, trade associations and linked entities?

Evidence for women's increasing empowerment – albeit from a low base – is found in a USDA Economic Research Service (Apr 2013) bulletin, 'Characteristics of Women Farm Operators and their Farms'. With first-time access to Census of Agriculture data from 1978 to 2007, Robert Hoppe and Penni Korb (USDA April 2013: iv–v) note: 'The share of US farms operated by women nearly tripled over the past three decades, from 5 percent in 1978 to 14 percent by 2007.' Especially significant is that women's operations increased in all sales classes. They add that when second operators are considered, women farmers neared 1 million (about 40 per cent of secondary women operators work off-farm 200 or more days a year). Concurrently, declines occurred in men's operation of farms – understandable when the number of farms, notably pastured dairy farms, declined rapidly via mergers into larger, often intensive monoculture or confined livestock dairy operations.

Is this evidence of the grass ceiling becoming more porous? Results are mixed. Hoppe and Korb (April 2013: iv) found women-operated farms in the US were generally very small with, from 1982, most having annual sales under $10,000. Growth in women-operated farms occurred mostly in that sales class, rising from about 60 per cent in 1982 to 75 per cent in 2007. Generally, the share of women-operated farms with sales under $10,000 was 20 per cent of male-operated farms in that sales class. In what could be described as breaking through the grass ceiling, 5 per cent of women-operated farms sold more than $100,000 in 2007. Hoppe & Korb (2007: iv) say: 'Most of these farms specialized in grains and oilseeds, specialty crops, poultry and eggs, beef cattle, or dairy.' About 50 per cent of women-operated farms with sales of at least $1 million were poultry and egg operations. It would be interesting to see how profitable these women's holdings remain in 2022, after decades in which US-based corporations such as Tyson Foods recruited thousands of family-scale poultry producers into contracted production, documented in the 2008 film *Food Inc.* The financial sustainability of women's farms in the COVID-19 pandemic begs research.

Perhaps linked to the Great Recession that began 2007–08, the 2012 US Census of Agriculture (UC Berkeley 1999; USDA 2014) revealed a nuanced relationship between aspirational farm women and the grass ceiling, as the number of female farm operators fell from 985,192 in 2007 to 969,672 in 2012 (–2 per cent). Total farm operators fell from 3.3 million to 3.2 million (–3 per cent). Yet, as farm operators of both sexes dwindled, women maintained a 30 per cent proportion of total farm operators in 2007 and 2012. This suggested women were consolidating gains in ag operations, in a small but notable turn toward gender equality. But the grass ceiling remained impermeable to many: 76 per cent of women-operated farms had sales less than $10,000 compared to 56 per cent for men; just 1 per cent of women-operated farms had sales of $1,000,000 or more, compared to 4 per cent for men (USDA NASS, 2012 Census of Agriculture).

Women, heavy machinery and technology

Recent research led by Sally Shortall (2017 et al., Shortall 2019) improves our understanding of how the grass ceiling in countries including Ireland, Scotland and the US, is made or unmade through generations of women's lives. Her work suggests conclusions on how girls' and women's past experiences with heavy machinery (and by inference, other technologies that may intimidate neophytes) can predict breakthroughs to empowerment. She has elucidated several strands of research on gender, and on bodies in society, relating to the grass ceiling. Shorthall was first author of the *Women in Farming and the Agriculture Sector* report for the Scottish Government (2017). The interviews addressed five key areas: 1. career paths, 2. daily life, 3. aspirations, 4. representation in ag organisations, and 5. farm succession. Focus groups also delineated these and associated questions. Scottish women respondents saw themselves in 'multiple, overlapping roles' (*WiFatAS* 2017: 39) with: '64% of main survey respondents identifying themselves as a "working woman", followed by "farmer's wife" (36%), "farmer" (33%), "homemaker" (33%), "career woman" (25%), "crofter" (16%), "caregiver" (13%) and "land manager" (9%).'

The report (*WiFatAS* 2017: 39–40) also found 27 per cent to 32 per cent of women in farming had university degrees, compared to about 16 per cent to 27 per cent of male farm operators. The percentage of women with university degrees was even higher among urban women who married male farmers. Such urban-originated women were apt to bring skills conducive to organizing on-farm activities such as hospitality or alternative food networks – but less keen on heavy machinery (and related technologies) in the production, processing and marketing aspects of regional development or globalization of agro-food networks (Raynolds 2004).

Relevant to this paper's exploration of the grass ceiling were many references in the Scottish report to technology involving heavy machinery (*WiFatAS* 2017: 15, 29, 39–40, 42, 54–5, 58). Only 9.5 per cent of women thought they had a role in major decisions such as new land or machinery development (*WiFatAS* 2017: 42). Notably, of women with on-farm aspirations, only 1.4 per cent wanted to work with heavy machinery. Less than one-quarter of women – 23.8 per cent – indicated that they wanted to run their own farm, while 29.3 per cent wanted a career where they could work with animals' (*WiFatAS* 2017: 54–5). According to the report (*WiFatAS* 2017: 58): 'Women not raised on farms are less interested in becoming involved in leadership of farming organisations (only 3%).' In a revealing statistic, women new to farms were interested in developing farm diversification activities – some 36 per cent, in comparison to 23 per cent of women raised on farms. They were typically keener on developing bed & breakfasts (B&Bs) or farm shops, rather than achieving greater economies of scale in core businesses such as crops or livestock production via heavy machinery.

The study (*WiFatAS* 2017: 58) led by Shorthall supports a conclusion from my own US-UK fieldwork (Scholten 2007a, 2011): On a continuum from Small-Organic to Family-Organic to Industrial-Organic operations on my Organic Agri-Farm Gender Scale, the grass ceiling is most impermeable to women's rise to top agricultural ownership and status on the cusp between Family-Organic and Organic-Industrial operations (see Tables 5.3a and 5.3b below). Talent for dealing with logistics, supply chains and socio-cultural barriers helps break the grass ceiling. The World Bank (2018) also notes that good relations with her bankers gave one third-generation poultry farmer access to capital and finance after Hurricane Sandy damaged her farm. Access to capital is even greater in the dairy sector, where familiarity and fondness for heavy machinery are markers of future achievement.

These conclusions are supported by interviews in Shortall's solo entry 'Planning the farmyard – Gender implications', in the *Routledge Companion to Rural Planning* (2019: 326–9, 328): 'While young people cannot drive cars until they are seventeen years old, exceptions are made for farm children who are allowed to drive heavy machinery at thirteen and fourteen years of age.' Early familiarity with passenger cars encourages grappling with farm equipment and vice-versa, in my US experience.

This helps explain why educated urban women who marry male farmers often initiate diversification into tourism, farm shops or farmers' markets, but with relatively less automotive experience than rural-born young women, seem less fixed on utilizing heavy machinery and other technologies to expand food or fibre production. Shortall et al.'s report (ScotGovt 2017: 28) explains: 'Women <u>not</u> raised on farms take on the same responsibilities as their more experienced counterparts (e.g., in livestock care, administration and machinery use), but were less likely to report contributing skills in machinery handling, and also livestock husbandry.' This makes sense if city-reared women accumulate knowledge on hospitality and retail industries, but little relating to farm machinery.

Women and farming across generations

Malcolm Gladwell's (2008) book *Outliers: The Story of Success* argues that in analysing top achievers, too much emphasis is put on individual talent or genius. He suggests more focus on origins, e.g., urban or rural, and what experience they bring to work. A key takeaway from *Outliers* is the idea that it requires 10,000 hours to achieve proficiency. This approximates twenty hours of work per week for ten years, about three hours a day. This dovetails with family-scale dairy farming. Consider that dairy girls and boys typically sit on their tractor-driving parents' laps from age of three or four (much like their nineteenth-century peers would have sat a horse), and older kids stand on the sideboard chatting with the driver. Children begin helping with chores from about the age of six. Chores may involve herding and feeding cattle, cleaning barns, planting crops, bucking bales and driving harvest wagons, assisting with calving, and testing milk for somatic cell counts (SCC). Youngsters also feed calves and wash cows' udders in milking before school, as well as putting in more houses in the evening milking and clean-up. Most kids want to drive a tractor and most learn. Years of adult supervision inculcate safe procedures. By the time they leave secondary school, ten years later, they have easily experienced 10,000 hours of dairy work. Training in family farm work – or in agricultural colleges – replaces kids' initial fears of noisy, potentially dangerous machinery with prideful competence in controlling tractors, mowers, milking machines, vacuum pumps and other technologies, building family success.

A longitudinal study of an extended family in Washington state bears this out (Scholten 2007, 2011). In the early 1950s, four brothers and one sister in one family married and with their spouses established dairy farms cut from forest land. Of a total of twenty-six boys and girls born among the extended family group, all learned to drive tractor at around the age of ten. They routinely performed potentially dangerous tasks such as hooking tractors to harvest wagons and driving them to storage barns. Soon they could plough fields, plant maize and mow hay. Not that those tasks could not be gendered: boys generally were assigned more work associated with, for example, cattle waste, than girls. Farm work engendered self-esteem: individuals of both genders manifested an attitude of 'Anything you can do, I can do better!' In family farm sustainability, succession is a crucial benchmark. In this case, two of the five farms were eventually inherited by daughters, and three by sons (although in all cases, spouses shared some farm tasks). It bears repeating that these women were groomed from childhood toward proficiency in farm skills. Pre-school girls or boys who sat on the laps of their tractor-driving parents had a headstart on their city cousins in the race toward farm management or ownership, 10,000 hours later.

Interviews with 'Ken' (pseudonym in Scholten 2002, 2007, 2014) of Ken & Jenny's Farm illustrated the advantage of childhood familiarity with machinery. (See Tables 5.3a and 5.4b below.) These represent 3 levels of operation: Small-Organic, Family-Organic, and Industrial-Organic. Ken inherited the family farm near Seattle and – after unprofitable years as a conventional dairy farm – converted it to an organic arable farm (Scholten 2002). Besides their core production of USDA organic-certified herbs for a German-based multinational corporation, they had an ancillary business selling organic compost regionally. Customers included urban-born women entrepreneurs who managed small flower, fruit and veg farms, which seldom used machinery heavier than a hand-guided rototiller. Ken used a truck, trailer and loader to deliver compost 300 miles away, recalling: 'These women ask, "how can you work with all this machinery?" I wonder how can they work without it.'

'Liv Smith' (pseudonym), an extension agent for a Pacific Northwest university (personal communication 26 Jun 2020) remembered harvests during the 1950s and 60s when women and children often preserved garden fruit, veg and meat in the humid house, while men, pre-teens and teenagers gathered silage and hay, driving tractors and wagons from fields to silos or haymows in barns. Smith recalled it was hot and uncomfortable work for women and kids canning glass jars of fruit, veg and meat with pressure cookers in the house: 'It was way more fun driving the hay wagon than in the kitchen canning with grandma. Usually better pay as well.'

Recently unearthed references, from Marilyn Loden in 1978, and Sally Shorthall in 2019, returned my gaze to previous consideration of the grass ceiling. This included qualitative observations by US informants such as Ken above – that women's resistance to machinery may block their adoption of economies of scale – impeding their progress through the grass ceiling (Tables 5.3a and 5.3b below. See also Scholten 2007a: 65). In years of thesis work this author took 10,000 photographs, but there were few examples of women driving tractors, or even two-handed roto-tillers. My recommendation? Teach the children!

Women in agriculture from 2000

Women and organic agriculture

While intensification and upscaling in US Food Power policies of the 1970s pushed women from agriculture, a countervailing turn to nature and quality heralded by the Organic Foods Production Act (OFPA 1990) pulled some back to farming (Goodman and DuPuis 2002). This happened simultaneously with the gradual shedding of both sexes from farm labour; for example, and as noted above, World Bank (Sep 2019) data show US Total ag employment fell from 2.777 per cent in 1991 to 1.41 per cent in 2019. Please consider: the recession (defined as two consecutive quarters of negative economic growth) in the administration of President George H. W. Bush, began July 1990 and continued to March 1991 (University of California, Berkeley 1999). Thus, the advent of the OFPA 1990 overlapped with that recession. Both female and male ag employment curves dropped until 1993 (1.151 per cent women; 3.761 per cent men), but women rebounded on a steeper curve than men by 1994 (women 1.5 per cent; men 3.818 per cent). Women's employment in ag rose to a new height in 1995 (women 1.521 per cent; men 3.772 per cent), and women maintained a comparative plateau until the drought year of 1999 (1.357 per cent women; 3.376 per cent men), according to the World Bank (2019).

Later, both women's and men's farm employment fell in 2000 (falls for women of 0.859 per cent; for men of 2.253 per cent). The dot-com bust of 2000, and 9/11 crisis of 2001, squeezed more jobs from ag in many countries. But OFPA (1990) and establishment of the USDA National Organic Program boosted US women's participation in the farmers' market and alternative food network boom. It also positioned women such as Maria Morgan, CEO of US firm Cascadian Organic under General Mills, and Rachel Rowlands, head of eponymous UK firm Rachel's Organic bought by Horizon USA, into globalized agro-food networks.

A look at organic agriculture allows a closer look at the (non-) permeability of the grass ceiling in this expanding sector. In a qualitative study of what motivates UK consumers to buy organic food, Aikaterini Makatouni (*British Food Journal* 2002, also 2001), found women pay more attention to organics than men. Supporting Makatouni are my Tables 4a and 4b below, quantified from 404 responses to my 2002–03 US-UK Food & Risk Survey. Of 226 people surveyed in the Newcastle area of Northern England, 62.02 per cent of seventy-nine women reported eating organics in their diets, compared to 50.34 per cent of 147 men. Of 178 people surveyed in the Seattle area, USA, 81.81 per cent of seventy-seven women reported eating organics in their diets, compared to 62.37 per cent of 101 men. Women in both the UK and US demonstrated greater affinity for organic food, compared to men, in higher reporting of serving organics in the last meal they hosted guests in their home – a revealing display of values. Of 226 area people surveyed in the Newcastle area, 35.44 per cent of seventy-nine women reported serving organics in the last meal they hosted guests in their home , compared to just 21.76 per cent of 147 men.

Parallel to intensification of US crops production, dairy farming upscaled from relatively small herds of fifty 50 pastured cows in 1970 to hundreds of them confined in concentrated animal feeding operations (CAFOs). Milking time per cow in new steel-and-glass pipeline milking parlours was faster and easier for farmers who – formerly in stanchioned barns – had to lift five-gallon (*c*. 45lbs or 20kg) buckets of milk from cows' belly straps, then pour it into steel buckets and hand carry them to a milk cooler. Standing on the same concrete, a milker could put a gentle hand on the animal's back and flanks, using voice to reassure her, as she munched hay and grain from the manger in front. Newer milking parlours limited eye-to-eye contact, weakening human–non-human relations, although

Table 5.2a Eat organic food (**2002–03, gendered**) (Scholten 2007a, 2011b: 2016).

Newcastle	Male	Female	Seattle	Male	Female
UK226 All	147 (**50.34%**)	79 (62.02%)	US178 All	101 (**62.37%**)	77 (**81.81%**)

Table 5.2b Guests served organics at last home meal (2002–03, gendered) (Scholten 2007a, 2011b: 233).

Newcastle	Male	Female	Seattle	Male	Female
UK226 All	32/147 (**21.76%**)	28/79 (**35.44%**)	US178 All	32/101 (**31.68%**)	35/77 (**45.45%**)

those might be re-established if farmers talked to cows and scratched their ears when cleaning the loafing shed.

Early proponents of confining cows in covered loafing sheds described lucky cows freed from muddy walks to pastures, lounging on sand or straw near a bovine salad bar. But bovine resilience suffered in confinement and from walking on concrete, resulting in weakened immune systems that harmed digestion, leg and hoof health, brought mastitis, laminitis, and – most terminal – infertility. Boosting cow milk yield 250 per cent from 1950 to 2014 stressed cows, accelerated their culling and shortened their lives. Knowledge of this concerned some older and women US dairy farmers who were discouraged by the new technologies and welcomed retirement in interviews with researchers (LeCompte-Mastenbrook 2004; Scholten 2002).

The Organic Valley dairy co-operative, founded 1988, joined Green allies in demanding a national organic certification programme in the US. Ironically, Greens won more allies after 1993, when the US Food and Drug Administration (FDA) approved Monsanto's synthetic dairy hormone. Mark Kastel – a former farm equipment salesman for International Harvester and J.I. Case, before health concerns turned him to sustainable farming – summariZed animal health problems of the GMO dairy peptide hormone BGH/rBST (recombinant Bovine Growth Hormone/ recombinant Bovine Somatotropin, branded Posilac) in his 1995 report for the non-profit group Rural Vermont. Such reports contributed to the decision by Canada's veterinary board to prohibit sale of rBGH/rBST when trials showed negative effects on bovine health, and it was also banned in Europe (Scholten 2014: 93; Scholten 1990: 190). Notwithstanding, the GMO drug boosted US dairy yield for years, before consumer opinion turned negative and co-operatives, including Darigold, asked farmer members to discontinue its use.

This was also true for animal welfarist members of Compassion in World Farming (2020), established in 1967 by UK dairy farmers Peter and Anna Roberts, who were vexed by intensive dairying's harm to animals, environment and people (*Guardian* 15 Nov 2006). CIWF was the first organisation to target farm animal welfare, and the Roberts' historic achievement in 1997 was recognition of animals as 'sentient beings' in the European Union Amsterdam Treaty of Protocol on Animal Welfare (*Guardian* 15 Nov 2006). In the post-Brexit era, UK recognition of animal sentience is wavering. In *Food and Animal Welfare*, Henry Buller and Emma Roe (2018) note EU recognition of animal sentience was written into the 2009 Lisbon Treaty, reflecting a shift in gaze to the subjective experience of the animal life lived, before slaughter. Yet, Buller and Roe (2018: 10) note: '…globally, the number of animals farmed and meat consumption itself continue to increase vertiginously.'

People for the Ethical Treatment of Animals (PETA), established in Maryland during 1980 – held the dairy sector's hooves to the fire of public opinion, and the industry began to respond. In Scandinavia, equipment maker DeLaval (2013) hosted a world longevity conference; the proceedings accepted that cows can live a quarter-century, but few outlived half a decade. Culling was seen by this author as a proxy for animal welfare in the book *US Organic Dairy Politics*, finding involuntary cull rates of 30–40 per cent customary in Canada, and even higher in China, Turkey and parts of the US (Scholten 2014: 20, 39, 49, 64–6, 125; DeLaval 2013). US liquid milk consumption peaked in the Baby Boomer generation, but many Generation Xers and Millennials were disillusioned with what their Boomer parents deemed nature's perfect food (DuPuis 2002). Millennials often chose plant-based drinks over bovine milk, which CiWF and PETA identified with zero-grazing and poor welfare (while organic milk from pastured herds increased market share). Dairy data service DHI-Provo (2013; now Amelicor) tracked a significant rise in US national culling rates from 36.7 to 42.7 per cent between 2004 and 2013.

Veterinarian Paul Biagiotti (2014), experienced in large and small conventional and organic dairy herds, wrote of a culling crisis of 44 per cent in Idaho megadairies, allowing average cows only a one-in-two chance of completing one full lactation. Inability to conceive was a prime reason for sending nearly half of cows to slaughter without birthing a second calf. This motivated some welfarists to theorize dairy as a feminist issue, with cows subject to cycles of artificial insemination (AI), birthing calves which are soon taken away, producing about 10,000 kg of milk per year. They then have to undergo chemical oestrus, and more AI-induced pregnancy if she is strong enough to conceive, in another round of what some see as lactic bondage.

Yet if feminists viewed intensive dairying as a manifestation of patriarchal technology, it was hardly kinder to male bovines. After the Second World War, tractors made male calves redundant for on-farm traction in many countries. In France young bulls became veal calves, but this was opposed by welfarists. Millennials who knew many bull calves were euthanized shortly after birth – if they did not spend truncated lives in the veal crates – understood welfarists saying 'Dairy is scary' (*Guardian* 30 May 2017; Scholten 1995), and more chose non-dairy products. Scientists developed 'sexed semen' that lowered the number of male calves born, but many remained superfluous to profits in the age of tractors.

Also working against longevity – and the pastoral idyll – was a sad outcome of Mad Cow disease: the progressive nature of BSE meant the risk of transmission to humans increased with bovine age. Thus 'dirty cows' suspected of carrying 'rogue prions' were subject to slaughter at earlier stages of their projected lifetimes (Scholten 2007: 189–97). Citing risks in the Mad Cow scandal, China banned British beef after 1996, when the UK admitted a bovine–human link in the BSE scandal. China also banned imports of US beef over thirty months old between 2001 and 2020 (*Global Times* 24 Feb 2020).

In *Food in Society* (2001: 243, 241–4) British geographers Peter Atkins and Ian Bowler noted knowledge of unsavoury aspects of dairy and meat production in the BSE era encouraged a 'gender bias' to vegetarianism among UK and Australian girls and young women, compared to boys and men.

In an article in *Frontiers in Psychology* (2018), Hamish J. Love and Danielle Sulikowski concluded: 'Men exhibited stronger associations than did women between meat and the concepts "healthy" and "delicious"', apparently as a social

Table 5.3a Seattle, US organic agri-farm gender scale.

SEATTLE, US ☐ ORGANIC AGRI-FARM GENDER SCALE

Bruce A. Scholten 2002-04 (17 June 20)

Scale & Products [*pseudonym*]	Network	Actors/CEO gender
Industrial-Organic (>$250,000/£125,000 gross income annually)		
Cascadian Farm-Small Planet Foods-General Mills; Cascadian-SPF & Muir Glen: 160 frozen & canned fruit, veg, ready meals. US Cheerios GMO/UK non-GMP. Organic Cheerios 'Purely O's' sold as Cascadian Farm (est. 1972). Cascadian linked to PCC coop Seattle.	Skagit farmshop (FS) nat'l supermarkets. USDA-NOSB links.	♂♂♀ Male Casc-SPF founder Gene Kahn sold to male MNC General Mills Cascadian CEO Maria Morgan 2003. ♀
Dean-Horizon-Rachel's Organic dairy: milk, yogurt, desserts ($250m sales 2005). Rachel's unknown in US. PCC Natural Markets boycott Horizon in 2006 re NoSB-USDA grazing rules.	Wal-Mart-US; UK supers. Dean plants in Spain	♂ Dean-Horizon-Rachel's Chair Greg Engles 2004-6.
Organic Valley: est 1988; co-op of 1010 family dairy farms from Minnesota to Whatcom Co, Washington ($245m sales 2005). Lost Wal-Mart contract to Horizon. Skagit Land Trust (2004) assists.	Family farms to supers & coops.	♂ 2004-06 CEO George Siemon, who retired 2019 w/ 1900 members.
Whole Foods: leads corporate natural & organic grocers e.g. Red Apple, Trader Joe's, Seattle's Central Market supers.	US & new UK chains.	♂ CEO John Mackey.
PCC Natural Markets (Puget Consumers Cooperative, est. 1972): 36k members (US #1). Goldie Caughlan (National Organic Standards Board) boycotts Horizon re pasture grazing rules.	8 Seattle area super-markets. NOSB links.	♂ Bob Cross Chair (2006) followed male chair in 2000.
Pioneer Organics: box scheme (est. 1997): supplies Full Circle Farm (Salmon Safe cert); vends with Seattle NFMA. Home box delivery to 5000 customers in Seattle & 1000 in Portland.	Puget Sound WA & Portland, OR.	♂ Male owner president Ronny Bell.
Badger Mountain Vineyard (WA): organic wine.	USA, Japan.	♂♂♂♀ Father, son, couple.

(continued)

Table 5.3a *Continued*

SEATTLE, US ▬ ORGANIC AGRI-FARM GENDER SCALE
Bruce A. Scholten 2002–04 (17 June 20)

Scale & Products (*pseudonym*)	Grass Ceiling?	Network	Actors/CEO gender
Family-Organic (<$250k)			
Seattle Neighbourhood Farmers Market Alliance (NFMA): 6 + city backed Farmers' Markets (FMs).		Seattle & statewide.	♀♀ Women-led by Chris Curtis, Karen Kinney.
***Ken & Jenny's Farm** (est. 1959): 90 acres: 40 types herbs, fruit, veg (e.g. beans, corn), compost, Whatcom Co. & region. No FMs.		Herb supplier to German MNC Flora.	♂♀ Male farmer. Wife keeps books. Seasonal Latin workers.
***Elm Hall Farm** (est. 1972): 47 acre fruit, flower, & veg. A pioneer family alternative food network (AFN) operation.		Whatcom–Seattle FMs, Slow Food.	♀♂ Woman, male partner & family.
***Alpen Dairy**: 1st Whatcom supplier to switch from Darigold coop to Organic Valley (CROPP) coop.		Regional – national.	♂♀ Man, wife & children.
***Artisan Farmstead Cheese**: artisanal cheedar, curd, feta, fromage blanc, gouda, paneer, quark on 300 cow Dutch dairy.		Farm shop; Whatcom–Seattle FMs, supers.	♂♀ ♂♀ 2 brothers & families.
***Sam & Wife Farm**: Cheese & butter to Puget Sound FMs & supermarkets.		Bellingham–Sea FMs.	♂♀ ex-Cascadian man & wife.
Small-Organic (<$50k)			
***Betty's Farm**: flowrs, fruit, herbs, veg to Skagit co-op, FMs & restaurants.		Skagit–Whatcom FMs.	♀ Betty – organic pioneer since 1970.
***Dandelion CSA Farm**: fruit, veg, eggs. Linked to PCC, NFMA & state apprentice programme.		King–Seattle FMs.	♀♂ woman & partner.
***Hi-Skies Farm**: plant starters.		Snohomish FMs.	♀♀ women, PT.
***Fireman's Wife**: flowers, veg.		Kitsap FMs.	♀♂ woman & husband.

signal of their keenness on 'hunting and meat provisioning' to primarily other rival men.

Gender increasingly marked food chains. The intensification of chemically dependent, potentially toxic inputs (*Economist* 2013) in GMO crops from rapeseed to wheat, plus additions of non-traditional commodities such as poultry feathers in dairy rations, were accompanied by heavier machinery – e.g., field tractors and freeway-sized tractor-trailers to deliver totally mixed rations (TMR) in dairy barns longer than football fields. Massive equipment dispelled romantic visions of pastoral farming, pushing some women from the ag sector, attracted by jobs in services or other industries.

Locating the grass ceiling *in the organic sector*

The Scottish Government report on *Women in Farming and the Agriculture Sector* led by Sally Shorthall (*WiFatAS* 2017: 58) supports a finding from my US-UK fieldwork in alternative food networks (Scholten 2007a): on a continuum from Small-to-Family- to Industrial-scale operations on my Organic Agri-Farm Gender Scales (**Tables 5a above & 5b below**), the grass ceiling is most resistant to women's rise to top agricultural ownership and status on the cusp between Family-Organic and Organic-Industrial operations.

This assessment was made by 2007, years before reading Shortall et al.'s Scottish study (*WiFatAS* 2017: 39–40), which found women from urban backgrounds keener on hospitality or alternative food networks – but less so on production, processing, and marketing involving heavy machinery in agro-food networks.

Market entry to Small-Scale actors is not prohibitive. Near Seattle, US, 'Betty's Farm' (pseudonym) grew flowers, herbs and veg on two acres of rented land. Near Newcastle, UK, 'Mum's Organic Meats' (pseudonym) relied less on financial investment that a woman's flexibility in linking a passionate grower of organic lamb and beef with quality-minded customers. However, the jump to the next level, of Family-Scale operations is costlier. In 1965 USA, the start-up cost for a forty-acre dairy farm with thirty cows was $250,000, and has multiplied since then. Thus, a woman pursuing success on the Family-Scale needs heavy capitalization, or an inherited operation such as Elm Hall farm near Seattle, US, or 'Cuthbert's Boxes' (pseudonyms) near Newcastle, UK.

The climb to and through the grass ceiling is fraught with stops along the way. But the jump to Industrial-Organic is the most complex, requiring world-quality products, and competitive nous, in a globalized market beset by fraud in imports such as soybeans, and poor monitoring and enforcement of domestic quality standards by the USDA (*Washington Post* 2018). The metaphor of a woman's grass ceiling is like a hurdle – but placement of hurdles can change according to events – or pandemics.

Table 5.3b Newcastle, UK, organic agri-farm gender scale.

NEWCASTLE, UK 🇬🇧 ORGANIC AGRI-FARM GENDER SCALE

Bruce A. Scholten 2002–04 (17 Jun 20)

Scale & Products (*pseudonym)	Network	Actors/Gender
Industrial-Organic (>$250,000 / £125.000 gross income annually)		
Dean–Horizon-Rachel's Organic: milk, yogurt, desserts. Rachel's was one of few UK farms to **refuse chemical inputs in WW [??]II; joined Soil Assoc. in 1947:** www.deanfoods.com; www. horizonorganic.com; www.rachelsorganic.co.uk	UK Horizon-Rachel's via **Dairy** Crest to Sainsbury, Morrison, Tesco Waitrose.	♂**Horizon acquired family** ♀♂ **Rachel & Gareth** 2004. ♂Dean bought Horizon-Rachel's 2010.
General Mills–**Cascadian Farms/Small Planet Foods:** frozen fruit, veg & ready meals. **General Mills Cheerios, etc.** whole grain in UK, but GM in US.	Skagit County Fshops, nat'l-global supermkts Gen. Mills global & UK.	♂♀ US Gen Mills CEO male. **Cascadian-SPF CEO Maria Morgan 2003.**
Cascadian-Small Planet Foods VP Sheldon Weinberg visited UK.		
Whole Foods: entered UK market 2004. The certified USDA organic grocer's niche is close to Waitrose. Sainsbury & Tesco blocked its UK supplies.	US & UK chains.	♂ **CEO John Mackey, vegan from Texas.** Mainly male mgt.
Waitrose follows Morrison & Safeway in Durham; Hexham & Edinburgh 2005: Subsidiary of John Lewis (est. 1904) with 64k co-op 'partners'. Revenue: £3bn; 184 branches 2006; 3.9% UK share (7% So. England; 16% share organics).	UK supermarkets; Spain (Dean). 'Owned' by 64k co-op 'partners'.	♂ Nat'l MD Steven D. Esom. Durham mgr ♂ Stacey Stump.
Out of this World: co-op supermarkets.	Ncl, Notts. Leeds, York.	♂ Male dir. 3 men/3 wom HQ.

Family-Organic (< £125k / $250k)

Oldfield's Restaurants: sources organic & local food from Cuthbert's et al in 15 mile radius. Cookery demos. Hosted 40 Slow Fooders (2006, £10/plate).	1 Newcastle, 1 Durham restaurant.	♂ CEO male with ♂♀ team of chefs, waiters, office staff.
*****Cuthbert's Boxes: home delivered organic & local fruit, veg, honey, juice, bread & local organic milk & butter. Meat discontinued 2006.**	County Durham	♀ woman leads w/ husband + farmer /entrepreneur partner.
Honey Tree: Organic greengrocer & food store began 1999. Wide range local & regional organics. Fruit & veg boxes, Aberdeen Angus, chicken. Hot & cold deli.	Newcastle, Tyne & Wear.	♀ woman leads.
Northumbrian Organic Producers (NOP) fruit, veg, lamb, pork, beef, etc. From Berwick-to-Tees: www.nop.org.uk/	Biodynamics. FARMA, UK Soil Association.	♀♂ ca. 40 farmers. 50% men, 50% women.

Small-Organic (<£25k / $50k)

Slow Food Durham (est. 2006) & Newcastle	Durham, Newcastle,.	♀ Women-led AFNs. Then ♂.
Durham Local Food Celebration 2005. Won Durham Council award for impact on local food networks.	Co. Durham AFNs	♀woman-led volunteers, et al.
*****Mary's Organic Meats (MOM's) 2002–3.** CSA-style home delivered local.	Co. Durham	♀ woman-led, husband helps.

How some informal vendors beat Covid in Nairobi

Dr Dorice Agol (2021: 8–9), a development consultant in the UK and East Africa, described how informal street vendors responded flexibly to the coronavirus lockdown in Nairobi, Kenya, when formal restaurants closed. Ms Zawadi (pseudonym) sells chapatis and tea in a kiosk under a tree, next to the six-lane bypass to Nairobi Airport, built by Chinese contractors. Zawadi explained: "My small business did very well – I received more customers than any other year since I began cooking, about five years ago." Profits from her business helped pay her son's university tuition for two semesters.

Observations

Destiny is politics as well as biology. The grass ceiling can be made and unmade according to societal attitudes, environmental factors and government policies. In the scenarios above, Nixon's Food Power policies of the 1970s effectively pushed some women from farming, while more men rallied to the USDA's challenge to 'get big or get out'. Conversely, the Organic Foods Production Act of 1990, and National Organic Program and certification of 2004 encouraged many women to join small-scale entrants in booming farmers' markets in the US, UK and other countries. An uptick in US women's employment in agriculture around 1994 supports this view (World Bank Sep 2019). On the Family-Organic scale, for example, certification encouraged 'Alpen Dairy' to join US co-operative Organic Valley. This was akin to certification by the UK Soil Association which helped Rachel's Organic dairy business prosper to the level that it was marketed by UK supermarkets nationwide, attaining Industrial-Organic status and attracted US buyer Horizon, then Dean Foods, and finally French company Lactalis (Scholten 2014). Bookending these events are President Trump's America First policies, which seem less bound by fiscal rectitude than readiness to invoke tariffs to spur trade concessions (CNBC 2018a).

Conventional US megadairies owners may have supported President Trump's attack on Canada's milk quota system as socialist. As aforementioned, the US organic sector was disrupted by the Trump administration's early-2017 rejection of previously negotiated welfare regulations – a unique selling point in organic marketing. A glut of organic milk – due to the US–Canada trade dispute, corporate megadairy consolidation of the organic sector, and animal abuse-wary Millennial and Gen Z consumers turning to non-dairy drinks – motivated some organic farmers to sell their cows and convert to growing oats for oat milk in New England (*edairynews* 2020a, b and c).

A litany of trade embargoes vis-à-vis countries such as China and Russia increased uncertainty in global dairy trade around 2014 when Russia invaded Crimea, and in 2022 when it invaded Ukraine. But it is worth remembering that co-operatives can respond flexibly to such events. Examples include collaboration among Arla and Omsco co-operatives in the EU and UK with Organic Valley in the US, resulting in cheese exports to China (Scholten 2017b.). Consider, also the success of women's dairy co-operatives in India (Basu 2009). India's premier co-operative Amul has added to its New Jersey facility, and another in New York supplied by regional farms, producing ghee and other products for Indo-American consumers. Just as literacy is rising in countries around the world, it is likely that better secondary school bio-chemistry studies will guide more young farmers, regardless of gender, to healthier solutions in crops and livestock farming.

Mom and pop farms' demise in the US

In March 2019, Charles Benbrook joined with the UK Soil Association, launching his monthly blog 'Letter from America', with a post titled 'US must shift towards agroecology' (2019). Benbrook's nod to smaller-scale, more labour-intensive regenerative agriculture, which is kinder to animals, environment and rural communities, contrasts the get-big-or-get-out neoliberalism of President Trump's Republican administration (Monbiot 2016, 2018; *Sustainable Food News* 2018). Bankrupted Wisconsin organic dairy farmers were galled by USDA data showing that for six organic dairy farms in Texas, average dollar sales per farm were 100 times greater than around Lake Champlain.

USDA Secretary Sonny Perdue did not placate the 90- Wisconsin organic dairy farmers cut adrift when processors switched from local milk to milk trucked from Texas megadairies 1,100 miles away. Perdue echoed the anti-socialist political rhetoric of his predecessor, Mike Pompeo, at the 2019 World Dairy Expo in Wisconsin, downplaying the loss of 818 (10 per cent) of the state's small, pastured dairy farms: 'In America, the big get bigger and the small go out.... I don't think in America we, for any small business ... have a guaranteed income or guaranteed profitability' (*Newsweek* 1 Nov 2019). Animal welfare? The USDA failed to poll cows whether they preferred life on a mom and pop farm's meadows – or inside a megadairy's sheds.

The Progressive response to Perdue was swift. In a *Dakota Free Press* (2019) article, 'Trump's Ag Secretary calls small farmers doomed un-American socialists', editor Cory Allen Heidelberger wrote: 'Earl Butz is back! (Did he ever really leave?) The Trump Administration here inescapably declares ... some of you (most of you, really, for the Butzian-Perduian-capitalist logic doesn't end) who've been working the cows and the land for generations are obsolete.'

On a 2020 visit to the European Union, Sonny Perdue admonished Common Agricultural Policy leaders to follow the US path on biotechnology (*Euractiv* 2020). That was unlikely, since US relations with traditional allies deteriorated in the Trump era, over differing scientific views on climate, food and health security; moreover, agroecology was becoming a stronger component of EU policy (ARC 2020). The COVID-19 pandemic and lockdowns compounded existing problems in the US dairy sector. US dairy farmers dumped 43 million gallons of milk on the ground in 2016 due to a glut, and thousands more have since sold their herds

(*Time* 2016; *Odairy* 2019). US gross domestic product dropped 30 per cent after coronavirus mitigations closed cafes, coffee shops, restaurants and schools in early 2020. Women and men in periurban food chains responded by organizing the direct marketing of foods, and outdoor dining with social distancing of two metres between tables. The coronavirus crisis bodes opportunities for women or men flexible enough to manage agri-farm operations in the post-COVID era.

The grass ceiling in flux?persists

The FAO's Agenda on Gender Equality reminds us that, as long as women are central in human reproduction, they juggle the weight of motherhood with agri-farm work. Primary responsibility for childcare is often an intrinsic part of grass ceiling that impedes mothers' empowerment. However, the ceiling has many facets; its permeability varies according to social attitudes, norms and structures. Parental leave for fathers as well as mothers is increasingly common worldwide, a prospect welcomed by many women (*Economist* 2020: 72; see also Mill 1836 and Kahneman and Tversky 1979). UK Prime Minister Boris Johnson likely would have taken paternity leave in June 2020, were the country not in pandemic lockdown (*Independent* 2020a).

What about the US? Statutes requiring minimum female participation on company boards of directors, common in Scandinavia, could spearhead such statutes there. Citing a study titled 'The New Dad: Take your leave' from Boston College (Harrington et al. 2014), a US Department of Labor (2014) policy brief noted paid parental leave was considered important by 90 per cent of highly educated professional fathers, considered very important by 60 per cent, and even higher by Millennials. Would parental leave become the norm in the farm sector? Elite heads of agribusinesses or co-operatives might get parental leave long before small-scale family farmers. But in a happy irony, many farm-based fathers already enjoy more meal times with pre-school children than do elite managers. That is one reason they choose to farm. In the 1950s we called those meal breaks breakfast, dinner and supper.

This discussion of the grass ceiling included findings by Sally Shortall et al. (2017) for the Scottish Government, and Malcolm Gladwell's 10,000-hour rule pinpointing experience as key to proficiency. Thus, farm-born girls who grow up with heavy machinery, learning the logistics of supplying alternative food networks in urban peripheries, or productivist global agro-food chains, have a head start on urban incomers, when beginning a dairy career. In this virtuous circle, daughters of female farm owners or managers are more likely to secure top positions themselves.

The future may require different skills for success, remaking the location and composition of the grass ceiling. Increasingly, women possess digital skills relevant to the precision farming of crops, and digitized robotic automated milking systems (AMS) which potentially reduce stress on humans and cows (Holloway, Bear and Wilkinson 2013 *AHV*, 2014 *JRS*). Rural geographers speculate that AMS robots could increase small-scale dairy profitability enough to lure women from town jobs back to full-time farm work.

If the globalized food system reverts to regionalized and localized food chains, as advocates of 'repeasantization' such as Jandouwe van der Ploeg (2009) recommend, there could be greater demand for labour in the agricultural sector, and more opportunities for women managers to transcend their grass ceiling.

US adoption of what Democratic Congresswoman Alexandria Ocasio-Cortez calls a Green New Deal could portend a re-location of the grass ceiling from its pre-COVID-19 height to a more accessible gateway (US Congress 7 Feb 2019; *Modern Farmer* 2019). This could admit more women and minorities to leadership in agri-farm enterprises. Meanwhile, Malcolm Gladwell's 10,000-hour rule suggests *practice makes perfect* for girls and boys.

Dairy in the twenty-first century: Empowered women and seaweed vs methane cow burps?

P.J. Atkins observes that one-third of world farming takes place generally in periurban areas. Today, trends vary between post-industrial and emerging economies. Republican US presidents encouraged capitalist consolidation, and the number of American dairy farms plunged from 3.5 million in 1950 to 29,000 today. Remaining farms and processors left metropoles for unpopulated areas with water (Scholten 2007a, 2014). Bucking intensification were small grazers in the Organic Valley co-operative, founded 1988. Periurban countertrends in Seattle (and Newcastle, UK) included alternative food networks of women and other small farmers selling local, organic food and dairy products. Emerging economy trends differ for cultural, environmental and political-economic reasons. India's White Revolution (Scholten 1997c, 2010c; World Bank 1998) showed that the post-colonial co-operative Amul model was an effective development tool for health, education and income for marginal women and children in farm families. Thus, the Amul model influences the East Africa Dairy Development project, helping meet demand in burgeoning territorial metropoles of Ethiopia, Eritrea, Tanzania, Kenya, Rwanda and Uganda.

Periurban EADD villages serve Nairobi consumption while supplying multinational food giant Nestlé (Scholten 2013b). Can dairying be sustained into the twenty-second century? The elephant, or milchcow, in the room is climate apocalypse: the 15 per cent of anthropogenic greenhouse gases – especially methane – emitted by ruminants is implicated in the rise of global temperatures past 1.5°C over pre-industrial levels (IPCC 2022). Fortunately, scientists say seaweed curbs methane cow burps. In the spirit of 'Empowering Rural Women' (FAO 2018) and the 2030 Agenda for Sustainable Development, women on all continents need investment and training to engage in growth, distribution and application of seaweed in cattle feed to better themselves – and the planet.

Chapter 6

CONCLUSIONS ON COWS, CLIMATE AND HUMANS IN THE TWENTY-FIRST CENTURY

Forthcoming are conclusions on animal welfare, respondents' views in the dairy survey, women's grass ceilings and continental dairy trends. The long-running discussion of dairy's methane (CH_4) scourge will also come into perspective.

This book prioritized its sub-themes first as ethics, then environment, and finally politics. Ethical concern for animals was an altruistic paean to liberating animals from intensive confinement in boring barns, sheds or feedlots, to express natural behaviours in herds grazing extensively on grass pasture, as envisioned in

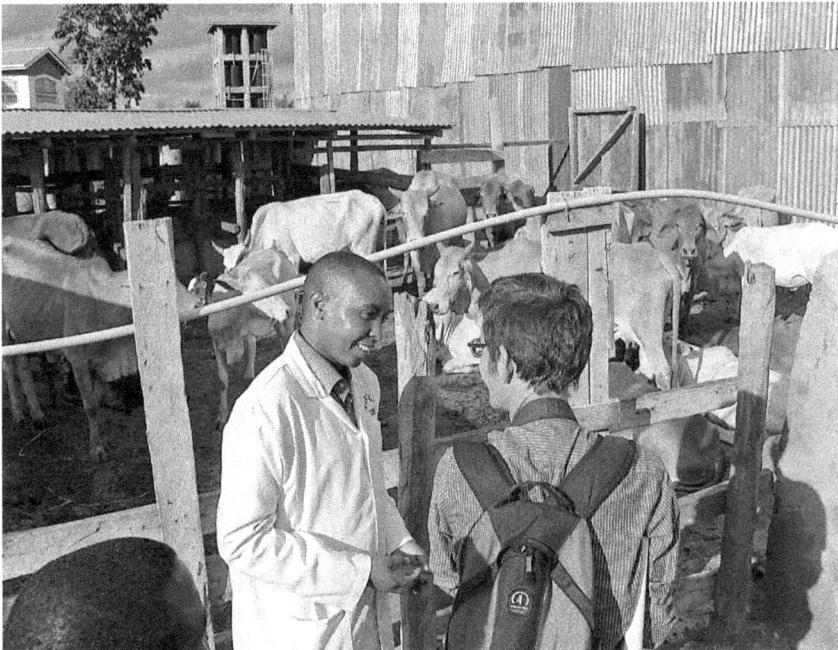

Figure 6.1 This farm hosted delegates from the 2012 Dairy Africa conference in Nairobi, Kenya. Beyond is the residence and rainwater silo. Dairying is growing in Africa and Asia, but climate change and drought threaten fodder production.

Figure 6.2 Norwegian Red cows in the Arctic Circle near Bodo go to fjords to flee mosquitoes, lick saltwater and eat seaweed. Evidence shows mixing seaweed in feed lowers ruminants' methane emissions, mitigating global warming.

the St Paul Declaration (IFOAM 2006; Scholten 2014: 288), and *The Cambridge Declaration on Consciousness* (*CDoC* 2012). That Eden-like vision still seemed faintly compatible with *Livestock's Long Shadow* (*LLS*), the FAO (2006: 96–7, 112) report by Steinfeld et al. estimating total livestock agriculture's greenhouse gases at 18 per cent of anthropogenic global GHGs, with livestock's subset of dairy responsible for less. (Note: in the livestock sector, FAO (2006: 96. 'Table 3.7 of Global methane emissions from enteric fermentation in 2004') estimated 15.69 per cent due to dairy cattle, compared to 50.16 per cent to other cattle, 9.23 per cent to buffalos, 9.44 per cent to sheep and goats, and 1.11 per cent to pigs.)

Recall, the FAO's 18 per cent assessment was challenged in a *World Watch Magazine* (2009) article by World Bank risk assessors Robert Goodland and Jeff Anhang, who claimed methodology errors by the FAO missed what they found: livestock agriculture's methane-rich emissions accounted for 51 per cent of the global warming potential (GWP) of anthropogenic greenhouse gas emissions. This put the onus of climate forcing on the livestock sector, not the Industrial Revolution, because Goodland and Anhang noted contemporary livestock production and land use for feed is scales higher than past eras. People joke that ivory-tower disputes are impassioned in inverse proportion to their triviality. But this dispute was existential, non-trivial. Suddenly, beef, dairy, pig and poultry farming – not carbon-burning petroleum energy and transport industries – were top villains in cataclysmic climate change, threatening civilization and survival of our grandchildren.

How could this be? Billions of bovines and other ruminants burped on Earth for millennia, before 1,000 BPE when China's *Book of Changes*, the *I-Ching*, mentioned petroleum discovered in brine drilling, via bamboo rods in salt production; the by-product oil was used on a small scale for lighting and lubrication. But humanity's carbon footprint deepened over three centuries: from the eighteenth, when wood and coal powered steam engines in factories, ships and trains, to the nineteenth century, when ships, trains, and autos switched to petroleum, and then the twentieth century, when propeller airliners became kerosene-guzzling jets.

Climate-change sceptics point out that Earth's atmospheric carbon content, surface temperatures and ocean levels fluctuated in past geologic epochs. The Intergovernmental Panel on Climate Change (IPCC 2019) responds that fluctuations follow wobbles in Earth's solar orbit. According to a report (IPCC 2018) coordinated by I.C. Prentice, pre-industrial era carbon dioxide atmospheric levels *c*. 1750 had been 280 ± 10 parts per million (ppm) for millennia. Since then, CO_2 levels have risen steadily, to 367ppm in 1999. Current CO_2 concentration is greater than during the previous 420,000 years, perhaps the most in 20 million years. Ominously, the rate of increase over the past century was unprecedented for 20,000 years. On the Ides of March 2021, Richard Betts, head of climate impacts at the UK Met Office Hadley Centre and University of Exeter (*Carbon Brief* 2021) wrote:

> Carbon dioxide … is now reaching levels 50% higher than when humanity began large-scale burning of fossil fuels during the industrial revolution. Recent measurements from the Mauna Loa observatory in Hawaii show … CO_2 levels exceeded 417 parts per million (ppm). Pre-industrial levels were about 278ppm.

The global scientific consensus was that the beginning of the Industrial Revolution around 1750 was the cusp of the Holocene epoch and what we now call the Anthropocene, in which the environment is dominated by human activities such as fossil-fuel extraction and the industries they fuel. Goodland and Anhang's (2009) paper blaming 51 per cent of GHGs on cows, pigs and chickens challenged the 18 per cent consensus on *Livestock's Long Shadow* (FAO 2006), but had few takers.

In the US, many Trump voters derided the climate crisis as woke left-wing political propaganda to advance social control, akin to intergovernmental social regulation in the COVID-19 pandemic. What is truth? In the 1970s some environmentalists feared industrial carbon loading would block sunlight, damaging crops like the 1883 eruption of Krakatoa, similar to what pacifists dubbed 'nuclear winter'. That doomsday scenario gave way to understanding that industry heats Earth in a greenhouse effect. More sophisticated analysis revealed the warming potential of methane. It wasn't just carbon-loading anymore.

Methodology

Chapter 3 mentioned that, like many scientific disputes, the climate debate between the FAO (2006, 2010) team of Steinfeld et al. claiming livestock emitted 14.5 per cent–18 per cent of GHGs (a subset of perhaps 2 per cent–5 per cent belonging to dairy), and the World Bank-linked duo of Goodland and Anhang (2009) claiming 51 per cent, quibbled over methodology, especially the balance of plant and animal respiration, along with land use.

Plants are not innocent of GHG emissions. Dr Charles Howie, my ecologist colleague in the Rural Geography Research Group (RGRG) of the Royal Geographical Society, has worked in Antarctica, Bangladesh (née Pakistan), Scotland and elsewhere. After a Master's at the Royal Agricultural College, and then earning a PhD, he advised on the curriculum of new An Giang University in Vietnam's rice-rich Mekong Delta, and consulted on tomato farming in Malawi. Howie explains rice is a top world staple food crop, but has downsides, as one of the lowest-protein grains. Rice is an emitter of greenhouse gases including nitrous oxide (N_2O), and when grown anaerobically in flooded paddies, produces much methane (Ruddiman 2005). So, rice research continues on cutting GHGs, and raising salinity tolerance in littoral areas with seawater rising due to climate change. Progress on these lines is ongoing in dairy-rice-fish systems in India and China (*Scientia Agricultura Sinica* 2009).

Got milk? Got science? Got peer review?

If the claim of World Bank risk assessors Goodland and Anhang (2009) that livestock industries emitted 51% of dangerous greenhouse gases had been valid, it would comprise an über-argument for veganism, or laboratory-grown substitutes for dairy and meat foods. Now, if the reader permits, is time for a comparison of epistemological problems in climate, animal welfare and current COVID-19 pandemic debates.

As noted above, the US dairy industry promoted itself with chirpy phrases like, 'Got Milk? Got Cookies?' The post-truth era has inured us to social media campaigns by populist groups (e.g., Q-Anon in the US) warning, for example, that vaccines for measles, mumps, rubella or coronavirus risk side-effects such as autism (*Economist* 2017). Myriad Internet sites suggest such medical interventions are vehicles for Deep State titans George Soros and Bill Gates to inject citizens with 5G microchips to enable surveillance.

Social media can entertain us, even when content is daft. We might agree it should welcome all opinions, even from all ex-presidents. But while activists and pundits amuse, serious problems like autism, fascism or climate apocalypse demand accurate information. In 2021, Republican Congress member Marjorie Taylor Greene, perhaps channelling the Scopes Monkey Trial of 1925, said: 'I don't believe in evolution ... I don't believe in that type of so-called science' (*Business Insider* 2021). She also demanded that Democratic President Biden – a Catholic who believes faith and reason can coexist – stop coronavirus vaccinations, and she only belatedly apologized for comparing mask requirements to Jewish suffering in the Nazi holocaust.

Got science? Scientists mitigate COVID-19 anti-vax paranoia by explaining that recent 5G chips are 19mm wide, thus unable to navigate the 0.25mm inside diameter of a 25-gauge needle (*Atlantic* 2021). On the other hand, if I'm wrong, and the Deep State really *has* reduced chips to such a Lilliputian scale, it explains the computer-chip shortage constraining global auto production in 2021!

Got peer review? Realistically, passionate activism can alter unhealthy status quos. But, having grown up on the periphery of a soil conservation movement led by farmers and advised by university biologists, I was baffled by rural dwellers blaming environmentalists for not dredging a river. Perhaps there was a conflict between biodiversity and flood control. But it illustrated the need for ethicists, environmentalists and politicians to marshal scientifically vetted facts, lest they cede credibility to their anti-science adversaries. Determining greenhouse gas emissions from ruminant supply chains, the livestock and dairy sectors and the huge impact of methane is a case in point.

FAO response to Goodland and Anhang (2009)

Tropical ecologist Robert Goodland (1938–2014) was called the conscience of the World Bank. From the mid-1970s, his consultancy probably saved millions of people from unnecessary projects such as dams that risked livelihoods and habitats. Yet, his claim with Jeff Anhang in (*World Watch Magazine* 2009) that the livestock sector accounted for 51 per cent of greenhouse gases (GHGs), fueled fanatic opposition by anti-dairy activists.

Outreach brought advice from sources including Dr Deepashree Kand, who researches dairy GHGs in India, Germany, Switzerland and the UK. She was featured in a hopeful front-page *New York Times* (2020) article, 'The business of burps: Scientists smell profit in cow emissions'. Kand kindly wrote to me that, after considering a number of scientific articles and their citations, she thought the livestock sector contributes somewhere around 18 per cent of GHG emissions. A couple of publications stated that livestock contributed round 14.8 per cent, which in her view was 'reasonable and close to 18%'. Kand, who shares this author's faith in peer review, added that Goodland and Anhang's (2009) claims of:

> 51% contributions are way too high; as rightly stated there may be an error in the calculations.

Kand recommended a paper by Herrero et al. (2011: 779–82), 'Livestock and greenhouse gas emissions: the importance of getting the numbers right', in *Animal Feed Science and Technology*. Mario Herrero has been associated with the International Livestock Research Institute (ILRI) in Nairobi, Kenya, and co-authors included Henning Steinfeld and Pierre Gerber from the classic (FAO

2006) *Livestock's Long Shadow*. Thus, Herrero et al. was an FAO counterattack of seventeen salvos on the World Bank-linked duo of Robert Goodland and Jeff Anhang, whose jarring claim implied the need for a shift to veganism. Herrero et al. (2011: 780) admitted livestock's 'substantial contribution to climate changing emissions' but stressed the need for 'providing human societies with food, incomes, employment, nutrients and risk insurance'. Herrero et al. (2011: 780) claimed Goodland and Anhang's 2009 article was 'non-peer reviewed' – a slight inviting a response – and faulted it on these points:

1. Introduction: The 'recent non-peer reviewed report published by the Worldwatch Institute (Goodland and Anhang 2009)', argued that livestock emitted 51 per cent of GHGs used flawed methodology and oversimplified the FAO (2006) estimate of 18 per cent.
2. Exclusion of carbon dioxide emissions from livestock respiration: Goodland and Anhang (2009) over-emphasized livestock respiration and CO_2 emissions, in a departure from IPCC and Kyoto climate-change guidelines.
3. Emissions from land-use change: Converting native grasslands and livestock pasture to plants for humans (even biofuel) threatened present carbon sequestration. Herrero et al. (2011: 782) also castigate Goodland and Anhang 2009) who 'erroneously assume that biofuel production is GHG neutral'.
4. Global warming potential (GWP) of methane: It is an ongoing debate, but the twenty-year number of GWP 72 assigned by Goodland and Anhang (2009 – not 2006 as published) may be methodologically too high. Herrero et al. (2011: 782) say the IPCC acknowledged the CH_4 atmospheric lifetime of twelve years, but did revise its GWP from 23 to 25 considering methane's indirect effects on ozone and water vapour. More research is needed on short-lived GHG methane compared to long-lived carbon dioxide.
5. Attribution of GHGs to livestock: Goodland and Anhang (2009) erroneously assume a 12 per cent increase in livestock production means a proportionate increase in GHG emissions, but production systems can become more efficient at higher production levels. Herrero et al. (2011: 781) state: 'For example, in Europe (EU-12), livestock production increased slightly between 1990 and 2002, while emissions of CH_4 and N_2O decreased 8–9%', and 'Denmark reduced its emissions of CH_4 and N_2O by 23% from 1990 to 2002, while maintaining dairy production output and increasing pig production by 27% (Danish EPA 2005)'.
6. Conclusions: Herrero et al. (2011: 781–2) write 'The magnitude of the discrepancy between the Goodland and Anhang (2006) paper and widely recognized estimates of GHG from livestock illustrates the need ... [for] accurate information about the link between agriculture and climate.'

Got peer review?

Goodland and Anhang's contentious 2009 claim appeared in *World Watch Magazine*, published by the Worldwatch Institute founded by Lester R. Brown, who earned relevant Master's degrees before 1964, when he advised USDA Secretary Orville Freeman in the Johnson administration. Brown's books and non-profit research entities won acclaim in global population, food and environmental sustainability movements. That said, *World Watch Magazine* was, perhaps, more focused on rallying political support than punctilious methodology in research. Goodland and Anhang's assertion could not have delighted investors in the fossil-fuel industry more!

Goodland and Anhang were properly given a response to Herrero et al. *in Animal Science and Feed Technology* (2012: 252–6) noting: 'They claimed that our *World Watch* article was not peer reviewed; but that is not so.' Though Goodland had officially retired, Anhang was attached to the World Bank, thus the article *was* subject to peer review – like the FAO, its sister agency under the UN, when Steinfeld and Gerber contributed to the disputed *Livestock's Long Shadow* (2006). Herrero et al. were offered the chance to respond to Goodland and Anhang's riposte, but declined.

A colourful account of this contretemps is made by Doug Boucher, of the Union of Concerned Scientists, on the UCS blog *The Equation* (UCS 2016). Boucher reviewed the 2015/2016 film *Cowspiracy*, promoted as 'The film that environmental organizations don't want you to see'. The premise was that livestock farming of meat, eggs, milk and fish triggered global warming – not fossil fuels. Boucher wrote that *Cowspiracy* claimed a conspiracy by environmentalists to hide the 'fact' revealed by 'two advisers from the World Bank' (i.e., Goodland and Anhang, but unnamed in the film) that 51 per cent of all GHGs are produced by animal farming – not 14.5 per cent–18 per cent, as the FAO maintained.

Boucher names World Bank-linked Goodland and Anhang, arguing that their methodology mistakenly counted CO_2 that farm animals breathe out – i.e., respiration – while ignoring the oxygen respired by plants. Methane from enteric fermentation, released by livestock and its subset of dairy, supplying a global population approaching 10 billion in the twenty-first century, does constitute a net GHG increase, admitted Boucher in *The Equation* (UCS 2016). But he faulted Goodland and Anhang for giving short-lived methane a weighting factor of seventy-two times CO_2, when twenty-five is reasonable.

Boucher (UCS 2016) claimed the world scientific community almost unanimously rejected the 2009 Goodland and Anhang study and their 51 per cent figure. Deploring the dearth of scientists cited in the *Cowspiracy* movie, Boucher hints the real conspiracy may be fake news by fossil-fuel industry publicists to tar livestock with the 51 per cent GHG brush. Anti-dairy activists might initially be attracted by claims that cows are über-polluters. But Boucher claimed there were tell-tale signs of queasiness by respected environmental organizations such as Greenpeace, which distanced itself from *Cowspiracy* by refusing interviews.

Transparency behoves organizations. Peer review of academic or scientific articles by experts maintains integrity of disciplines by eliminating articles of poor quality. The gold standard of peer review is double-blind review by anonymous, disinterested experts. That said, rumours persist of journals vulnerable to commercial pressure from food and energy sectors. That was an aspect of the media storm in the late 1990s, over Dr Arpad Pusztai's safety research on rats fed genetically modified potatoes (Smith 2003: 11–14, 25, 263; Scholten 2014: 15–16, 50).

Boucher wrote: 'Movies like *Cowspiracy* aren't believable, not only because of how they twist the science, but also because of what they ask us to believe: that the fossil-fuel industry – the Exxon-Mobils of the world – aren't the main cause of global warming … and that thousands of scientists have covered up the truth about the most important environmental issue of our time.'

Mitloehner on methane

Chapter 4 mentioned that researchers at Oxford Climate Society's now agree with Frank Mitloehner, director of ruminant emissions research at the University of California, Davis (2019), that the FAO (2010) estimate that the livestock sector contributes about 14.5 per cent to total anthropogenic greenhouse gas emissions (down from 18 per cent in FAO 2006) is reasonable. Further, they agree that dairy cows and other ruminants account for just 4 per cent of all greenhouse gases produced in the US, and beef cattle just 2 per cent of direct emissions. As director of the Clarity and Leadership for Environmental Awareness and Research (CLEAR) unit at UC Davis, GHG guru Mitloehner (27 Jun 2019 video) has amused Twitter followers by comparing Beyond Meat and Impossible Burgers to dog food, and claims that renouncing meat is 'not the environmental panacea many would have us believe'. He exudes confidence that ocean algae such as seaweed can mitigate cows' methane emissions.

Indeed, dairy methane may be contained if governments co-operate to achieve the aims of the 2015 Paris Agreement, because rich and poor countries have skin in the game, i.e., dairy sectors seeking better breeding and feeding technologies. However, by mid-2021, all continents were reporting climate disasters at such a rate that some fear it is likely Earth temperatures will be 1.5°C warmer than pre-industrial times (*Economist* 2021h).

Continental trends

For the moment, while the principals of the 2015 Paris Climate Agreement, and 2021 Glasgow COP26, respond to global warming, let us put the existential threat of ruminant methane on the back burner and focus on more empirical issues. Data on Milk & Milk Products 2010-20 compiled from the FAO (Table 6.1, based on FAO-UN 2014 and 2020) show production rises, except from China which shifted to imports from countries with a comparative advantage in dairying. China's twenty-first-century commitment to dairy was underscored in the COVID-19 pandemic, when four major dairy industry associations urged citizens to strengthen immune health by consuming dairy (*Food Navigator Asia* 2020).

Table 6.1 Milk and milk products production (1000 MT), FAO 2010–20.

(Table 6.1, is based on FAO-UN 2014 and 2020)		
	2010–12 ave. (FAO 2014)	**2016–18** ave. (FAO 2020)	**2020** forecast (FAO 2020)
World	743,535	823,234	860,125 (15.7% >2010)
Africa	45,108	48,024	46,954 (4.09%>2010)
Asia	276,764	334,869	361,986 (30.7%>2010)
China	41,879	32,663	34,124 (18.5%<2010)
	Lower Sino prod likely due to …	… 12–15 MT imports …	… from Oceania, EU & USA.
Europe	215,153	223,175	228,693 (6.3%>2010)
India	127,382	176,445	195,000 (53.1%>2010)
Oceania	27,590	31,067	31,372 (12.6%>2010)
S. America	65,038	61,615	61,524 (5.4%<2010)
US	89,118	97,605	100,793 (13.1% >2010)

To maintain imports, Chinese dairy giant Yili acquired the Westland dairy co-operative in New Zealand in 2021 (Xinhua 2021). With twice as many cows as its 10 million citizens, Antipodean NZ tops Germany, Netherlands, Belgium, US, France, Australia, UAE, UK and Poland in top ten milk exporters. Its strength grew under the aegis of the New Zealand Dairy Board, and the country's co-operative ethos persists (Campbell 2020; Le Heron 2018). After the advent of the World Trade Organization in 1995, NZDB merged with New Zealand Dairy Group and Kiwi Co-operative Dairies, to form Fonterra in 2001. Observers at the University of Auckland, some say Fonterra initially sought to build scale overseas but, amid high world milk prices, refocused on the domestic scene. Fear of foreign investment remains deep in New Zealand, though farmers were well compensated when Yili bought Westland.

Classical political economist David Ricardo might have toasted potential mutual gains in China's expanded global dairy trade as a rational policy change to enhance its food security. But is China vulnerable to charges of exploitation once directed at Americans? Contemporary critics of global trade, from public intellectual and Professor Emeritus of Linguistics Noam Chomsky at MIT, to Professor Emerita of African Studies at the University of Washington-Seattle, Lucy Jarosz (2014; Restrepo with Hensel 2019), worry that great power China's imports might imperil food sovereignty in poor countries.

In opposition to what Chomsky calls the US's corporate doctrine of power is the Alliance for Food Sovereignty in Africa. AFSA's Million Belay and Bridget Mugambe (*Scientific American* 2021) defend agroecology among millions of small-scale pastoralists, indigenous peoples, and women (see Chapter 5) – against Bill Gates' corporate GMO-and-glyphosate prescription of an Alliance for a Green Revolution in Africa (AGRA), lately promoted by the Cornell Alliance for Science. Belay and Mugambe claim that African and German civil society groups found no evidence of income increases among small-scale producers in the countries that AGRA serves. On the contrary, undernourishment and environmental increased as crop diversity declined, no doubt along with the biodiversity extolled by Rachel Carson (1962).

Food regimes

Twenty-first-century power asymmetries evoke the story of David and Goliath. In his article on 'New frontiers in agricultural geography', Guy Robinson (2018b: 1–48, 4) describes three world food regimes that help explain trade fluctuations in war and peace. The first, sparked by Britain's 1846 repeal of the Corn Laws, led to the Golden Age of trade, from 1870 to the First World War, based principally on exports from family farms in the New World linked to nation states in Europe (2018b: 4). The second, from the 1920s to the 1980s (despite a trough in the Great Depression between 1929 and 1939, and militarized trade and submarine warfare in the Second World War), involved 'production of durable food for the mass market, decolonization, consumerism, and the growth of forward and backward linkages from agriculture'. Guy Robinson (2018b: 4) notes that the 'putative third' food regime from the 1990s increased fresh and organic food trade. These flows eventually included China and Russia in the global capitalist system under the World Trade Organisation. Enhanced command-and-control systems, including satellite communications, GPS and the widening of the Panama Canal for container ships, reified this third food regime in growth of alternative agrifood networks for green consumers in the 'developed world through the growing sales from fair trade, organic, local, and specialty foods' (Robinson 2018a: 147-48). Robinson notes that enhanced trade even stimulated wine production in China.

Once stereotyped as dairy-averse, twenty-first-century century China (self-described by its ruling Communist Party, as Socialism with Chinese characteristics), has become the world's second-largest dairy importer, from near zero in 1977. Most Chinese are lactose-intolerant, but as in many markets, processing raw milk into yogurt, pizza cheese and UHT milk eases consumption, and growing availability of A2 milk, which lacks the A1 form of beta-casein, may make liquid milk potable to more Asians. According to the FAO, consumption of dairy products such as butter & ghee began with an intake rise from near zero in 1961 to 0.1kg per person in 1992 (Scholten 2010c: 115–18, 146, 159, 172).

Sino-dairy production increased when it absorbed thousands of US cows in the 1986 USDA herd buyout (Scholten 2014: 33, 167, 272), when like others, a friend sold their uneconomic family farm and began fishing on Puget Sound. China developed its dairy sector faster than any other country, joining the top ten world producers with 35 million tonnes in 2007. *Statistica* (2021) notes the average per capita consumption of milk products in China was 11.4kg in 2020.

Tariff disputes and embargoes have characterized relations among China, Russia, the US and EU countries since Russia's President Putin reclaimed Crimea and threatened the Ukraine, and since China's President Xi sent Muslim Uyghurs to political re-education camps. But if one country won't export milk, another one will. Call it the Exporter's Dilemma.

Recently, Chinese–Australian trade relations have coarsened. Above, Table 6.1 shows China's dairy production fell 18.5 per cent from 41,879 thousand metric tonnes (MT) over 2010–12 to a forecast 34,124 thousand MT in 2020, while domestic dairy consumption rose. Part of the explanation is that, as Australian dairy imports fell, China imported 12,00–15,000 MT of milk products from Fonterra in New Zealand, and Europe via the US (Chapters 1, 3, 4 and 5 mentioned Arla (EU), UK (Omsco) and US (Organic Valley) co-operatives working together to export cheese to China.).

The result is that despite disputes, contemporary global trade surpassed the 1870–1914 Golden Age – at least until 24 February 2022, when Russia invaded Ukraine. Like water seeking its own level, trade devises routes to source staples, and even inculcate new turns to so-called natural, quality and organic foods (Murdoch and Miele 1999; Murdoch, Marsden and Banks 2000; Robinson 2018b). But what is quality? Consumers may not realize their shiny, happy fruit and veg owe soilless hydroponics for their *natural* patina, a bone of contention by soil-loyal organicists. Robinson also notes food regimes are not globally homogenous, and that local characteristics of agricultural production can vary greatly while coexisting, depending on unique political and economic links. This makes it unlikely that all 7.8 billion Earthlings will soon go vegan.

In a similar vein, Geoff A. Wilson, author of the book *Multifunctionality* (2007: 273) represents the heterogeneity of farm types, scaling from hobby farms to transnational corporations, in an illustration titled the *Multifunctionality decision-making funnel*. Another example is what Felipe da Silva Machado (2020) calls the agricultural nexus around Rio de Janeiro, Brazil, where farmers' co-operatives facilitate commercial sustainability for a multiplicity of farm enterprises, including commercial exporters on small- to large-scales, when not overwhelmed by political, economic or health emergencies such as coronavirus.

Hamlet might have warned those touting simple solutions to climate problems: 'There are more things in heaven and earth, than are dreamt of in your philosophy.'

The next fifty years

Most experts and participants in the livestock sector, and dairy sub-sector, understand the need to reduce greenhouse gas emissions from ruminant's distinct problem of methane from enteric fermentation. Methane is a short-lived-climate-pollutant (SLCP; Cain et al. 2019; Lynch et al. 2021) in the atmosphere, but it is more problematic than everyday carbon dioxide or nitrous oxide, and has taken time to understand. Scientists in the Oxford University climate group, including Michelle Cain, John Lynch and Myles Allen, have taken CO_2-equivalent (CO_2-e) emissions standardized in the 2015 Paris Climate Agreement as Global Warming Potentials (GWP) over 100 years, and refined them as GWP*. They claim the GWP* (aka GWP star) is more accurate than the previous flawed model, because it differentiates between a flow gas, e.g., short-lived ruminant methane, which cycles through atmosphere in about nine years, compared to a long-lived stock gas such as carbon dioxide, which in fossil-fuel burning is a one-way force accumulating in the atmosphere for a millennium.

Frank Mitloehner (2017), air-quality specialist at University of California, Davis, agrees with the Oxford Climate Society that ruminant cows eat carbon-laden plants and belch or burp methane from enteric fermentation, which after about a decade converts to carbon molecules like those in plants previously eaten by cows – it's a closed cycle. Mitloehner is excited that California has proven how feed inputs such as seaweed, and anaerobic manure digesters, can minimize methane in dairying, effectively removing carbon accumulation from the atmosphere, and generating short-term cooling. However, Mitloehner warns that unless the IPCC and 2015 Paris Climate Agreement accept the GWP* system (with its short- and long-lived distinctions), 8,000-year-old ruminant farming could face legal extinction in the European Union.

Few dairy farmers have time for such (albeit serious) minutiae, and it is doubtful many gave any credence to Goodland and Anhang's exaggerated claims of ruminant emissions. As discussed, that was a clarion call to veganism – before being discrediting by the FAO and Union of Concerned Scientists (Herrero et al. 2011; Boucher 2016).

We have also established that top dairists generally accept estimates by the FAO (2006, 2010; also, Capper and Cady 2020) that livestock emit 14.5 per cent –18 per cent of GHGs. In 2018, the article 'Invited review: Learning from the future – A vision for dairy farms and cows in 2067', appeared in the *Journal of Dairy Science* (Britt et al. 2018: 3722–41.) The ten eminent co-authors, from the US, UK and Sweden, led by the late Dr Jenks Swann Britt, focused on industrialized countries, while expecting developing countries to continue modernization, including robot milkers and digital automation for cow health, milk quality control, and controlling GHGs including methane. Such a visionary dairy future might succeed what Robinson (2018b: 4) called a 'putative third regime'.

Britt et al. (2018) gave little reassurance to people nostalgic for the storybook USA of the 1950s, where 3,681,627 farms had many low-producing cows but also provided more single-family livelihoods – than 2022 USA, with under 30,000 farms (*Hoard's Dairyman* 2022; USDA June 2002 June by Don P. Blayne). The paper's future vision was that dairy farms would become bigger and more complex, coping with animal welfare, environmental and climate concerns as 'future generations become more displaced from ancestral connections to farming' (Britt et al. 2018: 3738).

It is worth mentioning that citizens clinging to the ideal of Jeffersonian democracy, i.e., of nations populated by small independent farmers, hoped labour-saving robot milking machines could make small farms economic again, as they remain in Canada's milk quota regime (seventy-seven cow herd average), and were in Europe's quota from 1984 to 2015. However, financial capitalization will be formidable in 2067, replacing most labour and even tractor-drivers with automation, integrated sensors and robotics. Rural dwellers seeking independent livelihoods may have to settle for gigs as hoof-trimmers, nutritionists or digital support, rather than ownership, as the total of farms ebbs.

Environment

Jenks Britt and his co-authors were anything but climate-change deniers. They envisioned innovations to mitigate climate as Earth's population climbed toward 10.4 billion in 2067 (earlier than some doomsayers expected), with 81 per cent or more of added population in Africa or Asia (Britt et al. 2018: 3722). Geographically, 'Temperature will increase in tropical and temperate zones, especially in the Northern Hemisphere' where 81 per cent of humans live today (2018: 3724). In North America, dairying would be pushed from the arid Southwest to the Upper Midwest, Great Lakes and central Canada. Ocean dampening would mitigate such effects in the Southern Hemisphere, but all continents would endure erratic drought and storms.

Ameliorating this shift might be the grail of clean, low-cost nuclear fusion for desalinisation of seawater (Britt et al. 2018: 3722) to benefit farmers and dairy cows in dry coastal regions. Fusion has been elusive, a sci-fi joke for decades as just forty years away, but Boeing, Lockheed, and the multinational ITER team in France are working on the problem. Record summer 2021 heat in Seattle (biggest US city with fewest air conditioners), Portland, Oregon, and Vancouver, Canada, tempted Pacific Northwesterners to buy AC units, which they once scorned as crutches for effete Californians. Fusion power could make AC affordable, but do nothing to suppress Canadian and US forest fires, *fin de siècle* harbingers of global warming, which from the early twenty-first century increasingly smudged West Coast cities. More thought is now given to cooling urban tree covers such as Seattle's Beacon Hill fruit forest. Forests as small as tennis courts, designed by ecologist Akira Miyawaki, can also help cool city neighbourhood air (*Economist* 3 July 2021).

Politics and ethics

The dairy vision 2067 co-authors addressed some concerns of activists in CiWF and PETA, and politicians supporting organics such as Senators Bernie Sanders and Patrick Leahy, as well as the duo of Senator Edward J. Markey and Representative Alexandria Ocasio-Cortez, who introduced legislation for a Green New Deal. The vision paper had little time for veganism, but acknowledged dairy critics (Britt et al. 2018: 3738):

> Many concerns of consumers are focused on practices that they perceive to be unnatural, including confining cattle, overuse of pharmaceuticals, weaning calves shortly after birth, overuse of chemical fertilizers and pesticides, and contamination of streams and sub-surface water with livestock waste.

Such admissions were refreshing, and like sages over the ages, they hinted a bright future (2018: 3738):

[P]ractices ... in the next 50 years will ameliorate ... concerns of consumers. There will be more zoning- and regulatory-based restrictions on farming, but demographic shifts to urban areas could also free up land resources ...

Some critics are troubled by the vision's implication that rural jobs and communities would dwindle amid urbanization. Others are heartened by hints of working with nature, forsaking blunt chemical and agro-pharmaceutical tools of the past, including penicillin in cows and glyphosate on forage. The vision entails studying herds as 'superorganisms' (Britt et al. 2018: 3737), or as units like hives, to understand why similar herds in close proximity have differing productivity, health and well-being. The authors say their new lens is not reductionist, as animal science has been hitherto, and they have cast their eyes more widely. What improving animals, crops and soils increasingly relies on is understanding microbial populations on the farm and 'managing epigenetic-mediated effects on animals and crops' (Britt et al. 2018: 3736); examples include gene editing for heat tolerance or reduction of methane excretion (a point we return to below).

Animal welfarists appreciate the authors' prediction that facilities will 'provide ways for early postpartum cows and new-born calves to interact for an extended period after birth' (Britt et al. 2018: 3737). Thriving calves usually drink plenty of their mother's colostrum. Future calf-specific products may inoculate colostrum for healthy 'microbiomes of gastrointestinal, mammary, and urogenital tracts' (2018: 3736). In this holistic scenario, creatures' microbiomes are matched to on-farm and outsourced feeds.

The article suggests emerging countries with permanent grasslands (2018: 3723) such as Mongolia will exert comparative advantages to graze cattle, perhaps marketed globally. This could be a boon to animal welfare, but overall, it supports 'sustainable intensification' (2018: 3739), and pastoralists reluctantly infer rich countries will confine many cows.

Tellingly, the vision paper (Britt et al. 2018) notes China has invested in 'dairy farms and processing facilities offshore in countries with more arable land per capita ... for import into China' (2018: 3723). Again, this helps explain the 18.5 per cent drop in China's Milk & Milk Products production, 2010–2020 in Table 6.1 above. Hopefully, this represents a healthy renunciation of mercantilism or zero-sum tactics in Sino trade policy.

Animal nutrition

Since *Hoard's Dairyman* magazine began in Wisconsin, USA, in 1885, it has been a conduit of scientific research to farmers, including my family. One of its best feed experts has been Michael F. Hutjens of the University of Illinois. Hutjens had a productivist but cautious outlook. When yield zealots proposed switching herds to 100 per cent high-energy grains and corn, he warned them to keep alfalfa and fibre in cows' rations (*Hoard's Dairyman* 10 Jan 2018), lest they explode.

Hutjens worked with Britt on the *Hoard's Dairyman* (2017) article, 'What will dairy cows and farms look like in 50 years?', preceding their later *Journal of Dairy Science* (2018) fifty-year vision report. Future crops could cut cow methane with highly-digestible feeds. Further examples of sustainable intensification include grazing systems with nitrogen-fixing legumes (e.g., clover, beans, peas) to cut chemical fertilizers. Development of perennial drought- and salt-tolerant maize and cane in no-till systems could help continuous soil carbon sequestration.

Organic fans may applaud adoption of GPS precision farming tech, e.g., planting polycultures of two or more crops in aesthetic swirls around hill and dale, to cut use of chemical insecticides and herbicides such as glyphosate. Chapter 1 noted debates on glyphosate in human breast milk. Will glyphosate be ubiquitous in fifty years?

Cow genetics

Observers in 1950, when average annual US milk production per cow was about 5,000 lbs, could have been surprised by 22,000 lbs in 2015 (*Hoard's Dairyman* 2018; Britt 2018). Now they might be shocked by predictions of an average 37,000 lbs per cow in 2066. That could be a brave new field where traditional animal husbandry is succeeded by gene editing, for cross-breeding between and among breeds in test tubes. Breeding services might primarily sell embryos, not semen as now.

Some animal welfarists and feminists see a projected annual average cow milk yield of 18 tonnes in 2067 as a nightmare. But mitigating this lactic largesse, an uncomfortable burden on the belly muscles of bovines, are improved robotic milking machines (Bear and Holloway 2016), to relieve cows at their discretion, two, three, four or more times a day. Computerized robot milkers would also monitor a cow's vital signs, appraise her milk for microbials, and reward her with tasty feed mixed to personal nutritional needs, in the spirit of treating all cows and their microbiomes on the farm as one superorganism (Britt et al. 2018: 3737). In 2015 one cow was noted to produce 75,000 lbs, but at an average of 37,000 lbs in 2067, Britt (2017 HD) estimates that just 1,300 to 1,900 herds could supply a projected 410 million Americans in 2066. Down from three million US herds in 1950, that is putting nearly all eggs – or rather, milk bottles – in a few baskets.

Human nutrition

The robust defence of livestock farming, including dairying, in Britt et al.'s vision paper (2018: 3722–3) was based largely on human nutrition, rejecting veganism in a world scrambling to feed 10 billion people:

> Dairy-based diets are superior to vegan, egg-and omnivore-based diets for ... croplands to feed the greatest number of people ... The advantage of dairy- and

egg-based diets over vegan-based diets is ... essential amino acids, and micronutrients ... missing in typical plant-based foods.

Henry Mance, author of *How to Love Animals* (2021: 71) disagrees, claiming pasture and land for feed 'animals currently account for 77% of the Earth's agricultural land, but they provide only 18% of our calories and only 37% of our protein'. He researched his thoughtful book by working in an abattoir, an intensive pig farm, accompanying a boar hunt, and other carnivorous pursuits. Eventually Mance went vegan, though his vegetarian wife (who called veganism a 'divorceable' offence) did not – even though Michelin recently awarded a star to a vegan restaurant in Bordeaux (*Forbes* 2021). Citing Johns Hopkins research, Mance writes (2021: 71) 'Worldwide, if everyone replaced just the dairy in their diets, food greenhouse gas emissions would fall by nearly a quarter', double the GHG savings if everyone eschewed red meat. Unusually, Mance urged consumers fearing global warming to first foreswear dairy, not meat. Indeed, the Johns Hopkins Center for a Livable Future (Reuters 17 Sep 2019) found diets with insects, fish and molluscs more nutritious than plant-based vegan diets with similar impacts on water, land use and GHGs. The study compared nine diets, including a weekly meatless day, as well as pescatarian and vegan menus in 140 countries.

Unsurprisingly, the fifty-year vision of dairying around 2067 by Britt et al. (2017, 2018) argues that dairy uses farmland efficiently, e.g., non-arable highlands in Britain's Pennine highlands. Their nutritional observation resonates to anyone familiar with tales of deprivation in socio-economic poverty, famine or wars: 'Even small amounts of animal source foods can improve the nutritional status of low-income households' (Britt et al. 2018: 722). Dairy's range of amino acids, iron, zinc, vitamin A, vitamin B-12, and calcium is difficult, and usually expensive, to replicate with vegan diets.

Critiquing the vision of 2067

Aspirations to improve cow health issues such as laminitis, mastitis and ketosis are laudable (Britt et al. 2018). As noted above, stress and poor condition, especially in high-producing cows, leading to inability to conceive a second calf, has devastated the longevity of dairy cows in the US, UK and other countries adopting confined or concentrated animal feeding operations. Descriptions of futuristic, larger dairy farms circa 2067 sound fabulous, evoking Walt Disney's pristine Tomorrowland theme park, even projections of space stations by Dr Wernher von Braun in the 1955–7 television series *Disneyland*. Dairying is not rocket science but, coincidentally, it was around 1957 that my Dutch-American relatives in California pushed the envelope of family farming to more intensive scales. These dairy memes spread north to Washington State. The 1960s began a transition from herds of fewer than fifty cows that spent the year grazing pasture, except for the coldest winter months, in Dutch-style stanchion barns with overhead haymows adjoining corn and grass silos.

The new model architecture featured an airy loafing shed, metal pole structures with flattish roofs over cows who were just short concrete walks away from feed bunks, jokingly called salad bars. Farmers, who had helped builders constructing each other's typically 34-foot by 80-foot wooden barns with peaked cedar shake roofs, debated individual cow resting stalls, open-plan bedded areas for chewing cud, maternity and calf pens, feeding areas, hay bales, grain carts, mechanization (often fragile) involving silo unloaders, milking parlours and the refrigerated bulk tank in the sanitized milk house.

It rains around Puget Sound, or the Salish Sea as it has become known again. Farmers sympathized with cows walking muddy lanes between pastures and barns. (Farmers in the Netherlands obviated the muddy transit with brick paths, but the practice was unused around Seattle.) Drawings of loafing sheds near feed bunks, salt licks, water tanks (cows need plenty), and maybe an acre of pasture outside for socializing on sunny days, looked ideal. The biggest dairy farms might even have a veterinarian on-site. *Bovine heaven?*

Well, it was better for some herds for some years, as US dairy exports flowed. But, as this book notes, the continual push to higher milk production rendered many cows infertile and culled to slaughter before their fourth birthday or second calf (Biagiotti 2013, 2014). Poor farmgate milk prices forced farmers to exceed originally planned density, which increased bullying of new or smaller cows, depressing their well-being and health. Water quality concerns around Seattle, Tacoma, and red tide scares for Puget Sound shellfish pushed development of multi-hundred cow mergers, then establishment of multi-thousand cow megadairies in semi-arid Eastern Washington, watered by the Columbia River.

As the 1950–60s dairy paradigm faded between Seattle and the Canadian border, the best dairy farmers told me: 'There are no bad farm managers anymore.' Remaining dairy farms merged into megadairies, or converted to berry farms (Scholten 2002). But, if someday, the 2067 vision of Britt et al. (2018) becomes as outdated as the loafing shed paradigm of the mid-twentieth century, humanity might survive climate Armageddon. Ethically driven politics might also keep some cows grazing pasture, at least part-time.

Whither methane?

Judith L. Capper and Roger Cady (2020) did not exaggerate when they wrote in the *Journal of Animal Science*: 'In 2006, the U.S. dairy industry, in conjunction with other livestock industries worldwide, was rocked by [the] assertion that livestock contributed more to global greenhouse gas (GHG) emissions than transportation'. Rocked is an understatement. It cast livestock and dairy farmers, who assumed they served an environmentally virtuous vocation, as rogues. At stake was climate stability, civilization and humanity. Therefore, it became easier to excuse animal confinement, if it were necessary in sustainable intensification.

Capper and Cady (2020) note the FAO (2006) report quantifying *Livestock's Long Shadow* as 18 per cent of total GHGs was trimmed by FAO to 14.5 per cent, after a critique by Maurice Pitesky, Kimberly R. Stackhouse and Frank M. Mitloehner in *Advanced Agronomy*, 'Clearing the air' (2009: 4). Thence, estimates for global livestock GHGs settled around 14.5 per cent, and dairy specifically about 2.9 per cent of GHG emissions, as mentioned in Chapter 2. For the US, Pitesky et al. (2009) estimate that agriculture made 32 per cent of anthropogenic methane emissions, 68 per cent of nitrous oxide emissions, and that 2.8 per cent is associated with livestock (i.e., enteric fermentation and manure management).

That 14.5 per cent GHG figure was, as we know from discussion above, temporarily challenged by the *World Watch Magazine* claim by Goodland and Anhang (2009) that 51 per cent of GHGs were from livestock, before the FAO (Gerber et al. 2013) rallied around the 14.5 per cent figure. As aforementioned, Deepashree Kand is among climate scientists, including the Oxford climate group, and Frank Mitloehner at UC Davis, who consider the total livestock sector emits 14–18 per cent (including its smaller dairy sub-sector).

Ruddiman's hypothesis on Holocene submerged rice and advent of the Anthropocene

Internet clickbait can bewilder people investigating anthropogenic greenhouse gases attributable to the livestock sector. *Plant Based News* (2021) trumpeted a report claiming, 'Animal agriculture responsible for 87% of greenhouse gas emissions'. It was based on a study (*Journal of Ecological Society* 2020–21) by Sailesh Rao, an electrical engineer who later founded Climate Healers promoting plant-based diets, noting that although humans have burned fossil fuels for 200 years, global warming is basically due to burning forests for 8,000 years. Rao has a point.

In partial agreement is William Ruddiman, an environmental scientist at the University of Virginia. A year before Livestock's *Long Shadow* (FAO 2006) was published, Ruddiman's article in *Scientific American* (2005: 45-53) asked, 'How did humans first alter global climate?'. In the context of Earth's wobbling axis on elliptical orbits around the Sun, he answered, 'As I see it, nature would have cooled earth's climate, but our ancestors kept it warm by discovering agriculture'.

Richard Blaustein (2015) explains that evidence for Ruddiman's hypothesis includes pre-historic carbon burning in forest clearance, methane-emitting submerged rice farming and cattle domestication, which began changing Earth's atmosphere at least 6,000 years ago. Kand and associates estimate that GHG emissions from ancient deforestation, cropping and cattle rearing were double those of Industrial Age emissions. This effectively resets the start of the Anthropocene epoch to a point long before the Industrial Age began around 1870. Perhaps the age of coal was the tipping point for global warming.

But, whether or not the Anthropocene began in the eighteenth century, or 10,000 BP, GHG stabilization is vital when the number of dairy- and meat-hungry humans edges toward 11 billion during this century. As noted above, methane is admittedly the Achilles' heel (hoof?) of dairy farming, but its profile as a short-lived climate pollutant means there may be enough time to avoid Climate Armageddon, by controlling enteric fermentation.

Chepeliev and global warming potentials

A relevant, recent study on 'Development of the Non-CO_2 GHG emissions database' by economist Maksym Chepeliev (2020) at Purdue University, incorporates global warming potentials (GWPs) from the Intergovernmental Panel on Climate Change (IPCC) Fourth Assessment Report (AR4), noting GHG emissions from land use activities and minor changes to the mappings between emission drivers and emission sources. For reference years 2004, 2007, 2011 and 2014, Chepeliev (2020: 2, 4, 10) addressed methane (16 per cent of total global GHGs, of which around one-third is emitted by cattle); nitrous oxide (16 per cent of total global GHGs, problematic in mis-managed manure); and fluorinated gases (F-gases, 2 per cent of total global GHGs, critical in livestock sector cold chains).

On the global level, agricultural and food sectors account for 46 per cent of all non-CO_2 GHG emissions, writes Chepeliev (2020: 10, 12), who quantifies them among: cattle (23 per cent), water supply & sewage (16 per cent), coal (10 per cent), paddy rice (6 per cent), petroleum and coke (6 per cent), oil (6 per cent), raw [liquid] milk (6 per cent), chemicals (5 per cent), other animal products (3 per cent), other grains (2 per cent), and other.

China, noted Chapeliev (2020: 12, 14) has the biggest global share of food-related GHG emissions (16.6 per cent), followed by India (12.2 per cent), the US (7.7 per cent) and Brazil (5.9 per cent). Per capita global GHGs from food and ag product final consumption is around 0.81 tCO_2-eq, but there is regional variation. Several European countries are below 0.7 tCO2-eq., including Austria, Bulgaria, Czech Republic, Hungary, the Netherlands, Romania and Slovakia. Emissions are higher in Canada (1.3 tCO2-eq.), the US (1.4 tCO2-eq.), Australia (2.2 tCO2-eq.) and New Zealand (2.5 tCO2-eq.). Latin America is characterized by higher-than-global-average food and ag per capita final consumption emissions. Sub-Saharan Africa has higher emissions than Northern Africa, because forage in arid regions in harder for cattle to digest than that in temperate regions.

Chapter 5 mentions that dairy biogas systems for smokeless cooking and lighting, being developed by co-operatives in India and Africa, can attenuate what has been an inexorable rise in methane and other emissions – while also empowering women. There is more on this below.

Data from the FAO (2010: 55) report *Greenhouse Gas Emissions from the Dairy Sector* indicate that global milk production, processing and transportation emit roughly 2.7 per cent of total anthropogenic emissions. (Estimates vary according to regional crop and fodder differences.) Global emissions attributed to dairy were around 4 per cent of total anthropogenic emissions, i.e., milk production, processing, transport, production of meat from dairy-related animals, and draught animals as used in India and elsewhere. Significantly, in the GHG lens, combined milk and meat production 'is particularly efficient in achieving low GHG emissions per unit of product, compared to pure beef production'.

Whether total livestock emissions do amount to 14.5 per cent of total anthropogenic GHGs, or are nearer the 18 per cent estimated in *Livestock's Long Shadow* (Steinfeld et al. 2006), grim resolution and political nous will be needed to coax nations' adherence to IPCC, Paris 2015 and COP26 commitments. The catastrophic floods that pushed tractors down European streets and destroyed bridges in Germany's Ahr Valley wine area, in June 2021, suggested no place is safe. Since US President Joe Biden re-joined 196 parties in the 2015 Paris Agreement on climate mitigation, adaptation and finance (for dairy biogas projects, etc.), chances are better that humanity might halt global warming to 1.5°C above pre-industrial levels. Failing that, shifting jet streams may drive billions more migrants from drought- and storm-stricken areas.

What shall we do, then?

The FAO (2013: 83) listed six guides to further limit livestock emissions, some of which are mentioned above in the discussion of Britt et al. (2018):

1. Reducing land use changes arising from pasture expansion and feed crop cultivation;
2. Improving feeding practices and digestibility of diets;
3. Improving grazing and pasture management to increase soil organic carbon (SOC) stocks;
4. Increasing yields, e.g., through genetics, feeding and animal health;
5. Improving manure management – reducing the use of uncovered liquid manure management systems (MMS), particularly in dairy systems; and
6. Increasing energy use efficiency, especially in post-farm part of the supply chain.

As the ranks of climate-change deniers thin, both traditional pastoralists, and productivists willing to countenance cow confinement in the name of sustainable intensification, broadly agree on such environmental goals. To research this book, the author cast his net wide for information. Relevant to point (2) above and to greenhouse gases, one source was Harsh Gohel, a graduate of the Institute of Rural Land Management in Anand (IRMA) who went on to work in banking and investing in women entrepreneurs in rural India. Gohel cited a report on India's National Dairy Plan Phase 1 (NDP-1 2020 Feb: 155; CSIRO 14 Oct 2016) noting 15–20 per cent reductions of methane from lactating animals by balancing feed to minimize acetates and butyrates, which are substrates of methane production in enteric fermentation of methane. Those are promising results on tailoring feed to bovine microbiomes, paralleling the FAO (2010: 46) study *Greenhouse Gas Emissions from the Dairy Sector*: 'If we assume an increase in milk production by 10%, parallel to the increased digestibility, the GHG emissions are reduced by 19.2% in the extensive system and by 15.4% in the intensive system.'

Balanced cattle feed (BCF) – sometimes accounts for 70 per cent of the cost of milk – has been a concern of India's Amul dairy co-operative, which built its first plant, assisted by Oxfam and FAO, and inaugurated by Prime Minister Shastri, in 1965. The Amul dairy co-operative has moved India's White Revolution toward zero-grazing, with tethered cattle fed balanced feed along with rice paddy stalks from the Green Revolution, but many cows, buffalo and goats still depend on roadside or (diminishing) forest grazing for nutrition. More digestible, nutrient-dense feed and/or supplements means less nutrient loss and better well-being for cows, which in turn improves incomes of marginal family farmers who are often women.

To address unbalanced nutritional intake of cows managed by poor farmers, Dr Milind Niphadkar, a cancer researcher with six patents on his CV, turned entrepreneur. Niphadkur established Occamy Bioscience (2021), named after one of J.R. Rowling's *Fantastic Beasts*. Espousing the Occam's Razor principle, which prioritizes simple, inexpensive solutions over complex ones – Occamy aims to provide affordable inputs (e.g., proteins, amino acids, vitamins and minerals) to marginal dairy farmers whose cows average only 987 litres per lactation, just 40 per cent of the global average of 2,200 litres. Seaweed has been mentioned as a GHG reducer in bovine research in Israel, the EU, US and UK – as well as Australia (CSIRO 14 Oct 2016). Working with microbiologist Ms. Saloni Godbole (MSc), and dairy nutritionist Dr Parag Ghogale, Dr Niphadkar (personal emails 20–4 May 2021) wrote to me to explain how additives and ingredients such as seaweed reduce acetates, butyrates and resulting methane.

Cows often turn up their noses at oilseeds – but they are cheap in India. So, Occamy's self-described team of scientists-turned-entrepreneurs blends tastier rapeseed deoiled cake as a main ingredient functioning as bypass protein (e.g., undigested corn or soy), to ensure synthesis of pyruvate that induces fat production. This is a boon to poor farmers and the environment. Ghogale added:

> We add a proprietary blend of microbes that ensure proper digestion of fibres in the rumen and also include bypass fat in some proportions. We have observed that regular feeding of our products reduces buffalo and cow burping :)

Methane is more than hot air. It could determine whether or not we return to Net Zero emissions before it is too late. In North-East England, Ewan Anderson, Emeritus Professor of Geopolitics at the University of Durham, alerted me to the Yorkshire Philosophical Society (YPS), and its Café Scientifique online Zoom seminar (3 March 2021) on the topic of 'Farming, Food and Climate Change – can we eat our way to a brighter future?' It was cutting-edge stuff. YPS speaker Neil Douglas Fuller, Technical Director of the Atlas Sustainable Soils Programme, acknowledged humanity's debt to nitrogen fertilizers for avoiding Malthusian starvation, but rued loss of biodiversity and, ironically, the halving of soil carbon content as our anthropogenic carbon footprint of intensive monoculture deepened. Fuller's illustrations showed Yorkshire farmers adopting practical measures like leguminous cover crops, to take carbon from the atmosphere and put it in soil, where it belongs. YPS Chair Catherine Brophy fielded questions from sixty virtual participants, including mine: 'In the year 2050, will dairy cows have to be intensively confined in feedlots – not grazing verdant Yorks and Durham fields?' Fuller's answer reassured pastoralists (and echoed Occamy's scientists): 'No. Much more can be done with soils, feed including seaweed, and so on' (CSIRO 2016; *The Lead* 2021).

YPS Chair Brophy later introduced me to Andrew Loftus, who explained the National Farmers' Union targets for Net Zero GHG emissions by 2040 – a decade before the UK government's 2050 target. Farming is pivotal as it acts both as a GHG emitter and a carbon sink. But reducing UK farms' 45.6 million MT of CO_2 (10 per cent of equivalent CO_2) will require agriculturalists to 'science the hell out of the problem' and develop best practices along food chains. Their vision entails cover crops as a nice green canopy feeding underground fungi, stopping soils from drying out, with earthworms building galleries for water and nutrient transport, sequestering huge chunks of carbon. The bad and good news is that methane comprises about 50 per cent of UK farm GHGs, but multiple possibilities exist for reductions. On his Yorkshire farm, Loftus keeps traditional suckler beef cattle and believes his beef is already carbon-neutral, depending on the system of carbon accounting used (*Agriland* 6 Aug 2020).

Loftus has worked along the supply chain, including meat processing and a major supermarket. He exuded excitement about the Oxford University climate group which is trying to ensure that global regulations do not needlessly penalize UK ruminant farming which is capable of GHG neutrality. In *Climate and Atmospheric Science,* Michelle Cain, John Lynch and Myles Allen (2019) announced their 'Improved calculation of warming-equivalent emissions for short-lived climate pollutants'. Michelle Cain (*Frontiers of Sustainable Food Systems* 3 Feb 2021) and John Lynch took conventional, standardized CO_2-equivalent (CO_2-e) emissions using Global Warming Potentials (GWP) over 100 years, and refined them with an alternative usage of GWP, denoted GWP*. Claiming the survival of Europe's livestock sector was at stake, Myles Allen exhorted the EU to change its methane calculation to the refined GWP* (*Agriland* 6 Aug 2020).

Climate science, and the mix of atmospheric GHGs, are dynamic. But consensus was strong among sources that Goodland and Anhang's 2009 *World Watch Magazine* article was simply wrong. The paper by Herrero (2011) and co-authors, including Steinfeld and Gerber of the original (FAO 2006) *Livestock's Long Shadow*, was sent out for comment. Dr Marek Szablewski, a mathematician in Durham University's Department of Physics, replied:

> These numbers are really difficult to pin down (GHGs) I think that as long as you cite where the figures are from it should be okay – the 18% does seem high. Your reference does seem to indicate this as reasonable.

Dairy's methane curse is yielding to science. In Chapter 3, Ethics and Animals, Query 5 posed: 'I would pay a little more for pasture-grazed dairy products and meat.' An organic dairy farm owner in North-East England replied that seaweed mixed in feed optimized environmental sustainability and cow welfare. Similarly, Australia's apex scientific arm CSIRO found that 100g per cow per day of red seaweed *Asparagopsis* mixed in regular feed cut methane emissions by 90 per cent. The South Australian Government has committed $1.5 million to support the new commercial seaweed industry for cows and sheep. Working with the Narungga Aboriginal Nation, the firm CH4 Global, cofounded by Steve Meller, will grow cold and warm water seaweed offshore (CSIRO 2016; *The Lead* 2020 and 2021).

In Washington State, USA, where dairy farms earn $1.2 billion per year, 10 per cent of all agricultural receipts, progress is sought in regenerative ag. University scientists work with farmers and state politicians on programmes to reduce fossil-fuel use via GPS-guided tractors, anaerobic digesters to transform dairy methane into energy, and worms in wastewater to convert 99 per cent of dairy waste into worm castings to boost soil health, according to the Darigold farmers' co-operative blog *The Daily Churn* (2020).

These ethical and environmental goals are widely shared, but the politics are problematic. In Seattle, Goldie Caughlan, retired spokesperson for Puget Consumer Cooperative Community Markets (PCC in Scholten 2014: 57, 86, 92, 101, 107, 110), the US's biggest consumer-owned food co-operative with 58,000 members, fears state funding for Big Ag can marginalize livelihoods of families in the alternative food networks that contribute to the co-operative. Civilization could be doomed without climate solutions, irrespective of socio-economic scale. However, as reported in Chapter 5, Amul, India's largest dairy co-op with 2.6 million farmers in Gujarat, works with marginal dairy farmers developing biogas, nutrient recycling and solar sites in villages (Scholten 2019b).

The UN-FAO's Henning Steinfeld told Darigold co-op's *Daily Churn* (2020) that the US dairy cow is a model of efficiency, with the country's current 9 million cows producing 60 per cent more than 25 million cows in the 1950s. Frank Mitloehner, the greenhouse gas expert from UC Davis, testified to the US Senate Committee on Agriculture, Nutrition and Forestry that this equated a two-thirds cut in carbon dioxide equivalents (CO_2e). Yet too many megadairies deny cows the grazing they need for the health, well-being and the longevity of their great-grandmothers. A better model is the Organic Valley co-operative, which promotes grazing and whose welfare practices incidentally appeal to ethical consumers.

However, even if enough political consensus is achieved, actions agreed to limit global warming to 1.5°C higher than pre-industrial times may be insufficient. Assessing recent climate disasters that have ravaged all continents – burned Australia, Canada, Siberia, Spain, Turkey; desiccated Africa; flooded Kerala in India; washed tractors down streets in Germany and Belgium; melted glaciers in the Alps and ice caps at the North and South Poles – *The Economist* (2021d) warned that even if we reach climate targets in previous COP and IPCC agreements, it still might not be enough: 'Three degrees of global warming is quite plausible and truly disastrous: Rapid emission cuts can reduce the risks but not eliminate them.'

Rudolph Steiner (1924a, b and c), a forerunner of organics, fought negative anthropogenic impacts on environment. It is unlikely Steiner knew of the ozone layer, but he would have lauded the 1987 Montreal Protocol that banned chlorofluorocarbons (CFC) to heal the hole in it. Now is time for politicians to mitigate global warming, as livestock and dairy sectors mix seaweed with feed to cut ruminant methane (ACIAGAR 2013; Britt et al. 2018). Crucially, states must cut subsidies to fossil-fuel industries, with cap-and-trade schemes to cut carbon equivalents while spurring conversion to cleaner solar-electric and hydrogen economies.

An honest proposal

Much of this narrative has dealt with dairy and livestock farming's downside of enteric fermentation. Methane is a mammoth problem, but amenable to more easily digestible grasses on pasture, and hay and silage fed with seaweed at the milking barn. Scientific research on dairy animals' microbiomes can also optimize their milk yield, health and well-being in their specific locations (Britt et al. 2018). As argued previously, better welfare is evidenced by improved longevity (Scholten 2014: 3, 6, 29, 52, 76, 91, 114, 121, 124–9, 179, 184, 196, 207, 211, 227, 235).

Former President Donald Trump had some good ideas. One was to make animal welfare standards the same for organic and conventional cattle. Trump's reasons, in January 2017, for shelving standards that had been negotiated meticulously by the National Organic Standards Board (NOSB) for a decade, are obscure. Trump critics might say it was deplorable inattentiveness to the suffering of other creatures, such as animals in factory farms, that triggered an assumption that what was good enough for one cow widget was good enough for another certified organic widget. But, taking this idea further, it would be ethical to guide reform of conventional confined CAFO dairying with the original letter and spirit of the US National Organic Program (NOP).

It is not too much to ask that conventional cows, like their organic sisters, follow the 2010 National Organic Program Pasture Rule, which mandates that organic cows graze pasture a minimum 120 days a year, and consume at least 30 per cent of their dry-matter intake on pasture. The spirit of the original rule was that cows exercise natural herding behaviours on pasture, with the chance to explore fresh paddocks solo or with friends, outside, weather permitting. So, as President Trump seemed to indicate, if the rules are good enough NOP cows, why not for conventional ones too?

Conventional megadairy owners should try rotational grazing one-third of their herd each day. A cow would enjoy at least ten days on pasture per month. How many would object on the basis that they lack sufficient pasture to graze lactating and dry cows 33 per cent of the time? Just as anti-trust laws force industrial monopolies to divest, megadairies could downsize herds and send extras to traditional dairy states like Wisconsin. This approximates a 2007 Supreme Court judgement against megadairies flouting organic rules in Idaho and Colorado (*New York Times* 2007, 2010; Scholten 2014: 31, 54–8, 101, 106 (Seattle boycott), 115, 210). Some farmers contend their fields are too muddy to permit 30 per cent grazing, but their welfare is so good that many milk cows live twelve years or more. If farm records prove this, an exemption could be in order – especially if they prominently display reassuring longevity data beside the farm mailbox.

In 2018, Californians passed Proposition 12, a ban on the sale of pork, eggs and veal calves raised in confined spaces in the state (*Economist* 2021i). Easing stocking densities might tempt some vegan Millennials and Gen Zers back to animal foods. Ultimately, if space is insufficient to allow animals to express natural behaviours such as grazing pasture, morality may require human conversion to plant- and laboratory-based diets. Ethical, environmentally sustainable farms, bankrupted by factory farms that push cows so brutally that they cannot conceive a second calf, have allies among consumers and activists promoting political action to reform dairying.

What's a failed vegan to do? My last fake meat burger tasted okay with vegan Gouda cheese. The absence of survivor's guilt was most welcome. More research is needed so, next to test are Pizza Hut's new vegetarian Beyond Meat pizzas (*Vegconomist* 29 July 2021). Meanwhile, the Intergovernmental Panel on Climate Change (IPCC) has signalled a Code Red for humanity; the report *titled AR6 Climate Change 2021: The Physical Science Basis* warns that average temperatures to 2.7°C above pre-industrial levels are possible by the end of the twenty-first century – even if we fulfil previous commitments on emissions cuts (IPCC 2021; *Economist* 2021f). Science fiction buffs tout geoengineering to balance atmosphere, but political hurdles alone make that riskier than tackling fossil-fuel emissions first.

Thomas Piketty, author of *Capital in the Twenty-first Century* (2013: 740–-3) seriously considers the threat of climate change, and estimates that damage to the environment could total 'dozens of points of global GDP per year'. British scholar Nicholas Stern urged investing 'at least five points of GDP a year right now to attempt to mitigate climate change in the future' (2013: 741). Piketty lauded Stern's 'reasonable' goal but asked, 'Do we really know what we ought to invest in and how we should organize our efforts' (2013: 743)? Green energy involving wind, solar and hydrogen are underway, but unlikely to halt backsliding to coal and petroleum, sparked by Russia's invasion of Ukraine on 24 February 2022. It is tempting to invest trillions of euros in fusion energy, cleaner than the fission reactor that has blighted Chernobyl since 1986. Yet, since the 1950s, science-fiction readers and cynics know fusion has always been forty years in the future Piketty (2013: 743) advises that it would be wiser to choose 'a balanced strategy that would make use of all available tools'.

It is the position of this book that an early, cost-effective tool against global warming can be development of easily digestible feeds and additives such as seaweed to reduce cow burps of ruminant methane. Considering that half the world's farmers are women facing low productivity, the spirit of 'Empowering Rural Women' (FAO 2018) and the 2030 Agenda for Sustainable Development urge agronomic training and investment to engage women on all continents in the growth, distribution and application of seaweed in cattle feed to better themselves

– and the planet. We can feed cows kelp and seaweed *now*, while developing fusion and sustainable energy as long-term solutions.

Best wishes to readers making ethical, environmental and political choices on animal welfare, biodiversity and human well-being. Climate apocalypse is a clear and present danger. The denouement of dairy farming in the twenty-first century will be a close-run thing.

BIBLIOGRAPHY

Abbott, Chuck (2020), 'USDA to buy as much excess milk and meat as possible, says Perdue', *Successful Farming*, 116 Apr.

Acorn Dairy (2019), 'Seaweed on the menu for our organic cows: A taste of the ocean to keep Acorn Dairy cows ship-shape and free from antibiotics', 12 Dec.

ACIAGAR (2013), 'Growing more food, efficiently and sustainably', by Peter Dixon of the Australian Centre for International Agricultural Research.

ADAS (2017), 'Grazed and confused? Latest report from the Food Climate Research Network questions the carbon sequestration potential of cattle grazing systems', Agricultural Development and Advisory Service (UK), 23 Oct.

Advances in Agronomy (2009), 'Clearing the air: Livestock's contribution to climate change', by Maurice Pitesky, Kimberly Stackhouse and Frank Mitloehner, in *Advances in Agronomy*, edited by Donald Sparks, Vol 103, 1–40, Burlington: Academic Press,

Agence-France Presse (2021), 'Michelin awards first star to vegan restaurant in France', 18 Jan.

Agol, Dorice (2021), 'This Corona virus (COVID-19) was somehow a blessing: Tales of street food vendors in Nairobi's informal settlements', *Rural Geography Research Group, RGRG Newsletter*, rgrg.co.uk/newsletter (accessed 29 Mar 22).

AHV (2020), 'Fight COVID-19 with dairy? China industry associations issue consumption guidelines to 'build immune resistance', by Pearly Neo, 17 Mar.

Albright, Jack L., and C.W. Arave (1997), *The behaviour of Cattle*. Egham, CABI.

Allied Market Research (2016), 'Meat substitute market – by product type (tofu, tempeh, textured vegetable protein, Quorn, Seitan), source (soy, wheat, mycoprotein), category (frozen, refrigerated, shelf-stable). February, *Global Opportunity Analysis and Industry Forecast, 2014–2020*.

Alston, Margaret (2000), *Breaking through the Grass Ceiling: Women, Power and Leadership in Agricultural Organisations*, Amsterdam: Harwood Academic.

Amul (2018),

Andrews, Kristin (2020), *How to Study Animal Minds*. Cambridge: Cambridge University Press (cites de Waal 1999.)

Animal Equality India (2017), 'In Photos: Study exposes horrific sexual abuse and torture in Indian dairy production', by AEI staff, 6 Dec.

ARC2020 (2020), 'Agroecology Europe forum: What is this thing called agroecology?', by Oliver Moore, Agricultural and Rural Convention.

Arla (2016), 'Organic milk to become more accessible with Arla organic farm milk launch', 15 Nov.

Atkins, Peter J. (1992), '"White poison?" The social consequences of milk consumption 1850–1930', *Social History of Medicine*, 5(2): 207–27.

Atkins, Peter J. (2000), 'The pasteurization of England: the science, culture and health implications of milk processing, 1900–1950', in *Food, science, policy and regulation in the 20th century*, edited by : D. Smith and J. Phillips, 37–51, London: Routledge.

Atkins, Peter J. (2001a), 'Milk consumption and tuberculosis in Britain', in A *Order and Disorder*, edited by A. Fenton, 83–95, East Linton: Tuckwell Press.

Atkins, Peter J. (2001b), 'The pasteurization of Britain: The science, culture and health implications of food processing', in *Science, Medicine and Food Policy,* edited by D. Smith and J. Phillips, London: Routledge.

Atkins, Peter J. (2010), *Liquid Materialities: A History of Milk, Science and the Law.* Farnham: Ashgate.

Atkins, Peter, and Ian Bowler (2001), *Food in Society: Economy, Culture, Geography.* London: Arnold.

Atkins, Peter J., and Philip A Robinson (2013), 'Coalition culls and zoonotic ontologies', *Environment and Planning A: Economy and Space,* 1 Jan. UK: Sage.

Atlantic (2014), 'How we get tall: Men grew four inches in 100 years', by Olga Khazan, 9 May.

Atlantic (2021), 'Putting microchips in vaccines Is a terrible idea, when you think about it. Let me explain', by James Heathers, 3 June.

Attfield, Robin (2006), 'Environmental sensitivity and critiques of stewardship', in *Environmental Stewardship: Critical Perspectives,* edited by R.J. Berry, 76–91, London: T & T Clark/Continuum.

Basu, Pratyusha (2009), *Villages, women, and the success of dairy cooperatives in India: Making place for rural development,* Amherst, NY: Cambria Press.

Basu, Pratyusha, and Bruce A. Scholten (eds, authors) (2012), Editorial: *Technological and social dimensions of the Green Revolution: Connecting pasts and presents, International Journal of Agricultural Sustainability,* 10(2), IJAS editor, Sir Jules Pretty.

Basu, Pratyusha, and Bruce A. Scholten (eds, authors) (2012), 'Crop-livestock systems in rural development: linking India's Green and White Revolutions', in *IJAS* 10(2).

Basu, Pratyusha, and Bruce A. Scholten (2013), *Technological and social dimensions of the Green Revolution: Connecting Pasts and Presents* [IJAS (2012) contents also in hardcover], Abingdon: Routledge.

BBC News (2010), 'China dairy products found tainted with melamine', 9 July.

BBC (2015), 'Milk: End of EU quota heightens UK farmers' fears', by Claire Marshall, 1 Apr.

BBC (2016), 'Brexit: EU says no compromise on freedom of movement.' 29 Jun.

BBC (2017a), 'David Attenborough – Blue planet [II] sequel [with methane volcanoes in Gulf of Mexico]', 2 Feb.

BBC (2017b), '100 Women: "Why I invented the Glass Ceiling phrase"', by Marilyn Loden, 13 Dec.

BBC (2018), 'Russian spy: Sergei Skripal collapsed alongside daughter', 6 Mar.

BBC (2020), 'Health – Fertility rate: 'Jaw-dropping' global crash in children being born', 15 Jul.

BBC (2021), 'Climate change: IPCC report is "code red for humanity"', 9 Aug.

Bear, Chris, and Lewis Holloway (2016), 'Resisting robots: Automated milking and emerging geographies of more-than-human resistance', PowerPoint at RGS-IBG, 1 Sep.

Beauchamp, Tom L., and R.G. Frey, eds (2014), *The Oxford Handbook of Animal Ethics* (*OHoAE*), Oxford: Oxford University Press.

Bellarby J., R. Tirado, T. Reyes, A. Leip, F. Weiss, J.P. Lesschen and P. Smith (2013), 'Livestock greenhouse gas emissions and mitigation potential in Europe', *Global Change Biology,* 19: 3–18.

Bellingham Herald (2017), 'Unusual building design paying dividends for cheese producer Appel Farms', by Dave Gallagher, 8 Jan.

Bellwood, Peter (2005), 'The beginnings of agriculture in Southwest Asia', in *First Farmers: The Origins of Agricultural Societies,* 44–68, Malden, MA: Blackwell.

Benbrook, Charles (1990) 'Monsanto Roundup Glyphosate almost doubled by 1990 compared to 1980'.

Benbrook, Charles (2007), 'Principles governing the long-run risks, benefits, and costs of agricultural biotechnology', in *Biodiversity and the law: Intellectual property, biotechnology, and traditional knowledge* (Chapter 11), edited by Charles McManis, US: Earthscan.

Benbrook, Charles (2010), *'Shades of green': User's manual – guide and documentation for a daily farm management system calculator,* Pullman, WA: The Organic Center.

Benbrook, Charles (2012a), *A Deeper Shade of Green: Lessons from Grass-based Organic Dairy Farms.* Washington DC: The Organic Center.

Benbrook, Charles (2012b), 'Impacts of genetically engineered crops on pesticide use in the U.S. – the first sixteen years', *Environmental Sciences Europe* 24:24.

Benbrook, Charles (2014), 'Shades of green dairy farm calculator webinar', 18 Mar.

Benbrook, Charles (2019), 'UK Soil Association and Dr Benbrook launch monthly "*Letter from America*"', Hygeia 12 Mar.

Benbrook, Charles, Cory Carman, E. Ann Clark, Cindy Daley, Wendy Fulwider, Michael Hansen, Carlo Leifert, Klaas Martens, Laura Paine, Lisa Petkewitz, Guy Jodarski, Francis Thicke, Juan Velez and Gary Wegner (2010), *A Dairy Farm's Footprint: Evaluating the Impacts of Conventional and Organic Farming Systems,* Pullman, WA: The Organic Center.

Benbrook, Charles, Gillian Butler, Maged A. Latif, Carlo Leifert and Donald R. Davis (2013), 'Organic production enhances milk nutritional quality by shifting fatty acid composition', *PLoS ONE* 8(12).

Benbrook, Charles and Rachel Benbrook (2018), 'The lowdown on Roundup, Part 1.' Children's Environmental Health Network. Available online: https://vimeo.com/225190429 (accessed 06 Jun 2018).

Benbrook, Charles, Donald R. Davis, Bradley J. Heins, Maged A. Latif, Carlo Leifert, Logan Peterman, Gillian Butler, Ole Faergeman, Silvia Abel-Caines, Marcin Baranski (2018), 'Enhancing the fatty acid profile of milk through forage-based rations, with nutrition modeling of diet outcomes', Food Science and Nutrition. Jan 2018.

Benbrook, Charles (2018), 'Roundup is safe enough to drink, right?' *Hygeia's Blog*, 18 Aug.

Betts, Richard (2021), 'Met Office: Atmospheric CO2 now hitting 50% higher than pre-industrial levels', *Carbon Brief: Clear on Climate*, 16 Mar.

Business Standard (2011), 'Sustainability of farm economy discussed at Amity University [book launch of Scholten 2010]', by Harish Damodaran with Asmita Bhardwaj, 5 Jan 2011, updated 20 Jan 2013.

Bhaskar, R.N. (2011), 'India's success with milk: Captivating saga of white revolution [by B.A. Scholten]', in *Governance Now*, Mumbai, 16 Dec.

Bhattacharjee, Ujjal, Danielle Jarashow, Thomas A. Casey, Jacob W. Petrich and Mark A. Rasmussen (2018), 'Using fluorescence spectroscopy to identify milk from grass-fed dairy cows and to monitor its photodegradation.' *Journal of Agricultural and Food Chemistry*, 22 Jan.

Biagiotti, Paul R. (2013), 'Overcrowding invites disease', *Hoard's Dairyman.* 25 Aug: 540.

Biagiotti, Paul R. (2014), 'Lack of longevity: Are we in a culling crisis?', *Progressive Dairyman.* 21 Feb.

Biagiotti, Paul R. (2016), *Practical Organic Dairy Farming: Management, Medical and Welfare Recommendations for Organic Dairy Producers*, Fort Atkinson, WI: *Hoard's Dairyman.*

Biagiotti, Paul R. (2017), 'Cow parallels to the human Paleo diet', *Hoard's Dairyman*, Dec: 752–3.

Binimelis, Rosa, Walter Pengue and Iliana Monterroso (2009), 'Transgenic treadmill: Responses to the emergence and spread of glyphosate-resistant johnsongrass in Argentina', *Geoforum*, 40(4): 623–33.

Blaustein, Richard J. (2015), 'William Ruddiman and the Ruddiman hypothesis', *Minding Nature*, 8(1): 44–9.

Bloomberg (2020), 'Bayer draws uncertain line under Roundup in $12 billion', by Jef Feeley and Tim Loh, 24 Jun.

Boston College Center for Work & Family (2014), *The New Dd: Take Your Leave*, by Brad Harrington, et al.

Boucher, Doug (2016), See UCS (2016).

Bowman, Michael (2019), 'Animals, humans and the international legal order: towards an integrated bioethical perspective', in *Animal Welfare and International Environmental Law: From conservation to compassion*, edited by Werner Scholz, 38–147, Cheltenham and Northampton, MA: Edward Elgar.

Britannica (1998), 'Livestock barns and shelters', in *Farm building – Agriculture*, by Roger Martinot, 28 Sep.

British Medical Journal (2019), 'Probable carcinogenicity of glyphosate [found by World Health Organization]', BMJ 2019;365:l1613.

British Social Attitudes (2015), 'Benefits and welfare: long-term trends or short-term reactions?', by P. Taylor-Gooby and E. Taylor (2015), in *British social attitudes: The 32nd report*, edited by J. Curtice and R. Ormston, 74–101, London: NatCen Social Research.

Britt, J.H., R.A. Cushman, C.D. Dechow, H. Dobson, P. Humblot, M.F. Hutjens, G.A. Jones, P.S. Ruegg, I.M. Sheldon and J.S. Stevenson (2018), 'Invited review: Learning from the future – a vision for dairy farms and cows in 2067', *Journal of Dairy Science*, 101(5): 3722–41. See also *Hoard's Dairyman* & *JDS*.

Brookings Institution (2017), 'Census shows a revival of pre-recession migration flows', by William H. Frey, Washington DC, 30 Mar.

Buller, Henry J. (2013), 'Animal geographies 1', *Progress in Human Geography*, 38(2):308–18.

Buller Henry J. (2015), 'Animal geographies II: Methods', *Progress in Human Geography*, 39(3): 374–84.

Buller, Henry, and Emma Roe (2018), *Food and Animal Welfare: Producing and Consuming Valuable Lives*, London: Bloomsbury.

Business Insider (2015), 'How a startup that makes fake meat from plants caught the attention of Bill Gates and the founders of Twitter', by Madeline Stone, 15 Aug.

Business Insider (2018), 'Incredible photos of New York City when it was covered in farmland', by Leanna Garfield, 17 Jan.

Business Insider (2021), 'Rep. Marjorie Taylor Greene says she doesn't believe in the "so-called science" of evolution', by Yelena Dzhanova, 12 Jun.

Business Standard (2011), 'Sustainability of farm economy discussed at Amity University [book launch of Scholten 2010]', by Harish Damodaran with Asmita Bhardwaj, 5 Jan 2011, updated 20 Jan 2013.

Butler, Justine (2015), 'Why milk is a feminist issue: What goes on behind the closed doors of the modern intensive dairy farm?' *Viva! 60*, Winter. [This online source lacks page numbers.]

CiWF (2017), 'The cruel truth behind Parmesan that is hard to stomach', Compassion in World Farming, 27 Nov.

CNBC (2018a), 'Trump slaps China with tariffs on up to $60 billion in imports', by Kevin Breuninger and Kayla Tausche, 22 Mar.

CNBC (2018b), Bill Gates and Richard Branson are betting lab-grown meat might be the food of the future', by Rick Morgan, 23 Mar.

CSIRO (2016), 'Seaweed could hold the key to cutting methane emissions from cow burps', by Michael Battaglia, *CSIROscope*, Australian Government, 14 Oct. Also, *The Lead* 30 July.

Cain, Michelle, John Lynch, Myles R. Allen, Jan Fuglelstvedt, David J. Frame and Adrian H. Macey (2019), 'Improved calculation of warming-equivalent emissions for short-lived climate pollutants', *Climate and Atmospheric Science, 2*(29).

Caja, Gerardo, Andreia Castro-Costa and Christopher H. Knight (2016), 'Engineering to support well-being of dairy animals', *Journal of Dairy Research,* 136–47.

Cambridge Declaration on Consciousness (2012), *CDoC* by Philip Low and edited by Jaak Panksepp, Diana Reiss, David Edelman, Bruno Van Swinderen, Philip Low and Christof Koch. Proclaimed Cambridge, UK, 7 July 2012, at Francis Crick Memorial Conference on Consciousness in Human and non-Human Animals. On CBS -TV *60 Minutes.* (See Low et al. below).

Campbell, Hugh (2020), *Farming Inside Invisible Worlds: Modernist Agriculture and Its Consequences,* London: Bloomsbury Academic.

Candler, Wilfred, and Nalinia Kumar (1998), *India: The dairy revolution*, The World Bank, Washington DC.

Capper, Jude L., R.A. Cady and D.E Bauman (2009), 'The environmental impact of dairy production: 1944 compared with 2007', *Journal of Animal Science, 87*(6): 2160.

Capper, Jude L. (2012), 'Can buying local food really save the planet?', *Hoard's Dairyman,* 25 Jan: 43.

Capper, Jude L. (2012), 'Comparing the environmental impact of conventional, natural and grass-fed beef production systems' *Animals, 2*(2): 127–43.

Capper, Jude L. (2013), 'Should we reject animal source foods to save the planet? A review of the sustainability of global livestock production', *South African Journal of Animal Science, 43*(3).

Capper, Jude (2017), 'A sustainable future for livestock farming – how do dietary choices, production systems and consumer perceptions intersect?', Vet BVA webinar, 22 Nov.

Capper, Jude (2018a), 'Is grass always greener?' Shropshire Grassland Society, Shrewsbury, UK.

Capper, Jude (2018b), 'Crying over spilt milk: sustainability, efficiency and the industry's need for myth-busting', Semex Glasgow, 15 Jan.

Capper, Jude L. (2018c), 'Progress and prospects in optimized dairy husbandry', 5th DairyCare conference Thessaloniki, Greece, 20 Mar.

Capper, Jude (2020), 'A decade of continuous improvement – how far has U.S. dairy production come?' ASAS Webinar, 12 Feb.

Capper, J. L., E. Castaneda-Gutierrez, R.A. Cady and D.E. Bauman (2008), 'The Environmental impact of recombinant bovine somatotropin (rBST) use in dairy production', Proceedings of the National Academy of Sciences, *105*(28): 9688–73.

Capper, Jude L., R. A. Cady and D. E. Bauman (2009), 'Efficiency of dairy production and its carbon footprint', University of Florida IFAS.

Capper, Jude L., and Roger A. Cady (2020), 'The effects of improved performance in the U.S. dairy cattle industry on environmental impacts between 2007 and 2017', *Journal of Animal Science, 98*(1), Jan.

Carbon Brief (2021), 'Met Office: Atmospheric CO2 now hitting 50% higher than pre-industrial levels', by Richard Betts, 16 Mar.

Carrington, Damian (2018), 'Avoiding meat and dairy is "single biggest way" to reduce your impact on Earth', *Gurardian*, 31 May.

Carson, Rachel (1962), *Silent Spring*, USA: Houghton Mifflin.

Chase, Larry E., Lane O. Ely and Michael F. Hutjens (2006), 'Major advances in extension education programs in dairy production', *Journal of Dairy Science 89*(5), May: 1147–54.

Chepeliev, Maksym (2020), "Development of the Non-CO$_2$ GHG Emissions Database for the GTAP Data Base Version 10A," GTAP Research Memoranda 5993, Center for Global Trade Analysis, Department of Agricultural Economics, Purdue University.

Chomping Climate Change (2014) 'In Memoriam: Robert Goodland (1939–2013), co-founder of CCC'. Available online: http://www.chompingclimatechange.org/in-memorium-robert-goodland/ (accessed 16 May 2021).

Chomsky, Noam (2021) 'Noam Chomsky – Neoliberalism, democracy and the climate crisis 2021', www.oxfordclimatesociety.com (1:04:30) streamed live 22 Feb 2021: https://www.youtube.com/watch?v=WZ81-McOgdM (accessed 4 Jun 2021).

Chemosphere (2018), 'Glyphosate and the key characteristics of an endocrine disruptor: a review', by Juan Munoz, Tammy Bleak and Gloria Calaf, 11 Sep 2018.

Common Dreams (2021), 'Mexico's decision to ban glyphosate has rocked the agribusiness world. GM corn presidential decree comes despite intense pressure from industry, U.S. authorities', 24 Feb 2021.

Compassion in World Farming (2017), 'The cruel truth behind Parmesan that is hard to stomach', by Emma Slawinski, Director of Campaigns.

Conversation (2022), 'Giant ancient sharks had enormous babies that ate their siblings in the womb', by Tom Fletcher, University of Leicester, 11 Jan.

Conway, Gordon (2013), 'Sustainable agricultural intensification: A practical solution for the global development agenda.' *Huffington Post*, 18 Apr.

Coop News (2017), 'Organic Valley farmers' co-op grows membership to 2,000 families', 12 Jan.

Cornucopia Institute (2014), 'Photo gallery: Redland Dairy, Farwell, Texas, 17 Ma.

Cornucopia Institute (2015), 'Conventional cows on organic Dairies? USDA's proposed Origin of Livestock Rule could create new loophole', by Will Fantle.

Cornucopia Institute (2018a), 'Organic Checkoff proposed by USDA to the dismay of farmers', 19 Jan.

Cornucopia Institute (2018b), 'The origin of livestock: Conventional cows on organic dairies', in *The Industrialization of Organic Dairy: Giant Livestock Factories and Family Farms Sharing the Same Organic Label* (18–19, 1–68).

Cornucopia Institute (2021), 'The top issues impacting organic policy in 2021', 14 Jan.

Cowspiracy: The Sustainability Secret (2014), Documentary by Kip Andersen and Keegan Kuhn. Cited Goodland and Anhang's (2009 *WW*) estimate that livestock emit 51 per cent of GHGs.

CowSignals Training (2018), '5 topics to improve animal welfare and farmer welfare', by J. Driessen, 20 Mar.

Crunchbase (2020), '[List of top] Organic female founded companies'.

Cummins, Ronnie (2020), *Grassroots Rising: A Call to Action on Climate, Farming, Food, and a Green New Deal*, 11 Feb, US: Amazon.com.

Daily Mail (2012), 'Do animals have a sense of humour? It's no laughing matter . . .', by Peter Lewis, (Review of *Why Animals Matter* by Marian Stamp Dawkins), 25 May.

Daily Mail (2016), 'Waitrose to ban factory farmed cows from producing milk for its supermarkets as it targets animal welfare', by Sean Poulter, 2 Feb.

Dairy Business (2009), 'USDA survey provides a glimpse of organic milk and crop production: Organic dairies represented 3.5% US herds, 2.1% of cows and 1.5% of milk volume in 2008', by Dave Natzke.

Dairy Farmers of Washington (2014), 'Facts about the Washington dairy Industry 2005–2014', Washington Dairy Products Commission.

Dairy Group (2010), *Dairy Cow Housing*. Report for Arla, Morrisons and Dairy Co., Aug 2012, Somerset: New Agriculture House.

Dairy Herd Improvement (2013), 'Rolling herd average – % cows leaving the herd', by Ladd Muirbrook, Table and chart 2004–2013, Provo, UT: DHI (rebranded as amelicor.com).

Dairy Herd Improvement Association (DHIA) (2013), 'DHI Glossary', Aug.

Dairy Herd Management (2018), 'Anti-dairy commercial runs during closing ceremony of Olympics', by Wyatt Bechtel.

Dairy India Yearbook (2007), *Dairy India 2007: 6th Edition*, Edited by Sharad Gupta, 838pp, New Delhi: https://www.iimb.ac.in/node/4158

Dairy Site (2013), 'EU-funded research into precision livestock farming', 2 Dec. [N.B. PF dairy failed.]

Dakota Free Press (2019), 'Trump's ag secretary calls small farmers doomed un-American socialists', 3 Oct.

Damásio, Antonio R. (1994/2006), *Descartes' Error: Emotion, Reason, and the Human Brain*, London: Vintage.

Darigold (2020) 'A climate solution hiding in plain sight', by Tafline Laylin, *The Daily Churn*, 24 Feb.

Davis, Janet M. (2016), *The Gospel of Kindness: Animal Welfare and the Making of Modern America*, Oxford: Oxford University Press.

Dawkins, Marian Stamp (1998), *Through Our Eyes Only? The Search for Animal Consciousness,* UK, Oxford: Oxford University Press.

Dawkins, Marian Stamp (2007), *Observing Animal Behaviour: design and analysis of quantitative data*, UK, Oxford: Oxford University Press.

Dawkins, Marian Stamp (2012a), *Why Animals Matter: Animal Consciousness, Animal Welfare, and Human Well-being,* Oxford: Oxford University Press.

Dawkins, Marian Stamp (2012b), *What Do Animals Want? A Conversation with Marian Stamp Dawkins*, in *Edge*, 31 Oct.

DeLaval (2013), *Cow longevity conference 2013 proceedings,* Tumba, Sweden: DeLaval International.

Denver Post (2017), 'A USDA investigation or just an appointment? Few details emerge from inquiry into Boulder-based organic milk company', by Peter Whoriskey, 22 Dec.

Dettloff, Paul (2019), *Dr. Paul Dettloff's Complete Guide to Raising Animals Organically*, Greeley, CO: Acres USA.

de Waal, Frans B.M. (1999) 'Anthropomorphism and anthropodenial', *Philosophical Topics*, 27(1): 255–280. In Kristin Andrews (2020) *How to Study Animal Minds*, Cambridge: Cambridge University Press.

Didanna, Habtamu Lemma, Ashenafi Mengistu, Taddese Kuma and Berhanu Kuma (2018), 'Improving milk safety at farm-level in an intensive dairy production system: Relevance to smallholder dairy producers', *Food Quality and Safety 3*: 135–43.

Domingo. J.L. (2000), 'Health risks of genetically modified foods: Many opinions but few data', *Science* 288, 9 Jun: 1748–9.

DuPuis, E. Melanie (2002, updated 2015), *Nature's Perfect Food: How Milk Became America's Drink*. New York: New York University Press.

DuPuis, E. Melanie (2015), *Dangerous Digestion: The Politics of American Dietary Advice*. Berkeley, CA: Universit of California Press.

Dugdill, Brian T., Anthony Bennett, Joseph Phelan and Bruce A. Scholten (2013), 'Dairy industry development programmes: Their role in food and nutrition security and poverty reduction.' In *Milk and dairy products in human nutrition*, Food and Agricultural Organization of the United Nations, Rome: FAO-UN: 313–54. Free online: https://www.yumpu.com/en/document/read/40797937/3snq2aaot

Eastern Daily Press (2020), 'Why farmers need to 'pre-bunk' myths about meat production', by Chris Hill, 28 Nov.

Economist (2006), 'Freedom fried: The four freedoms on which the European Union is based are under threat', 9 Feb 2006.

Economist (2010), 'There is hope for forests, but mankind needs to move faster', 23 Sep 2010.

Economist (2013), "GM maize, health and the Séralini affair: Smelling a rat', 1 Dec 2013: 86.

Economist (2016), 'Art of the lie: Post truth politics in the age of social media', (Leader) 10 Sep.

Economist (2017a), 'Banyon: Goring the law: Ugly row about sacred cows undermines India's judiciary', 28 Jan.

Economist (2017b), 'Agriculture and energy: Electric fields: [Norwich] A maize boom', 16 Sep: 29.

Economist (2017c), 'What's in New Zealand's water? Cows are warming the planet', 30 Nov.

Economist (2020), 'Free exchange – Economists discover the power of social norms', 08 Feb: 72.

Economist (2021a), 'Put a plug in it: Governments should set targets to reduce methane emissions', 3 Apr.

Economist (2021b), 'A new use for microwaves: If you can have microwave ovens, why not microwave boilers?', 10 Apr: 77-78.

Economist (2021c), 'Urban environments: Could miniature [Miyawaki] forests help air-condition cities?, 3 July.

Economist (2021d), 'What's the worst that could happen? Three degrees global warming is quite plausible and truly disastrous: Rapid emission cuts can reduce the risks but not eliminate them', 24 July: 15–17.

Economist (2021e), 'Solar geoengineering: It that cannot be named: Geoengineering is a hot topic – and was underplayed in the IPCC's report', 14 Aug: 66.

Economist (2021f), 'Why curbing methane emissions will help fight climate change: It's a more powerful greenhouse gas than carbon dioxide, and should be easier to control', 14 Aug.

Economist (2021g), 'Economic & financial indicators: Currency Units per US$',18 Aug: 72.

Economist (2021h), 'Not all about the carbon: Why curbing methane emissions will help fight climate change: It's a more powerful greenhouse gas than carbon dioxide, and should be easier to control', 14 Aug.

Economist (2021i), 'Animal welfare: The bacon crunch: California's new regulations may raise the price of pork', 21 Aug: 29

Economist Intelligence Unit (2017) *Fixing Food*. EIU project developed with Barilla Center for Food and Nutrition (BCFN)'.

edairynews (2020), 'The dairy industry is collapsing before our eyes. This is why', 14 Feb.

edairynews (2020), 'The decline of "America's Dairyland" is fundamentally changing Wisconsin's rural landscape', 11 Mar. Excerpt: Jim 'Goodman family . . . milking cows in Wisconsin since 1889.'

edairynews (2020b), '"Let dairy die" activists may face jail time, sex offender list for protesting Bernie Sanders', 11 Mar.

Epoch Times (2016), 'The history that shaped the standard American diet', by Conan Milner, 14 Mar.

Eurostat (2019), 'News: Females in the field: more women managing farms across Europe', European Commission, 08 Mar 2019.

Express (2016), 'Nearly two-thirds of farmers back Brexit, new poll reveals', by Greg Heffer, 29 Apr.

Euractiv (2019), 'FAO official: 'Veganism is certainly not for everyone', by Sarantis Michalopoulos, 6 Jun 2019.

Euractiv (2020), 'US agriculture chief urges EU to listen to science, not fear-mongering NGOs', by S. Michalopoulos, 4 Feb.

Euronews (2018), 'Bayer and Monsanto in merger deal', 21 Mar.

Eurostat (2017), 'Milk and milk product statistics', in *Agriculture, forestry and fishery statistics*, Oct.

Eurostat (2019), 'Females in the field: more women managing farms across Europe', European Commission.

Extension (2016), 'Minimizing the risk for ketosis in dairy herds', Coop extension service, Kansas City.

Factchecker (2017) '3 Years of Swachh Bharat: 50 million more toilets', by Devanik Saha.

FAO (2014), 'Milk and milk products', Comm markets monitoring, Oct, Rome. Rome. ct'http://www.fao.org/fileadmin/templates/est/COMM_MARKETS_MONITORING/Dairy/Documents/OCTOBER_2014_FO_DAIRY.pdf

FAO-UN (2018), 'Empowering rural women, powering agriculture', *2030 Agenda for Sustainable Development*, 1 Dec.

FAO-STAT (2012), 'The female face of farming', Rome.

FAO-UN (1987), 'Useful conversion factors – Appendix 4', ISBN 92-5-101328-1, Rome: FAO-UN.

FAO-UN (2003), 'WTO Agreement on Agriculture: The implementation experience', ID 127659. (White, Green, Blue, Brown, Yellow Revolutions), by Anil Sharma, Rome: FAO-UN.

FAO-UN (2005), 'From the Green Revolution to the Gene Revolution. How will the poor fare?', by Prabhu Pingali and Terri Raney, Rome: FAO-UN.

FAO-UN (2006), *Livestock's Long Shadow: Environmental Issues and Options*, by Henning Steinfeld, Pierre Gerber, Tom Wassenaar, Vincent Castel, Mauricio Rosales and Cees de Haan, Rome: FAO-UN.

FAO-UN (2007), *Organic Agriculture and Food Security*, by Nadia El-Hage Scialabba, International Conference on Organic Agriculture and Food Security, Rome (3–5 May), Rome: FAO-UN.

FAO-UN (2010), *Greenhouse Gas Emissions from the Dairy Sector: A Life Cycle Assessment*, by Pierre Gerber (Coordinator, FAO), Theun Vellinga, Klaas Dietze, Alessandra Falcucci, Guya Gianni, Jerome Mounsey, Luigi Maiorano, Carolyn Opio, Daniela Sironi, Olaf Thieme and Viola Weiler. Advisory Group on methodology and data, Chair Henning Steinfeld. Rome: FAO-UN.

FAO-UN (2013a), *Greenhouse Gas Emissions from* Ruminant *Supply Shains: A Global Life Cycle Assessment*, by C. Opio, Pierre Gerber, A. Mottet, A. Falcucci, G. Tempio, M. MacLeod, T. Vellinga, B. Henderson, & H. Steinfeld, Rome: FAO-UN.

FAO-UN (2013b), *Dairy Industry Development Programmes: Their Role in Food and Nutrition Security and Poverty Reduction,* by Brian T. Dugdill, Anthony Bennett, Joe Phelan and Bruce A. Scholten, in *Milk and Dairy Products in Human Nutrition,* Rome: FAO-UN. Download: http://www.fao.org/3/i3396e/i3396e.pdf.

FAO-UN (2013c), *Tackling Climate Change Through Livestock: A Global Assessment of Emissions and Mitigation Opportunities,* edited by P.J. Gerber, Henning Steinfeld, B. Henderson, A. Mottet, C. Opio, A. Dijkman, A. Falucci and G. Tempio, Rome: FAO-UN.

FAO-UN (2014), *Food Outlook,* Serial Title: Food Outlook, Series number: 1560-8182|0251-1959, Rome.

FAO-UN (2020), *Food Outlook: Biannual report on global food markets,* 13 Nov.

FAO-OECD (2021) /OECD-FAO Agricultural Outlook 2021–2030, 'World per capita consumption of processed and fresh dairy products in milk solids may rise from ca. 13 kg/cap to 15 kg/cap, 2018-30.Farm Animal Welfare Council (1997)', 'Five freedoms', in *FAWC Animal Welfare Council Annual Report* (3797), 179–80.

Farm Journal (2016), 'Why is Temple Grandin concerned about the dairy industry?', by Anna-Lisa Laca, 28 Apr.

Farm Journal's Milk (2020), 'How one Washington dairy farmer turned a liability Into a profit center', by Anna-Lisa Laca, 13 Mar.

Farmers Weekly (2017), 'Farmers fear Brexit backslide after shock election result', by Philip Case, 9 Jun.

Farming Online (2017), 'Dairy farmers: UK workers won't make up for Brexit losses', 27 Jun.

Farming UK (2015), 'Morrisons launches milk that gives customers the choice to pay more to support farmers.'

Ferdman, Roberto A. (2016), Why a top animal science expert [Temple Grandin] is worried about the milk industry', *Washington Post,* 21 Apr.

FiBL-IFOAM (2020), *The World of Organic Agriculture Statistics and Emerging Trends 2020,* edited by Helga Willer, Bernhard Schlatter, Jan Trávníÿek, Laura Kemper and Julia Lernoud: Research Institute of Organic Agriculture (FiBL, Frick, Switzerland) and International Federation of Organic Agricultural Movements (IFOAM, Bonn, Germany).

FiBL-IFOAM (2021), *The World of Organic Agriculture: Statistics and Emerging Trends 2021,* edited by Helga Willer, Jan Trávníček, Claudia Meier, Bernhard Schlatter. FiBL (Switzerland) and IFOAM (Germany).

Flachowsky, Gerhard, Andrew Chesson and Karen Aulrich (2005), 'Animal nutrition with feeds from genetically modified plants', *Archives of Animal Nutrition,* 59:1–40.

Food Revolution Network (2012), 'The truth about grassfed beef', 19 Dec.

Food Inc. (2008), *Food Inc.,* directed by Robert Kenner, UK: Dogwoof Pictures.

Food Navigator Asia (2020), 'Fight COVID-19 with dairy? China industry associations issue consumption guidelines to "build immune resistance"', by Pearly Neo, 17 Mar.

Forbes (2020), 'Gates Foundation leads $45 million funding round for new pesticide venture Enko', by Jenny Splitter, 19 Jun.

Forbes (2021), 'Michelin star awarded to vegan restaurant for first time ever', by Alex Ledsom, 19 Jan.

Frontiers in Psychology (2018), 'Of meat and men: Sex differences in implicit and explicit attitudes toward meat', by Hamish J. Love and Danielle Sulikowski, *9*(20) 559.

Forbes (2021), 'Michelin Star awarded to vegan restaurant for first time ever', by Alex Ledsom, 18 Jan.

Futurism (2018), 'Switzerland rules that you must stun your food before you kill it', by Kristin Houser.

Garrison, Ann (2020), 'The Gates foundation's "Green Revolution" in Africa: Agribusiness wins, small scale farmers lose', by Ann Garrison, 15 July 2020.

Gates, Bill (2021), *How to Avoid a Climate Disaster*, New York: Allen Lane.

Gladwell, Malcolm (2008) *Outliers: The Story of Success*, London: Little, Brown and Company.

Global Times (2020), 'China lifts ban on US beef imports in accordance with phase-one deal', 24 Feb 2020.

Gano, L.B., M. Patel and J.M. Rho (2014), 'Ketogenic diets, mitochondria, and neurological diseases', *Journal of Lipid Research*, Nov 2014 (11): 2211–28.

Gao, Helen (2017), 'Opinion: Red century: How did women fare in China's communist revolution?', by Helen Gao, *New York Times*, 25 Sep 2017.

Gehm, Bill (2012), 'Watch mastitis in first-calf heifers', CoPulsation System, 7 Mar 2018.

Gerber, P.J., H. Steinfeld, B. Henderson, A. Mottet, C. Opio, J. Dijkman, A. Falcucci and G. Tempio (2013), *Tackling Climate Change Through Livestock*, Rome: FAO-UN.

Gillespie, Katie A. (2014a), 'Sexualized violence and the gendered commodification of the animal body in Pacific Northwest US dairy production', *Gender, Place & Culture*, 2(10): 1321–37.

Gillespie, Kathryn Anne (2014b), *Reproducing Dairy: Embodied Animals and the Institution of Animal Agriculture*, PhD, University of Washington, USA. Available online: https://digital.lib.washington.edu/researchworks/handle/1773/26271 (accessed 29 May 2018).

Glatzle, Albrecht (2014), 'Questioning key conclusions of FAO publications "Livestock's Long Shadow" (2006) appearing again in "Tackling Climate Change Through Livestock" (2013)', *Pastoralism*, 4(1).

Goodland, Robert (2009) 'Forests, fisheries, agriculture: A vision for sustainability', Expert consultation on greenhouse gas emissions and mitigation potentials in the agriculture, forestry and fisheries sectors, UN-FAO Rome, Italy, 2–4 Dec: Brief-for-FAO-Expert-Consultation-December-2009.pdf (chompingclimatechange.org; accessed 3 Jun 2021).

Goodland, Robert, and Jeff Anhang (2009), 'Livestock and climate change', *Worldwatch Institute*, Nov/Dec 2009. [IPCC recommends a 20-year time-frame, increasing methane's GWP.]

Goodland, Robert, and Jeff Anhang (2011), 'Livestock and greenhouse gas emissions: The importance of getting the numbers right, by Herrero et al., *Animal Feed Science and Technology*, 166–167, 779–782' (doi: 10.1016/j.anifeedsci.2011.12.028). Online: http://dx.doi.org/10.1016/j.anifeedsci.2011.12.028.

Goodland, Robert, and Jeff Anhang (2012) 'Comment to the Editor on "Livestock and greenhouse gas emissions: The importance of getting the numbers right by Herrero et al. in *Anim. Feed Sci. Technol.* 166–167, 779–782)", *Animal Feed Science and Technology*, 172(3–4): 252–6.

Goodland, Robert (2013a), 'Lifting livestock's long shadow', *Nature Climate Change*, 3, 2.

Goodland, Robert (2013b), 'A fresh look at livestock greenhouse gas emissions and mitigation potential in Europe.' *Global Change Biology*, 20: 2042–4. Available online: https://onlinelibrary.wiley.com/doi/epdf/10.1111/gcb.12454; see also: http://www.chompingclimatechange.org/ (accessed 06 Feb 2021).

Goodman, David, and E. Melanie DuPuis (2002), 'Knowing food and growing food: Beyond the production-consumption debate in the sociology of agriculture." *Sociologia Ruralis* 42: 5–22.

Grain (2020), 'Harvard's land grabs in Brazil are a disaster for communities', by Rede Social de Justiça e Direitos Humanos, 18 May.

Grandin, Temple (1989), 'Behavioural principles of livestock handling.' *Professional Animal Scientist*, Dec: 1–11.

Grandin, Temple (2010), 'Dr. Grandin speaks out on animal welfare issues: 'I divide animal welfare concerns into . . . #1: Abuse and neglect, #2: Boredom and restrictive environments'.

Grandin, Temple (2013), 'Reducing fear improves milk production', *Hoard's Dairyman*, 12 Dec: 684.

Grandin, Temple, and Mark Deesing (2002, updated 2003), 'Distress in animals: Is it fear, pain or physical stress?', Paper to American Board of Veterinary Practitioners – Symposium 17 May 2002. Paper updated Sep. 2013: http://www.grandin.com/welfare/fear.pain.stress.html

Grandin, Temple, and Catherine Johnson (2005), *Animals in Translation*. New York: Scribner.

Grandin, Temple, and Catherine Johnson (2009). *Animals Make Us Human: Creating the Best Life for Animals,* New York: Houghton Mifflin.

Grant, R. (2009), 'Stocking density and time budgets', *Proceedings: Western Dairy Management Conference,* in *Dairy Group 2010*: 7–17.

Green America (2013), 'EPA raises levels of glyphosate residue allowed in food', 22 July.

Grigg, D. B. (1975), 'The world's agricultural labour force 1800–1970', *Geography 60*(3): 194–202.

Guardian (2006), 'Peter Roberts: Founder and director of Compassion in World Farming', 15 Nov.

Guardian (2010), 'UK farmers face dilemma over 8,100-cow "super-dairy" . . . will . . . destroy smaller rural-based family farms . . ', by Tom Levitt, 22 Sep.

Guardian (2012), 'Female face of farming', 2 Mar.

Guardian (2014a), 'Russia responds to sanctions by banning western food imports', by Jennifer Rankin, 7 Aug.

Guardian (2014b), 'Russian food import ban leaves shoppers unaffected – or a bit peeved', by Alec Luhn, 7 Aug.

Guardian (2016), 'The anthropocene epoch: scientists declare dawn of human-influenced age', by Damian Carrington, 29 Aug.

Guardian (2017a), 'Dairy is scary. The public are waking up to the darkest part of farming', by Chas Newkey-Burden, 30 Mar.

Guardian (2017b), 'Farms hit by labour shortage as migrant workers shun "racist" UK', by Damian Carrington, 22 Jun.

Guardian (2017c), 'Fox says public won't accept lower food standards in chlorinated chicken row', by Jessica Elgo, 7 Nov.

Guardian (2017d), 'I wrote about farmers' suicides – and the reaction has been overwhelming', 17 Dec.

Guardian (2018a), 'Revealed: industrial-scale beef farming comes to the UK', by Andrew Wasley and Heather Kroeker, 29 May

Guardian (2018b), 'Avoiding meat and dairy is 'single biggest way' to reduce your impact on Earth', by Damian Carrington, 31 May.

Guardian (2018c) 'Avoiding meat and dairy is single biggest way to reduce your impact on earth?', by Damian Carrington, 31 Jun.

Guardian (2021), 'Revealed: Monsanto owner and US officials pressured Mexico to drop glyphosate ban', by Carey Gillam, 16 Feb.

Gupta, P.R. (2000), 'Traditional Milk Products from India', Dairy India Yearbook, from FAO E-mail conference on Small Scale Milk Collection and Processing in Developing Countries, 29 May–28 July 2000.

Harper, L.A., O.T Denmead, J.R. Freney and F.M. Byers (1999), 'Direct measurements of methane emissions from grazing and feedlot cattle', *Journal of Animal Science*, 77: 1392–1401.

Hartman Group (1997), *The Hartman report: Food and Environment – A Consumer's Perspective, Phase II,* Winter, Bellevue, WA: THG.

Hartman Group (2004), 'Organic food & beverage trends 2004: Lifestyles, language & category adoption', THG.

Hartman Group (2006), 'Organic 2006: Consumer attitudes & behaviour, five years later & into the future', THG.

Harvey, David R. (1997), 'Chapter 1: The role of markets in the rural economy', In: *The rural economy and the British countryside*, (eds) P. Allanson and M.C. Whitby.

Harvey, David R. (2003), 'Agri-environmental relationships and multifunctionality: Further considerations', The *World Economy*, 26 (5): 705–725.

Hemsworth, Paul, Grahame Coleman, J.L. Barnett and S. Dowling (2002), 'The effects of cognitive behavioural intervention on the attitude and behaviour of stockpersons and the behaviour and productivity of commercial dairy cows.' *Journal of Animal Science*, 80(1): 68–78.

Herrero, M., P. Gerber, T. Vellinga, T. Garnett, A. Leipe, C. Opio, H.J. Westhoek, P.K. Thornton, J. Olesen, N. Hutchings, H. Montgomery, J.-F. Soussanai, H. Steinfeld, T.A. McAllister (2011), Livestock and greenhouse gas emissions: The importance of getting the numbers right', 'Livestock and greenhouse gas emissions: The importance of getting the numbers right. *Animal Feed Science and Technology*, 166: 779–782.

Hoard's Dairyman (1998), 'The behaviour of cattle', by Jack L. Albright and C.W. Arave, Nov: 787.

Hoard's Dairyman (2012), 'Expert panel addresses Idaho dairy hidden camera investigation', 11 Oct. (N.B. Centre for Food Integrity created Animal Care Review with Temple Grandin, CSU.)

Hoard's Dairyman (2013), 'Reducing fear improves milk production', by Temple Grandin, 12 Dec: 684.

Hoard's Dairyman (2015a), 'Robotics are becoming conventional', by *Hoard's Dairyman* staff, Nov: 719.

Hoard's Dairyman (2015b), 'The comfortable cow is a human illusion', by Don Hogland and Bonnie Beaver, Nov: 735.

Hoard's Dairyman (2016a), 'EU milk flood keeps rising', by Dennis Halladay, 9 May.

Hoard's Dairyman (2016b), 'Farm plastic could be greener', by Bruce A. Scholten, 25 Sep: 579.

Hoard's Dairyman (2017a), 'What will dairy cows and farms look like in 50 years?: In the future, cows could produce between 37,000 to 78,000 pounds of milk per year', by Jack Britt et al., 25 Apr.

Hoard's Dairyman (2017b), 'Cow parallels to the human Paleo diet', by Paul R. Biagiotti, Dec: 752–3.

Hoard's Dairyman (2018), 'Keep some alfalfa in the ration', by Michael F. Hutjens, 10 Jan: 15.

Hoard's Dairyman (2018), 'Supply management', letter in Opinions, brickbats, bouquets, by HH Barlow II, 10 May: 298.

Hoard's Dairyman (2019), 'Washington State dairy ambassadors selected', by Washington State Dairy Women, 28 Jun.

Hoard's Dairyman (2022), 'Dairy farm numbers slide below 30,000', HD Intel, March 3, 2022: https://hoards.com/article-31603-dairy-farm-numbers-slide-below-30000. html?utm_medium=email&utm_campaign=220303-93Thursday&utm_ content=220303-93Thursday+CID_621b760267c0748760a0eb4cdc914e6c&utm_ source=Intel&utm_term=Read%20More

Hobby Farms (2015), 'How to use brewer's waste as animal feed', by Nick Straus, 9 Jan.

Hoekman, Bernard, and Michel Kostecki (1995), *The Political Economy of the World Trading System: From GATT to WTO*, Oxford: Oxford University Press.

Holloway, Lewis, Christopher Bear and Katy Wilkinson (2013), 'Robotic milking technologies and renegotiating situated ethical relationships on UK dairy farms', *Agriculture and Human Values, 30*: 185–199.

Holloway, Lewis, and Chris Bear (2014), 'Animals, technologies and people in rural spaces', *Journal of Rural Studies, 33*: 95–8.

Holloway, Lewis, Chris Bear and Katy Wilkinson (2014), 'Re-capturing bovine life: Robot–cow relationships, freedom and control in dairy farming', *Journal of Rural Studies, 33*: 131–40.

Howard, Philip (2014), 'Organic industry structure: Acquisitions and alliances – Top 100 Food Processors in North America (Who owns organic?)', graphic in Scholten (2014): 74.

Howitt, Richard E., Duncan MacEwan, Josué Medellín-Azuara, Jay R. Lund and Daniel A. Sumner (2015), 'Economic analysis of the 2015 drought for California agriculture', Center for Watershed Sciences, UC Davis.

Huffington Post (2015), 'Monsanto advocate says Roundup is safe enough to drink, then refuses', by Nick Visser, 27 Mar.

Hutjens, Michael F. (2018), 'Keep some alfalfa in the ration', *Hoard's Dairyman*, 10 Jan: 15.

Hygeia Analytics (2016), 'Organic milk and meat enhances the nutritional quality of human breast milk', 14 Dec (accessed 18 Dec 2016. See also: *British Journal of Nutrition* (2007).

Hygeia (2018), 'Bayer announces plans to shed the Monsanto name – But will the new Bayer differ from the old Monsanto?', 5 Jun 2018.

IFOAM (2006), 'The St. Paul Declaration: On the occasion of the first IFOAM international conference on animals in organic production', University of Minnesota, 26 Aug,

IFOAM (2017), 'Dairy co-operatives empower farmers vis-à-vis processors & traders in US, UK & India' by Bruce Scholten, PowerPoint at IFOAM Delhi organic world congress, Panel 7.B Fairness for all in the value chain! Available online: https://owc. ifoam.bio/2017/. See also Scholten (2018b).

IFOAM (2006) 'The St. Paul Declaration: On the occasion of the first IFOAM international conference on animals in organic production', University of Minnesota, 23–25 Aug.

IJAR (2018), 'Role of women in agriculture', by Basavaraj Patil and V. Suresh Babu. *International Journal of Applied Research*, 4(12): 109–14.

IJAS (2020), 'Changing agricultural stubble burning practices in the Indo-Gangetic plains: is the Happy Seeder a profitable alternative?', by Alwin Keil, P. P. Krishnapriya, Archisman Mitra, Mangi L. Jat, Harminder S. Sidhu, Vijesh V. Krishna and Priya Shyamsundar: 128–15.

ILRI (2000), 'Gender roles and child nutrition in livestock production systems in developing countries: A critical review.' Socioeconomics and Policy Research Working Paper 27, by F.K. Tangka, M.A. Jabbar and B.I. Shapiro. International Livestock Research Institute, Nairobi, Kenya.

Inside Climate News (2019), 'What Is Nitrous Oxide and Why Is It a Climate Threat? Despite its increasing role in global warming and effect on the ozone layer, little has been done to rein in this climate pollutant. One big reason: ag', by Sabrina Shankman, 11 Sep.

India in Pixels (2014), 'Percentage of population that is vegetarian in Indian states', Union Government Sample Registration System B.S., Census Dir., GoI, via A.S. Chatterjee and D. Ghosh.

IPCC (2018), *The Carbon Cycle and Atmospheric Carbon Dioxide*, Intergovernmental Panel on Climate Change,

IPCC (2019), *Climate Change and Land: An IPCC Special Report on Climate Change, Desertification, Land Degradation, Sustainable Land Management, Food Security, and Greenhouse Gas Fluxes in Terrestrial Ecosystems*, Intergovernmental Panel on Climate Change, Edited by P.R. Shukla, J. Skea, E. Calvo Buendia, V. Masson-Delmotte, H.-O. Pörtner, D. C. Roberts, P. Zhai, R. Slade, S. Connors, R. van Diemen, M. Ferrat, E. Haughey, S. Luz, S. Neogi, M. Pathak, J. Petzold, J. Portugal Pereira, P. Vyas, E. Huntley, K. Kissick, M. Belkacemi and J. Malley. Available online: www.ipcc.ch (accessed 4 Jun 2021).

IPCC (2021), *AR6 Climate Change 2021: The Physical Science Basis*, Contribution of Working Group I to the Sixth Assessment Report of the Intergovernmental Panel on Climate Change, [Masson-Delmotte, V., P. Zhai, A. Pirani, S. L. Connors, C. Péan, S. Berger, N. Caud, Y. Chen, L. Goldfarb, M. I. Gomis, M. Huang, K. Leitzell, E. Lonnoy, J. B. R. Matthews, T. K. Maycock, T. Waterfield, O. Yelekçi, R. Yu and B. Zhou (eds.)]. Finalized 6 Aug 2021. Cambridge University Press.

Independent (2017), 'Swiss town denies passport to vegan anti-cowbell campaigner', 11 Jan.

Independent (2020a), 'Boris Johnson set to take paternity leave', by Andrew Woodcock, 29 Apr.

Independent (2020b), 'My generation? Millennials, Baby Boomers, Gen X and Gen Z: The cut-off years for each generation. And don't forget Xennials, Gen. Alpha or Gen. Jones', by Helen Wolf, 22 Jul.

Independent (2020c), 'Mitch McConnell warns of Democrats' war on hamburgers', 28 Aug.

Ipsos-MORI (2018), 'An exploration into diets around the world', by Pippa Bailey, Head of Innovation, Ipsos MORI, Aug.

Jarvis, Helen (2006), *Work–life City Limits: Comparative Household Perspectives,* London: Palgrave.

Jarosz, Lucy (2008), 'The city in the country: Growing alternative food networks in metropolitan areas', *Journal of Rural Studies, 24*: 231–44.

Jarosz, Lucy (2014), 'Comparing food security and food sovereignty discourses', *Dialogues in Human Geography 4*(2): 168–81.

Journal of Applied Ecology (2021), 'Roundup causes high levels of mortality following contact exposure in bumble bees', by Edward A. Straw, Edward N. Carpentier & Mark J. F. Brown, 6.

Journal of Animal Science (2002), 'The effects of cognitive behavioral intervention on the attitude and behavior of stockpersons and the behavior and productivity of commercial dairy cows', by Paul H. Hemsworth, Grahame Coleman, J. L. Barnett,. S. Borg and S. Dowling, February 2002. *JAS* 80(1):68–78.

Journal of Animal Science (2011), 'Enteric methane production and greenhouse gases balance of diets differing in concentrate in the fattening phase of a beef production system', by M. Doreau, H.M.G. van der Werf, D. Micol, H. Dubroeucq, J. Agabriel, Y. Rochette, C. Martin, *JAS* 07 March.

Journal of Animal Science (2020), 'The effects of improved performance in the U.S. dairy cattle industry on environmental impacts between 2007 and 2017', by Judith L. Capper and Roger Cady, *JDS 98*(1).

Journal of Dairy Research (2016), 'Engineering to support well-being of dairy animals', by Gerardo Caja, Andreia Castro-Costa and Christopher H. Knight. Cambridge University Press, 23 May: 136–47.

Journal of Bioethical Inquiry (2013), 'Bioethics and nonhuman animals', by Rob Irvine, Chris Degeling, Ian Kerridge and Rob Irvine, *10*(4): 435–40.

Journal of Dairy Science (1999), 'Effects of milk fever, ketosis, and lameness on milk yield in dairy cows', by P.J. Rajala-Schultz, Y.T. Gröhn and C.E. McCulloch, Feb: 288–94.

Journal of Dairy Science (2006), 'Major advances in extension education programs in dairy production', by Larry Chase, Lane Ely & Michael Hutjens, *89*(5): 1147–54.

Journal of Dairy Science (2014a), 'A case study of the carbon footprint of milk from high-performing confinement and grass-based dairy farms', by D. O'Brien, J. L. Capper, P. C. Garnsworthy, C. Grainger and L. Shalloo, *97*: 1835–51.

Journal of Dairy Science (2014b), 'Invited review: Enteric methane in dairy cattle production: Quantifying the opportunities and impact of reducing emissions', by J. R. Knapp, G. L. Laur, P. A . Vadas, W. P. Weiss and J. M. Tricarico, *97*: 3231–61.

Journal of Dairy Science (2018a), 'Detection of lameness in dairy cows using a grooming device', by R. Mandel et al., *101*(2), Feb: 1511–17.

Journal of Dairy Science (2018b), 'Invited review: Learning from the future—A vision for dairy farms and cows in 2067', by J.H. Britt, R.A. Cushman, C.D. Dechow, H. Dobson, P. Humblot, M.F. Hutjens, G.A. Jones, P.S. Ruegg, I.M. Sheldon and J.S. Stevenson, 101(5): 3722–41.

Journal of Ecological Society (2020–2021), 'Animal agriculture is the leading cause of climate change', by Sailesh Rao, founder of Climate Healers.

Kahneman, Daniel, and Amos Tversky (1979), 'Prospect theory', *Econometrica, 47*(2): 263–292.

Kahneman, Daniel, and Amos Tversky (1979), 'Prospect theory: An analysis of decision under risk' (Tversky's 1979 paper 'Prospect theory' counters John Stuart Mill's homo economicus.

Kansas City Star (2020), 'Missouri charmer led double life, masterminded one of the biggest frauds in farm history', by Mike Hendricks, 12 Jan.

Karreman, Hubert J. (2004/2nd edn 2007), *Treating Dairy Cows Naturally: A Handbook for Organic and Sustainable Farmers*. Austin, TX: Acres USA.

Karreman, Hubert J. (2011), *The Barn Guide to Treating Dairy Cows Naturally,* Austin, TX: Acres USA.

Karreman, Hubert J. (2013), 'Meet Hubert Karreman – CowSignals trainer for Organic Valley, Pennsylvania', Video: https://youtu.be/q_yRsc1JiW0 (accessed 25 Mar 2021).

Kastel, Mark (1995), 'Down on the farm: The real BGH story: Animal health problems, financial troubles', Rural Vermont: Rural Education Action Project.

Keating, Mark (2009), 'Genesis of the USDA's National Organic Program: History of organic agriculture', 4 Nov.

Knapp, J.R., G. L. Laur, P. A. Vadas, W. P. Weiss and J. M. Tricarico (2014) *Journal of Dairy Science* (2014), 'Invited review: Enteric methane in dairy cattle production: Quantifying the opportunities and impact of reducing emissions', *97*: 3231–61.

Knickel, Karlheinz, Henk Renting and Jan Douwe van der Ploeg (2004), 'Multifunctionality in European agriculture', in *Sustaining Agriculture and the Rural Economy*, edited by F. Brouwer, 81–103, Cheltenham: Edward Elgar.

Lancet (2015), 'Potential burden of antibiotic resistance on surgery and cancer chemotherapy antibiotic prophylaxis in the USA', by R. Laxminarayan, et al., *Lancet Infectious Diseases*, 15(12): 1421–37.

Lancet (2020), 'Editorial: COVID-19 in the USA: a question of time', 395, 18 Apr.

Lang, Tim, and Michael Heasman (2004), *Food Wars*. London: Earthscan.

Lappé, Frances Moore (1971, 2nd edn 1991), *Diet for a Small Planet,* New York City: Ballantine.

Lead, The (2020), 'Methane-busting seaweed farms on track for 2021 production', by Andrew Spence, 01 Dec.

Lead, The (2021), 'Methane-busting seaweed industry begins growing in South Australia', 30 Jul.

Lebergott, S. (1966), 'Labor force and employment, 1800–1960', in *Output, employment, and productivity in the United States after 1800*, edited by Dorothy S. Brady, Cambridge, MA: National Bureau of Economic Research (NBER).

LeCompte-Mastenbrook, Joyce (2004), 'Making sense of place: Narratives of migration, milk and modernity in a Northwest Washington dairy community [aka Dutch-Whatcom-Stewardship]', BA thesis (interviewed Bastian Scholten). Seattle: University of Washington Anthropology Department.

LeDoux, Joseph (2015), 'The amygdala Is NOT the brain's fear centre', *Psychology Today*, 19 Aug.

Le Heron, Richard (2018), 'Dairying in question', in *New Biological Economies*, eidted by E. Pawson, 20–40, Auckland: Auckland University Press.

Loden, Marilyn (2017), '100 women: Why I invented the glass ceiling phrase', BBC News, 13 Dec.

Low, Philip et al. (2012), *The Cambridge Declaration on Consciousness*, written by Philip Low and edited by Jaak Panksepp, Diana Reiss, David Edelman, Bruno Van Swinderen, Philip Low and Christof Koch. *CDoC* proclaimed Cambridge, UK, 7 July 2012, Francis Crick Memorial Conference on Consciousness in Human and non-Human Animals, Churchill College, University of Cambridge, by Low, Edelman and Koch. The Declaration was signed by participants in the presence of Stephen Hawking. The signing ceremony was memorialized by CBS *60 Minutes.*

Lymbery, Philip, with Isabel Oakeshott (2014), *Farmageddon*, London: Bloomsbury.

Lynch, John, Michelle Cain, David Frame and Raymond Pierrehumbert (2021), 'Agriculture's contribution to climate change and role in mitigation Is distinct from predominantly fossil CO_2-emitting sectors', *Frontiers in Sustainable Food Systems, 4.*

MIDFT (2022), 'Memorial lecture series', [Scholten 2019 photo], Mansinhbhai Institute of Dairy & Food Technology, http://preview.midft.com/memorial-lecture-series, Last Update 01 Apr, 2022.

Makatouni, Aikaterini (2001), 'What motivates consumers to buy organic food in the UK? Results from a qualitative study', *Organic Research* 1, April, www.organic-research.com/Pdfs/.

Makatouni, Aikaterini (2002), 'What motivates consumers to buy organic food in the UK? Results from a qualitative study', *British Food Journal* 104(1): 345–352.

Machado, Felipe da Silva (2020), *Relational rural geographies, resilience, and narratives of small-scale fruit farming in the metropolitan countryside of Rio de Janeiro, Brazil*, University of Plymouth.

Mance, Henry (2021), *How to Love Animals: In a Human-shaped World*, London: Jonathan Cape.

Mandel, R., H. Harazy, L. Gygax, C. J. Nicol, A. Ben-David, H. R. Whay, and E. Klement (2018), 'Short communication: Detection of lameness in dairy cows using a grooming device', *Journal of Dairy Science* 101:1511–1517.

(2018a), 'Detection of lameness in dairy cows using a grooming device', by R. Mandel et al., *101*(2), Feb: 1511–17.

Mbogho, Stephen Gichovi, K. Munei, M.K. Komen and J.M. Mohammed (2016), 'The factors that influence beef cattle marketing efficiency and the behavior of pastoralists: A case study in Kenya', *World Journal of Research and Review*, 3(2): 51–8.

McCartney, Mary (2017), 'Black bean burgers [recipe], © Meat Free Monday 2017.

McGuire, Michelle K. (2015), 'U.S. breast milk is glyphosate free', Washington State University study in *ScienceDaily*, 23 July: 1285–90.

McGuire, Michelle K., Mark A McGuire, William J Price, Bahman Shafii, Janae M Carrothers, Kimberly A Lackey, Daniel A Goldstein, Pamela K Jensen and John L Vicini (2016), 'Glyphosate and aminomethyl-phosphonic acid are not detectable in human milk', *American Journal of Clinical Nutrition (AJCN)*, *103*(5): 1285–90. Doi: 10.3945/ajcn.115.126854. Epub 30 Mar 2016.

McKenzie, Jessica (2019), 'The misbegotten promise of anaerobic digesters', *New Food Economy*, 3 Dec.

Meadow, R. H. (1996), 'The origins and spread of agriculture and pastoralism in northwestern South Asia', in D. R. Harris, *Origins and Spread of Agriculture and Pastoralism in Eurasia*, 390–412, London: UCL.

Meat + Poultry (2018), 'Animal welfare groups join lawsuit over organic livestock rule [OLPP]', by *Meat + Poultry* staff, Washington DC, 12 Apr.

Merriam-Webster (1995), *Webster's Ninth New Collegiate Dictionary*, Springfield, MA.

MIDFT (2020), 'Reducing carbon footprint in the dairy industry (Edition-II)', webinar 5 Nov 2020, India: Mehsana District Co-operative Milk Producers' Union Ltd.

MIDFT (2019), 'Women empowerment: Taking care of rural milk producers, most of whom are women'.

Mill, John Stuart (1836), 'On the definition of political economy and on the method of investigation proper to it.' After Aristotle, Mill described rational man, i.e., Homo economicus.

Mitloehner, Frank (2017), 'Rethinking Methane', video (4:57) by Frank Mitloehner, Director, UC Davis CLEAR Center.

Mitloehner, Frank (2019), 'Trivia quiz: following are the ingredients of three food/feed items. Two of them are fake burgers (namely @ImpossibleFoods burger and @BeyondMeat burger, respectively) and the third is premium dog food. Can you pick the latter?', Twitter, 27 Jun.

Modern Farmer (2019), 'Ocasio-Cortez's green new deal', by Brian Barth, 20 Jan.

Monbiot, George (2016), 'Neoliberalism, the ideology at the root of all our problems, *Guardian*, 15 Apr.

Monbiot, George (2018), 'Resist a US trade deal. Your life may depend on it', *Guardian*, 14 Feb.

Moon, Jennifer (2015), 'Can Whatcom's small farms help reconstruct our local food system?', in WhatcomWatch, 20 Nov.

Morgan, Dan (1979), *Merchants of Grain*, New York: Viking.

Morgan, Kevin, Terry Marsden and Jonathan Murdoch (2006), *Worlds of Food: Place, Power, and Provenance in the Food Chain*, New York: Oxford University Press.

Morris, C., and Lewis Holloway (2014), 'Genetics and livestock breeding in the UK: Co-constructing technologies and heterogeneous biosocial collectivities', *Journal of Rural Studies*, *33*: 150–60.

Murdoch, Jonathan, and Mara Miele (1999), 'Back to nature: Changing worlds of production in the food system', *Sociologia Ruralis*, *39*: 465–84.

Murdoch, Jonathan, Terry Marsden and Jo Banks (2000), 'Quality, nature, and embeddedness: Some theoret-ical considerations in the context of the food sector', *Economic Geography*, *76*(2): 107–25.

Muslim Mirror (2016), 'Indira Nooyi: A Tamil brahmin who heads world's largest cow-meat supplier company', 8 Aug.

NBC News (2018), 'Mexico will impose 20 percent tariffs on U.S. pork', by Ben Popken, 5 Jun.

Nature (2020), 'Global human-made mass exceeds all living biomass', by Emily Elhacham, Liad Ben-Uri, Jonathan Grozovski, Yinon M. Bar-On and Ron Milo, 9 Dec.

Nation (2018), 'Is the USDA the latest site of corporate takeover in the Trump administration?', by Jasper Craven, 13 Mar.

National Dairy Council (2013), 'NDC blasts PETA got zits anti-dairy campaign', by Mark Astley, 10 Apr.

National Institutes of Health (2013), 'Why obesity Is a health problem', updated 13 Feb.

Natural Society (2014), '3 studies proving toxic glyphosate found in urine, blood, and even breast milk', by Mike Barrett, 4 May.

New Yorker (2019), 'Can a Burger Help Solve [CH4 &] Climate Change?', by Tad Friend, 23–30 Sep.

New York Times (2007), '[Colorado's Aurora] organic dairy agrees to alter some practices', by Andrew Martin, 30 Aug.

New York Times (2010), 'New pasture rules issued for organic dairy producers', by Matt Staver, 12 Feb.

New York Times (2020), 'The Business of Burps: Scientists [e.g., Dr Deepashree Kand] smell profit in cow emissions', 5 May.

NFFC (2020), 'Farm and environmental organizations rebuke new USDA regulatory review', National Family

NIRD (2018), 'Role of women in agriculture', by Panchayati Raj and Venkatachalapathi Suresh Babu, National Institute of Rural Development.

NOFA (2006), 'Putting politics out to pasture', by Steve Gilman, Northeast Organic Farming Association, *The Natural Farmer 2*(69): 7–8.

NPR (2006), 'A conversation with Temple Grandin', on *Talk of the Nation*, National Public Radio, 20 Jan 2006.

NPR (2016), 'Life expectancy In US drops for first time in decades', 8 Dec 2016.

Occamy Bioscience (2021), 'All about cattle feed business'.

Odairy (2007), 'Ed Maltby applauds Cornucopia re decertification of Vander Eyck Dairy', Spring, ODAIRY@LISTSERV.NODPA.COM.

Odairy (2017), 'Francis Thicke comments on exiting the NOSB', 3 Nov.

Odairy (2018), 'Safety net for dairy farmers', 6 Jun 2018 via Nodpa, and USDA 4 Jun 2018 'Margin protection program for dairy'.

Odairy (2019), 'Organic dairy in crisis: Where do we go from here?', by Ed Maltby, NODPA and Abby Youngblood, National Organic Coalition (NOC), OEFFA, 14 Feb.

Odairy (2021), 'USDA announces annual count of certified operations', via USDA NOP Organic Integrity Database, 27 Jan.

Odairy (2022), 'USDA published a Final Rule on Origin of Livestock', by Ed Maltby, ODAIRY@LISTSERV.NODPA.COM, 29 Mar.

OECD-FAO (2016), *OECD-FAO agricultural outlook 2016–2025*, by Organization of the Economically Developed Countries and the Food and Agriculture Organization of the United Nations, 4 Jul.

Omsco, OV and Eko (2019), *Global Organic Dairy Market Report 2019*, UK.

Open India (2011), 'Greed Revolution?', by Sumithra Prasanna, 19 May.

Organic Eye (2019), 'ActionAlert! USDA: Stop "organic" factories from milking conventional dairy cows', by OrganicEye, cofounded by Mark Kastel, 13 Nov. Available online: https://organiceye.org/action-alert-usda-stop-organic-milking-conventional-dairy-cows/ (accessed 13 Nov 2019).

organic-market.info (2006), '1st IFOAM conference on animals in organic production advances global organic livestock sector [St. Paul Declaration]', 14 Sep.

Organic Valley (2018), 'Here's our story: It all started in 1988: We were a handful of Midwest family farmers and we were fed up with the state of American agriculture. Family farms were going extinct', by Coulee Region Organic Produce Pool (CROPP) co-operative.

Osman, Loren H. (1985), *W. D. Hoard: A Man for His Time*. Fort Atkinson, WI: W. D. Hoard & Sons Co.

Oxford Handbook of Animal Ethics (2011) *OHoAE*, edited by Tom L. Beauchamp and R.G. Frey, Oxford: Oxford University Press.

Peer J (2018), 'Agrichemicals and antibiotics in combination increase antibiotic resistance evolution', by B. Kurenbach, A.M. Hill, W. Godsoe, S. van Hamelsveld and J.A. Heinemann, 12 Oct.

PETA (2017), 'Our mission statement', by Katherine Sullivan, People for the Ethical Treatment of Animals, updated 11 May.

Pew Research Center (2016), 'The new food fights: U.S. public divides over food science: Differing views on benefits and risks of organic foods, GMOs . . ', 1 Dec.

Phillipov, Michelle and Michael K. Goodman (2017), 'The celebrification of farmers, *Celebrity Studies*, 8(2): 346–50.

Pitesky, Maurice, Kimberly R. Stackhouse and Frank M. Mitloehner (2009), 'Clearing the air: livestock's contribution to climate change', *Advanced Agronomy*, 103: 3–40.

Piketty, Thomas (2013) *Capital in the Twenty-first Century*, London and Cambridge, MA: Belknap Press.

Plant Based News (2021), 'Impossible Foods slashes grocery price of plant-based meat', 3 Feb.

Plant Based News (2021), 'Animal agriculture responsible for 87% of greenhouse gas emissions, finds new report: Climate Healers says UNFAO has underestimated . . ', by Liam Giliver, 4 May.

PLOS Biology (2019), 'If a fish can pass the mark test, what are the implications for consciousness and self-awareness testing in animals?', by M. Kohda et al., 7 Feb.

Pollan, Michael (2001), 'Behind the organic-industrial complex', *New York Times Magazine*, 13 May.

Pollan, Michael (2008), *In Defense of Food*, New York: Penguin Press.

Pollan, Michael (2009), *The Omnivore's Dilemma*, New York: Penguin Press.

Pollan, Michael (2013), *Cooked: A Natural History of Transformations*, New York: Penguin Press.

Poore, Joseph, and T. Nemecek (2018), 'Reducing food's environmental impacts through producers and consumers', *Science* 360(6392): 987–92.

Portlandia (2011), 'Ordering the chicken', video satirizing political correctness, 25 Jan.

Porter, Michael E. (1979), 'How competitive forces shape strategy', *Harvard Business Review*, Mar-Apr: 79–93.

Porter, Michael E. (2008), 'The five competitive forces that shape strategy', *Harvard Business Review* 86/1 Jan: 78–93.

Pretty, Jules (2009), *Reaping the Benefits: Science and the Sustainable Intensification of Global Agriculture*, Royal Society Report by Ian Crute et al.

Pretty, Jules, et al. (2011), *Save and Grow: A Policymaker's Guide to the Sustainable Intensification of Smallholder Crop Production*, UN-FAO.

Progressive Dairyman (2013), 'Your cows are talking to you . . .?', by Amanda Meneses, 9 Aug.

Progressive Dairyman (2019), 'Keeping kelp in front of cows on grass,' by Brittany Olson, 18 Mar. (Also, NODPA 29 Apr 2019.)

Quanta (2018), 'A "self-aware" fish raises doubts about a cognitive test', by Elizabeth Preston, 12 Dec.

Qureshi, Yasmin (2021), 'Animal sentience in law', by Labour MP for Bolton, UK, 17 Feb 2021.

Radford, Mike (2001), *Animal Welfare Law in Britain: Regulation and responsibility*, Oxford: Oxford University Press.

Raynolds, Laura T. (2004), 'The globalization of organic agro-food networks', *World Development*, 32(5): 725–43.

Rajala-Schultz, P. J., Y. T. Grohn and C. E. McCulloch (1999), 'Effects of milk fever, ketosis, and lameness on milk yield in dairy cows', *Journal of Dairy Science* 82, No. 2: 288–294.

Real Organic Project (2020), 'Jean-Paul Courtens on farming and climate', Thetford, VT, 15 Jan.

Reed, Matt J. and Holt, Georgina, eds (2006), *Sociological Perspectives of Organic Agriculture: From Pioneer to Policy*, Egham: CABI.

Reese, Jacy (2018), *The End of Animal Farming*, Boston, MA: Beacon Press.

Restrepo, Rivera J., with J. Hensel (2019), *The ABC of Organic Agriculture*, by Lane Farm, Ragnas Farm, UK.

Reuters (2019) 'Vegetarian diets not always the most climate-friendly, researchers say [at Johns Hopkins Center for a Livable Future, cited by Henry Mance (2021)]', by Thin Lei Win, 17 Sep.

Reuters (2020), 'Bayer faces 4th U.S. Roundup cancer trial in Monsanto's hometown', by Tina Bellon, 24 Jan.

Reuters (2021), 'After three years of haggling, EU farm deal expected this week', by Kate Abnett, 26 May.

Rist, Lukas, et al. (2007), 'Influence of organic diet on the amount of conjugated linoleic acids in breast milk', in *British Journal of Nutrition*.

Ritzer, George (1993, 2004), *The McDonaldization of Society*, Thousand Oaks, CA: Pine Forge Press.

Riverford Organic Farms (2021), 'What is a Devon farmer, who doesn't speak French, doing buying a farm in West France?', by Guy Watson, riverford.co.uk, 26 Apr.

Robinson, Guy M., ed. (2008), *Sustainable rural systems: Sustainable agriculture and rural communities*, Farnham and Burlington, VT: Ashgate (from IGU-RGS-IBG Conf, Glasgow, 2004).

Robinson, Guy M., ed. (2018a), 'Globalization of agriculture', *Annual review of resource economics*, 10(1): 133–60.

Robinson, Guy M. (2018b), 'New frontiers in agricultural geography: Transformations, food security, land grabs and climate change', *Boletin de la Asociacion de Geografos Espanoles*, 78: 1–48.

Robinson, Guy, and Doris A. Carson, eds (2016), *Handbook on the Globalisation of Agriculture* (Handbooks on Globalisation series), Cheltenham and Northampton MA: Edward Elgar.

Robinson, Paul (2010), *Improving fertility in the high-yielding dairy cow*. Newcastle University: Nuffield Farming Scholarships Trust

Rodale Institute (2011), *The Farming Systems Trial: Celebrating 30 Years*, Kutztown, PA: Rodale Institute.

Roverso, Giovanni (2020), 'Washington Conservation Corps replenishing Bellingham's waterways since 1999', *Whatcom Watch*, 30 Dec.

Ruddiman, William (2005), 'How did humans first alter global climate?' *Scientific American* 292: 46–53.

Ruddiman, William (2017), 'Geographic evidence of the early anthropogenic hypothesis', *Anthropocene* 20: 4–14.

Rural Vermont (1995), 'Down on the farm: The real BGH story animal health problems, financial troubles', by Mark Kastel, Vermont: Rural Education Action Project.

Rushen, Jeff, and Anne Marie de Passille (2013), 'The Importance of improving cow longevity.' University of British Columbia Dairy Education and Research Centre, Agassiz, BC, Canada. Article in DeLaval (2013) *Cow Longevity Conference Proceedings*: 3–21: Tumba, Sweden: DeLaval Int'l AB. Excerpt: Canada average culling 30–40%; worse in China, Mexico, Sweden: 3–4.

Schlosser, Eric (2001), *Fast Food Nation: The Dark Side of the All-American Meal*, New York: Houghton Mifflin.

Scholten, Bruce A. (1989a), 'Milk quotas help melt Europe's butter mountain', *Hoard's Dairyman*, 10 Jan: 91.

Scholten, Bruce A. (1989b), 'BST burdens EC decision makers', *Hoard's Dairyman*, 10 Mar: 183, 194.

Scholten, Bruce A. (1989c), 'USA Chancen für Milchquoten: Mit dem US$ überschüsse steigen', *Württembergisches Wochenblatt für Landwirtschaft/BWL (WWL/BWL)*, 26 Aug: 10.

Scholten, Bruce A. (1990a), 'Animal welfare a rising farmer concern in Europe', *Hoard's Dairyman*, 25 Feb: 190.

Scholten, Bruce A. (1990b), 'Pesticide und die Agrar-Umwelt Politik in USA [Pesticides/ ag-enviro policy USA]', *VDI nachrichten [VDI news]*, Düsseldorf: Verein der Deutschen Ingenieren, 6 Sep: 6, 12.

Scholten, Bruce A. (1990c), 'Wird Bush Umwelt-Präsident [Will Bush veto GMO crops?]' (*WWL/BWL*), 20 Oct: 8.

Scholten, Bruce A. (1990d), 'Europe's milk quotas . . . Six years down the Road', *Hoard's Dairyman*, July: 587.

Scholten, Bruce A. (1995), 'Veal protests rock UK.' *Hoard's Dairyman*, 25 Mar: 217.

Scholten, Bruce A. (1997a), 'Brits bat around appearance of countryside', *Hoard's Dairyman*, 10 Mar: 181.

Scholten, Bruce A. (1997b), 'US dairy 2000: Bye-bye this American guy', *Dairy News*, London. 21 Nov: 6–7.

Scholten, Bruce A. (1997c), *International Dairy Product Aid & Trade 1960s–1990s: Focusing on the EU and India in Operation Flood*, MA by research, Durham University, UK.

Scholten, Bruce A. (1999), 'India's winning the White Revolution: The success of India's Operation Flood will soon make it the world's top producer of milk', *Hoard's Dairyman*, 10 Apr: 287.

Scholten, Bruce A. (2002), 'Organic-industrial complex or herbal remedy? A case near Seattle and Vancouver', *UK Organic Research: Proceedings of the Colloquium of Organic Researchers*, University of Aberystwyth, 22–5 Mar.

Scholten, Bruce A. (2004), 'A Grass Ceiling is haunting America's rural economy: Comparing a US alternative agro-food network to those in the UK and Germany', presentation, 2nd Anglo-German Rural Geographers on 'Rural multifunctionality: Perspectives from policy-making, implementation and practice', University of Exeter, UK, July (viz. AAG 2004 Philadelphia paper). Scholten, 'Grass ceiling', cited in G.A. Wilson (2007) *Multifunctional Agriculture*, CABI: 355

Scholten, Bruce A. (2006a), 'Farmers' market movements in the UK & US: Consumers on rural spaces in urban places', unpublished paper, Association of American Geographers (AAG) annual meeting, Chicago, 8–11 Mar 2006, Rural Geography Specialty Group (RGSG) session convened by Peter Nelson (Middlebury College) and Randall Wilson (Gettysburg College).

Scholten, Bruce A. (2006b), 'Firefighters in the UK and the US: Risk perception of local and organic food', *Scottish Geographical Journal 122*(2): 130–48.

Scholten, Bruce A. (2006c), 'Motorcyclists in the USA & the UK: Risk perceptions of local and organic food', in Reed and Holt (2006).

Scholten, Bruce A. (2006d), 'Polytunnel perversity & cow confinement: Organic rules shape farmscapes', PowerPoint, RGS-IBG session by Helen Moggridge and Kate Mahoney, London, 31 Aug–1 Sep.

Scholten, Bruce A. (2007a), *Consumer Risk Reflections on Organic and Local Food in Seattle, with Reference to Newcastle upon Tyne*, PhD thesis, Durham University Geography Department (UK). Available online: http:durham.academia.edu/ BruceScholten.

Scholten, Bruce A. (2007b), 'Dirty cows: Perceptions of BSE/vCJD', in *Dirt: New Geographies of Cleanliness and Contamination*, edited by Rosie Cox and Ben Campkin, London: I. B. Tauris.

Scholten, Bruce A. (2007c), 'USDA organic pasture wars: Shaping farmscapes in Washington State and beyond', presentation and chapter in *Proceedings, 6th Quadrennial meeting of British, Canadian & American Rural Geographers* (2010), Eastern Washington University, Spokane, 15–20 July. Dick Winchell, Doug Ramsey, Rhonda Koster and Guy M. Robinson (eds), Canada: Brandon University (RDI).

Scholten, Bruce A. (2007d), 'Dirty cows: Perceptions of BSE/vCJD', chapter in Rosie Cox and Ben Campkin (eds.), *Dirt: New geographies of cleanliness and contamination*, London: I. B. Tauris.

Scholten, Bruce (2007e), 'Meeting PR Gupta in April 1998', *Dairy India 2007*, Ed. 6; edited by S. Gupta: viii–ix.

Scholten, Bruce (2007f), "Organics in the green hills of India', *Dairy India 2007*, Ed. 6; edited by S. Gupta: 41.

Scholten, Bruce A. (2008), 'Lies on the milk label: Consumer boycotts in the USDA organic pasture war', presentation for 'The lie of the land: Rural lies, myths and realities' for Rural Geography Research Group (RGRG) session convened by Gareth Enticott (Cardiff University) and Keith Halfacree (Swansea Univ.), Royal Geographical Society (RGS-IBG) meet (27–29 Aug 2008), London.

Scholten, Bruce A. (2010a), 'Pasture in the biofuel boom: Rescaling of FRG, UK and US organic dairy farms?', in *Globalization and rural transitions in Germany and the UK*, edited by Ingo Mose, Guy Robinson, Doris Schmied, Geoff Wilson, Göttingen: Cuviller Verlag.

Scholten, Bruce A. (2010b), 'USDA organic pasture wars: Shaping farmscapes in Washington State and beyond', in *Geographical Perspectives on Sustainable Rural Change*, edited by Dick Winchell, Doug Ramsey, Rhonda Koster and Guy M. Robinson, Brandon, Manitoba: Brandon University Rural Development Institute.

Scholten, Bruce A. (2010c), *India's White Revolution: Operation Flood, Food Aid and Development*, London: I. B. Tauris-Bloomsbury.

Scholten, Bruce A. (2011a), 'Cooperative dairy development in India & Africa', *Agrarian revolutions & rainfed agriculture: White & Green*. Roundtable hosted by Amity University Uttar Pradesh & Durham University Geography Dept UK. Keynote for book launch of *India's White Revolution* (Scholten 2010c), organised by Dr Asmita Bhardwaj, 5 Jan: Article 'Sustainability of farm economy discussed at Amity University', by Harish Damodaran, *Business Standard*.

Scholten, Bruce A. (2011b), *Food and Risk in the US and UK: Seattle and Newcastle Academics, Firefighters, Motorcyclists and Others Reflect on Organic and Local Dood*, Saarbrücken: LAP-Lombard.

Scholten, Bruce A. (2013a), *U.S. organic dairy politics survey*. Available online: http://www. surveymonkey. com/s/83QSVHP.

Scholten, Bruce A. (2013b), 'Development through dairying: An East African case study', *Geography Review*, 27(2): 26–9.

Scholten, Bruce A. (2014), *U.S. Organic Dairy Politics: Animals, pasture, people, and agribusiness*, New York: Palgrave Macmillan/Springer.

Scholten, Bruce A. (2015), 'The White Revolution and its role in dual economies', in *Edgar Elgar Handbook on the Globalization of Agriculture*, edited by Guy Robinson and Doris Carson, 461–82, Cheltenham and Northampton, MA: Edward Elgar.

Scholten, Bruce A. (2016b), 'Farm plastic could be greener', *Hoard's Dairyman*, 25 Sep: 579.

Scholten, Bruce A. (2017a), 'Brexit plagues farm labor', *Hoard's Dairyman*, 25 Aug: 508.

Scholten, Bruce A. (2017b), 'Dairy co-operatives empower farmers vis-à-vis processors & traders in US, UK & India.' PowerPoint, Royal Geographical Society (& IBG) conference, London, 1 Sep. Also, IFOAM Delhi organic world congress, Panel 7.B Fairness for all in the value chain! 10 Nov: Https://owc.ifoam.bio/2017/, update 6/ Dec/2017.

Scholten, Bruce A. (2018a), 'Philosophy, politics, and technology morph dairyscapes', RGS-IBG Cardiff, 28–31 Aug 2018, presentation on CAFOs and pastures linked to this book, *Dairy Farming in the 21st Century.*

Scholten, Bruce A. (2018b), 'Organics matter in New Delhi [IFOAM world congress]', *Rural History Today,* online: http://www.bahs.org.uk/RHT.html) RHT-Scholten 2018 spring-IFOAM matters in Delhi. Also: https://www.academia.edu/36605410/ARTICLE_ IFOAM_2017_Organics_Matter_in_New_Delhi_9_ (last accessed 11 Nov 2017).

Scholten, Bruce A. (2019a), 'Dairy farmers' co-ops co-operating globally? Reaching India's green hills?' Lecture to B.Tech dairy students & faculty, 10 April. Anand, Vidya Dairy. Also Mansinhbhai Patel Memorial Lecture, 15 Apr 2019, MIDFT, Mehsana, Dudhsagar Dairy.

Scholten, Bruce A. (2019b), 'Editorial: Economic incentives key to Indian farmers' co-operative energy-groundwater nexus', *RGRG Newsletter*, Summer, 19 Jun 2019, p.1. Available online: https://rgrg.co.uk/wp-content/uploads/2020/11/RGRG-News-Summer-19Jun19rpr.pdf

Scholten, Bruce A. (2019c), 'Dairy Farming in the 21st Century: Ethics, Environment, and Politics', Survey Monkey https://www.surveymonkey.co.uk/r/R3KR8W5. Constructed after US National Institutes of Health (NIH) Office of Extramural Research certified that Bruce Scholten successfully completed the NIH Web-based training course 'Protecting Human Research Participants.' Date of completion: 27 February 2017. Certification Number: 2338308.

Scholten, Bruce A. (2021), 'No Trojan Cow', in *The Utterly Butterly Milkman: A Birth Centenary Commemorative*, curated by Nirmala Kurien, 314–17.

Scholten, B. A., and Brian T. Dugdill (2012), 'Avoiding dairy aid traps: The cases of Uganda, India and Bangladesh', chapter in *Challenging Post-Conflict Environments*, edited by Alpaslan Ozerdem and Rebecca Roberts, Farnham: Ashgate.

Scholten, B. A., and Pratyusha Basu, eds (2012), *Technological and social dimensions of the Green Revolution: Connecting pasts and presents*, special issue of *International Journal of Agricultural Sustainability*, 10(2), *IJAS* editor Jules Pretty; special issue co-edited by Scholten and Basu. Introduction, and article 'Crop-livestock systems in rural development: Linking India's Green and White Revolutions', by Basu & Scholten. Our issue joins our 2009 and 2010 AAG (Association of American Geographers) and RGS-IBG (Royal Geographical Society with IBG) session presenters, discussing tech, neoliberalism, GMOs, and dairy cooperatives.

Scholten, B. A., and Pratyusha Basu, eds (2013), *Technological and social dimensions of the Green Revolution: Connecting pasts and presents*, Routledge *IJAS* special-issue-as-book (hb/pb), 7 Apr 2013.

Scholz, Werner, ed. (2019), *Animal Welfare and International Environmental Law: From Conservation to Compassion*, Cheltenham and Northampton, MA: Edward Elgar. See Michael Bowman (2019).

Science (2000), 'Health risks of genetically modified foods: Many opinions but few data', by J. L. Domingo. 9 Jun 2000, 288: 1748–9.

Science (2018), 'Reducing food's environmental impacts through producers and consumers', by Joseph Poore and T. Nemecek *Science*, *360*(6392): 987–92.

ScienceDaily (2015), 'US breast milk is glyphosate free: Study is first independently verified look for the presence of Roundup ingredient in human milk', by Michelle K. McGuire, Washington State University.

Scientia Agricultura Sinica (2009), 'Methane and nitrous oxide emissions from rice-fish and rice-duck complex ecosystems and the evaluation of their economic significance', by YUAN Wei-ling, CAO Cou-gui, LI Cheng-fang, ZHAN Ming, CAI Ming-li, WANG Jin-ping, (Huazhong Agricultural University, Wuhan 430070), *SAS 42*(6): 2052–60.

Scientific American (2021), 'Bill Gates should stop telling Africans what kind of agriculture Africans need', by Million Belay, Bridget Mugambe, 06 Jul.

Scientific Reports (2017), 'Dairy cows value access to pasture as highly as fresh feed', by Mariana von Keyserlingk, A.A. Cestari, B. Franks, J.A. Fregonesi and D.M. Weary, *SR 7*: 44953.

Scottish Government (2017), [*aka* Shortall et al.] (2017), *Women in Farming and the Agriculture Sector: Research Report: Findings and Recommendations from Research into the Role of Women in Farming and the Agriculture Sector in Scotland*, by Professor Sally Shortall, Centre for Rural Economy, Newcastle University, Newcastle Upon Tyne, and Lee-Ann Sutherland, Annie McKee, Jonathan Hopkins, Social, Economic and Geographical Sciences (SEGS) Group, James Hutton Institute, Craigiebuckler, Aberdeen. Published: 23 Jun, 187pp. Available online: https://www.gov.scot/publications/women-farming-agriculture-sector/pages/16/ (accessed 17 Mar 2020).

Scruton, Roger (1998), *Animal Rights and Wrongs*. London: Metro Books (Demos).

Seattle Eater (2020), 'Washington Supreme Court decision grants farm workers overtime pay', by Gabe Guarente, 5 Nov.

Séralini, Gilles-Eric, Emilie Claira, Robin Mesnagea, Steeve Gressa, Nicolas Defargea, Manuela Malatestab, Didier Hennequinc and Joël Spiroux de Vendômoisa (2012), 'Long term toxicity of a Roundup herbicide and a Roundup-tolerant genetically modified maize', *Food and Chemical Toxicology, 50*(11): 4221–31. Retracted by Elsevier.

Séralini, Gilles-Eric, et al. (2014), 'Republished study: Long-term toxicity of a Roundup herbicide and a Roundup-tolerant genetically modified maize'. *Environmental Sciences Europe, 26*(1): 14.

Shortall et al. (2017), *Women in Farming and the Agriculture Sector* (Scottish Government study).

Shortall, Sally (2019), 'Planning the farmyard – gender implications', in *Routledge Companion to Rural Planning*, edited by Mark Scott, Nick Gallent and Menelaos Gkartzios, 326–9, Abingdon and New York: Routledge.

Shah, Tushaar (2018), 'Solar pumps and South Asia's energy-groundwater nexus', Tushaar Shah, Abhishek Rajan, Gyan Prakash Rai, Shilp Verma and Neha Durga, *Environmental Research Letters, 13*(11): 1–12.

Singer, Peter (1975, 2nd edn 1990), *Animal Liberation*. New York: Random House.

Singer, Peter (2002), *One World: The Ethics of Globalization*, New Haven, CT: Yale University Press.

Sky News (2017), 'Government draft tougher animal cruelty laws after sentience row', by John Craig, 12 Dec.

Smith, Jeffrey M. (2003), *Seeds of Deception: Exposing Industry and Government Lies About the Safety of Genetically Engineered Foods*, Fairfield, IA: Yes Books.

Smith, Jeffrey M. (2009), 'You're appointing who [Monsanto-linked- Michael Taylor]? Please Obama, say it's not so!', *Huffington Post*, 23 Jul.

Snopes (2019), 'Are ingredients in 'Impossible' and 'Beyond Meat' burgers indistinguishable from dog food?, 16 Aug.

Spiegel, Marjorie (1988), *The dreaded comparison: Human and animal slavery*. London: Heretic

Statista (2021a), 'Dairy cattle livestock numbers in New Zealand 2010–2020', by L. Granwal, 29 Jan. Available online: https://www.statista.com/statistics/974482/new-zealand-dairy-cattle-numbers/ (accessed 28 Feb 2021).

Statista (2021b), 'Unprecedented growth in China's milk consumption in 2020', via SEO Agency China, 16 Oct.

Statista (2021), 'Market revenue of plant-based meat worldwide from 2016 to 2026 (in billion US dollars)', 9 Dec.

Steiner, Rudolf (1924a), 'Report to members of the anthroposophical society after the agriculture course', Dornach, Switzerland, 20 June 1924', in M. Gardner (1993), *Spiritual Foundations for the Renewal of Agriculture by Rudolf Steiner*, 1–12, Kimberton, PA: 'Bio-Dynamic Farming and Gardening Association', *Journal of Organic Systems*, 6(1): 2011.

Steiner, R. (1924b), 'To All Members: The Meetings at Breslau and Koberwitz; the Waldorf School; the longings of the Youth.' *Anthroposophical Movement* 1: 17–18.

Steiner, R. (1924c), 'To All Members: The Meetings at Koberwitz and Breslau.' *Anthroposophical Movement* 1: 9–11.

Steinfeld, Henning, Pierre Gerber, Tom Wassenaar, Vincent Castel, Mauricio Rosales and Cees de Haan (2006), *Livestock's Long Shadow*. See: FAO-UN.

Stevenson, Adlai (1952), 'Let's not forget the farmer', Museum of the Moving Image.

Successful Farming (2020), 'USDA to buy as much excess milk and meat as possible, says Perdue', by Chuck Abbott, 16 Apr.

Sundaresan, C. S. (2014), *Farm Value Chains: For Sustainable Growth and Development*, New Delhi: Regal.

Sustainable Food News (2018), 'State's [Texas] "organic mega dairy farms" supplying [Wisconsin] processors 1,100 miles away', by *Sustainable Food News*, 15 Mar.

Taylor-Gooby, Peter, and Eleanor Taylor (2015), 'Benefits and welfare: long-term trends or short-term reactions?', in *British Social Attitudes 32*, edited by J. Curtice and R. Ormston, 74–101, London: NatCen Social Research.

Taylor-Puckett, Olivia (2018), 'Markets and infrastructure: Women and farmers markets', in *Women Farmers Weekly*, Lawrence Farmers' Market, Kansas, 8 Aug.

Telegraph (2021a), 'More than 170 feared dead as Himalayan glacier crashes into dam in northern India', by Samaan Lateef and Jessica Abrahams, 8 Feb.

Telegraph (2021b), 'Exclusive: Government must live up to its promise to enshrine animal sentience in law', by Helena Horton, 23 Mar.

Time (2016), 'Dairy farmers pour out 43 million gallons of milk due to surplus', by Melissa Chan, 13 Oct.

Times Literary Supplement (1995), 'Review of Damásio, *Descartes' error: Emotion, reason, and the human brain* (1994), review by Daniel C. Dennett in *TLS*, 25 Aug: 3–4.

Times of India (2015), 'Brahmin priests have historically eaten beef in India: Kancha Ilaiah', by Anahita Mukherji, 30 Nov.

Trauger, Amy, and J.L. Fluri (2019), *Capitalism and Inequality in the Global Economy*, London and New York: Routledge.

UBC (2017), 'Dairy farmers should rethink a cow's curfew, say UBC researchers [Dan Weary and Mariana von Keyserlingk]', by Corey Allen, University of British Columbia, 23 Mar.

UCS (2016), 'Movie Review: There's a vast Cowspiracy about climate change', by Doug Boucher, in *The Equation* blog, Union of Concerned Scientists, 10 June.

UK Met Office (Mar 2021), 'Met Office: Atmospheric CO_2 now hitting 50% higher than pre-industrial levels', by Richard Betts, Met Office Hadley Centre and University of Exeter, on Carbon Brief, 16 Mar.

University of California, (UC) Davis (2019), 'Cows and climate change: Making cattle more sustainable', by Amy Quinton, June 27, mentions Prof. Mitloehner. Available online: https://www.ucdavis.edu/food/news/making-cattle-more-sustainable (accessed 16 Feb 2022).

University of California, Berkeley (1999), '1990–92 early 1990s recession', in 'Slaying the dragon of debt' research project by the Regional Oral History Office of the Bancroft Library at UC Berkeley.

University of Ghana (2017), 'Breaking the glass ceiling', by Lydia Aziato (Dean, School of Nursing).

UN (1948), *The Universal Declaration of Human Rights* (UDHR), Proclaimed by the United Nations General Assembly in Paris, 10 Dec.

UN-FAO (2014), 'Review of animal welfare legislation in the beef, pork, and poultry industries', by Peter Stevenson, Daniela Battaglia, Carmen Bullon and Arianna Carita. Rome: UN-FAO.

UN-FAO (2016), *OECD-FAO Agricultural Outlook 2016–2025*, by the OECD and UN-FAO, Rome: UN-FAO.

UN-FAO (2018), *The Future of Food and Agriculture – Alternative Pathways to 2050*. Summary. Rome: UN-FAO.

UN-FAO (2018), *Empowering Rural Women, Powering Agriculture: FAO's Work on Gender*. Rome: UN-FAO.

UN (2017), *2017 Revision of world population prospect.*

UN (n.d.), 'The 17 goals', United Nations, Department of Economic and Social Affairs Sustainable Development.

Universal Declaration for Animal Welfare (2000), UDAW proposed 2000 by World Animal Protection; previously called World Society for the Protection of Animals, which acts as its Secretariat.

US Congress (2019), 'House resolution 109: Recognizing the duty of the federal government to create a green new deal', 7 Feb.

USDA (2001), USDA Farm typology, Figure 3.4, by Newton & Hoppe, in Scholten (2007; 2011: 120).

USDA (2002), 'The changing landscape of US milk production', by Don P. Blayne, SBN 978, June.

USDA (2005), 'The twentieth centurytransformation of U.S. agriculture and farm policy', by Carolyn Dimitri, Anne Effland and Neilson Conklin, *ERS Economic Information Bulletin 3.*

USDA (2011), 'Vietnam colossal growth in the dairy industry', by Quan Tran and Alex M. Vigil. USDA Foreign Agricultural Service 25 Mar.

USDA (2012), *U.S. Statistics on Women and Minorities on Farms and in Rural Areas,* compilers Mary V. Gold and Becky Thompson, AFSIC, National Agricultural Library, USDA, Beltsville, MD.

USDA-ERS (2013), *Characteristics of women farm operators and their farms,* by Robert Hoppe and Penni Korb, EIB-111, USDA Economic Research Service. April 2013.

USDA-AMS (2014), 'Number of U.S. farmers' markets continues to rise' [AMS 4 Aug 2014 update: 'rose to 8,284 in 2014, up from 3,706 in 2004 and 1,755 in 1994.']

USDA[-NASS] (2014), 'Women farmers control 7% of U.S. farmland, account for 3% of sales', USDA, National Agricultural Statistics Service. ACH12–12/Sep. 2014.

USDA (2016–17), 'USDA's 2016 certified organic survey'. Oct, No .2017–6.

USDA[-FAS] (2017), 'US top 10 agricultural exports in 2017: Dairy products: pc consumption, US (annual) last updated 5 Sep 2017', (646 pounds in 2016, up from 539 pounds in 1975):

USDA[-NASS] (2018), 'Rate per cow, 2008–17: US: 12% increase over the past 10-year period', 21 Feb.

USDA (2018), *Organic Dairy Market News,* 5–9 Mar 2018, information gathered 26 Feb–09 Mar, 85, Report 10. (Also, *Sustainable Food News,* 15 Mar 2018: 'Some Wisconsin organic dairy processors have switched from sourcing local milk to milk trucked from Texas ...')

USDA (2018 Mar 15), 'USDA: Texas "organic mega dairy farms" supplying processors 1,100 miles away', by Ed Maltby <emaltby@COMCAST.NET> 15mar18 Today at 16:55 From: Mark Kastel [mailto:kastel@mwt.net] Sent: Thursday, March 15, 2018 12:02 PM To: Independent Odairy.

USDA (2018), 'Top U.S. agricultural exports in 2017', 23 Mar 2018, USDA ... (Cotton, Dairy, Fruits, Veg, Grain.

USDA (2018 May 15), *Milk production: National agricultural statistics service NASS.* Report contains number of milk cows, production per cow, and total milk production for major milk producing states and US; number of milk cows and total milk production for all states and U.S.; number of licensed dairy herds for all states and U.S. Coverage: 11 Nov 1931–18 May 2018.

USDA (2018), 'Margin protection program for dairy', 4 Jun.

USDA (2019), *Peer Review of the AMS National Organic Program (NOP).*

USDA (2019), 'Socially disadvantaged farmers: Race, Hispanic origin & gender: Beginning, limited resource, socially disadvantaged, and female farmers', USDA-ERS, 7 Nov.

USDA (2020), 'Consolidation in U.S. dairy farming', by James M. MacDonald, Jonathan Law, and Roberto Mosheim, ERR-274, July.

USDL (1995), *Federal glass ceiling commission. Solid investments: Making full use of the nation's human capital.* U.S. Department of Labor, 1 Nov: 13–15.

USDL (2014), *Paternity leave: Why parental leave for fathers Is so important*, US Department of Labor.

USEPA (n.d.), 'Animal feeding operations: Animal feeding operations (AFO) and concentrated animal feeding operations (CAFO)', EPA.

US News & World Report (2019), 'Ag secretary: No guarantee small dairy farms will survive', AP, 1 Oct.

Van der Ploeg, Jan Douwe (2009), *The New Peasantries: Struggles for Autonomy and Sustainability in an Era of Empire and Globalization,* London: Earthscan.

Van der Ploeg, Jan Douwe (2010), 'The peasantries of the twenty-first century', *Journal of Peasant Studies*, 37(1): 1–30. [Cited in Trauger and Fluri 2019: 73]

Van der Ploeg, Jan Douwe (2020), 'Farmers' upheaval, climate crisis and populism', *Journal of Peasant Studies* 47(3): 589–605.

Van der Ploeg, Jan Douwe (2020), 'Farmers' upheaval, climate crisis and populism', *Journal of Peasant Studies*, 47(3): 589–605.

Vegconomist (2012), 'Beyond Meat and Pizza Hut expand partnership, but why is it not vegan?', 29 Jul.

Vegconomist (2020), 'ALDI Nord and ALDI SÜD Harmonise Vegan Range & Announce Promotions, 18 Mar.

Vegconomist (2020), 'Pizza Hut partners with Beyond Meat, is first to offer plant-based meat pizza across whole of USA [cheese source not stated]', Nov. 10.

Vellinga, T. V., R.L.M. Schils, M.H.A. De Haan, A. Evers and A. VandenPol- van Dasselaar (2009), 'Implementation of GHG mitigation on intensive dairy farms', *Livestock Science* 137(1–3): 185–95.

Visak, Tatjana, Robert Garner and Peter Singer (2015), *The Ethics of Killing Animals.*

Waldau, Paul (2011), *Animal Rights: What Everyone Needs to Know*, Oxford: Oxford University Press.

Walker, Alice (1988), *Preface in: The Dreaded Comparison: Human and Animal Slavery, by Marjorie Spiegel,* UK: New Society Publishers.

Wall Street Journal (2018), 'Here's to really good fat! Fat is fashionable now, prompting a deluge of ultra-rich dairy products billed as healthy and delicious', by Jane Black, 3–4 Mar: D7, D9.

Washington Post (2016), 'Why a top animal science expert is worried about the milk industry', by Roberto A. Ferdman, 21 Apr.

Washington Post (2017a), 'Investigative report documents rampant corruption at USDA "Organic" program', by Mark Taylor, 8 Jun.

Washington Post (2017b), 'USDA closes investigation into a massive organic farm – but what did it check?' by Peter Whoriskey, 28 Sep (Bruce Scholten quoted.). Available online: https://www.washingtonpost.com/news/wonk/wp/2017/09/28/usda-closes-investigation-into-a-massive-organic-farm-but-what-did-it-check/?utm_term=.577fb043fc47 (accessed 28 Sep 2017).

Washington Post (2017c), 'Organic food fraud leads Congress to weigh bill doubling USDA oversight: amid growing scepticism of "organic" food products, new legislation would roughly double the budget for USDA oversight of the industry', 21 Dec.

Washington Post (2017d), 'A USDA investigation or just an appointment? Few details emerge from inquiry into Boulder-based organic milk company', by Peter Whoriskey. See also *Denver Post*, 22 Dec.

Washington Post (2018), 'USDA officials said they were guarding against organic food fraud. Congress decided they need help', by Peter Whoriskey, 20 Dec.

Watson, Guy (2021), 'What is a Devon farmer, who doesn't speak French, doing buying a farm in West France?', in *Wicked Leeks*, Riverford Organic Farms, riverford.co.uk, 26 Apr.

Women Farmers Weekly (2018), 'Markets and infrastructure: Women and farmers markets', by Olivia Taylor-Puckett, Manager of Lawrence Farmers' Market, Kansas, 8 Aug. United States. Congress. House. Committee on Agriculture · 1990 · Agricultural laws and legislation

Washington State Dairy Federation (1990), 'Testimony of Bastian Scholten, President WSDF, Formulation of the 1990 Farm Bill: Hearings before the House Agriculture Subcommittee on livestock, dairy and poultry, Seattle, Washington, 9 Jan 1990.'

Washington State University (2015), 'U.S. breast milk is glyphosate free: Study is first independently verified look for the presence of Roundup ingredient in human milk', study leader Michelle McGuire, *ScienceDaily*, 23 July: 1285–1290. Available online: https://www.sciencedaily.com/releases/2015/07/150723133120.htm (accessed 5 Sep 20).

Wasley, Andrew and Heather Kroeker (2018), 'Revealed: industrial-scale beef farming comes to the UK', *Guardian*, 29 May.

Wathes, Christopher M., Henry Buller, Heather Maggs and Madeleine L. Campbell (2013), 'Livestock production in the UK in the 21st century: A perfect storm averted?' Special issue, The Future of Farm Animal Welfare, *Animals*, 2013, *3*(3): 574–83.

Whatcom Watch (2015), 'Can Whatcom's small farms help reconstruct our local food system?', by Jennifer Moon, 20 Nov.

Whatcom Watch (2020), 'Washington Conservation Corps replenishing Bellingham's waterways since 1999', by Giovanni Roverso.

Whatmore, Sarah (2002), *Hybrid Geographies: Natures, Cultures, Spaces*, London: Sage.

Whiten, Andrew (2021), 'The burgeoning reach of animal culture', *Science*, 372: 6537.

Wilson, Geoff A. (2007), *Multifunctional Agriculture: A transition Theory Perspective*, New York: Oxford University Press, and CABI, Wallingford.

Wilson, Geoff A. (2011), *Community Resilience and Environmental Transitions*, London: Earthscan.

Wilson, G.A., G. Robinson, D. Schmied and I. Mose, eds (2010), *Globalization and Rural Transitions in Germany and the UK*. Proceedings, Anglo-German Rural Geographers meeting 2008, Universität Oldenburg. Göttingen: Cuvillier Verlag.

Wohleben, Peter (2017), 'The Inner Life of Animals, by Peter Wohlleben. Review by Richard Kerridge. Friday 20 October 2017 – a revolution in how we regard other species.'

World Bank (1998), *India: The dairy revolution*, by Wilfred Candler and Nalinia Kumar, Washington DC.

World Bank (2017), *Employment in agriculture (% of total employment) (modelled ILO estimate)* International Labour Organization, ILOSTAT database. Data retrieved in Nov 2017.

World Bank (2019), Employment in agriculture, (% of total employment) (modelled ILO estimate). Int'l Labour Organization, ILOSTAT database.

World Watch Magazine (2009), 'Livestock and climate change: What if the key actors in climate change are cows, pigs, and chickens?', by Robert Goodland and Jeff Anhang,

Worldwatch Institute. Available online: https://www.cabdirect.org/cabdirect/abstract/20093312389 (accessed 19 Mar 2018).

World Watch Magazine (2010), 'Critical comments and responses [to WWM (2009), 'Livestock and climate change'], March/April 2010.

Xinhua (2021), 'Chinese dairy giant Yili acquisitions New Zealand's Westland'. Available online: http://www.xinhuanet.com/english/2019–08/01/c_138276017.htm

Zalasiewicz, J., M. Williams, W. Steffen and P. Crutzen (2010), 'The new world of the Anthropocene', *Environmental Science and Technology 44*: 2228–31.

INDEX